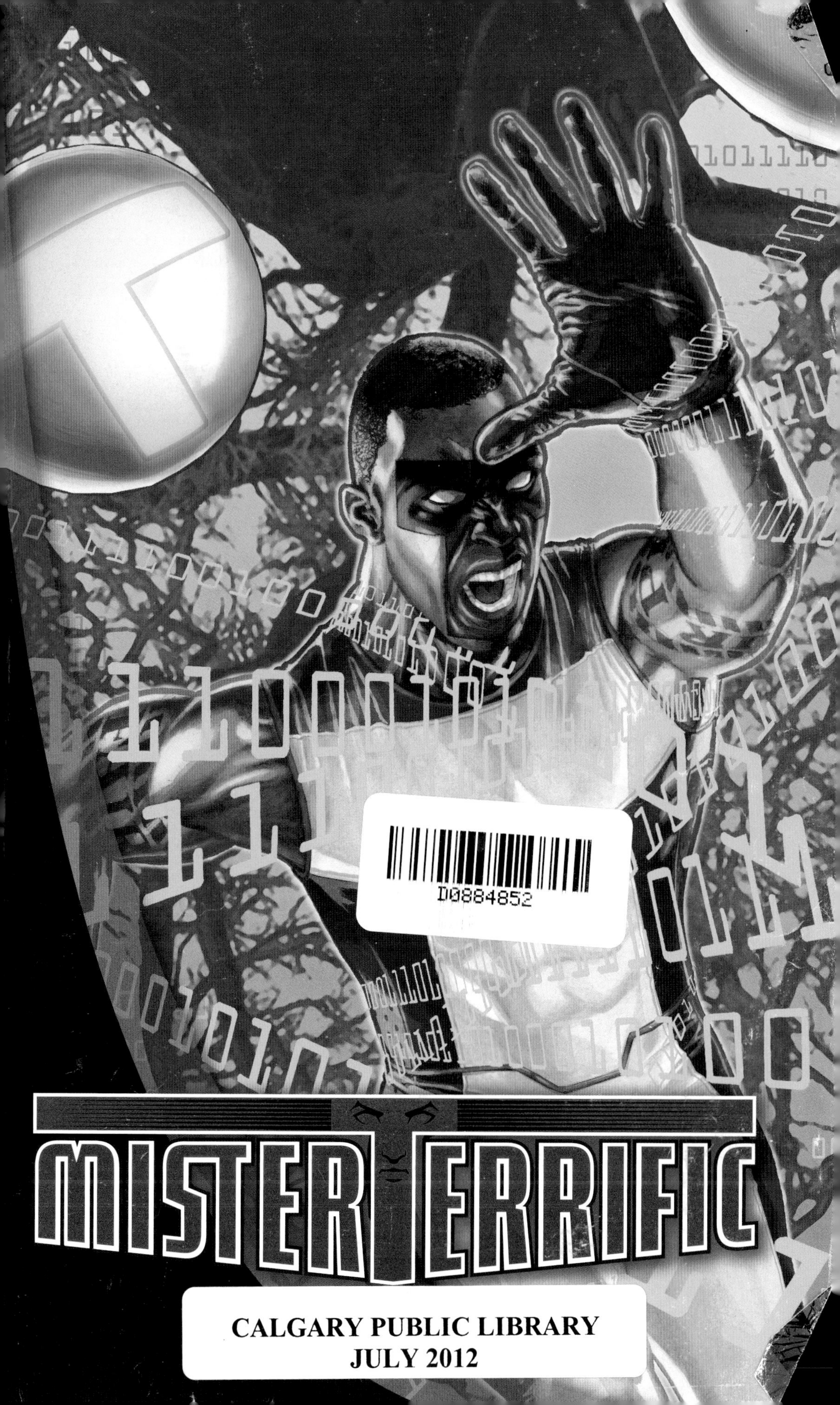
MISTER TERRIFIC

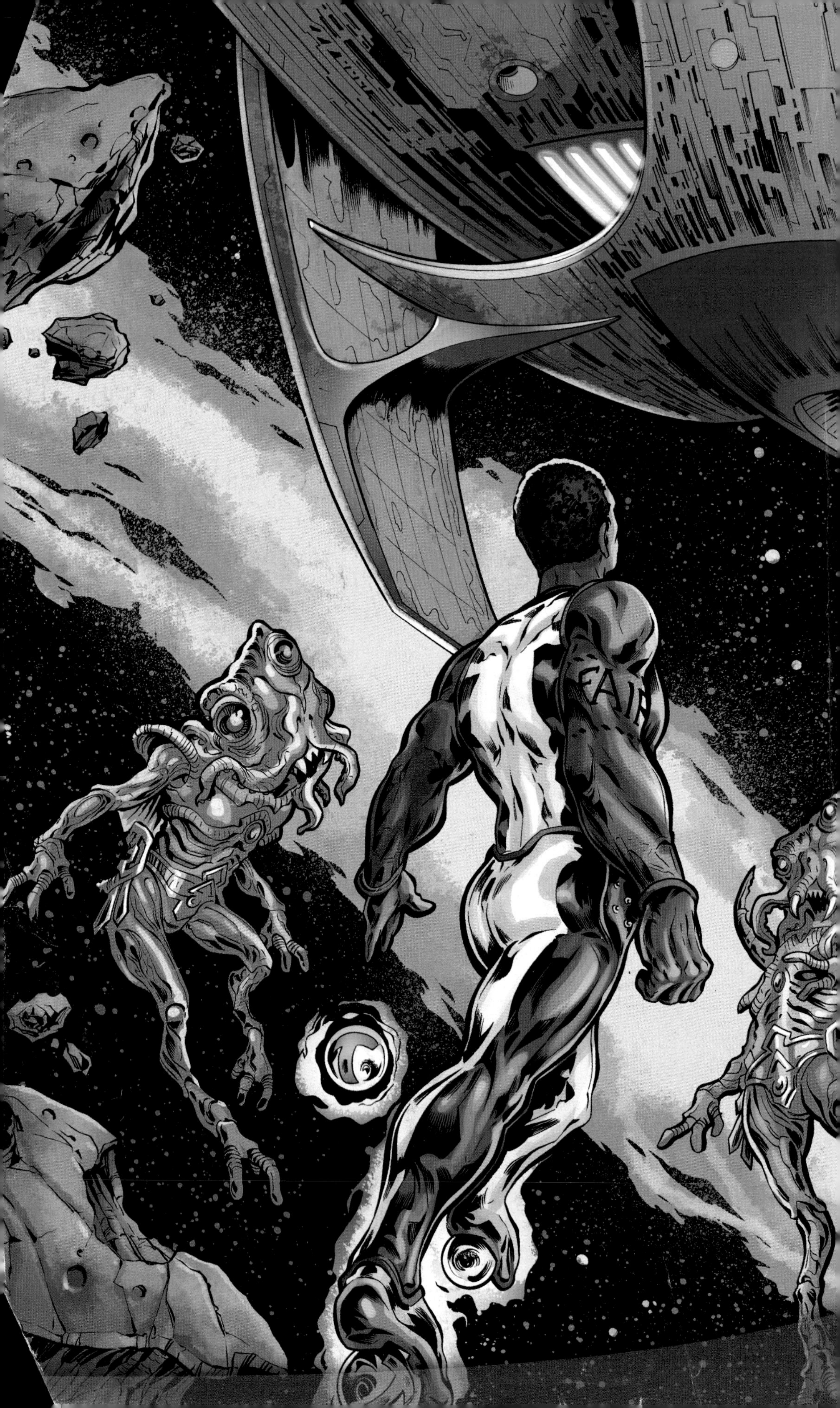

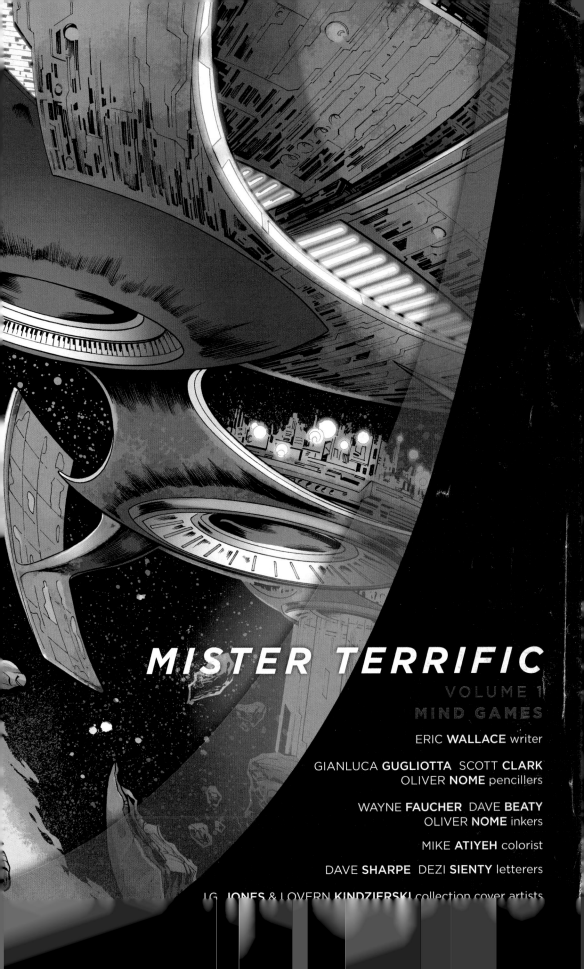

MISTER TERRIFIC

VOLUME 1
MIND GAMES

ERIC **WALLACE** writer

GIANLUCA **GUGLIOTTA** SCOTT **CLARK**
OLIVER **NOME** pencillers

WAYNE **FAUCHER** DAVE **BEATY**
OLIVER **NOME** inkers

MIKE **ATIYEH** colorist

DAVE **SHARPE** DEZI **SIENTY** letterers

J.G. **JONES** & LOVERN **KINDZIERSKI** collection cover artists

JOEY CAVALIERI Editor – Original Series   KATE STEWART Assistant Editor – Original Series   ROWENA YOW Editor
ROBBIN BROSTERMAN Design Director – Books   ROBBIE BIEDERMAN Publication Design

BOB HARRAS VP – Editor-in-Chief

DIANE NELSON President   DAN DIDIO and JIM LEE Co-Publishers
GEOFF JOHNS Chief Creative Officer
JOHN ROOD Executive VP – Sales, Marketing and Business Development
AMY GENKINS Senior VP – Business and Legal Affairs   NAIRI GARDINER Senior VP – Finance
JEFF BOISON VP – Publishing Operations   MARK CHIARELLO VP – Art Direction and Design
JOHN CUNNINGHAM VP – Marketing   TERRI CUNNINGHAM VP – Talent Relations and Services
ALISON GILL Senior VP – Manufacturing and Operations   DAVID HYDE VP – Publicity
HANK KANALZ Senior VP – Digital   JAY KOGAN VP – Business and Legal Affairs, Publishing
JACK MAHAN VP – Business Affairs, Talent   NICK NAPOLITANO VP – Manufacturing Administration
SUE POHJA VP – Book Sales   COURTNEY SIMMONS Senior VP – Publicity
BOB WAYNE Senior VP – Sales

MISTER TERRIFIC VOLUME 1: MIND GAMES
Published by DC Comics. Cover and compilation Copyright © 2012 DC Comics.
All Rights Reserved.

DC Comics, 1700 Broadway, New York, NY 10019
A Warner Bros. Entertainment Company.
Printed by RR Donnelley, Salem, VA, USA. 5/11/12. First Printing.
ISBN: 978-1-4012-3500-0

Certified Chain of Custody
At Least 25% Certified Forest Content
www.sfiprogram.org
SFI-01042
APPLIES TO TEXT STOCK ONLY

Library of Congress Cataloging-in-Publication Data

Wallace, Eric, 1969-
Mister Terrific volume one: mind games / Eric Wallace, Gianluca
Gugliotta, Wayne Faucher.
p. cm.
"Originally published in single magazine form in Mister Terrific
1-8"—T.p. verso.
ISBN 978-1-4012-3500-0
1. Graphic novels. I. Gugliotta, Gianluca. II. Faucher, Wayne. III.
Title. IV. Title: Mind games.
PN6728.M55W35 2012
741.5'973—dc23
2012002250

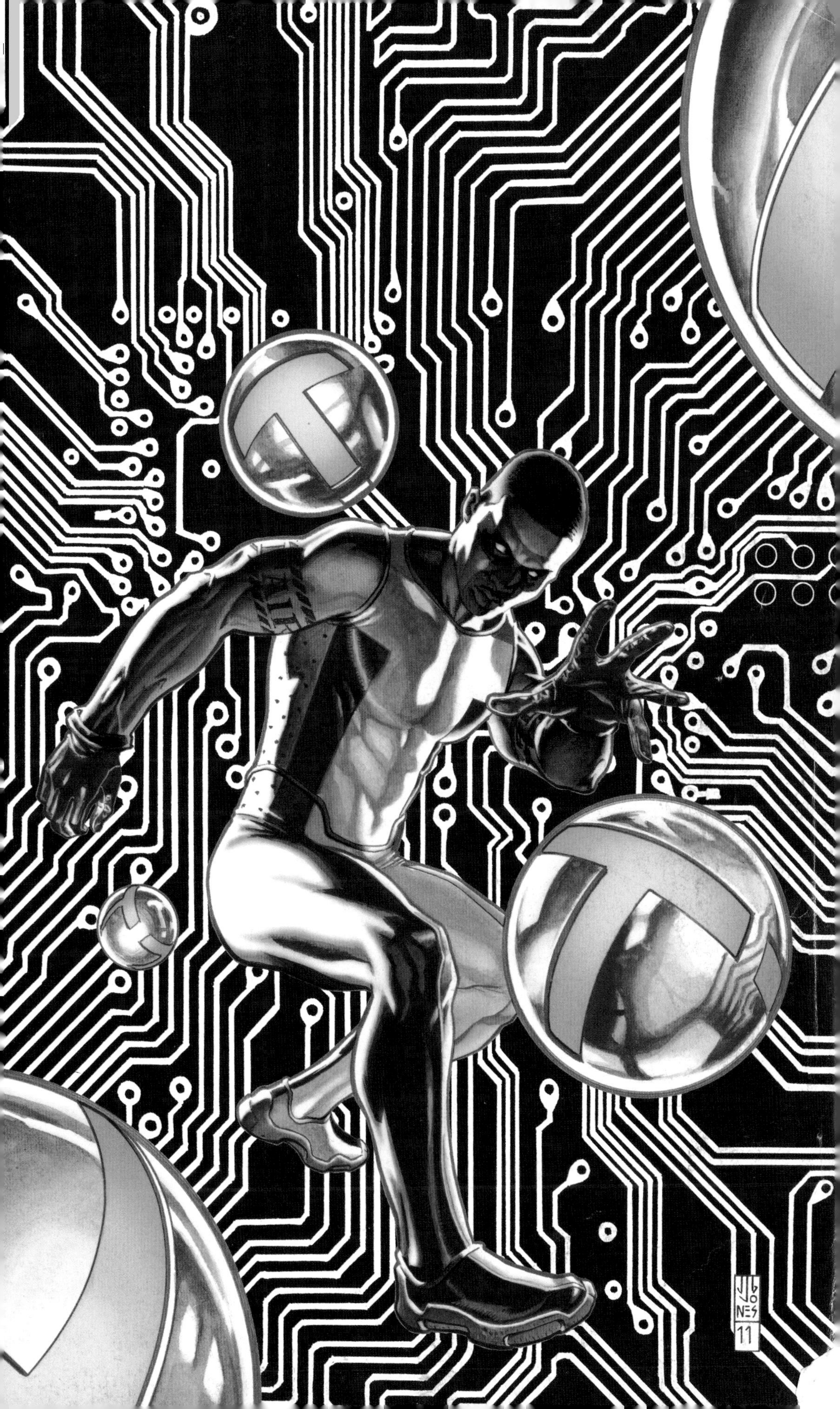
JG JONES
11

SOFTWARE UPDATE

ERIC WALLACE writer **GIANLUCA GUGLIOTTA** penciller **WAYNE FAUCHER** inker
cover art by **J.G. JONES** with colorist **LOVERN KINDZIERSKI**

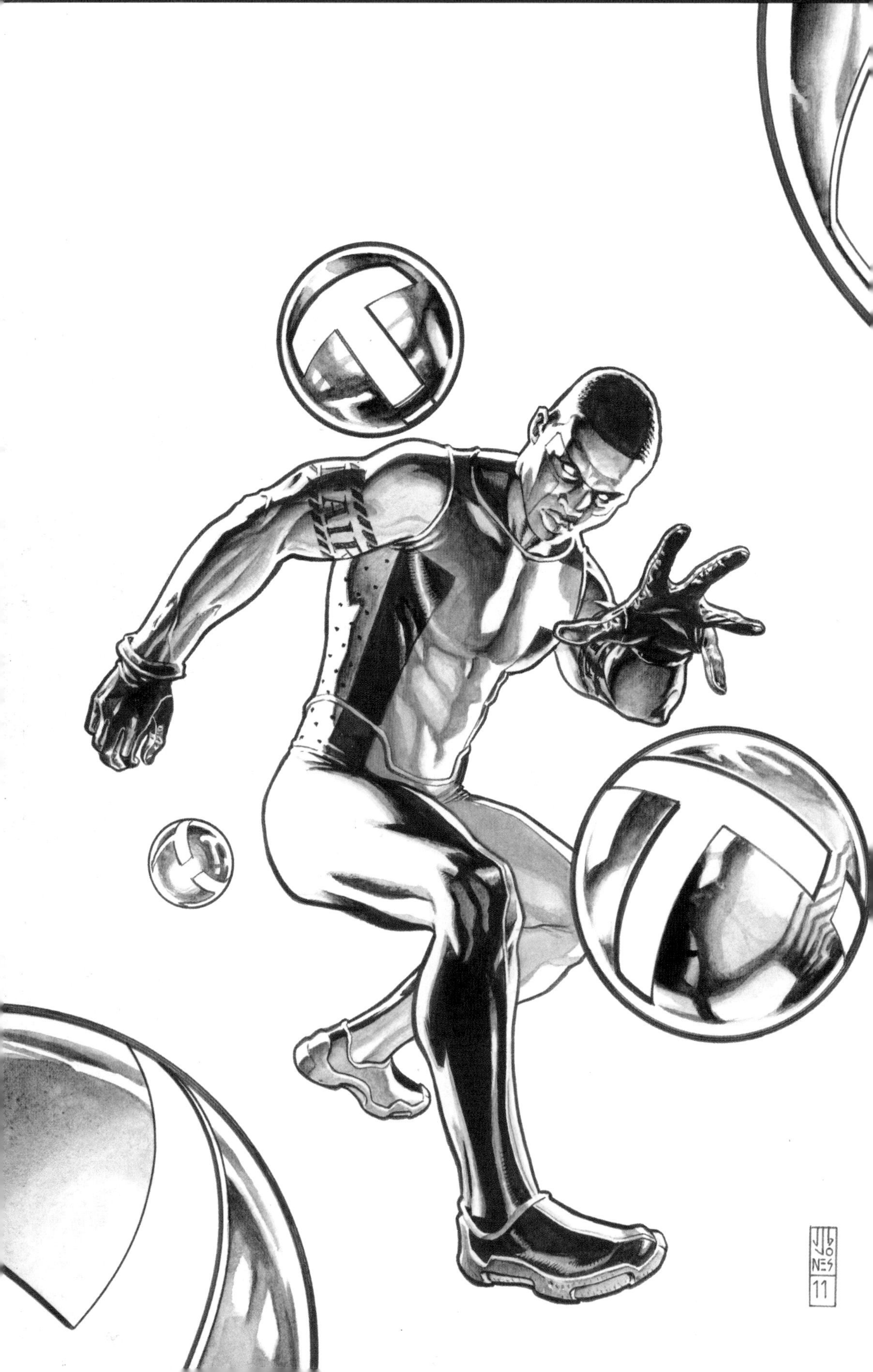

JG JONES
11

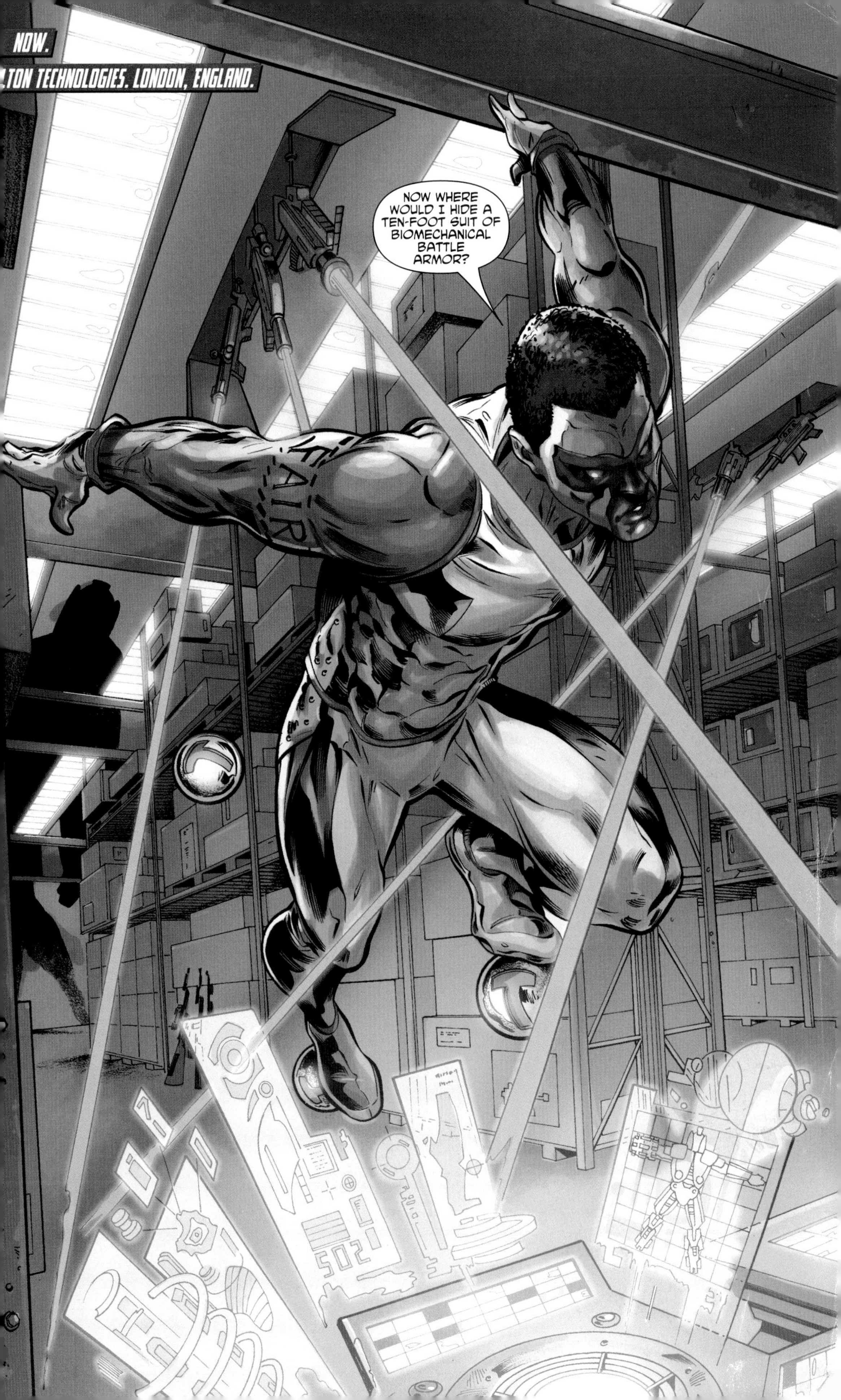
NOW.
...TON TECHNOLOGIES. LONDON, ENGLAND.
NOW WHERE WOULD I HIDE A TEN-FOOT SUIT OF BIOMECHANICAL BATTLE ARMOR?

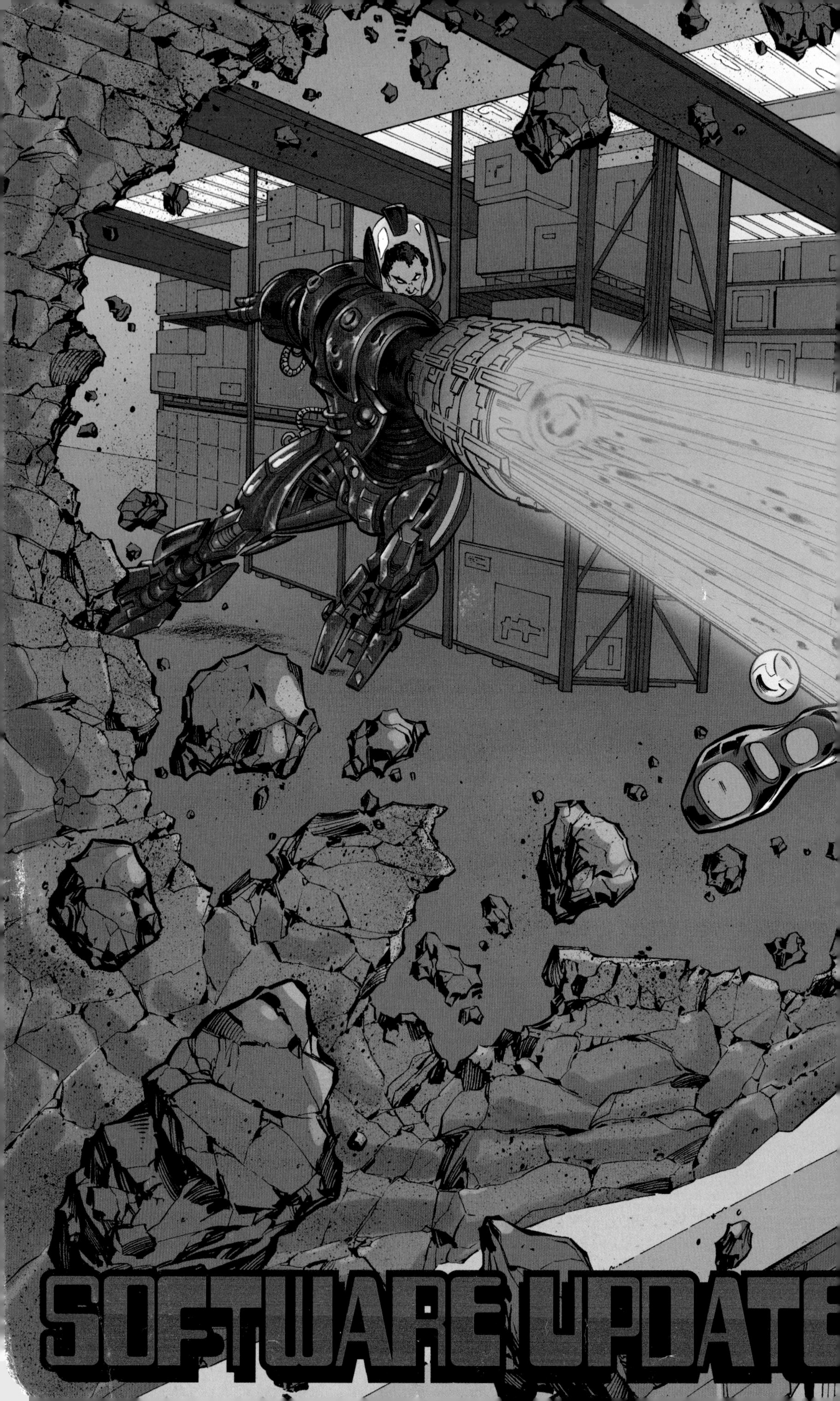
SOFTWARE UPDATE

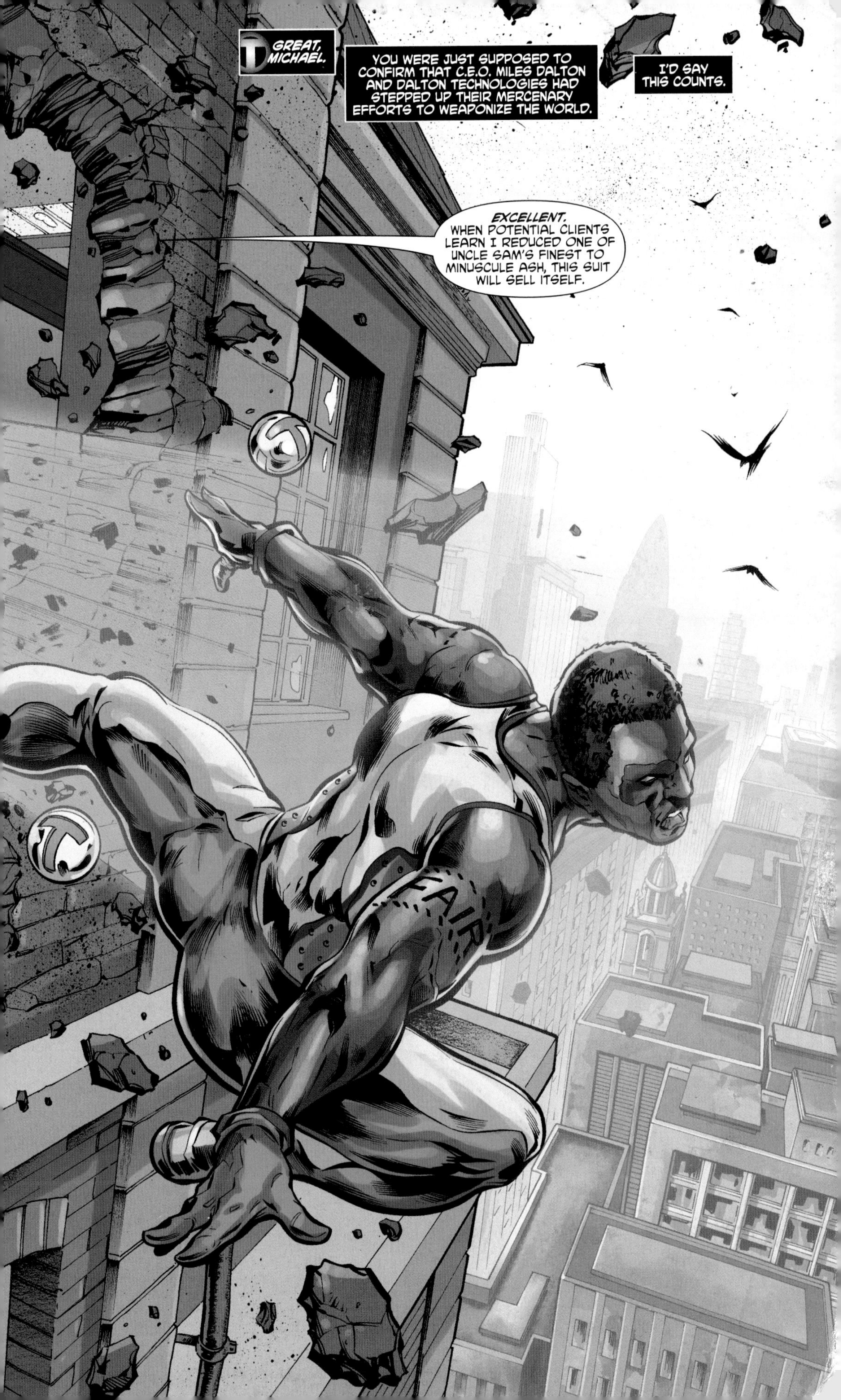

GREAT, MICHAEL.
YOU WERE JUST SUPPOSED TO CONFIRM THAT C.E.O. MILES DALTON AND DALTON TECHNOLOGIES HAD STEPPED UP THEIR MERCENARY EFFORTS TO WEAPONIZE THE WORLD.
I'D SAY THIS COUNTS.
EXCELLENT. WHEN POTENTIAL CLIENTS LEARN I REDUCED ONE OF UNCLE SAM'S FINEST TO MINUSCULE ASH, THIS SUIT WILL SELL ITSELF.
FAIR

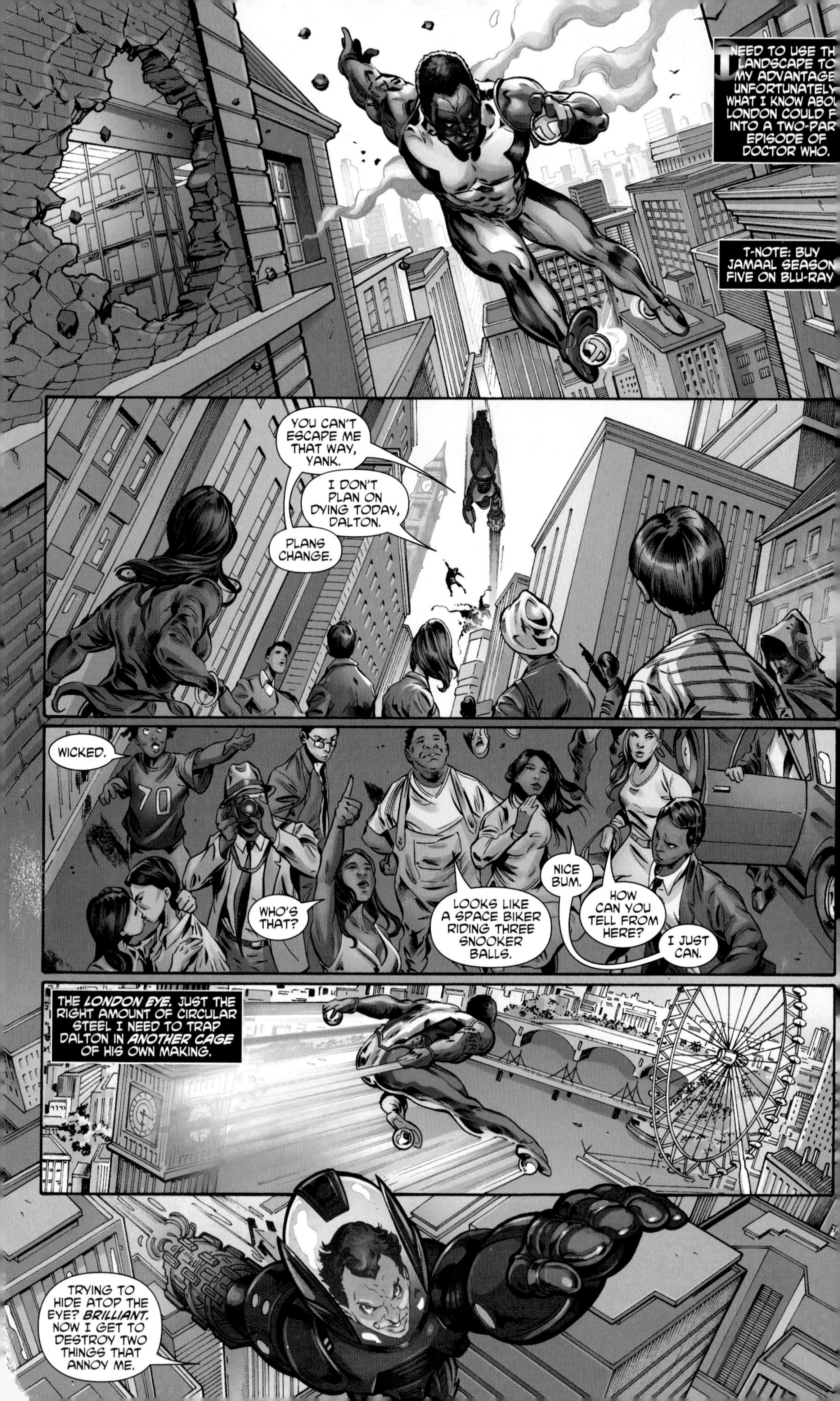

NEED TO USE TH LANDSCAPE TO MY ADVANTAGE UNFORTUNATELY WHAT I KNOW ABOU LONDON COULD F INTO A TWO-PAR EPISODE OF DOCTOR WHO.
T-NOTE: BUY JAMAAL SEASON FIVE ON BLU-RAY
YOU CAN'T ESCAPE ME THAT WAY, YANK.
I DON'T PLAN ON DYING TODAY, DALTON.
PLANS CHANGE.
WICKED.
WHO'S THAT?
LOOKS LIKE A SPACE BIKER RIDING THREE SNOOKER BALLS.
NICE BUM.
HOW CAN YOU TELL FROM HERE?
I JUST CAN.
THE *LONDON EYE.* JUST THE RIGHT AMOUNT OF CIRCULAR STEEL I NEED TO TRAP DALTON IN *ANOTHER CAGE* OF HIS OWN MAKING.
TRYING TO HIDE ATOP THE EYE? *BRILLIANT.* NOW I GET TO DESTROY TWO THINGS THAT ANNOY ME.

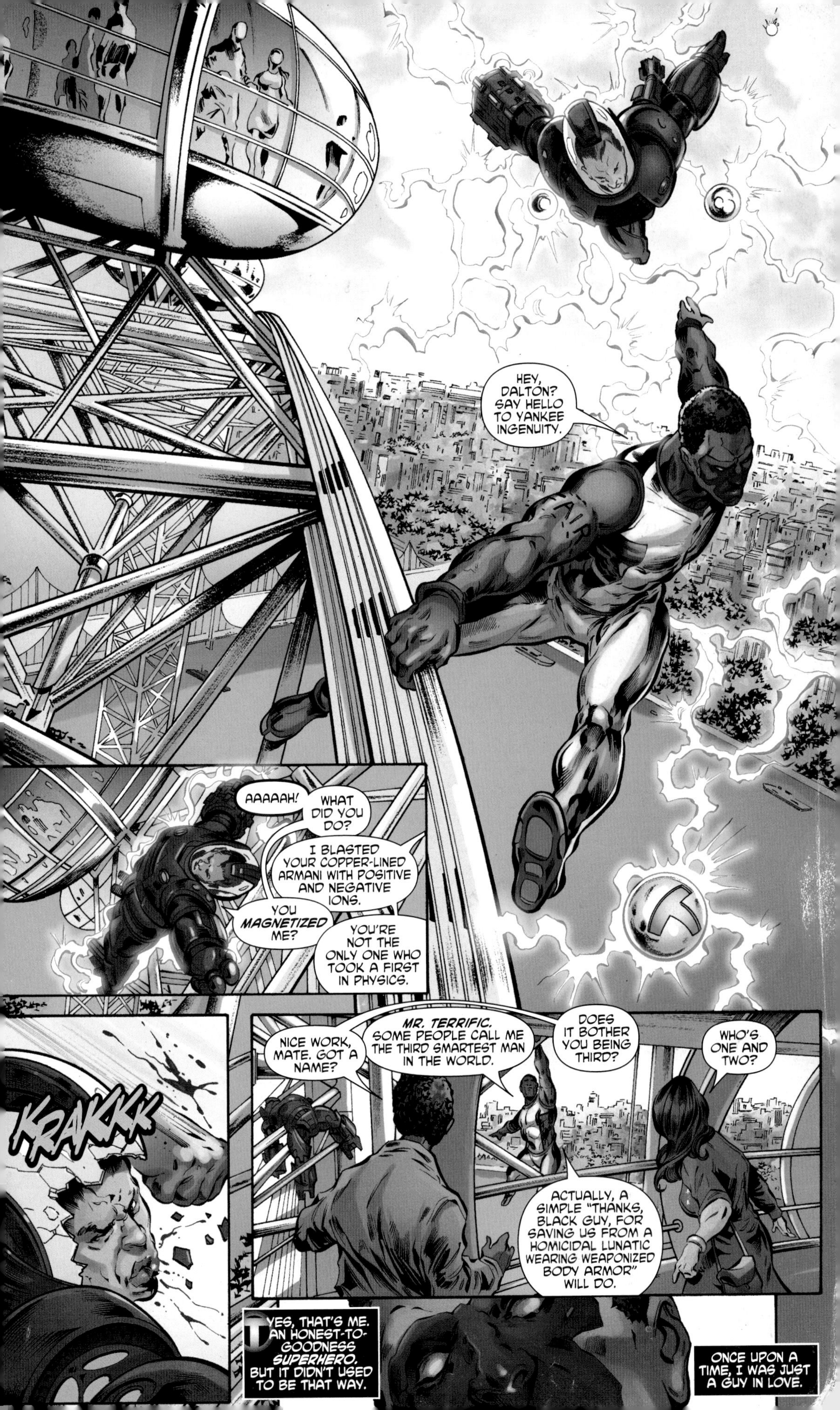
HEY, DALTON? SAY HELLO TO YANKEE INGENUITY.
AAAAAH!
WHAT DID YOU DO?
I BLASTED YOUR COPPER-LINED ARMANI WITH POSITIVE AND NEGATIVE IONS.
YOU *MAGNETIZED* ME?
YOU'RE NOT THE ONLY ONE WHO TOOK A FIRST IN PHYSICS.
KRAKKK
NICE WORK, MATE. GOT A NAME?
MR. TERRIFIC. SOME PEOPLE CALL ME THE THIRD SMARTEST MAN IN THE WORLD.
DOES IT BOTHER YOU BEING THIRD?
WHO'S ONE AND TWO?
ACTUALLY, A SIMPLE "THANKS, BLACK GUY, FOR SAVING US FROM A HOMICIDAL LUNATIC WEARING WEAPONIZED BODY ARMOR" WILL DO.
YES, THAT'S ME. AN HONEST-TO-GOODNESS *SUPERHERO.* BUT IT DIDN'T USED TO BE THAT WAY.
ONCE UPON A TIME, I WAS JUST A GUY IN LOVE.

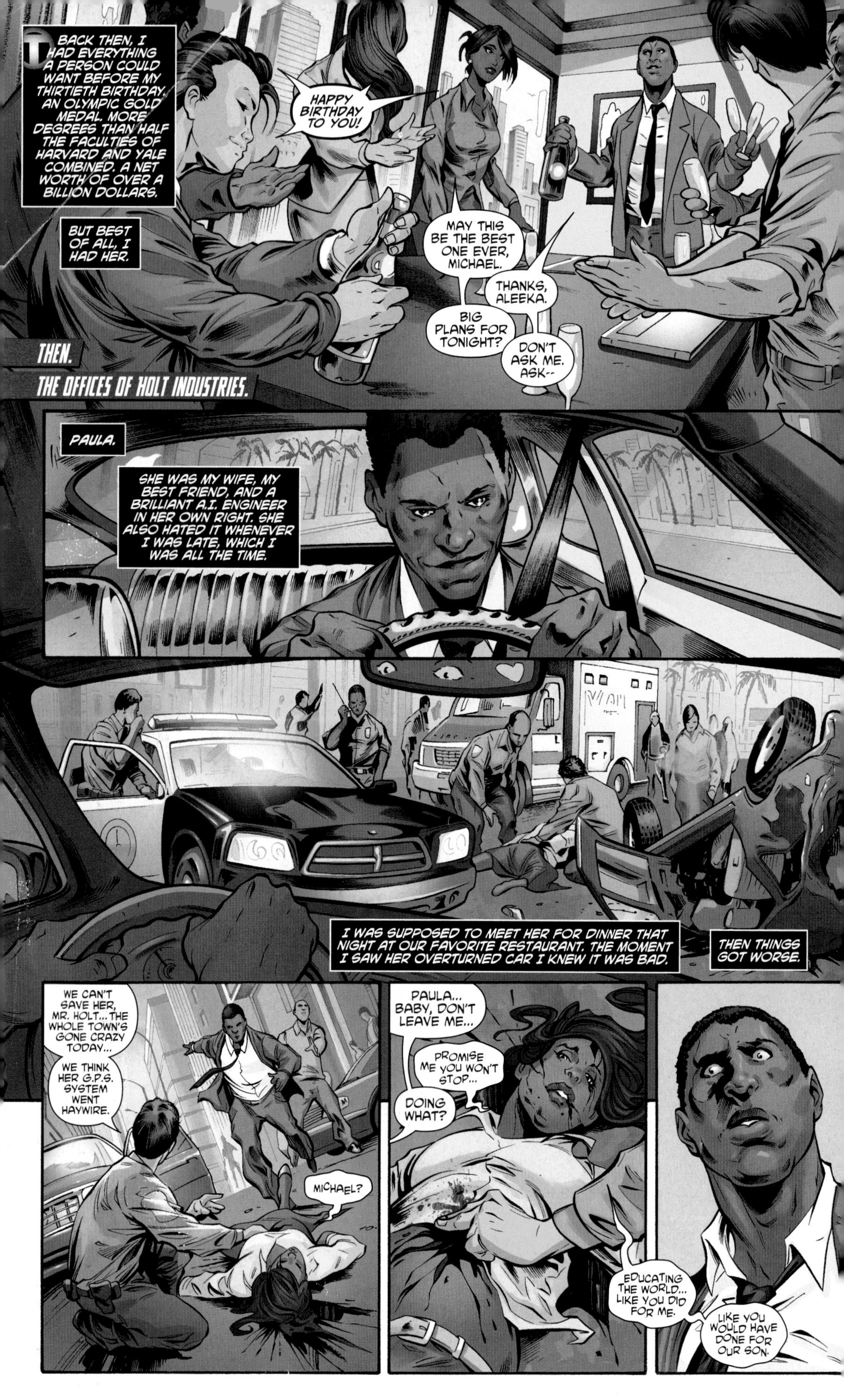
BACK THEN, I HAD EVERYTHING A PERSON COULD WANT BEFORE MY THIRTIETH BIRTHDAY. AN OLYMPIC GOLD MEDAL. MORE DEGREES THAN HALF THE FACULTIES OF HARVARD AND YALE COMBINED. A NET WORTH OF OVER A BILLION DOLLARS.
BUT BEST OF ALL, I HAD HER.
HAPPY BIRTHDAY TO YOU!
MAY THIS BE THE BEST ONE EVER, MICHAEL.
THANKS, ALEEKA.
BIG PLANS FOR TONIGHT?
DON'T ASK ME. ASK--
THEN.
THE OFFICES OF HOLT INDUSTRIES.
PAULA.
SHE WAS MY WIFE, MY BEST FRIEND, AND A BRILLIANT A.I. ENGINEER IN HER OWN RIGHT. SHE ALSO HATED IT WHENEVER I WAS LATE, WHICH I WAS ALL THE TIME.
I WAS SUPPOSED TO MEET HER FOR DINNER THAT NIGHT AT OUR FAVORITE RESTAURANT. THE MOMENT I SAW HER OVERTURNED CAR I KNEW IT WAS BAD.
THEN THINGS GOT WORSE.
WE CAN'T SAVE HER, MR. HOLT... THE WHOLE TOWN'S GONE CRAZY TODAY...
WE THINK HER G.P.S. SYSTEM WENT HAYWIRE.
MICHAEL?
PAULA... BABY, DON'T LEAVE ME...
PROMISE ME YOU WON'T STOP...
DOING WHAT?
EDUCATING THE WORLD... LIKE YOU DID FOR ME.
LIKE YOU WOULD HAVE DONE FOR OUR SON.

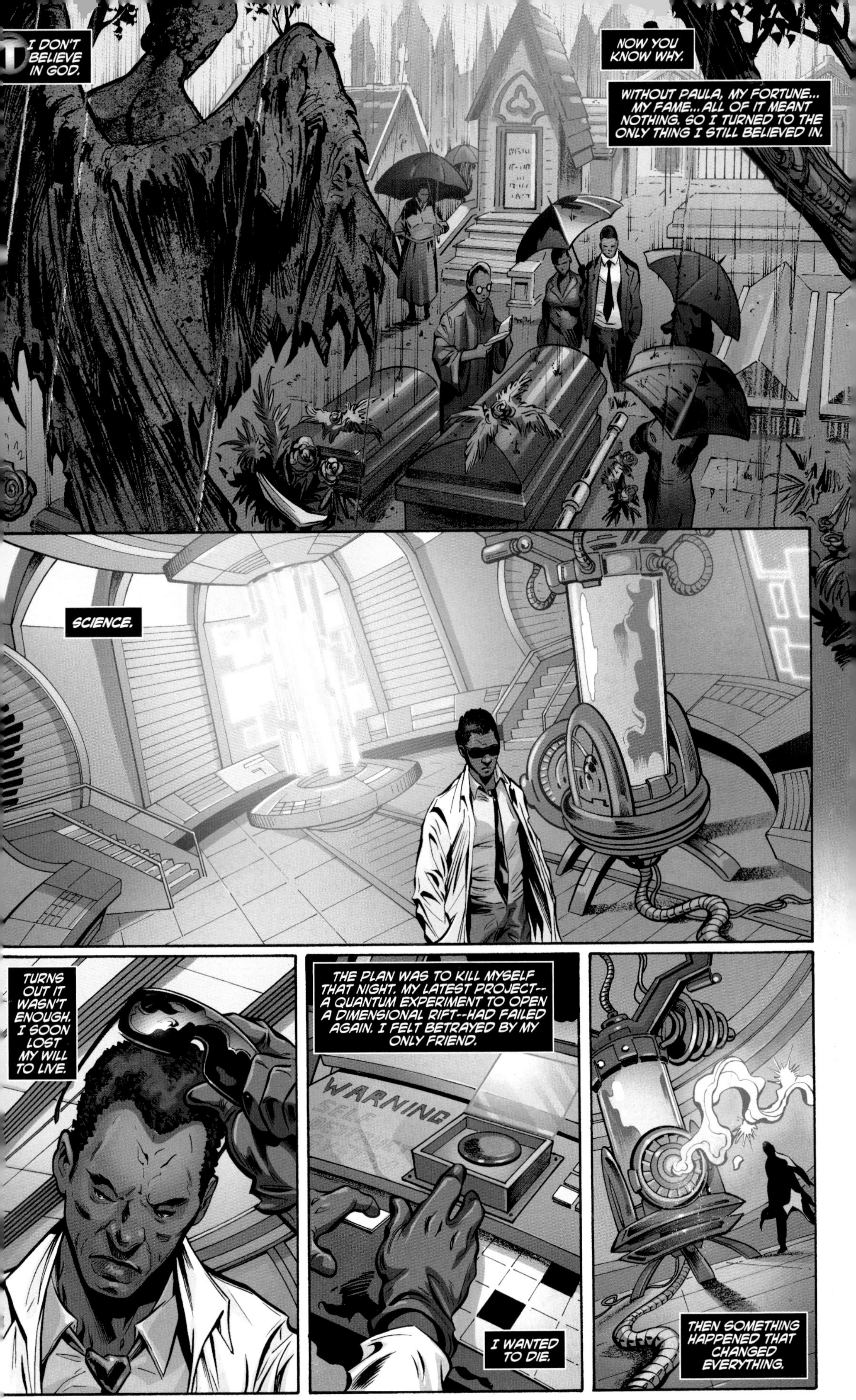
I DON'T BELIEVE IN GOD.
NOW YOU KNOW WHY.
WITHOUT PAULA, MY FORTUNE... MY FAME...ALL OF IT MEANT NOTHING. SO I TURNED TO THE ONLY THING I STILL BELIEVED IN.
SCIENCE.
TURNS OUT IT WASN'T ENOUGH. I SOON LOST MY WILL TO LIVE.
THE PLAN WAS TO KILL MYSELF THAT NIGHT. MY LATEST PROJECT-- A QUANTUM EXPERIMENT TO OPEN A DIMENSIONAL RIFT--HAD FAILED AGAIN. I FELT BETRAYED BY MY ONLY FRIEND.
WARNING
I WANTED TO DIE.
THEN SOMETHING HAPPENED THAT CHANGED EVERYTHING.

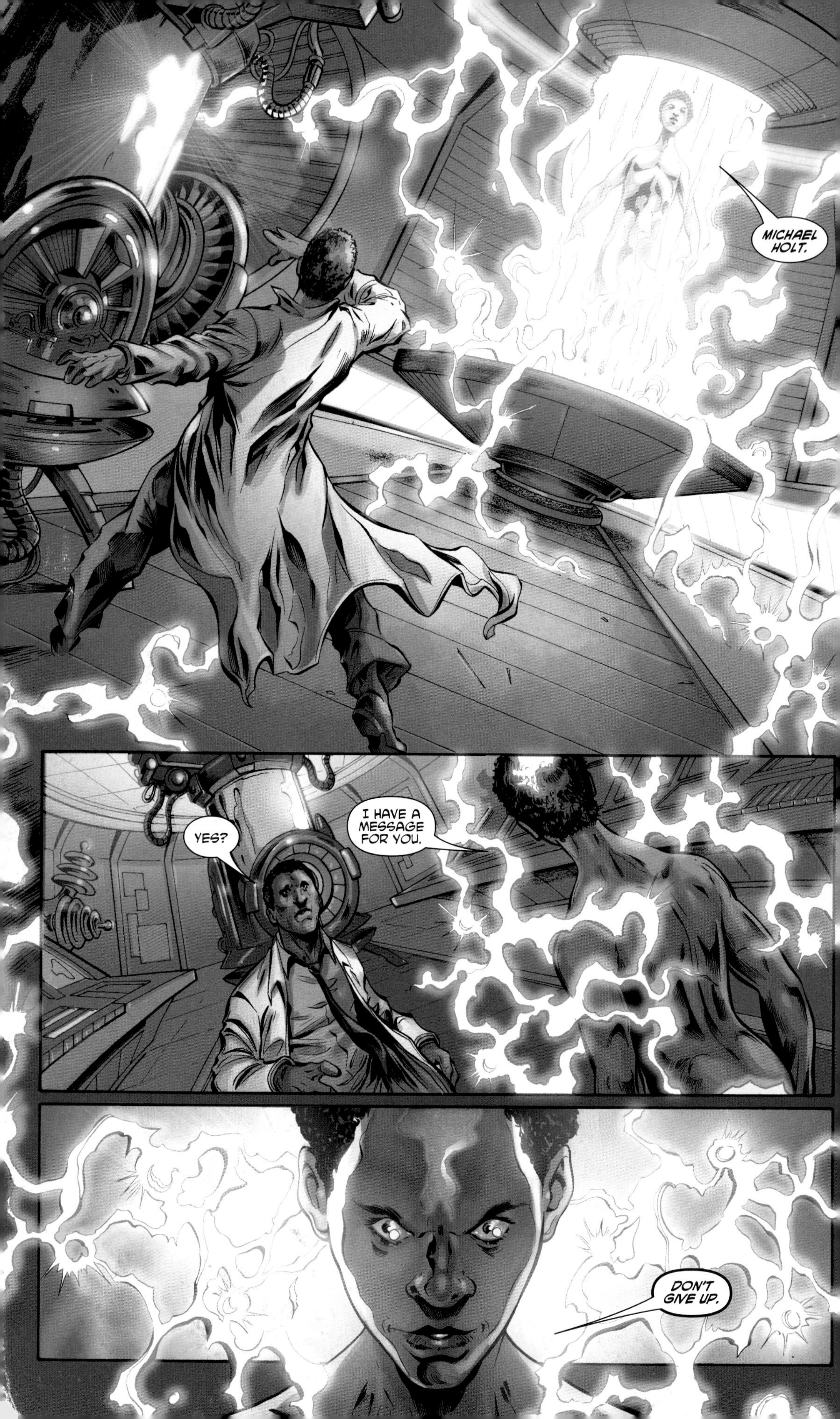
MICHAEL HOLT.
YES?
I HAVE A MESSAGE FOR YOU.
DON'T GIVE UP.

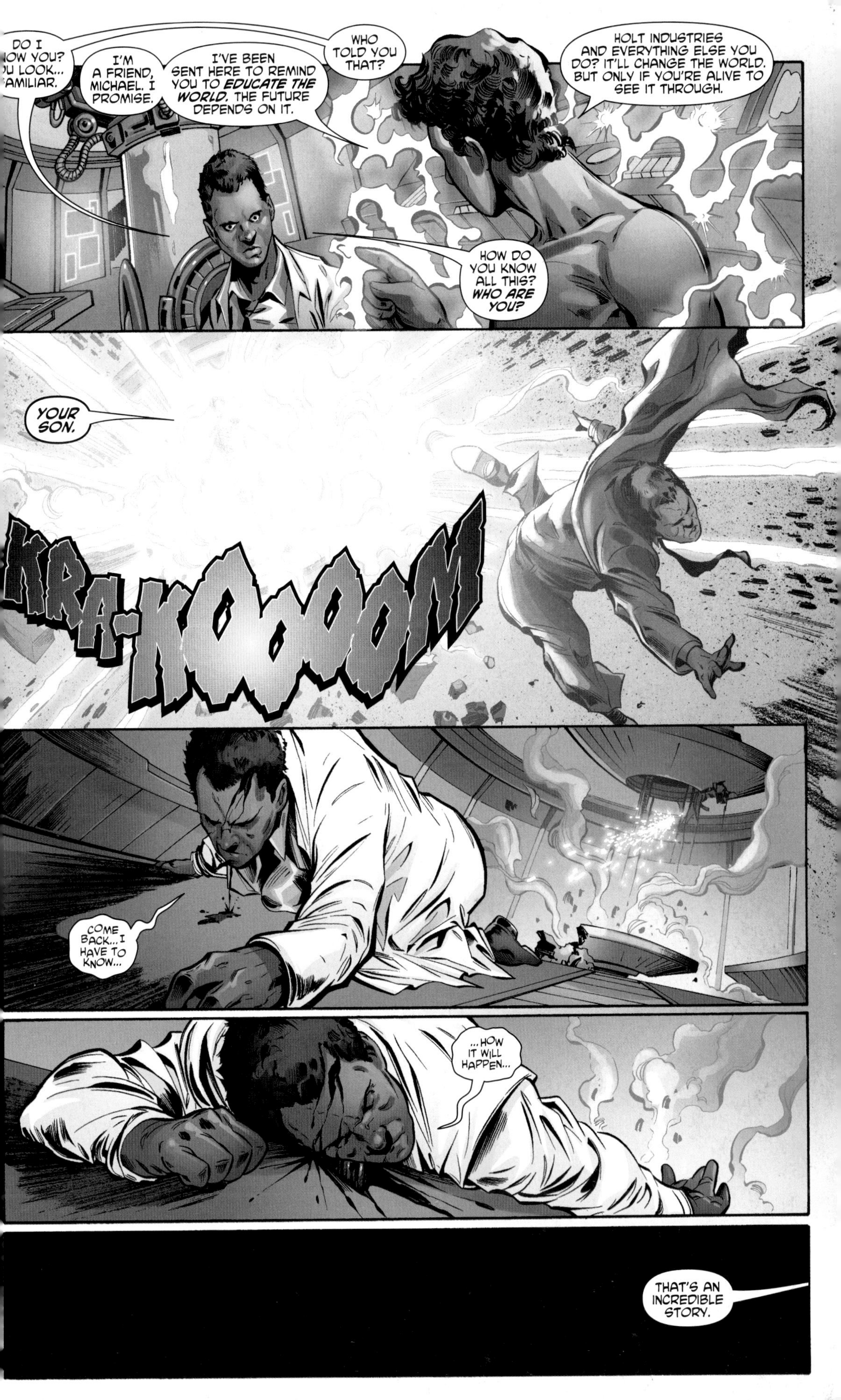
DO I
NOW YOU?
OU LOOK...
AMILIAR.
I'M A FRIEND, MICHAEL. I PROMISE.
I'VE BEEN SENT HERE TO REMIND YOU TO EDUCATE THE WORLD. THE FUTURE DEPENDS ON IT.
WHO TOLD YOU THAT?
HOLT INDUSTRIES AND EVERYTHING ELSE YOU DO? IT'LL CHANGE THE WORLD. BUT ONLY IF YOU'RE ALIVE TO SEE IT THROUGH.
HOW DO YOU KNOW ALL THIS? WHO ARE YOU?
YOUR SON.
KRA-KOOOOM
COME BACK...I HAVE TO KNOW...
...HOW IT WILL HAPPEN...
THAT'S AN INCREDIBLE STORY.

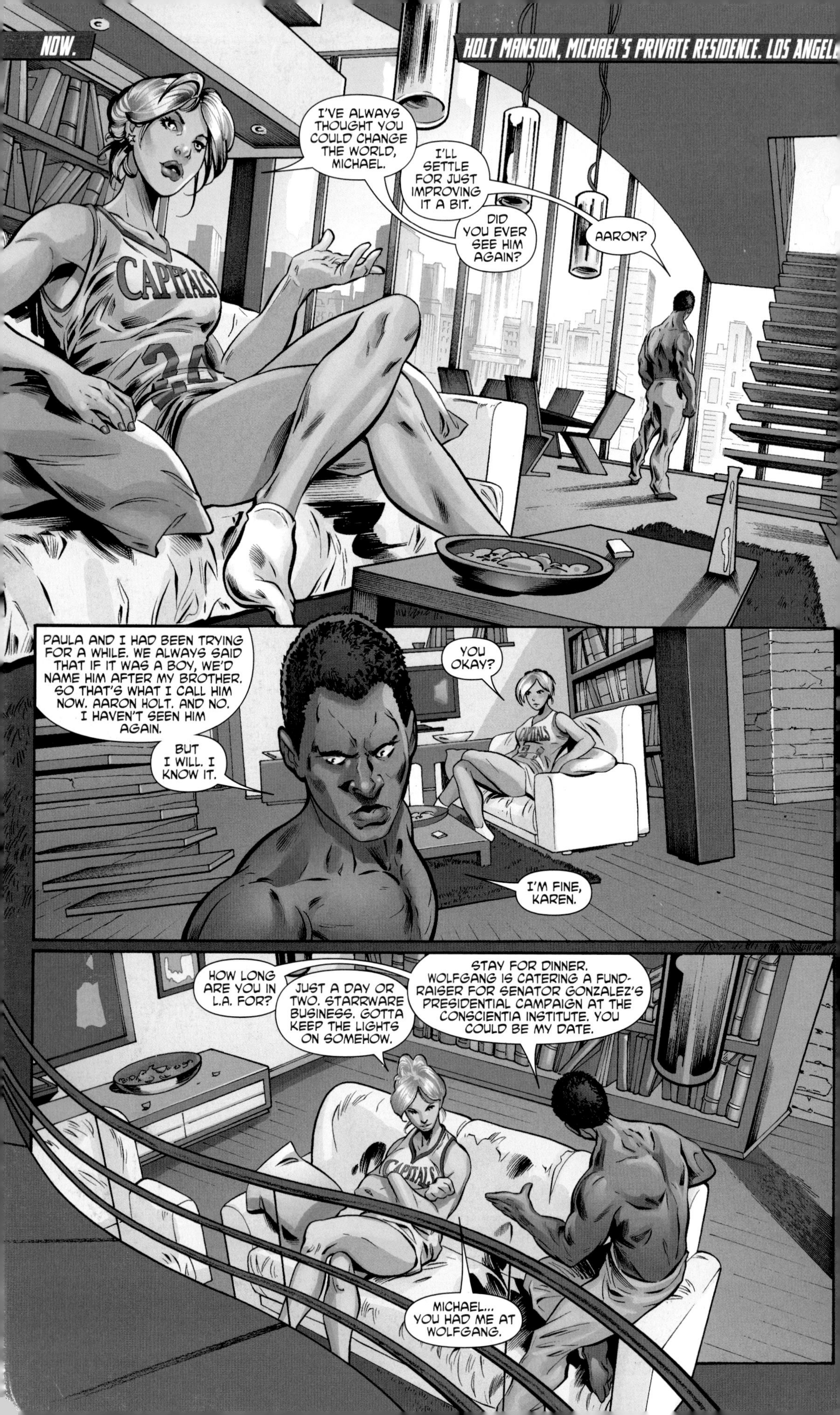
NOW.
HOLT MANSION, MICHAEL'S PRIVATE RESIDENCE. LOS ANGEL
I'VE ALWAYS THOUGHT YOU COULD CHANGE THE WORLD, MICHAEL.
I'LL SETTLE FOR JUST IMPROVING IT A BIT.
DID YOU EVER SEE HIM AGAIN?
AARON?
CAPITALS
PAULA AND I HAD BEEN TRYING FOR A WHILE. WE ALWAYS SAID THAT IF IT WAS A BOY, WE'D NAME HIM AFTER MY BROTHER. SO THAT'S WHAT I CALL HIM NOW. AARON HOLT. AND NO. I HAVEN'T SEEN HIM AGAIN.
BUT I WILL. I KNOW IT.
YOU OKAY?
I'M FINE, KAREN.
HOW LONG ARE YOU IN L.A. FOR?
JUST A DAY OR TWO. STARRWARE BUSINESS. GOTTA KEEP THE LIGHTS ON SOMEHOW.
STAY FOR DINNER. WOLFGANG IS CATERING A FUND-RAISER FOR SENATOR GONZALEZ'S PRESIDENTIAL CAMPAIGN AT THE CONSCIENTIA INSTITUTE. YOU COULD BE MY DATE.
MICHAEL... YOU HAD ME AT WOLFGANG.

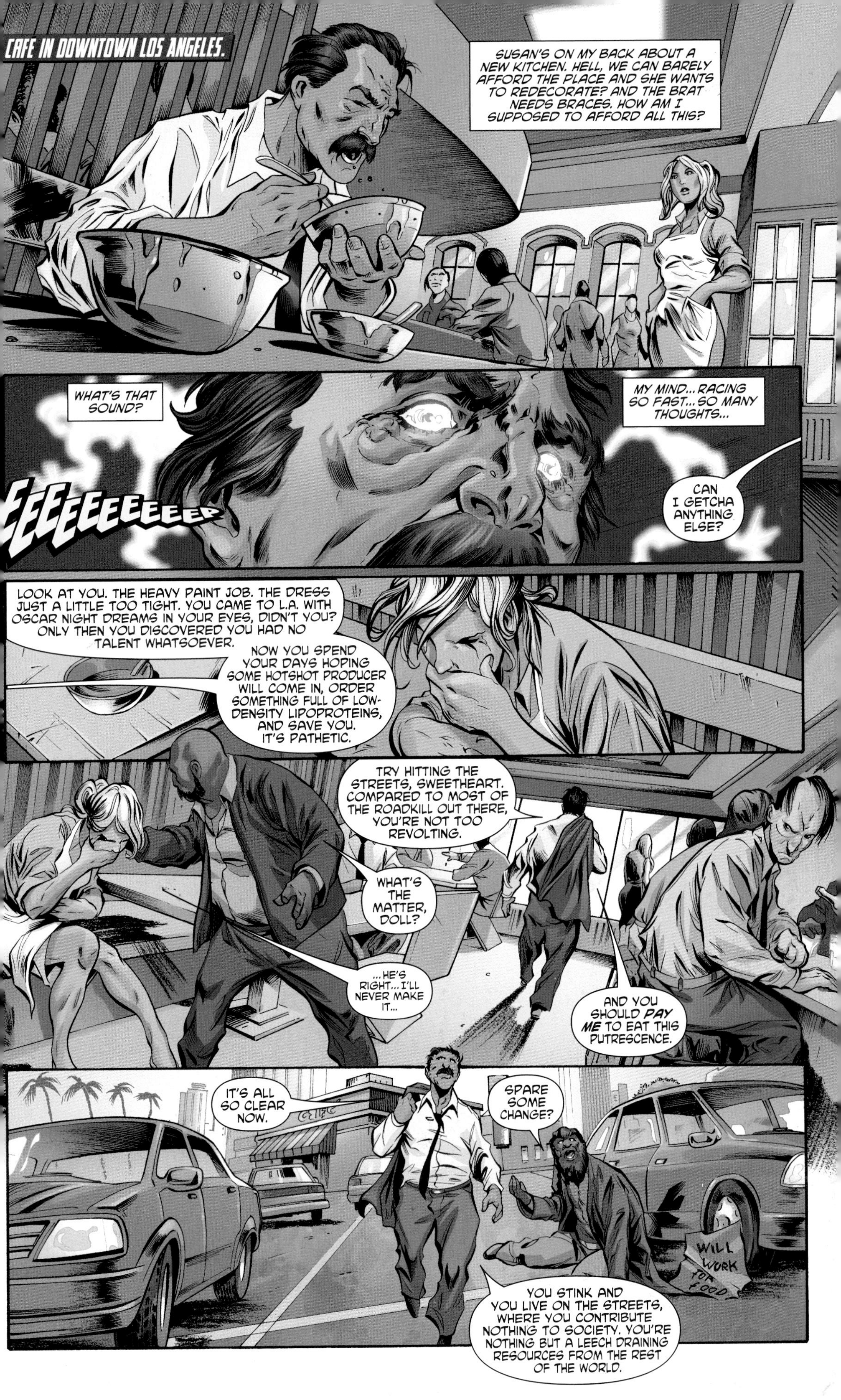

CAFE IN DOWNTOWN LOS ANGELES.
SUSAN'S ON MY BACK ABOUT A NEW KITCHEN. HELL, WE CAN BARELY AFFORD THE PLACE AND SHE WANTS TO REDECORATE? AND THE BRAT NEEDS BRACES. HOW AM I SUPPOSED TO AFFORD ALL THIS?
WHAT'S THAT SOUND?
MY MIND... RACING SO FAST... SO MANY THOUGHTS...
EEEEEEEEEEEP
CAN I GETCHA ANYTHING ELSE?
LOOK AT YOU. THE HEAVY PAINT JOB. THE DRESS JUST A LITTLE TOO TIGHT. YOU CAME TO L.A. WITH OSCAR NIGHT DREAMS IN YOUR EYES, DIDN'T YOU? ONLY THEN YOU DISCOVERED YOU HAD NO TALENT WHATSOEVER.
NOW YOU SPEND YOUR DAYS HOPING SOME HOTSHOT PRODUCER WILL COME IN, ORDER SOMETHING FULL OF LOW-DENSITY LIPOPROTEINS, AND SAVE YOU. IT'S PATHETIC.
TRY HITTING THE STREETS, SWEETHEART. COMPARED TO MOST OF THE ROADKILL OUT THERE, YOU'RE NOT TOO REVOLTING.
WHAT'S THE MATTER, DOLL?
...HE'S RIGHT... I'LL NEVER MAKE IT...
AND YOU SHOULD PAY ME TO EAT THIS PUTRESCENCE.
IT'S ALL SO CLEAR NOW.
SPARE SOME CHANGE?
WILL WORK FOR FOOD
YOU STINK AND YOU LIVE ON THE STREETS, WHERE YOU CONTRIBUTE NOTHING TO SOCIETY. YOU'RE NOTHING BUT A LEECH DRAINING RESOURCES FROM THE REST OF THE WORLD.

COME BACK HERE, YOU JERK!

OH, MAN.

PROBLEM SOLVED.

"HIS NAME IS *EDGAR HOLOWITZ*."

LOS ANGELES POLICE DEPARTMENT, HOLLYWOOD DIVISION.

WE CHECKED WITH HIS OFFICE. HE WAS FINE THIS MORNING. THEN THE GUY TAKES A LUNCH BREAK AND SUDDENLY--

--HE GOES NUTS.

HAS HE BEEN WRITING SYMBOLS LIKE THESE ALL DAY?

YUP. LOOKS LIKE SOME KINDA SCIENCE GIBBERISH. FIGURED SINCE THAT'S YOUR BEAT, WE'D BETTER CALL YOU IN.

YOU DID THE RIGHT THING. THIS IS EXACTLY THE KIND OF SITUATION I ENVISIONED WHEN I PROVIDED THE L.A.P.D. WITH A WAY TO CONTACT ME SECURELY. SEE THESE INTEGERS?

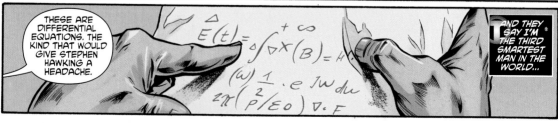

THESE ARE DIFFERENTIAL EQUATIONS. THE KIND THAT WOULD GIVE STEPHEN HAWKING A HEADACHE.

AND THEY SAY I'M THE THIRD SMARTEST MAN IN THE WORLD...

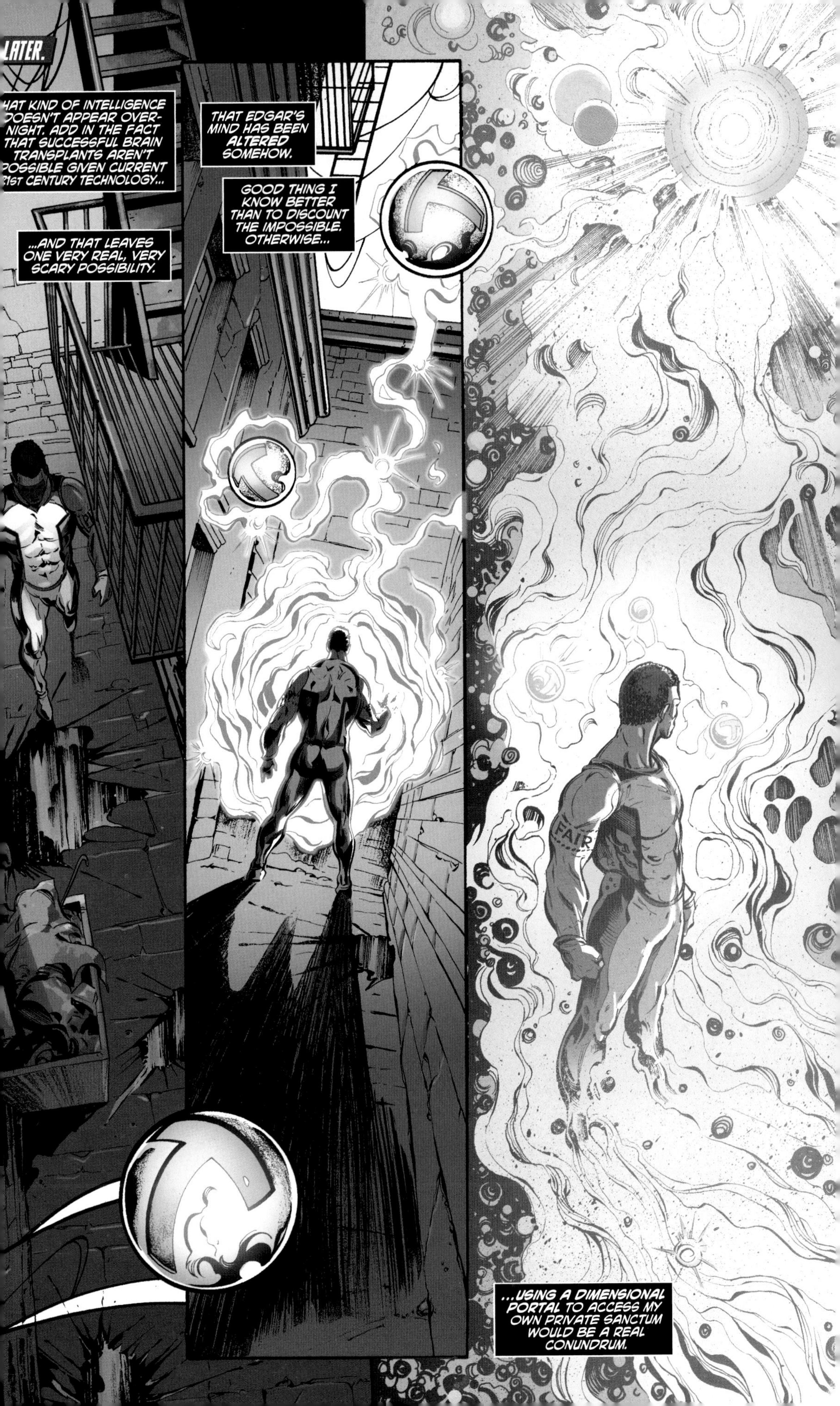
LATER.
HAT KIND OF INTELLIGENCE DOESN'T APPEAR OVER-NIGHT. ADD IN THE FACT THAT SUCCESSFUL BRAIN TRANSPLANTS AREN'T POSSIBLE GIVEN CURRENT 21ST CENTURY TECHNOLOGY...
...AND THAT LEAVES ONE VERY REAL, VERY SCARY POSSIBILITY.
THAT EDGAR'S MIND HAS BEEN ALTERED SOMEHOW.
GOOD THING I KNOW BETTER THAN TO DISCOUNT THE IMPOSSIBLE. OTHERWISE...
FAIR
...USING A DIMENSIONAL PORTAL TO ACCESS MY OWN PRIVATE SANCTUM WOULD BE A REAL CONUNDRUM.

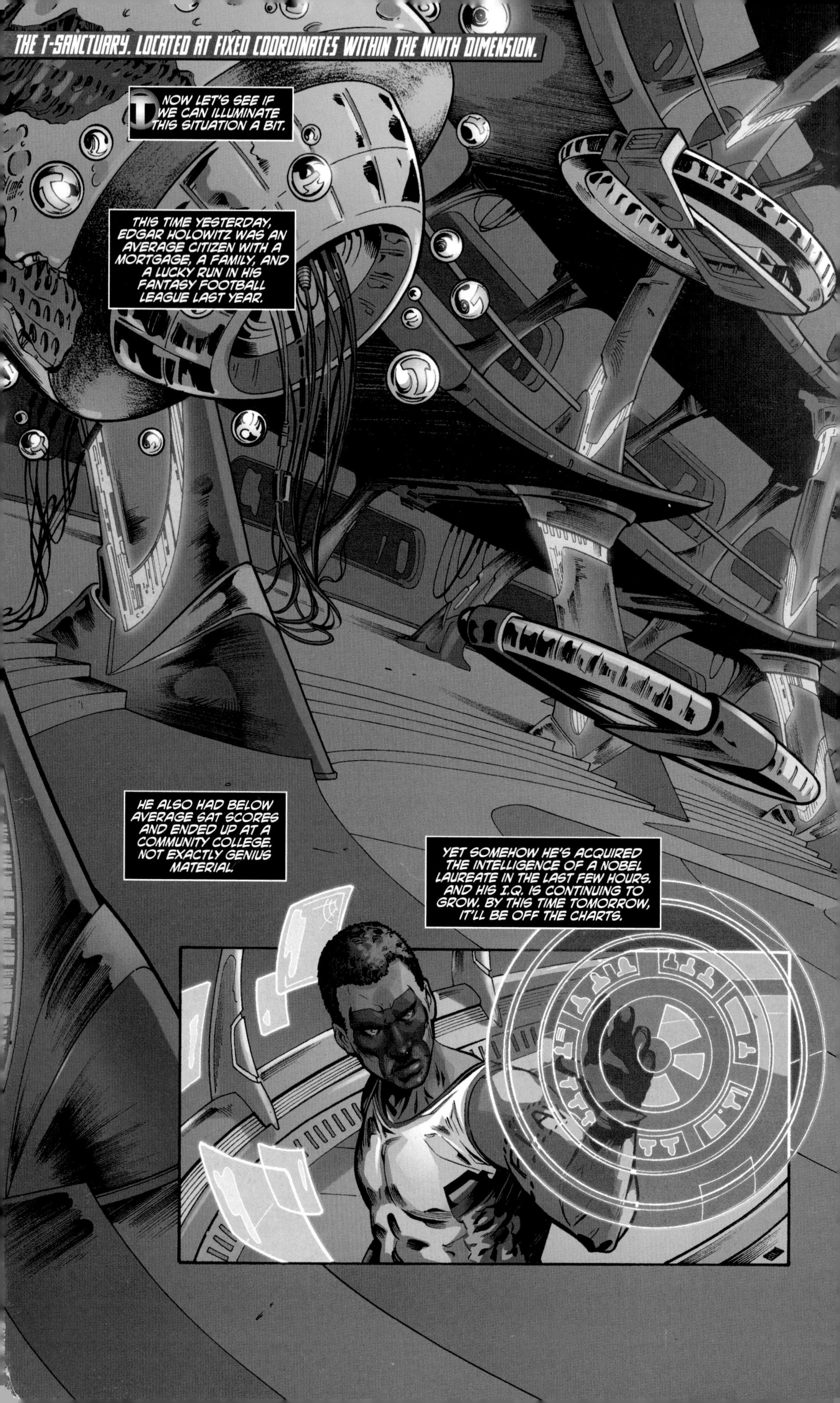

THE T-SANCTUARY. LOCATED AT FIXED COORDINATES WITHIN THE NINTH DIMENSION.
NOW LET'S SEE IF WE CAN ILLUMINATE THIS SITUATION A BIT.
THIS TIME YESTERDAY, EDGAR HOLOWITZ WAS AN AVERAGE CITIZEN WITH A MORTGAGE, A FAMILY, AND A LUCKY RUN IN HIS FANTASY FOOTBALL LEAGUE LAST YEAR.
HE ALSO HAD BELOW AVERAGE SAT SCORES AND ENDED UP AT A COMMUNITY COLLEGE. NOT EXACTLY GENIUS MATERIAL.
YET SOMEHOW HE'S ACQUIRED THE INTELLIGENCE OF A NOBEL LAUREATE IN THE LAST FEW HOURS. AND HIS I.Q. IS CONTINUING TO GROW. BY THIS TIME TOMORROW, IT'LL BE OFF THE CHARTS.

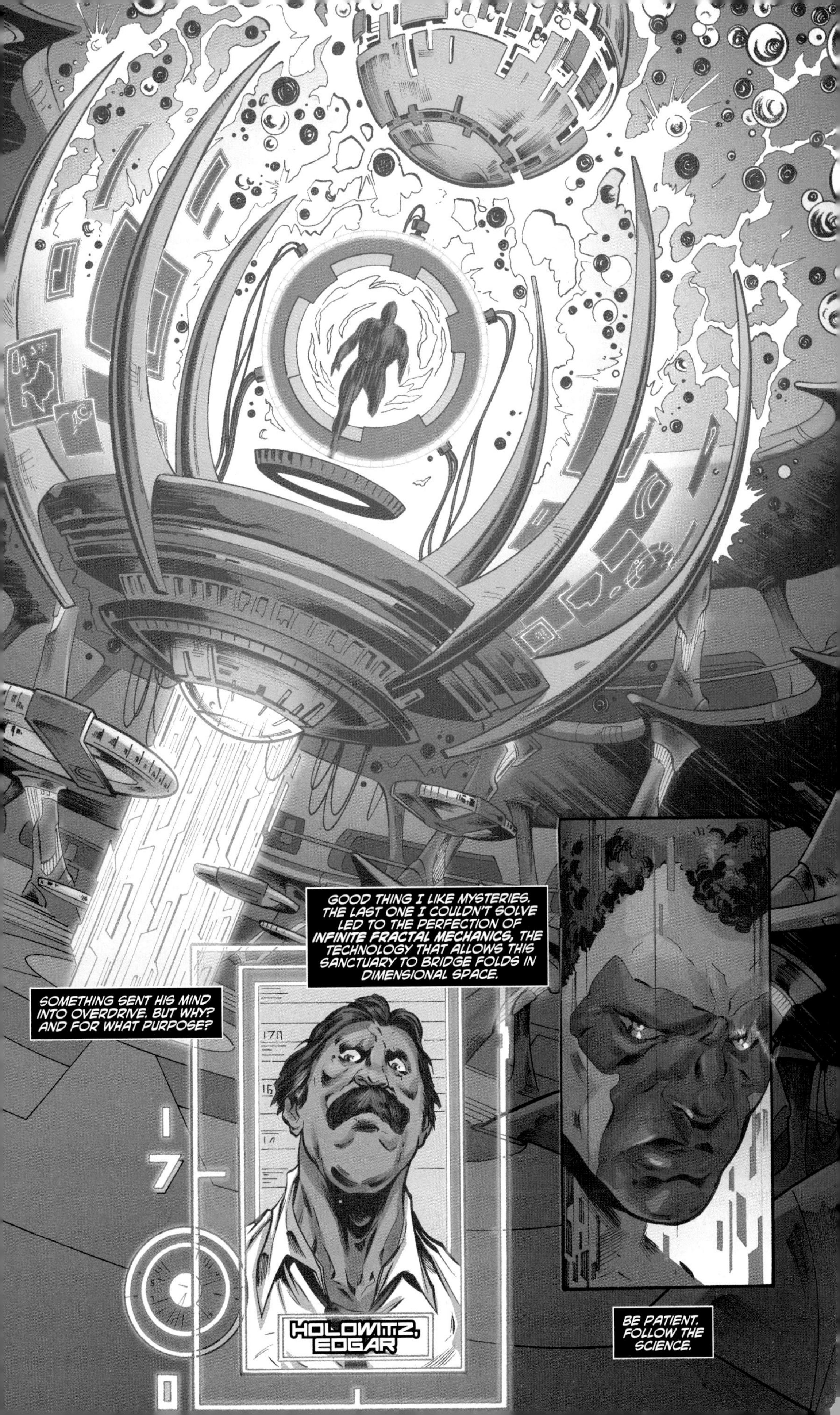
SOMETHING SENT HIS MIND INTO OVERDRIVE. BUT WHY? AND FOR WHAT PURPOSE?
GOOD THING I LIKE MYSTERIES. THE LAST ONE I COULDN'T SOLVE LED TO THE PERFECTION OF INFINITE FRACTAL MECHANICS, THE TECHNOLOGY THAT ALLOWS THIS SANCTUARY TO BRIDGE FOLDS IN DIMENSIONAL SPACE.
HOLOWITZ, EDGAR
BE PATIENT. FOLLOW THE SCIENCE.

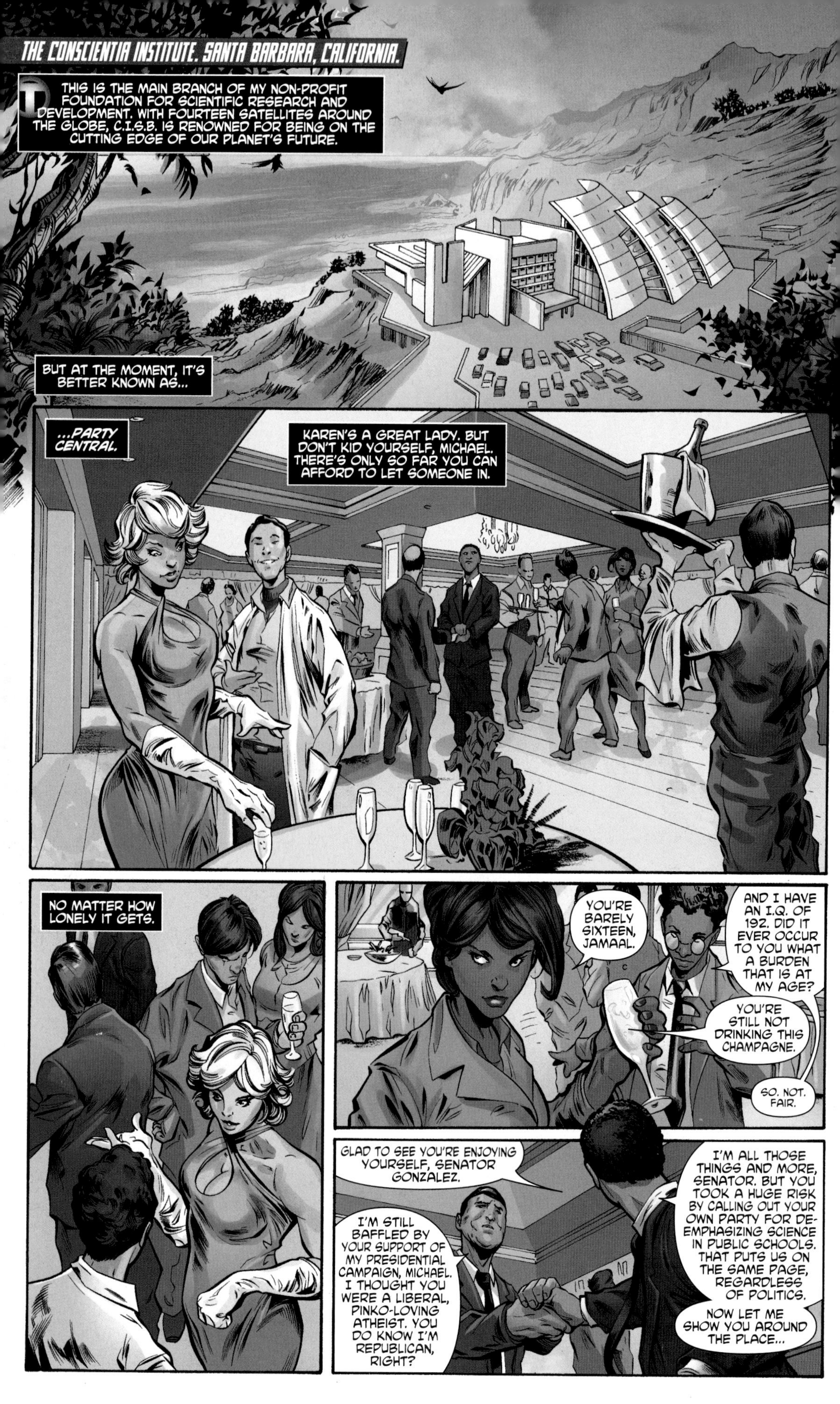

THE CONSCIENTIA INSTITUTE. SANTA BARBARA, CALIFORNIA.
THIS IS THE MAIN BRANCH OF MY NON-PROFIT FOUNDATION FOR SCIENTIFIC RESEARCH AND DEVELOPMENT. WITH FOURTEEN SATELLITES AROUND THE GLOBE, C.I.S.B. IS RENOWNED FOR BEING ON THE CUTTING EDGE OF OUR PLANET'S FUTURE.
BUT AT THE MOMENT, IT'S BETTER KNOWN AS...
...PARTY CENTRAL.
KAREN'S A GREAT LADY. BUT DON'T KID YOURSELF, MICHAEL. THERE'S ONLY SO FAR YOU CAN AFFORD TO LET SOMEONE IN.
NO MATTER HOW LONELY IT GETS.
YOU'RE BARELY SIXTEEN, JAMAAL.
AND I HAVE AN I.Q. OF 192. DID IT EVER OCCUR TO YOU WHAT A BURDEN THAT IS AT MY AGE?
YOU'RE STILL NOT DRINKING THIS CHAMPAGNE.
SO. NOT. FAIR.
GLAD TO SEE YOU'RE ENJOYING YOURSELF, SENATOR GONZALEZ.
I'M STILL BAFFLED BY YOUR SUPPORT OF MY PRESIDENTIAL CAMPAIGN, MICHAEL. I THOUGHT YOU WERE A LIBERAL, PINKO-LOVING ATHEIST. YOU DO KNOW I'M REPUBLICAN, RIGHT?
I'M ALL THOSE THINGS AND MORE, SENATOR. BUT YOU TOOK A HUGE RISK BY CALLING OUT YOUR OWN PARTY FOR DE-EMPHASIZING SCIENCE IN PUBLIC SCHOOLS. THAT PUTS US ON THE SAME PAGE, REGARDLESS OF POLITICS.
NOW LET ME SHOW YOU AROUND THE PLACE...

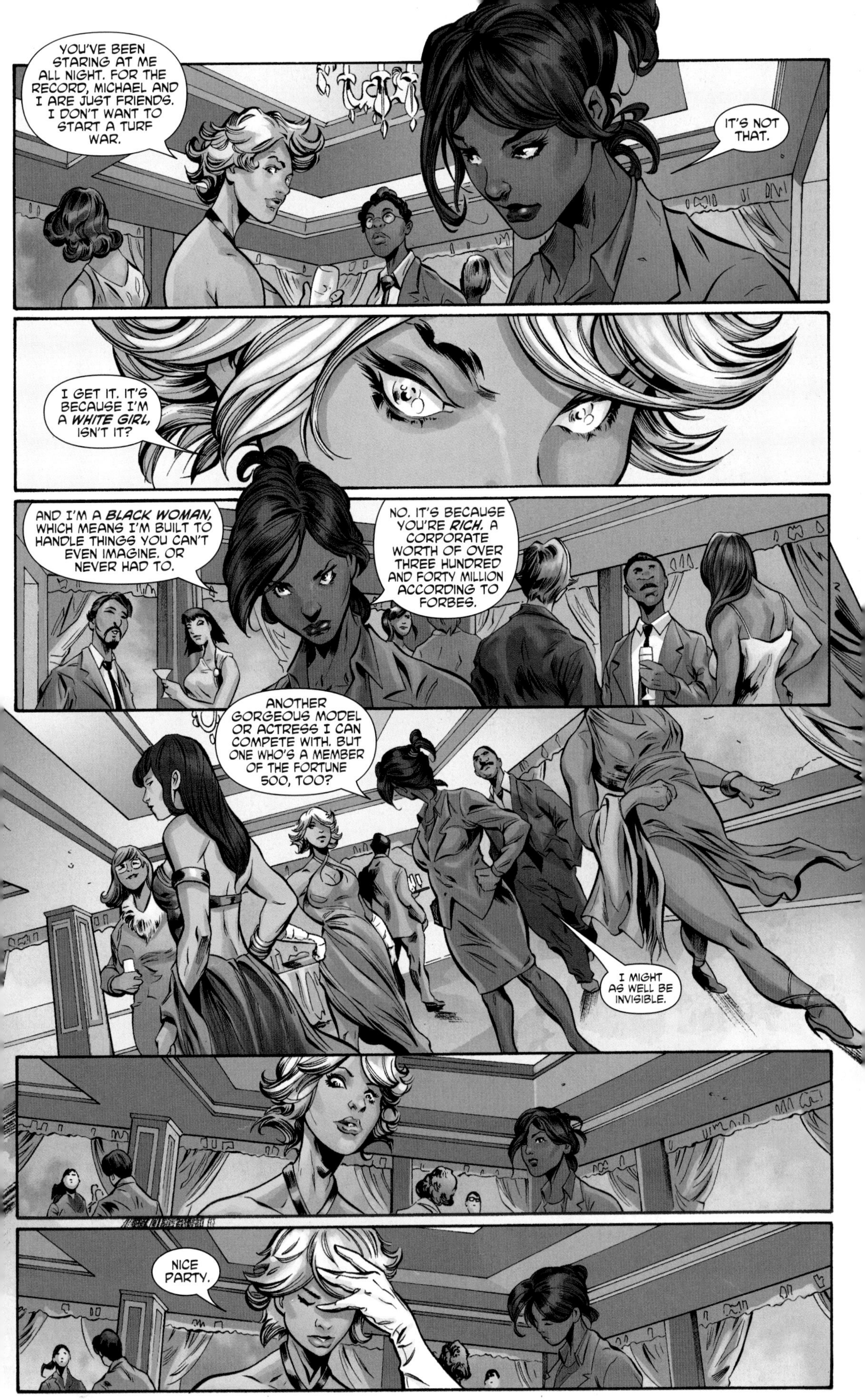

YOU'VE BEEN STARING AT ME ALL NIGHT. FOR THE RECORD, MICHAEL AND I ARE JUST FRIENDS. I DON'T WANT TO START A TURF WAR.
IT'S NOT THAT.
I GET IT. IT'S BECAUSE I'M A *WHITE GIRL,* ISN'T IT?
NO. IT'S BECAUSE YOU'RE *RICH.* A CORPORATE WORTH OF OVER THREE HUNDRED AND FORTY MILLION ACCORDING TO FORBES.
AND I'M A *BLACK WOMAN,* WHICH MEANS I'M BUILT TO HANDLE THINGS YOU CAN'T EVEN IMAGINE. OR NEVER HAD TO.
ANOTHER GORGEOUS MODEL OR ACTRESS I CAN COMPETE WITH. BUT ONE WHO'S A MEMBER OF THE FORTUNE 500, TOO?
I MIGHT AS WELL BE INVISIBLE.
NICE PARTY.

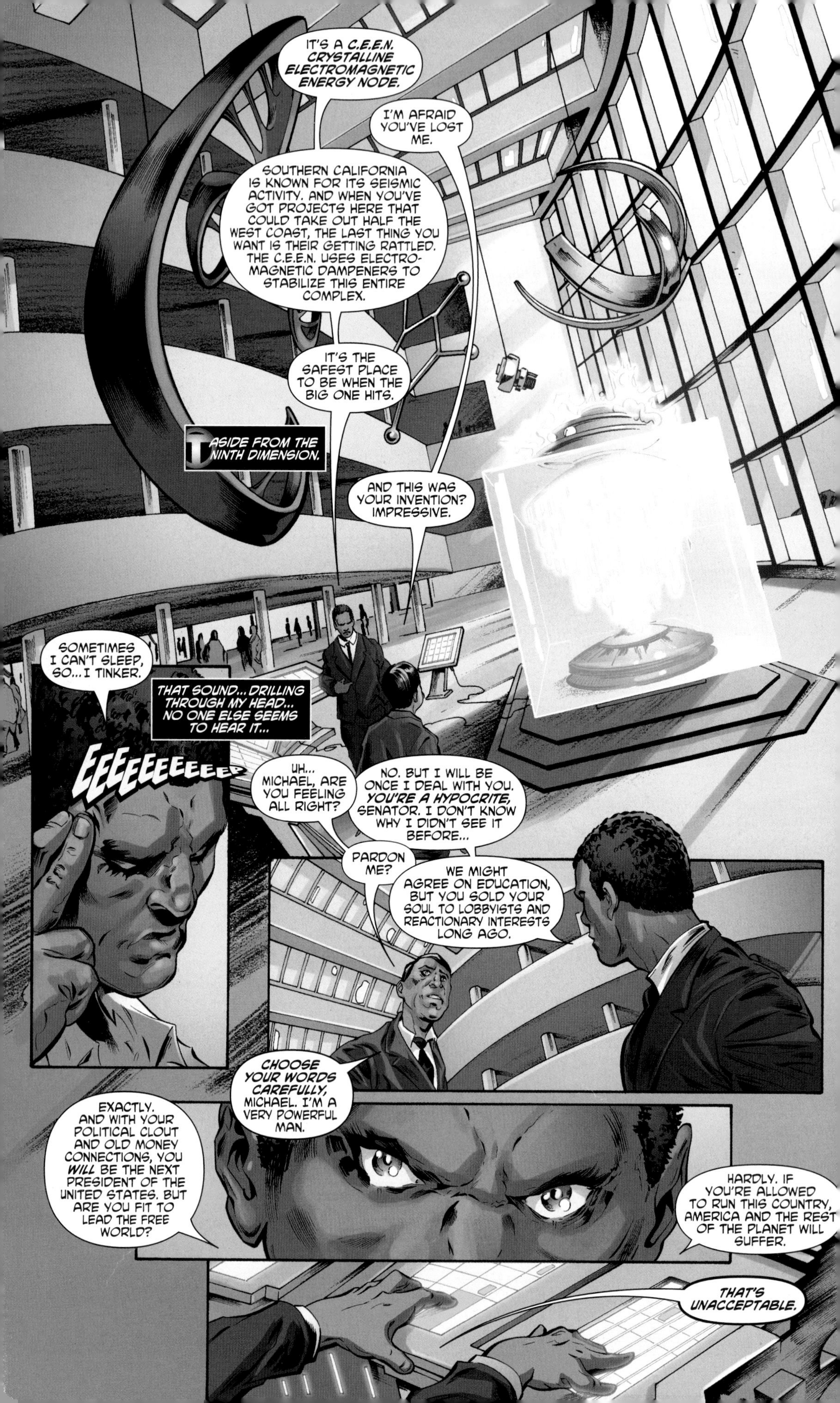

IT'S A C.E.E.N. CRYSTALLINE ELECTROMAGNETIC ENERGY NODE.
I'M AFRAID YOU'VE LOST ME.
SOUTHERN CALIFORNIA IS KNOWN FOR ITS SEISMIC ACTIVITY. AND WHEN YOU'VE GOT PROJECTS HERE THAT COULD TAKE OUT HALF THE WEST COAST, THE LAST THING YOU WANT IS THEIR GETTING RATTLED. THE C.E.E.N. USES ELECTRO-MAGNETIC DAMPENERS TO STABILIZE THIS ENTIRE COMPLEX.
IT'S THE SAFEST PLACE TO BE WHEN THE BIG ONE HITS.
ASIDE FROM THE NINTH DIMENSION.
AND THIS WAS YOUR INVENTION? IMPRESSIVE.
SOMETIMES I CAN'T SLEEP, SO...I TINKER.
THAT SOUND...DRILLING THROUGH MY HEAD... NO ONE ELSE SEEMS TO HEAR IT...
EEEEEEEEEEEP
UH... MICHAEL, ARE YOU FEELING ALL RIGHT?
NO. BUT I WILL BE ONCE I DEAL WITH YOU. YOU'RE A HYPOCRITE, SENATOR. I DON'T KNOW WHY I DIDN'T SEE IT BEFORE...
PARDON ME?
WE MIGHT AGREE ON EDUCATION, BUT YOU SOLD YOUR SOUL TO LOBBYISTS AND REACTIONARY INTERESTS LONG AGO.
CHOOSE YOUR WORDS CAREFULLY, MICHAEL. I'M A VERY POWERFUL MAN.
EXACTLY. AND WITH YOUR POLITICAL CLOUT AND OLD MONEY CONNECTIONS, YOU WILL BE THE NEXT PRESIDENT OF THE UNITED STATES. BUT ARE YOU FIT TO LEAD THE FREE WORLD?
HARDLY. IF YOU'RE ALLOWED TO RUN THIS COUNTRY, AMERICA AND THE REST OF THE PLANET WILL SUFFER.
THAT'S UNACCEPTABLE.

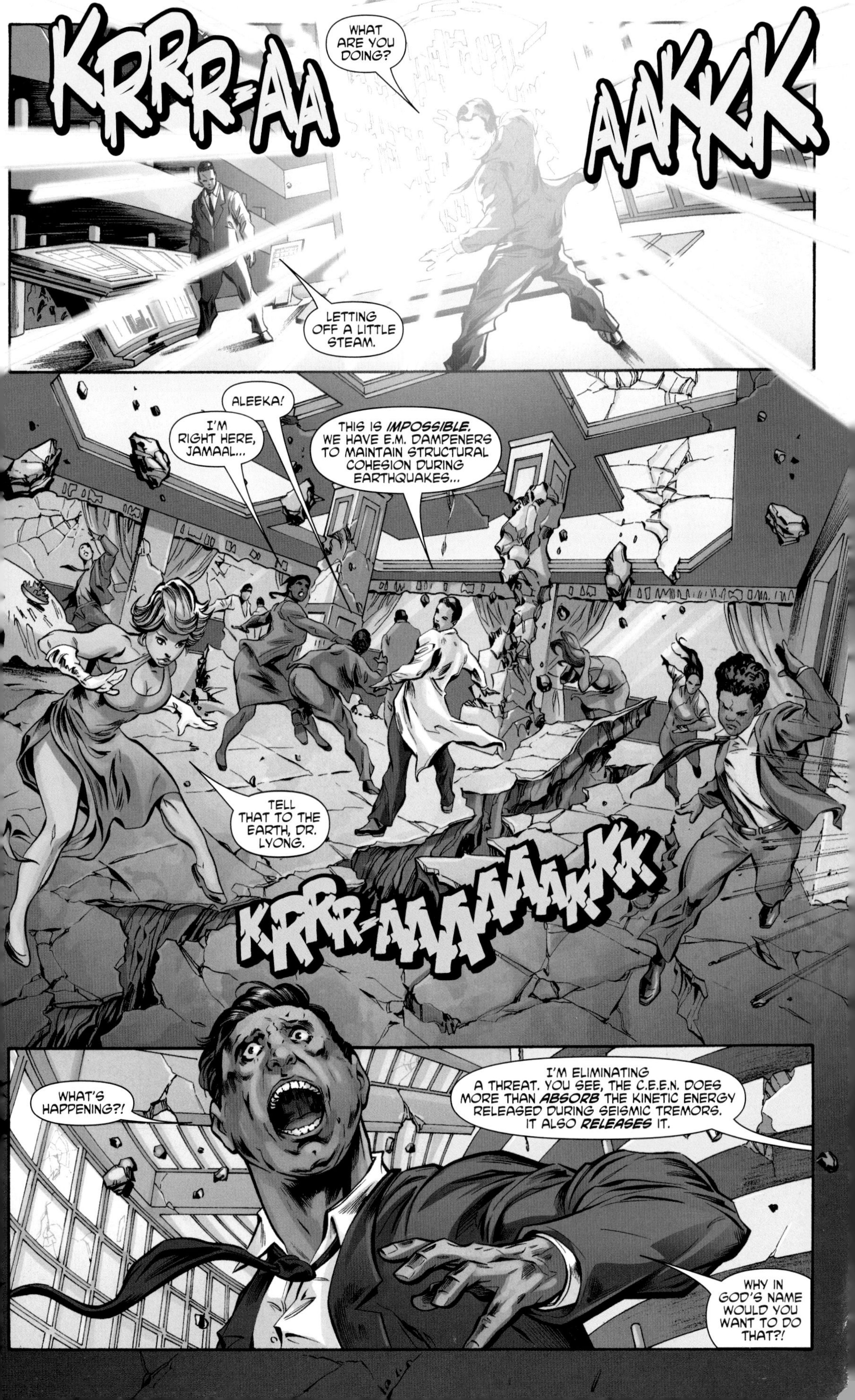
KRRR-AA
WHAT ARE YOU DOING?
AAKKK
LETTING OFF A LITTLE STEAM.
ALEEKA!
I'M RIGHT HERE, JAMAAL...
THIS IS IMPOSSIBLE. WE HAVE E.M. DAMPENERS TO MAINTAIN STRUCTURAL COHESION DURING EARTHQUAKES...
TELL THAT TO THE EARTH, DR. LYONG.
KRRR-AAAAAAKKK
WHAT'S HAPPENING?!
I'M ELIMINATING A THREAT. YOU SEE, THE C.E.E.N. DOES MORE THAN ABSORB THE KINETIC ENERGY RELEASED DURING SEISMIC TREMORS. IT ALSO RELEASES IT.
WHY IN GOD'S NAME WOULD YOU WANT TO DO THAT?!

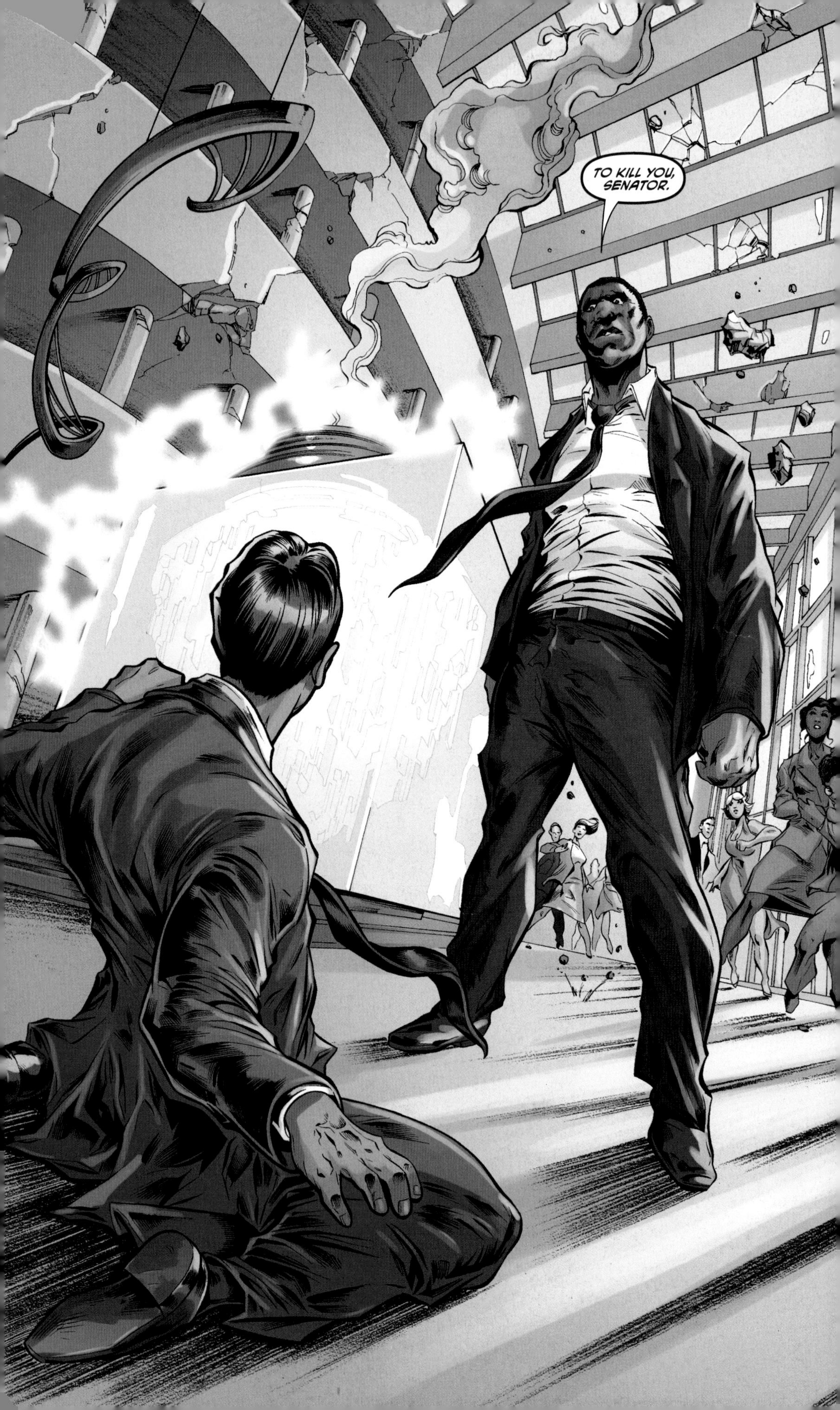
TO KILL YOU, SENATOR.

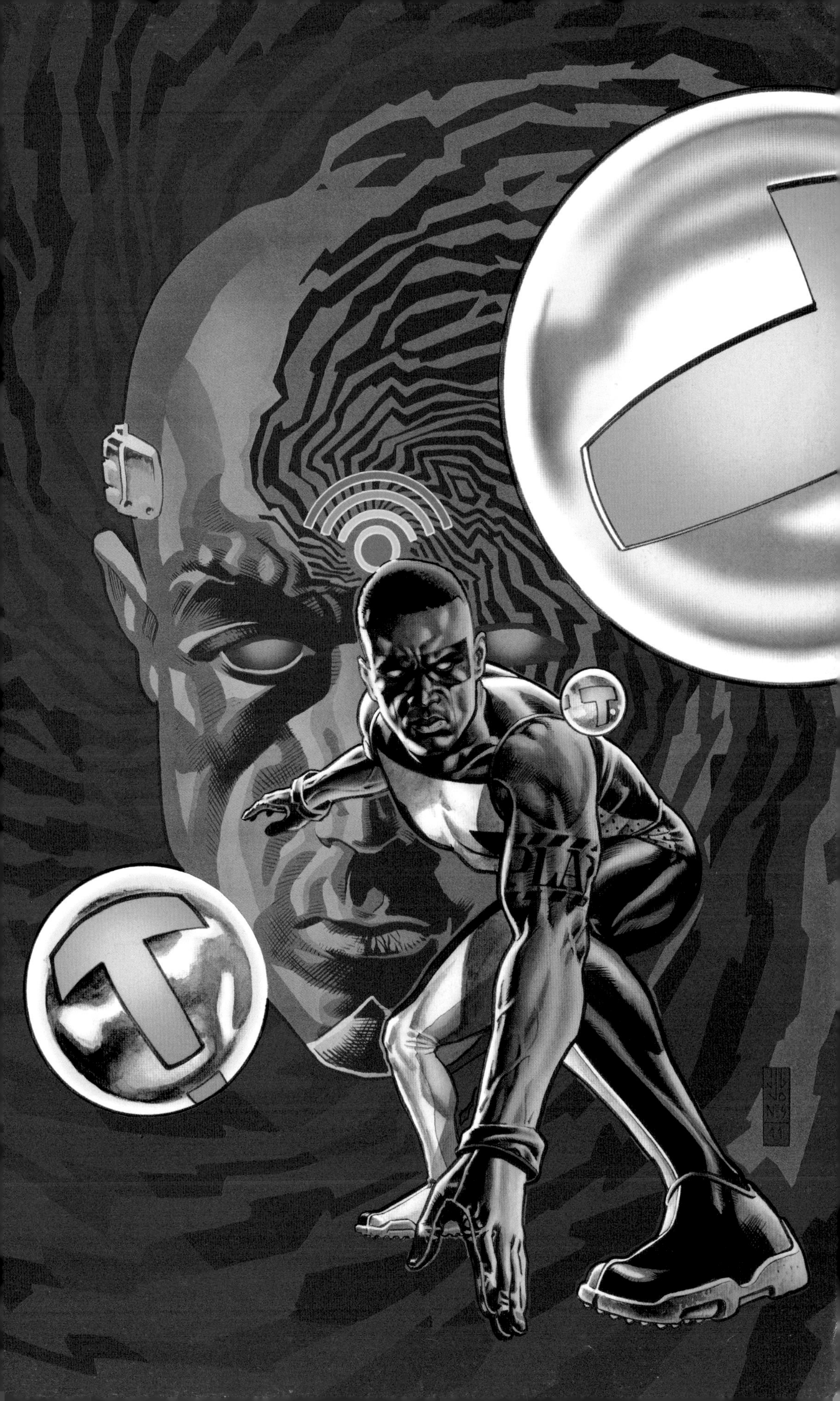

BLINDED BY SCIENCE

ERIC WALLACE writer **GIANLUCA GUGLIOTTA** penciller **WAYNE FAUCHER** inker
cover art by **J.G. JONES** with colorist **LOVERN KINDZIERSKI**

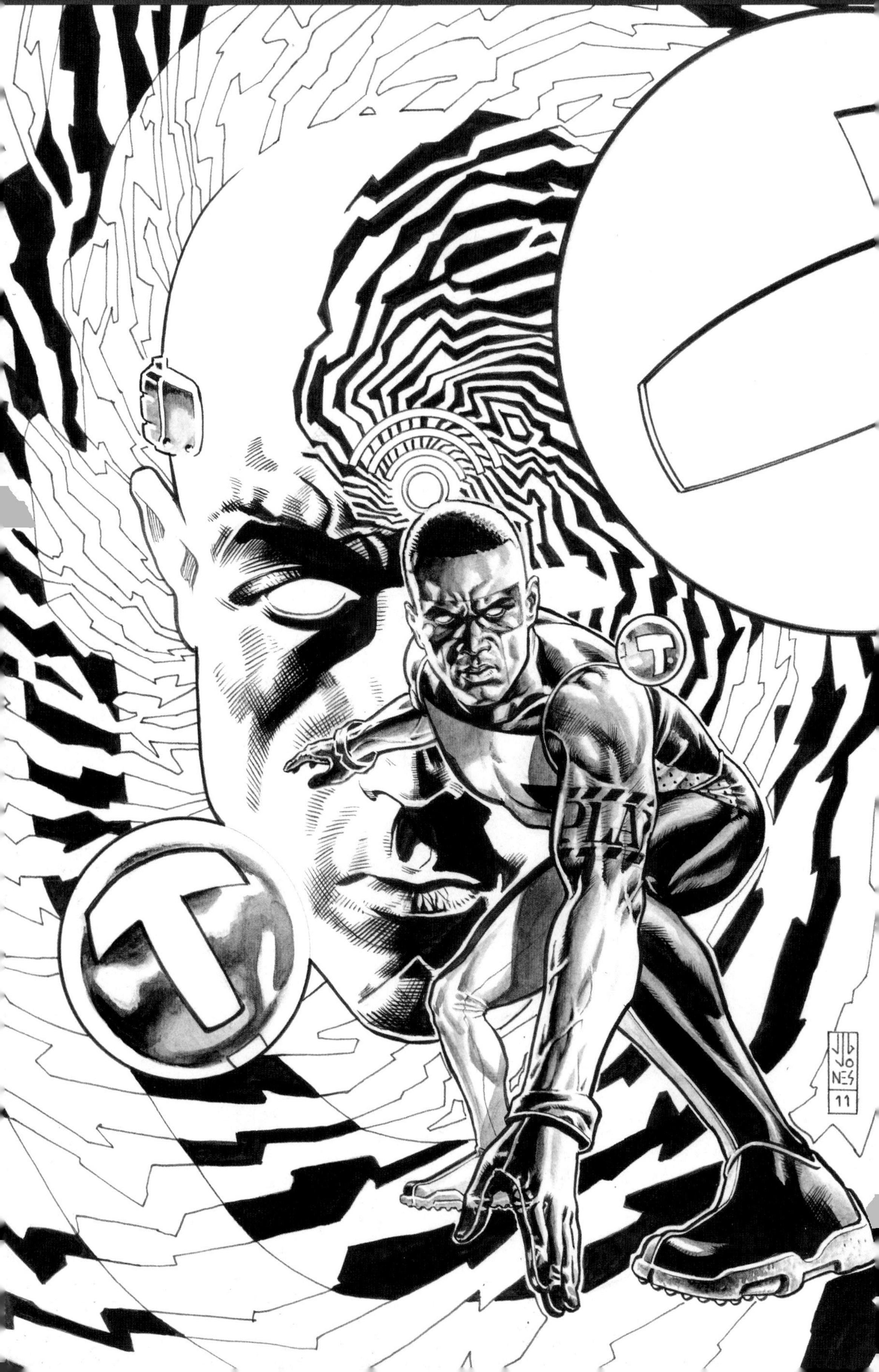

JG JONES
11

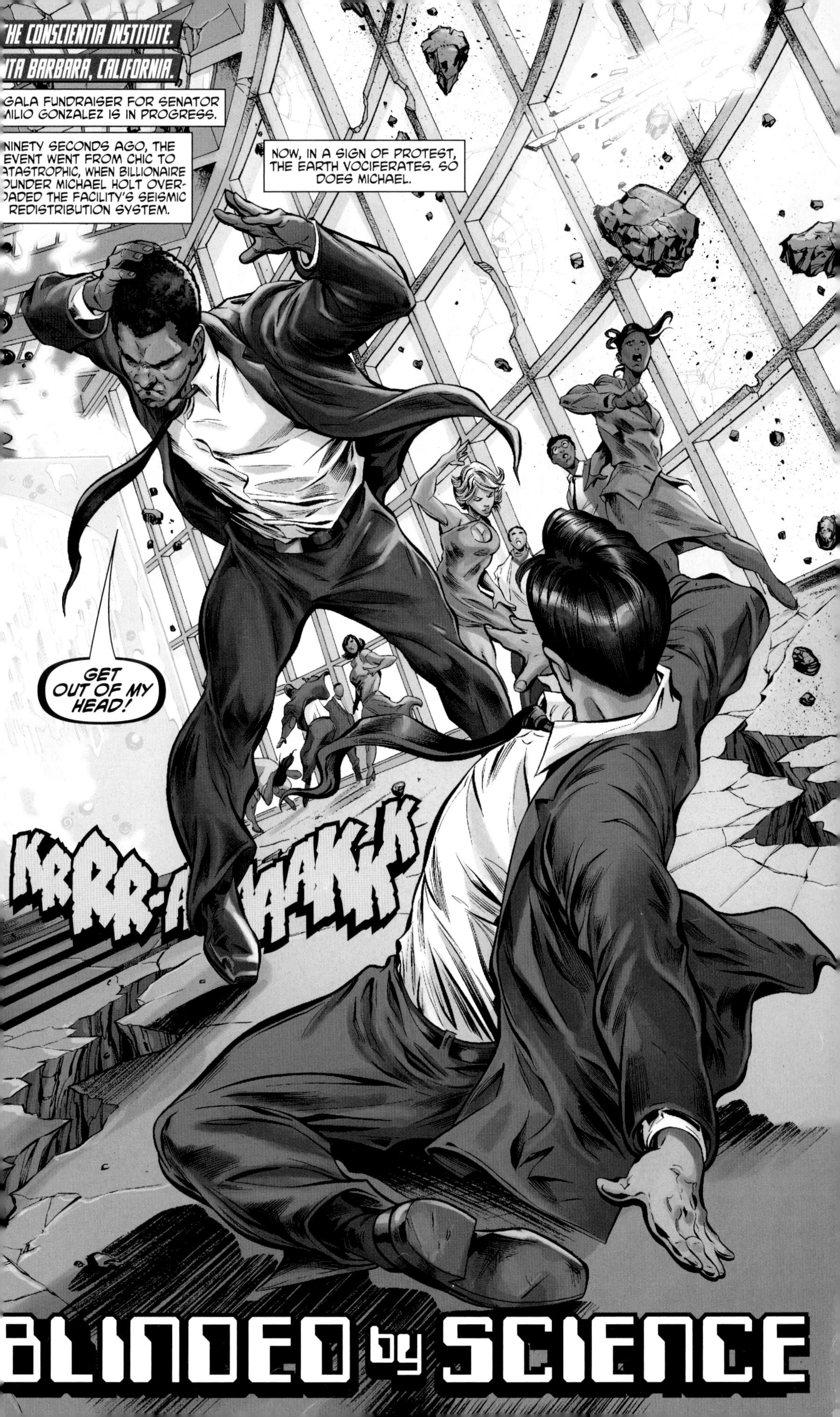
HE CONSCIENTIA INSTITUTE.
ITA BARBARA, CALIFORNIA.
GALA FUNDRAISER FOR SENATOR MILIO GONZALEZ IS IN PROGRESS.
NINETY SECONDS AGO, THE EVENT WENT FROM CHIC TO ATASTROPHIC, WHEN BILLIONAIRE OUNDER MICHAEL HOLT OVER-OADED THE FACILITY'S SEISMIC REDISTRIBUTION SYSTEM.
NOW, IN A SIGN OF PROTEST, THE EARTH VOCIFERATES. SO DOES MICHAEL.
GET OUT OF MY HEAD!
BLINDED by SCIENCE

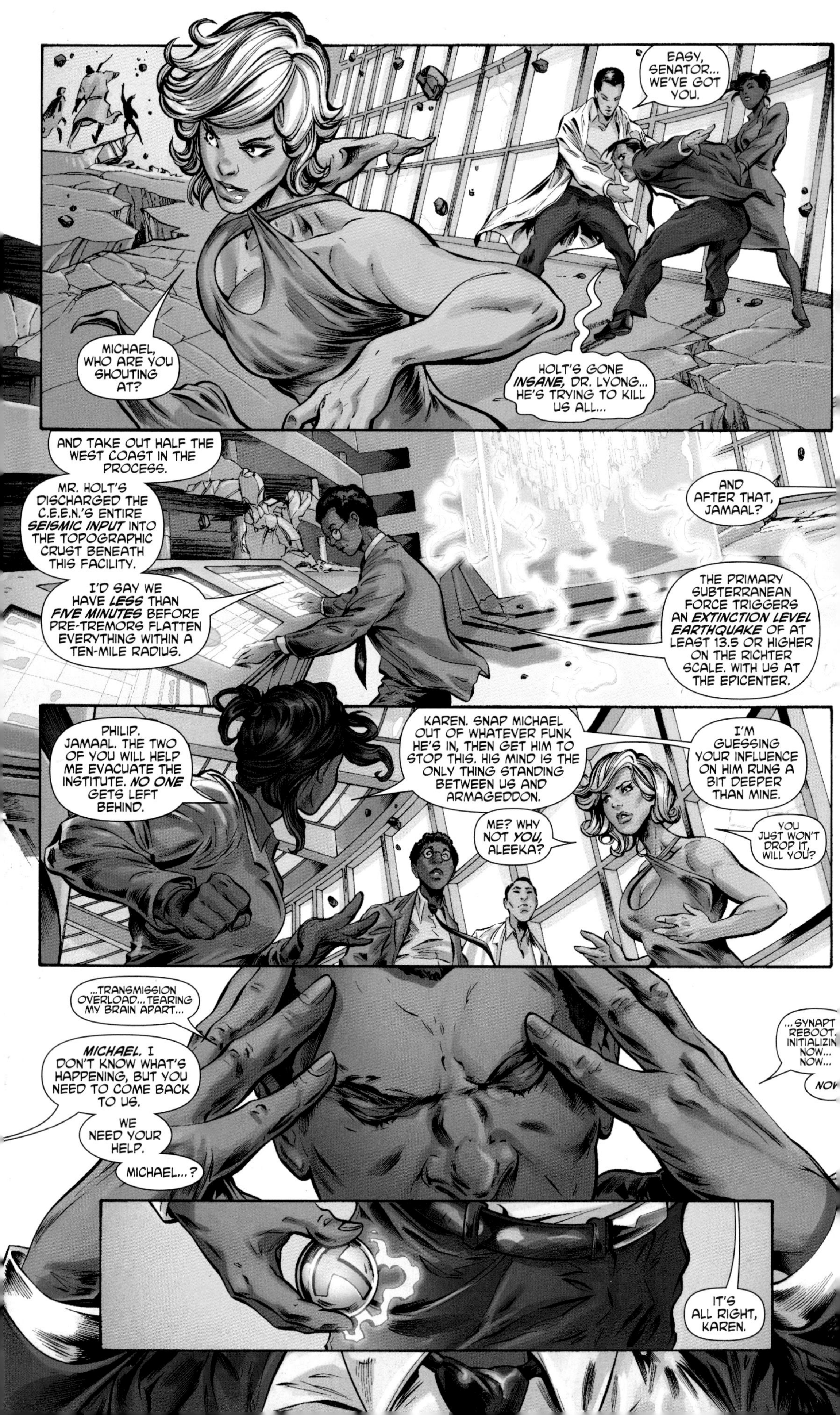

EASY, SENATOR... WE'VE GOT YOU.
MICHAEL, WHO ARE YOU SHOUTING AT?
HOLT'S GONE *INSANE,* DR. LYONG... HE'S TRYING TO KILL US ALL...
AND TAKE OUT HALF THE WEST COAST IN THE PROCESS.
MR. HOLT'S DISCHARGED THE C.E.E.N.'S ENTIRE *SEISMIC INPUT* INTO THE TOPOGRAPHIC CRUST BENEATH THIS FACILITY.
I'D SAY WE HAVE *LESS* THAN *FIVE MINUTES* BEFORE PRE-TREMORS FLATTEN EVERYTHING WITHIN A TEN-MILE RADIUS.
AND AFTER THAT, JAMAAL?
THE PRIMARY SUBTERRANEAN FORCE TRIGGERS AN *EXTINCTION LEVEL EARTHQUAKE* OF AT LEAST 13.5 OR HIGHER ON THE RICHTER SCALE. WITH US AT THE EPICENTER.
PHILIP. JAMAAL. THE TWO OF YOU WILL HELP ME EVACUATE THE INSTITUTE. *NO ONE* GETS LEFT BEHIND.
KAREN. SNAP MICHAEL OUT OF WHATEVER FUNK HE'S IN, THEN GET HIM TO STOP THIS. HIS MIND IS THE ONLY THING STANDING BETWEEN US AND ARMAGEDDON.
ME? WHY NOT *YOU,* ALEEKA?
I'M GUESSING YOUR INFLUENCE ON HIM RUNS A BIT DEEPER THAN MINE.
YOU JUST WON'T DROP IT, WILL YOU?
...TRANSMISSION OVERLOAD... TEARING MY BRAIN APART...
MICHAEL. I DON'T KNOW WHAT'S HAPPENING, BUT YOU NEED TO COME BACK TO US.
WE NEED YOUR HELP.
MICHAEL...?
IT'S ALL RIGHT, KAREN.

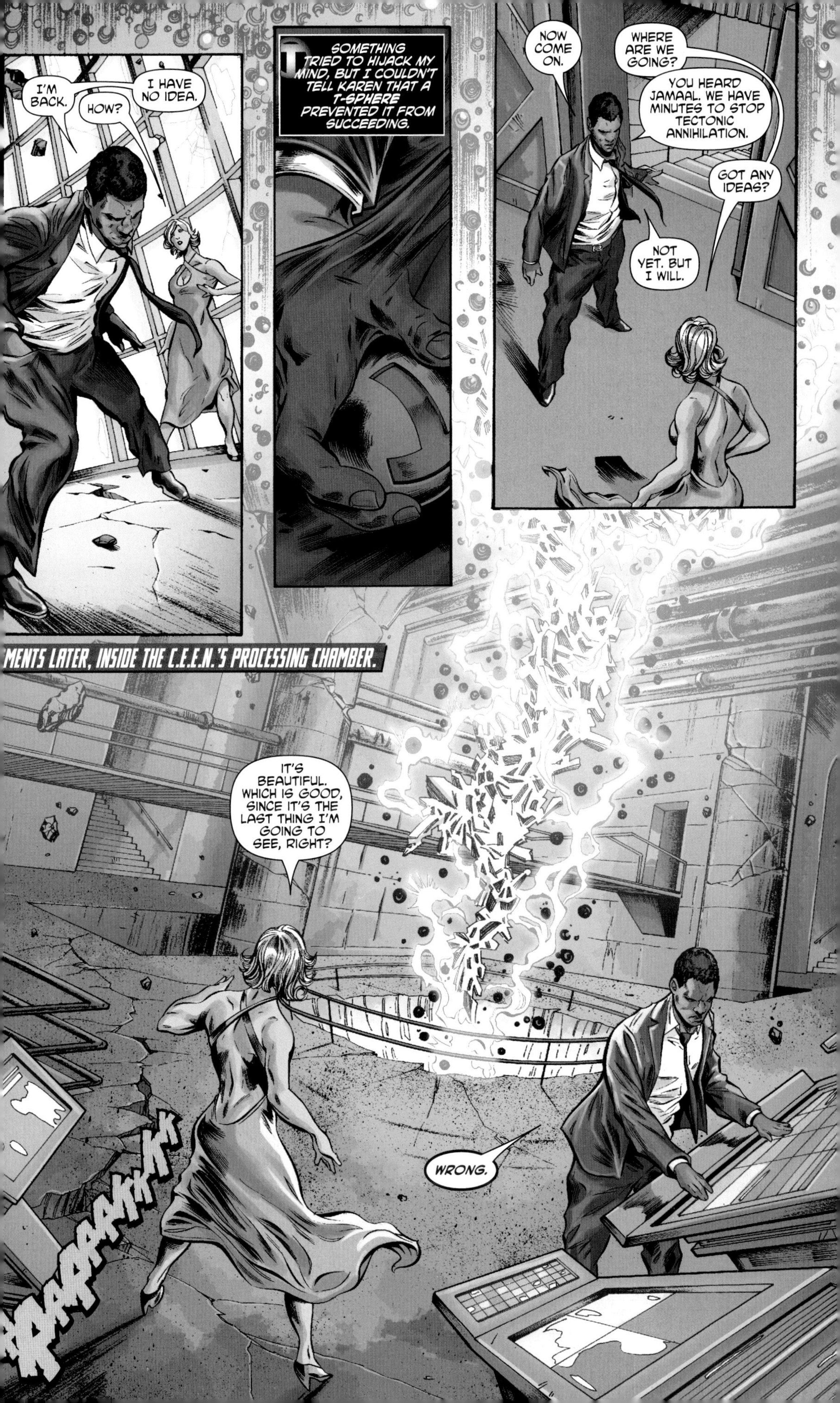
I'M BACK.
HOW?
I HAVE NO IDEA.
SOMETHING TRIED TO HIJACK MY MIND, BUT I COULDN'T TELL KAREN THAT A T-SPHERE PREVENTED IT FROM SUCCEEDING.
NOW COME ON.
WHERE ARE WE GOING?
YOU HEARD JAMAAL. WE HAVE MINUTES TO STOP TECTONIC ANNIHILATION.
GOT ANY IDEAS?
NOT YET. BUT I WILL.
MENTS LATER, INSIDE THE C.E.E.N.'S PROCESSING CHAMBER.
IT'S BEAUTIFUL. WHICH IS GOOD, SINCE IT'S THE LAST THING I'M GOING TO SEE, RIGHT?
WRONG.
RRAAAKKKK

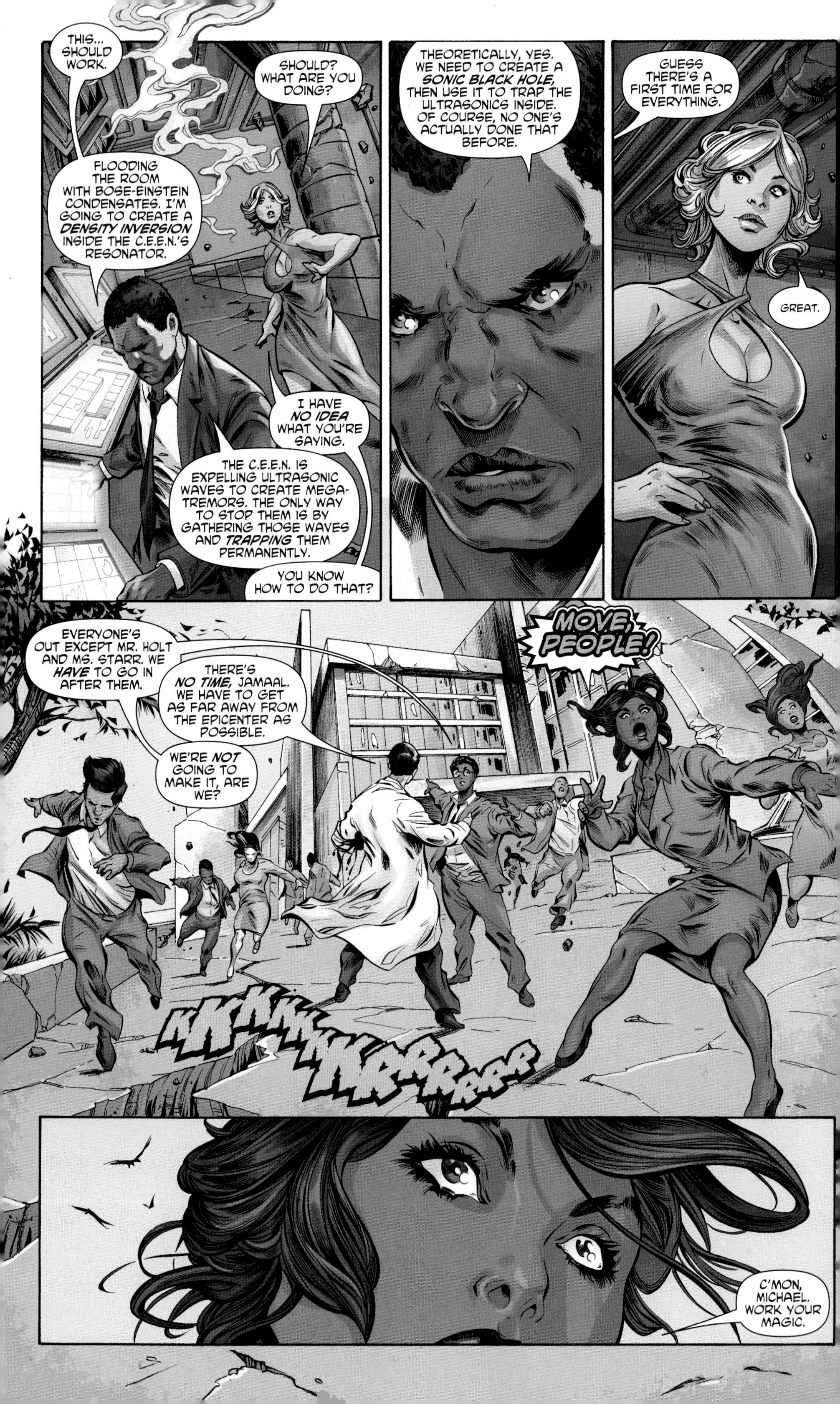
THIS... SHOULD WORK.
SHOULD? WHAT ARE YOU DOING?
FLOODING THE ROOM WITH BOSE-EINSTEIN CONDENSATES. I'M GOING TO CREATE A DENSITY INVERSION INSIDE THE C.E.E.N.'S RESONATOR.
I HAVE NO IDEA WHAT YOU'RE SAYING.
THE C.E.E.N. IS EXPELLING ULTRASONIC WAVES TO CREATE MEGA-TREMORS. THE ONLY WAY TO STOP THEM IS BY GATHERING THOSE WAVES AND TRAPPING THEM PERMANENTLY.
YOU KNOW HOW TO DO THAT?
THEORETICALLY, YES. WE NEED TO CREATE A SONIC BLACK HOLE, THEN USE IT TO TRAP THE ULTRASONICS INSIDE. OF COURSE, NO ONE'S ACTUALLY DONE THAT BEFORE.
GUESS THERE'S A FIRST TIME FOR EVERYTHING.
GREAT.
EVERYONE'S OUT EXCEPT MR. HOLT AND MS. STARR. WE HAVE TO GO IN AFTER THEM.
THERE'S NO TIME, JAMAAL. WE HAVE TO GET AS FAR AWAY FROM THE EPICENTER AS POSSIBLE.
WE'RE NOT GOING TO MAKE IT, ARE WE?
MOVE, PEOPLE!
KKKKKKKKRRRRRRR
C'MON, MICHAEL. WORK YOUR MAGIC.

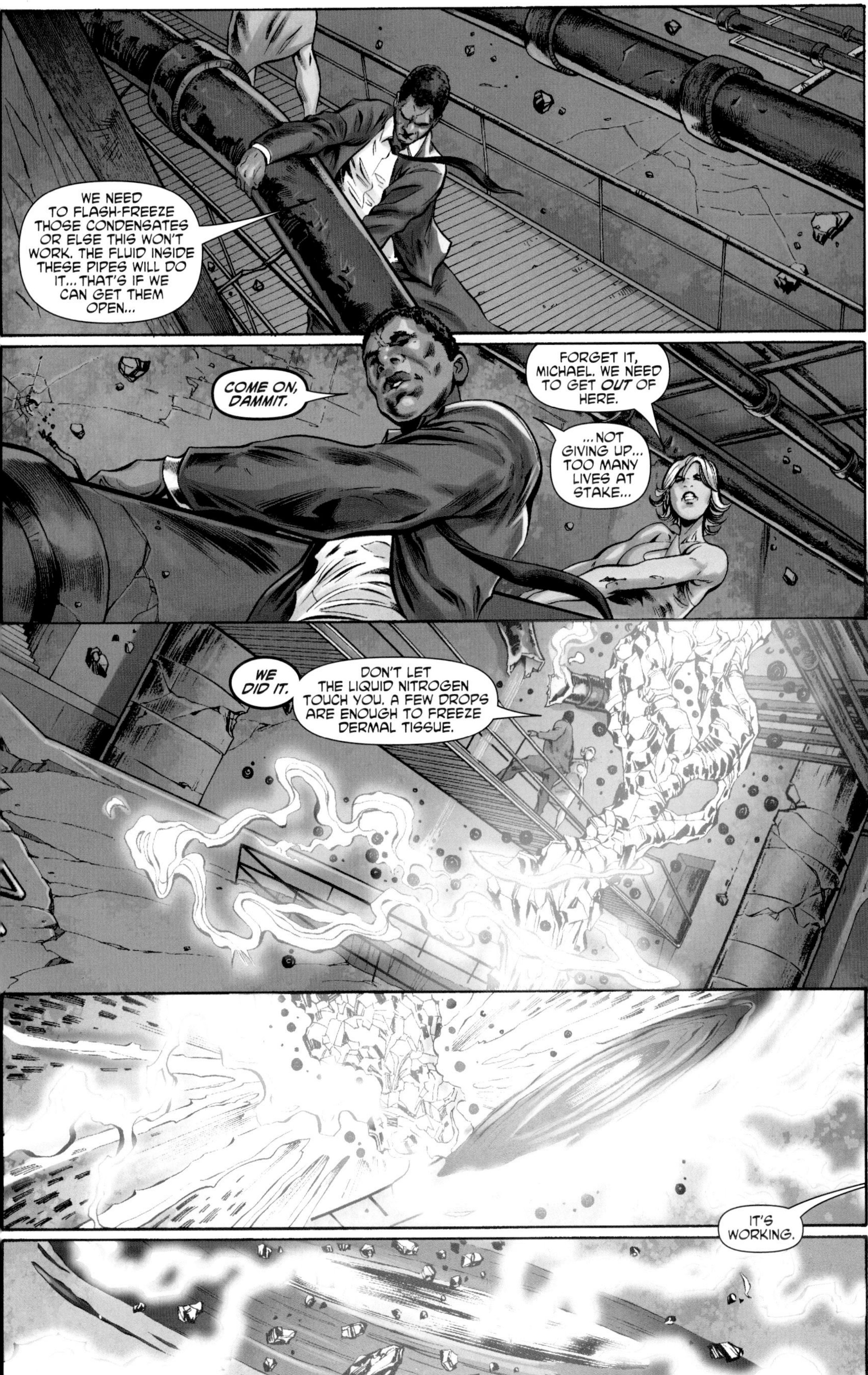
WE NEED TO FLASH-FREEZE THOSE CONDENSATES OR ELSE THIS WON'T WORK. THE FLUID INSIDE THESE PIPES WILL DO IT... THAT'S IF WE CAN GET THEM OPEN...
COME ON, DAMMIT.
FORGET IT, MICHAEL. WE NEED TO GET OUT OF HERE.
...NOT GIVING UP... TOO MANY LIVES AT STAKE...
WE DID IT.
DON'T LET THE LIQUID NITROGEN TOUCH YOU. A FEW DROPS ARE ENOUGH TO FREEZE DERMAL TISSUE.
IT'S WORKING.

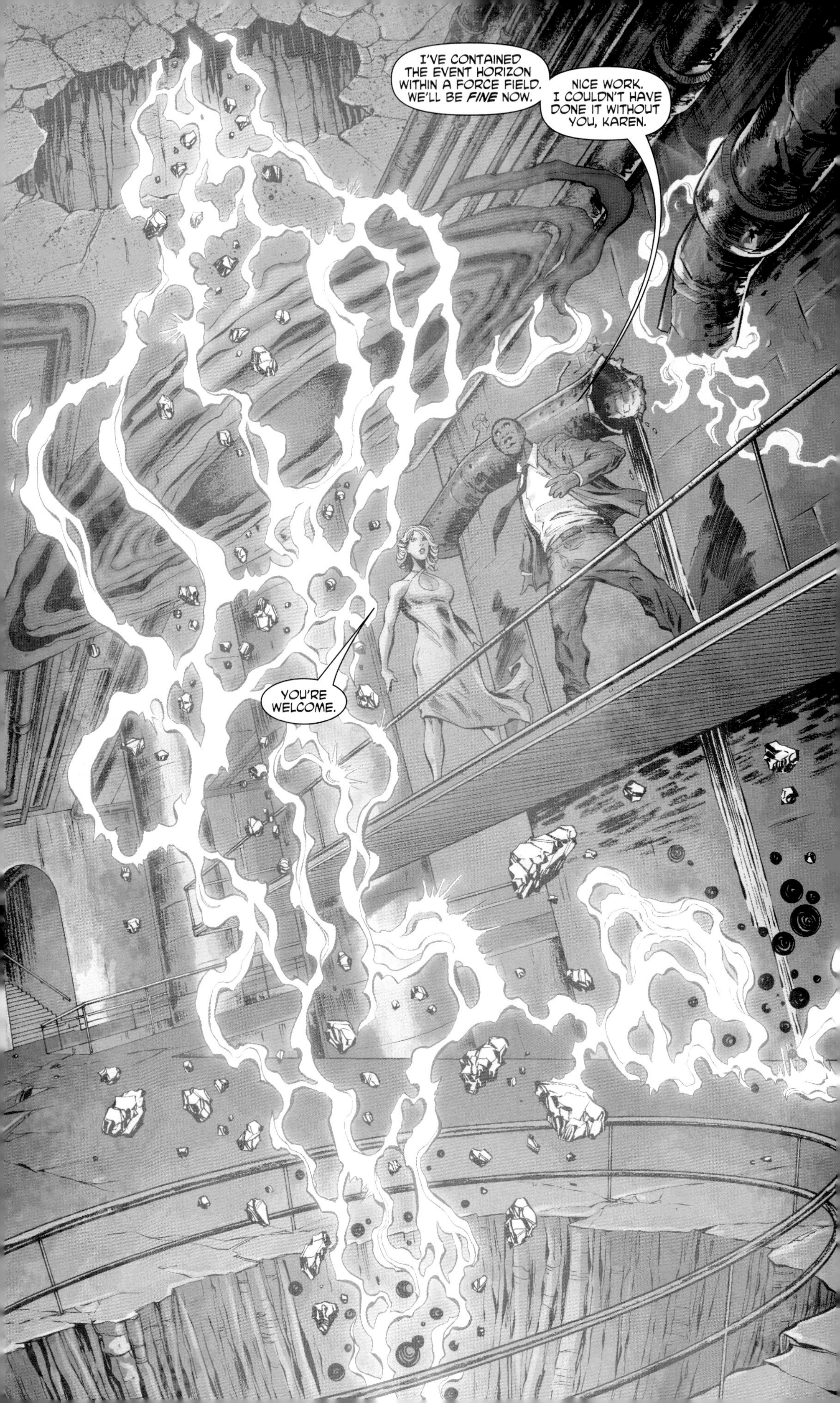
I'VE CONTAINED THE EVENT HORIZON WITHIN A FORCE FIELD. WE'LL BE *FINE* NOW.
NICE WORK. I COULDN'T HAVE DONE IT WITHOUT YOU, KAREN.
YOU'RE WELCOME.

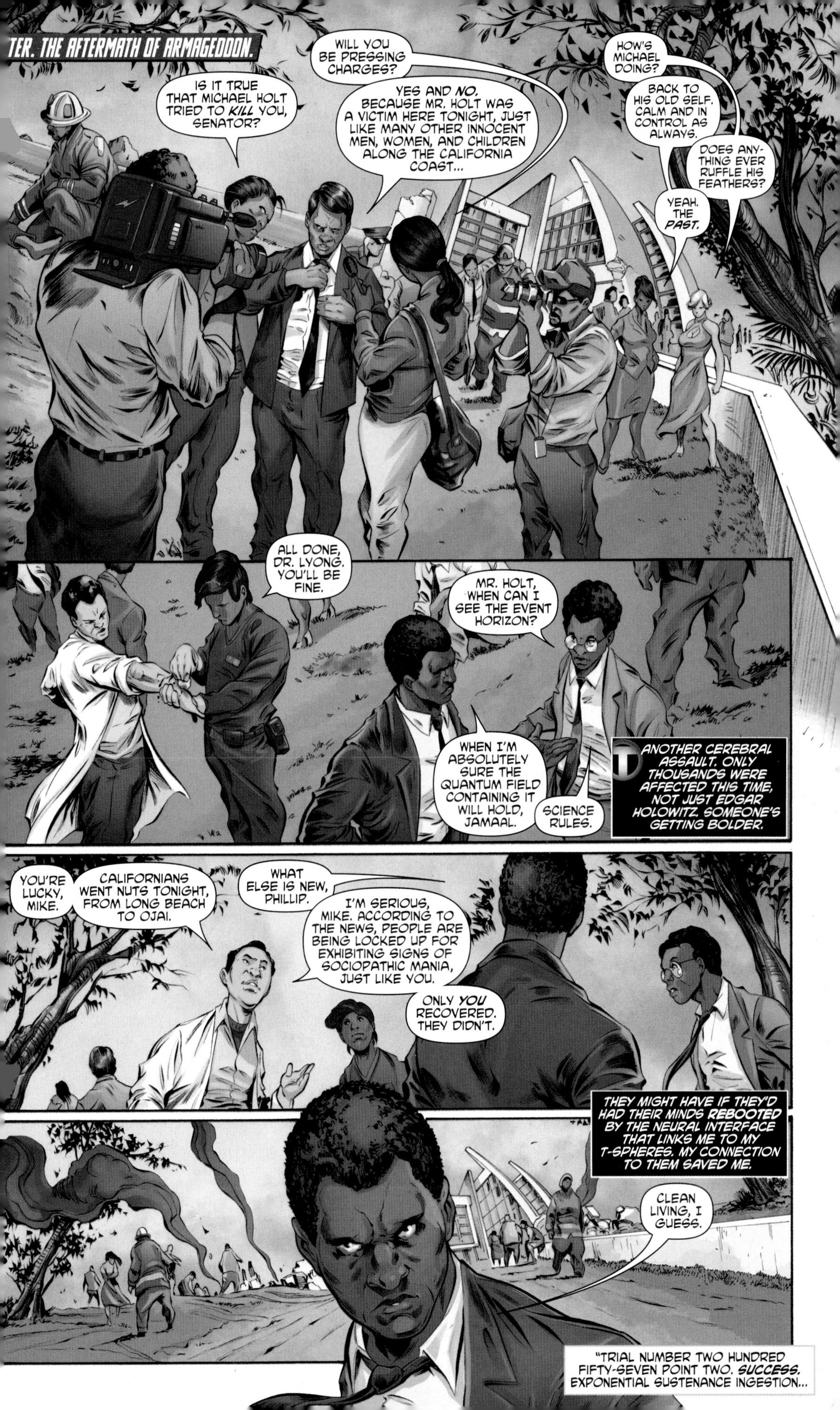
TER. THE AFTERMATH OF ARMAGEDDON.
IS IT TRUE THAT MICHAEL HOLT TRIED TO KILL YOU, SENATOR?
WILL YOU BE PRESSING CHARGES?
YES AND NO. BECAUSE MR. HOLT WAS A VICTIM HERE TONIGHT, JUST LIKE MANY OTHER INNOCENT MEN, WOMEN, AND CHILDREN ALONG THE CALIFORNIA COAST...
HOW'S MICHAEL DOING?
BACK TO HIS OLD SELF. CALM AND IN CONTROL AS ALWAYS.
DOES ANY-THING EVER RUFFLE HIS FEATHERS?
YEAH. THE PAST.
ALL DONE, DR. LYONG. YOU'LL BE FINE.
MR. HOLT, WHEN CAN I SEE THE EVENT HORIZON?
WHEN I'M ABSOLUTELY SURE THE QUANTUM FIELD CONTAINING IT WILL HOLD, JAMAAL.
SCIENCE RULES.
ANOTHER CEREBRAL ASSAULT. ONLY THOUSANDS WERE AFFECTED THIS TIME, NOT JUST EDGAR HOLOWITZ. SOMEONE'S GETTING BOLDER.
YOU'RE LUCKY, MIKE.
CALIFORNIANS WENT NUTS TONIGHT, FROM LONG BEACH TO OJAI.
WHAT ELSE IS NEW, PHILLIP.
I'M SERIOUS, MIKE. ACCORDING TO THE NEWS, PEOPLE ARE BEING LOCKED UP FOR EXHIBITING SIGNS OF SOCIOPATHIC MANIA, JUST LIKE YOU.
ONLY YOU RECOVERED. THEY DIDN'T.
THEY MIGHT HAVE IF THEY'D HAD THEIR MINDS REBOOTED BY THE NEURAL INTERFACE THAT LINKS ME TO MY T-SPHERES. MY CONNECTION TO THEM SAVED ME.
CLEAN LIVING, I GUESS.
"TRIAL NUMBER TWO HUNDRED FIFTY-SEVEN POINT TWO. SUCCESS. EXPONENTIAL SUSTENANCE INGESTION...

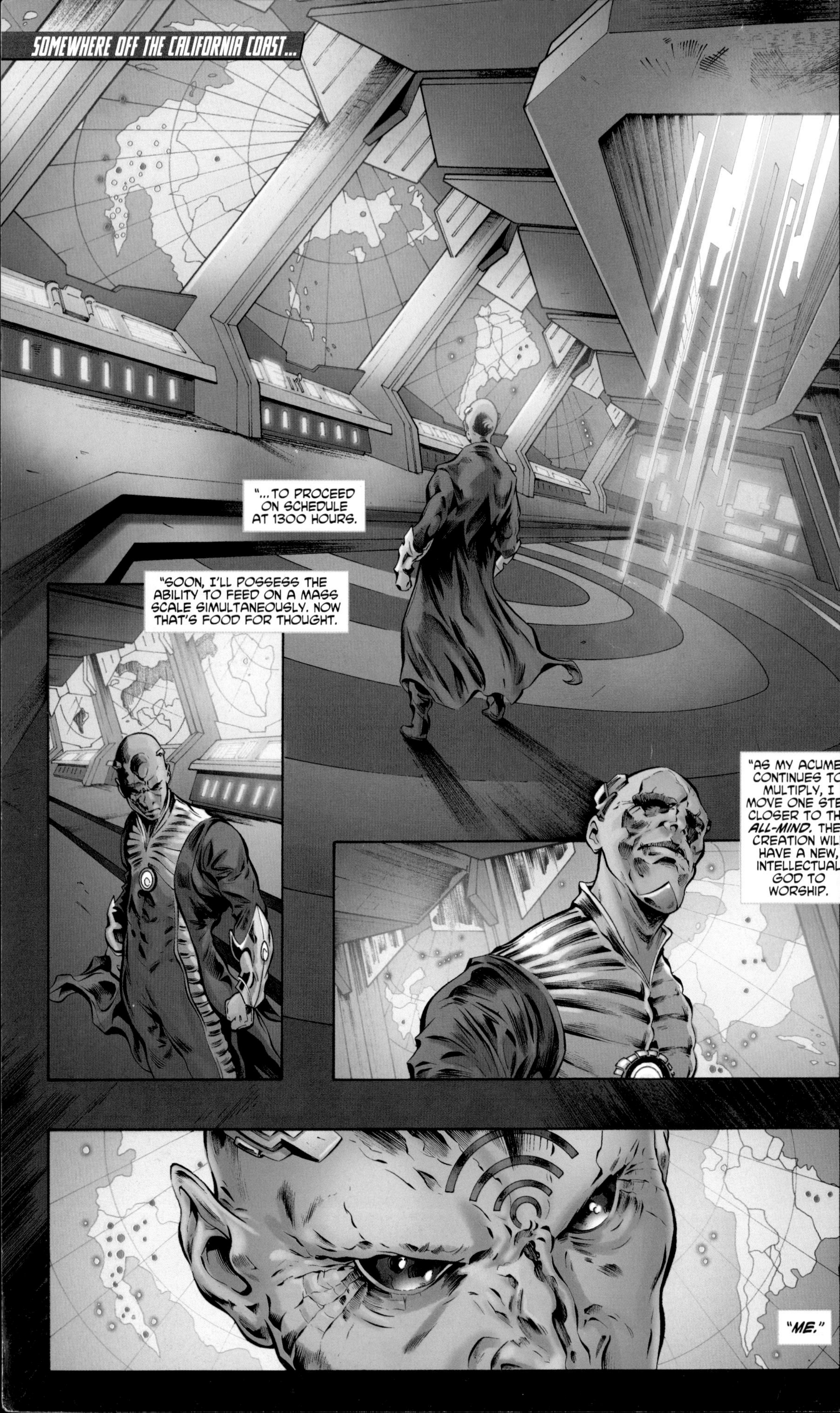
SOMEWHERE OFF THE CALIFORNIA COAST...
"...TO PROCEED ON SCHEDULE AT 1300 HOURS.
"SOON, I'LL POSSESS THE ABILITY TO FEED ON A MASS SCALE SIMULTANEOUSLY. NOW THAT'S FOOD FOR THOUGHT.
"AS MY ACUME CONTINUES TO MULTIPLY, I MOVE ONE STE CLOSER TO TH ALL-MIND. THE CREATION WIL HAVE A NEW, INTELLECTUAL GOD TO WORSHIP.
"ME."

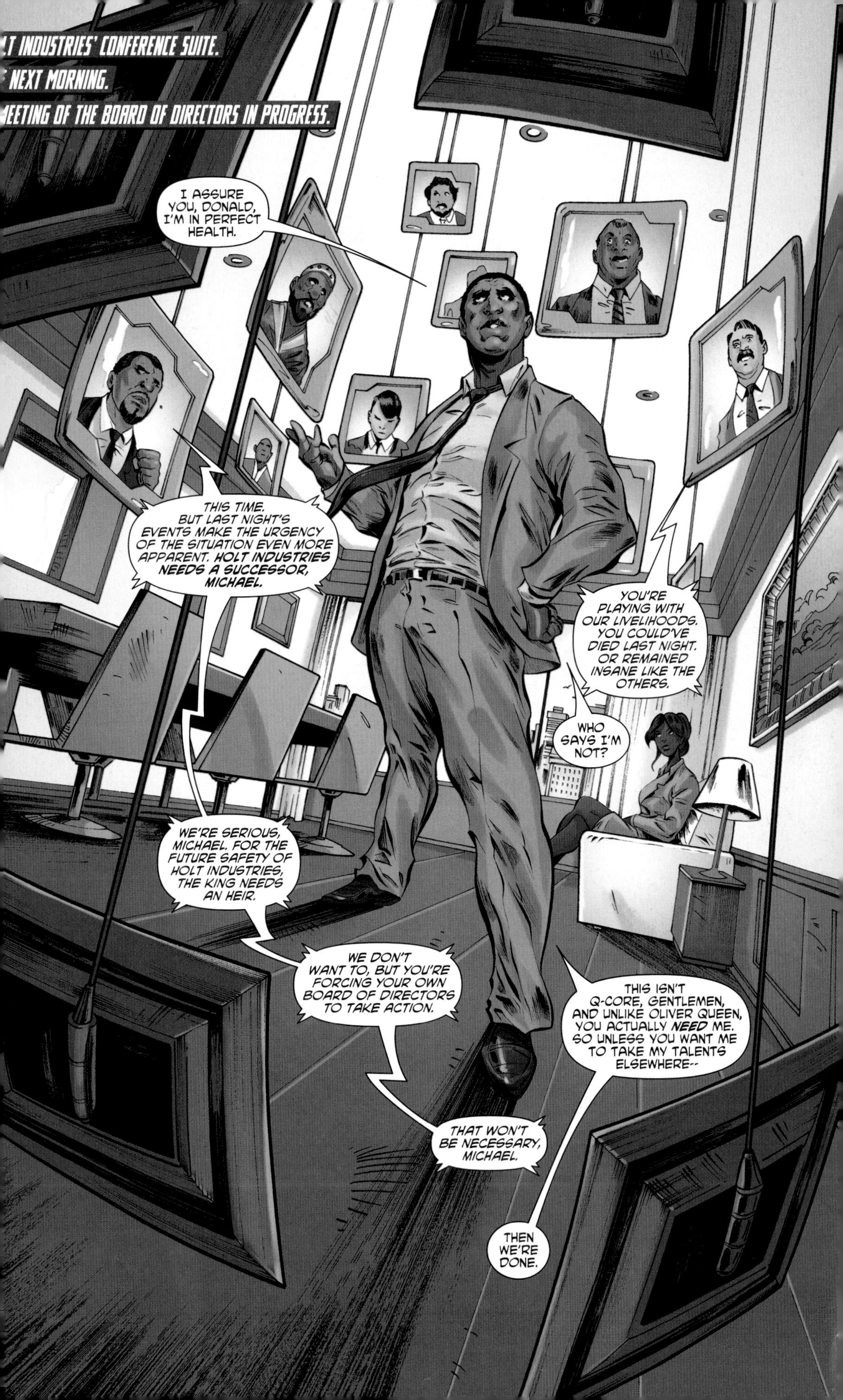

LT INDUSTRIES' CONFERENCE SUITE.
NEXT MORNING.
EETING OF THE BOARD OF DIRECTORS IN PROGRESS.
I ASSURE YOU, DONALD, I'M IN PERFECT HEALTH.
THIS TIME. BUT LAST NIGHT'S EVENTS MAKE THE URGENCY OF THE SITUATION EVEN MORE APPARENT. HOLT INDUSTRIES NEEDS A SUCCESSOR, MICHAEL.
YOU'RE PLAYING WITH OUR LIVELIHOODS. YOU COULD'VE DIED LAST NIGHT. OR REMAINED INSANE LIKE THE OTHERS.
WHO SAYS I'M NOT?
WE'RE SERIOUS, MICHAEL. FOR THE FUTURE SAFETY OF HOLT INDUSTRIES, THE KING NEEDS AN HEIR.
WE DON'T WANT TO, BUT YOU'RE FORCING YOUR OWN BOARD OF DIRECTORS TO TAKE ACTION.
THIS ISN'T Q-CORE, GENTLEMEN, AND UNLIKE OLIVER QUEEN, YOU ACTUALLY NEED ME. SO UNLESS YOU WANT ME TO TAKE MY TALENTS ELSEWHERE--
THAT WON'T BE NECESSARY, MICHAEL.
THEN WE'RE DONE.

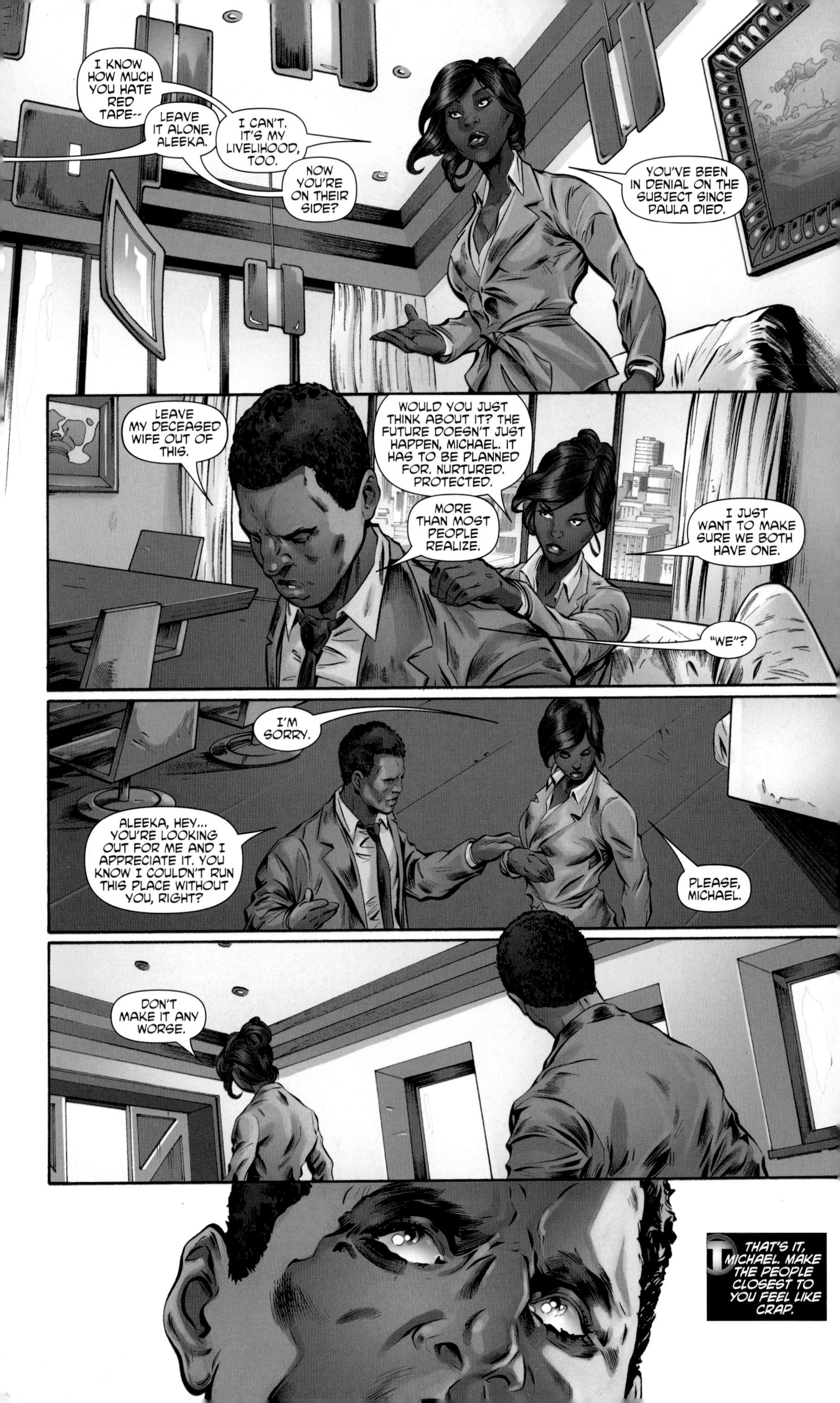
I KNOW HOW MUCH YOU HATE RED TAPE--
LEAVE IT ALONE, ALEEKA.
I CAN'T. IT'S MY LIVELIHOOD, TOO.
NOW YOU'RE ON THEIR SIDE?
YOU'VE BEEN IN DENIAL ON THE SUBJECT SINCE PAULA DIED.
LEAVE MY DECEASED WIFE OUT OF THIS.
WOULD YOU JUST THINK ABOUT IT? THE FUTURE DOESN'T JUST HAPPEN, MICHAEL. IT HAS TO BE PLANNED FOR. NURTURED. PROTECTED.
MORE THAN MOST PEOPLE REALIZE.
I JUST WANT TO MAKE SURE WE BOTH HAVE ONE.
"WE"?
I'M SORRY.
ALEEKA, HEY... YOU'RE LOOKING OUT FOR ME AND I APPRECIATE IT. YOU KNOW I COULDN'T RUN THIS PLACE WITHOUT YOU, RIGHT?
PLEASE, MICHAEL.
DON'T MAKE IT ANY WORSE.
THAT'S IT, MICHAEL. MAKE THE PEOPLE CLOSEST TO YOU FEEL LIKE CRAP.

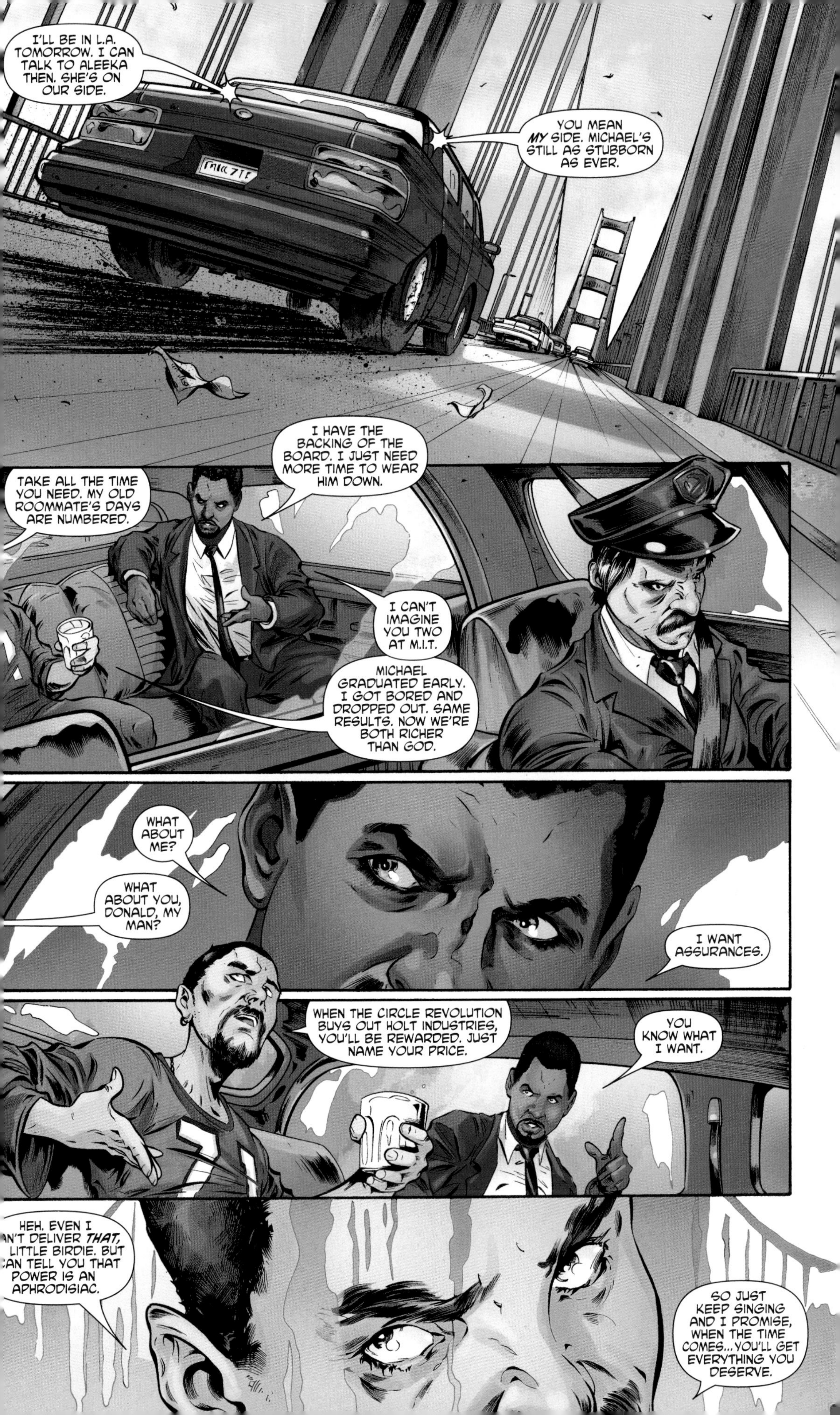
I'LL BE IN L.A. TOMORROW. I CAN TALK TO ALEEKA THEN. SHE'S ON OUR SIDE.
YOU MEAN *MY* SIDE. MICHAEL'S STILL AS STUBBORN AS EVER.
TAKE ALL THE TIME YOU NEED. MY OLD ROOMMATE'S DAYS ARE NUMBERED.
I HAVE THE BACKING OF THE BOARD. I JUST NEED MORE TIME TO WEAR HIM DOWN.
I CAN'T IMAGINE YOU TWO AT M.I.T.
MICHAEL GRADUATED EARLY. I GOT BORED AND DROPPED OUT. SAME RESULTS. NOW WE'RE BOTH RICHER THAN GOD.
WHAT ABOUT ME?
WHAT ABOUT YOU, DONALD, MY MAN?
I WANT ASSURANCES.
WHEN THE CIRCLE REVOLUTION BUYS OUT HOLT INDUSTRIES, YOU'LL BE REWARDED. JUST NAME YOUR PRICE.
YOU KNOW WHAT I WANT.
HEH. EVEN I AN'T DELIVER *THAT,* LITTLE BIRDIE. BUT CAN TELL YOU THAT POWER IS AN APHRODISIAC.
SO JUST KEEP SINGING AND I PROMISE, WHEN THE TIME COMES...YOU'LL GET EVERYTHING YOU DESERVE.

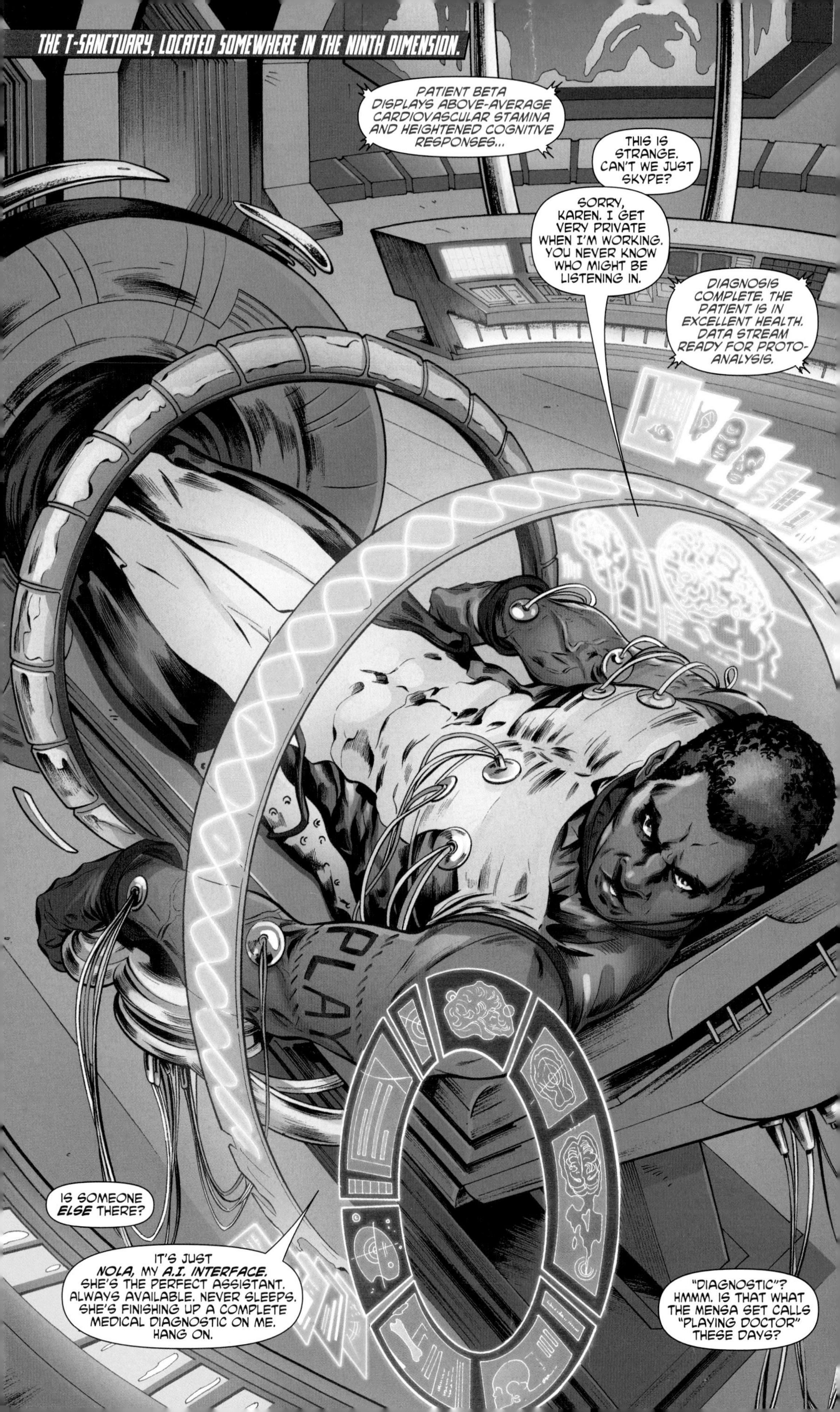
THE T-SANCTUARY, LOCATED SOMEWHERE IN THE NINTH DIMENSION.
PATIENT BETA DISPLAYS ABOVE-AVERAGE CARDIOVASCULAR STAMINA AND HEIGHTENED COGNITIVE RESPONSES...
THIS IS STRANGE. CAN'T WE JUST SKYPE?
SORRY, KAREN. I GET VERY PRIVATE WHEN I'M WORKING. YOU NEVER KNOW WHO MIGHT BE LISTENING IN.
DIAGNOSIS COMPLETE. THE PATIENT IS IN EXCELLENT HEALTH. DATA STREAM READY FOR PROTO-ANALYSIS.
IS SOMEONE *ELSE* THERE?
IT'S JUST *NOLA,* MY *A.I. INTERFACE.* SHE'S THE PERFECT ASSISTANT. ALWAYS AVAILABLE. NEVER SLEEPS. SHE'S FINISHING UP A COMPLETE MEDICAL DIAGNOSTIC ON ME. HANG ON.
"DIAGNOSTIC"? HMMM. IS THAT WHAT THE MENSA SET CALLS "PLAYING DOCTOR" THESE DAYS?

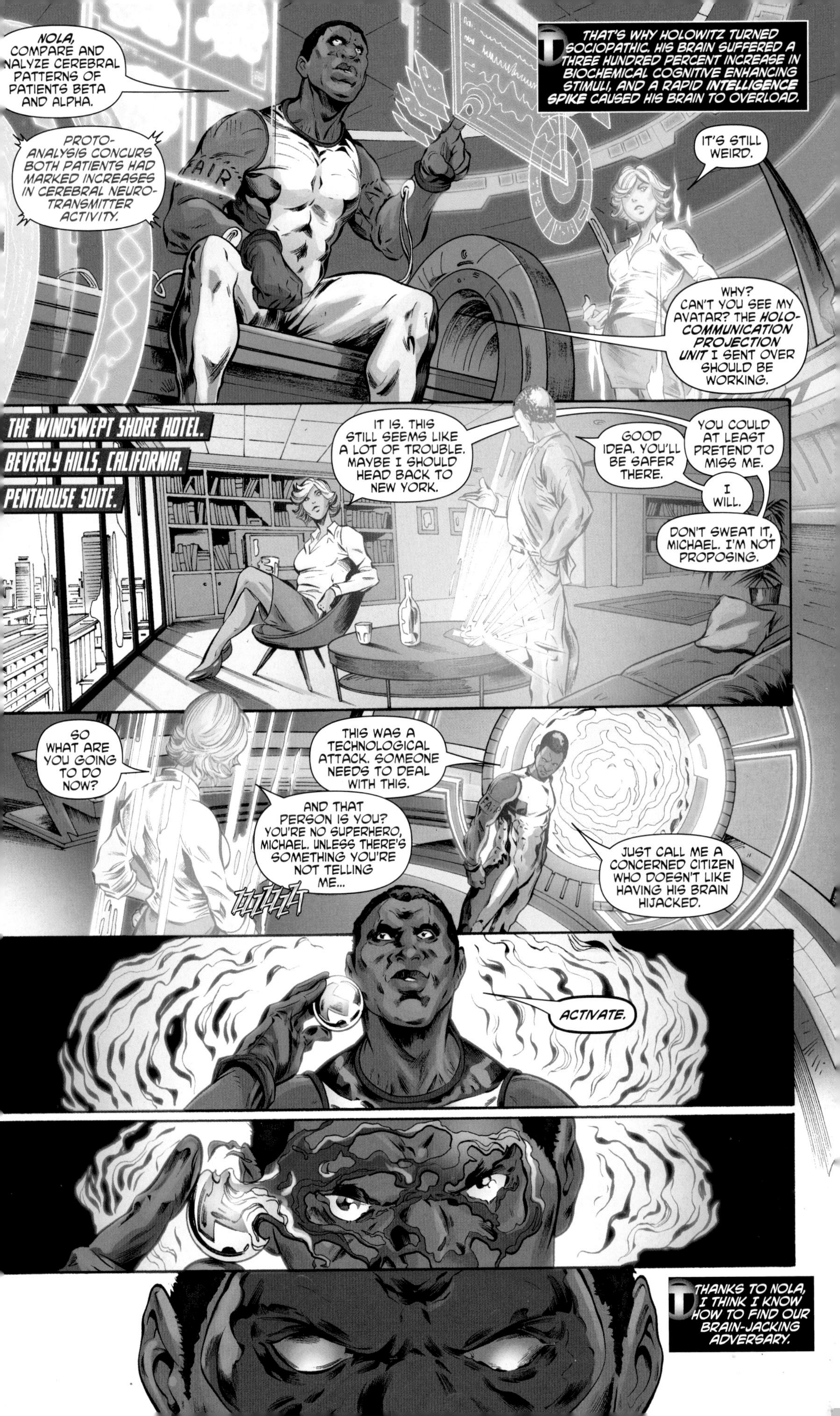
NOLA, COMPARE AND ANALYZE CEREBRAL PATTERNS OF PATIENTS BETA AND ALPHA.
THAT'S WHY HOLOWITZ TURNED SOCIOPATHIC. HIS BRAIN SUFFERED A THREE HUNDRED PERCENT INCREASE IN BIOCHEMICAL COGNITIVE ENHANCING STIMULI, AND A RAPID INTELLIGENCE SPIKE CAUSED HIS BRAIN TO OVERLOAD.
PROTO-ANALYSIS CONCURS BOTH PATIENTS HAD MARKED INCREASES IN CEREBRAL NEURO-TRANSMITTER ACTIVITY.
IT'S STILL WEIRD.
WHY? CAN'T YOU SEE MY AVATAR? THE HOLO-COMMUNICATION PROJECTION UNIT I SENT OVER SHOULD BE WORKING.
THE WINDSWEPT SHORE HOTEL.
BEVERLY HILLS, CALIFORNIA.
PENTHOUSE SUITE.
IT IS. THIS STILL SEEMS LIKE A LOT OF TROUBLE. MAYBE I SHOULD HEAD BACK TO NEW YORK.
GOOD IDEA. YOU'LL BE SAFER THERE.
YOU COULD AT LEAST PRETEND TO MISS ME.
I WILL.
DON'T SWEAT IT, MICHAEL. I'M NOT PROPOSING.
SO WHAT ARE YOU GOING TO DO NOW?
THIS WAS A TECHNOLOGICAL ATTACK. SOMEONE NEEDS TO DEAL WITH THIS.
AND THAT PERSON IS YOU? YOU'RE NO SUPERHERO, MICHAEL. UNLESS THERE'S SOMETHING YOU'RE NOT TELLING ME...
JUST CALL ME A CONCERNED CITIZEN WHO DOESN'T LIKE HAVING HIS BRAIN HIJACKED.
TZZZZZT
ACTIVATE.
THANKS TO NOLA, I THINK I KNOW HOW TO FIND OUR BRAIN-JACKING ADVERSARY.

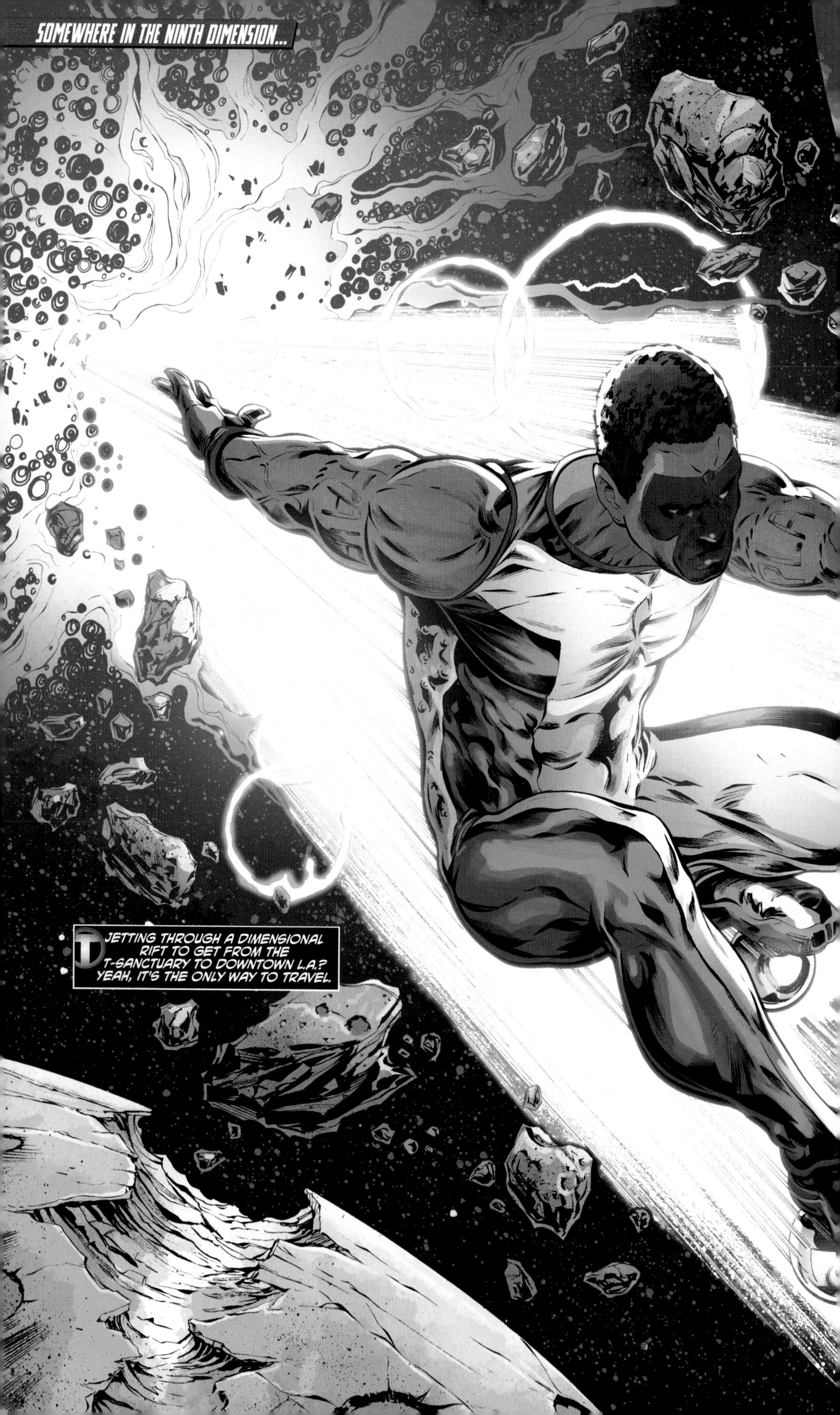
SOMEWHERE IN THE NINTH DIMENSION...
JETTING THROUGH A DIMENSIONAL RIFT TO GET FROM THE T-SANCTUARY TO DOWNTOWN L.A.? YEAH, IT'S THE ONLY WAY TO TRAVEL.

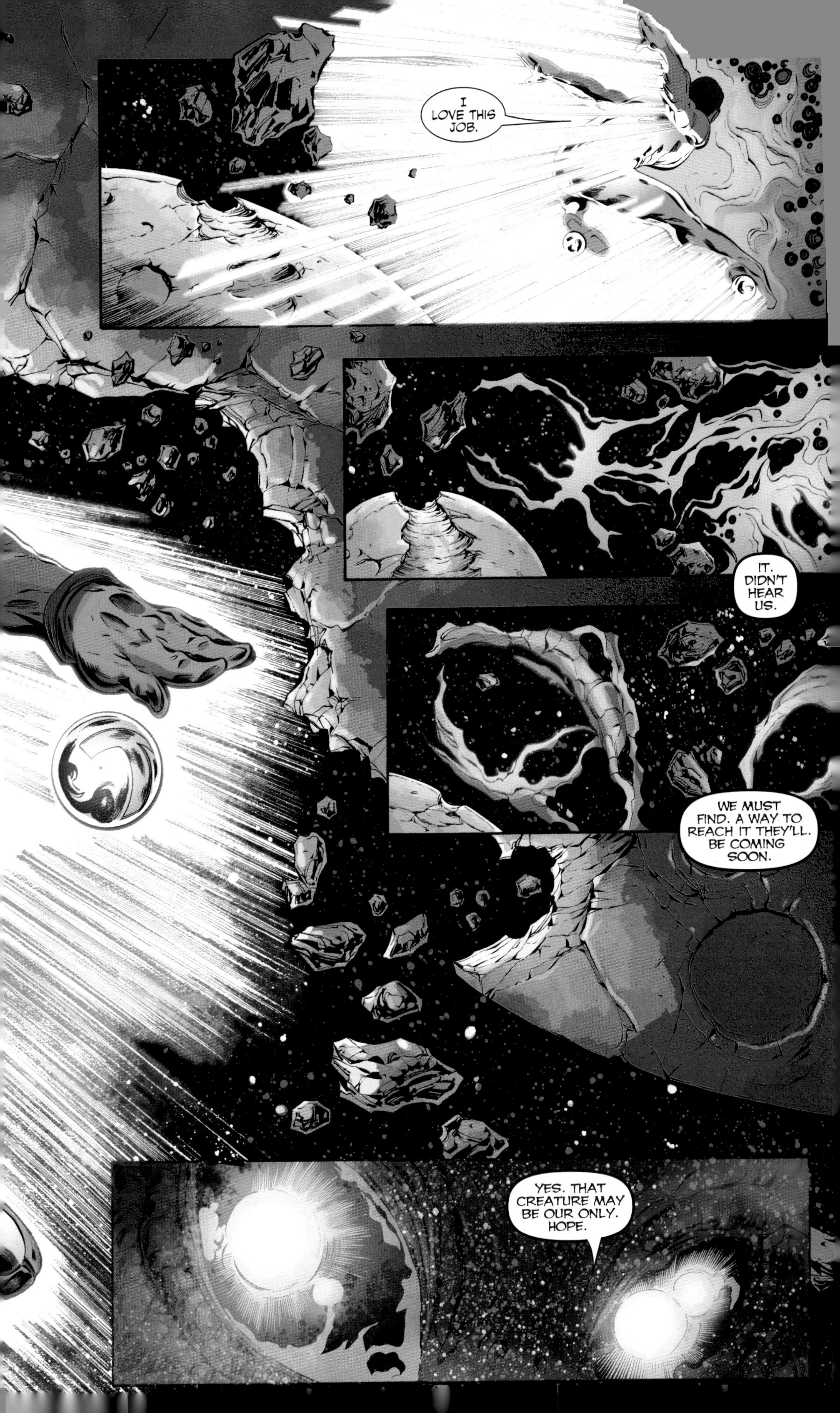
I LOVE THIS JOB.
IT. DIDN'T HEAR US.
WE MUST FIND. A WAY TO REACH IT THEY'LL. BE COMING SOON.
YES. THAT CREATURE MAY BE OUR ONLY. HOPE.

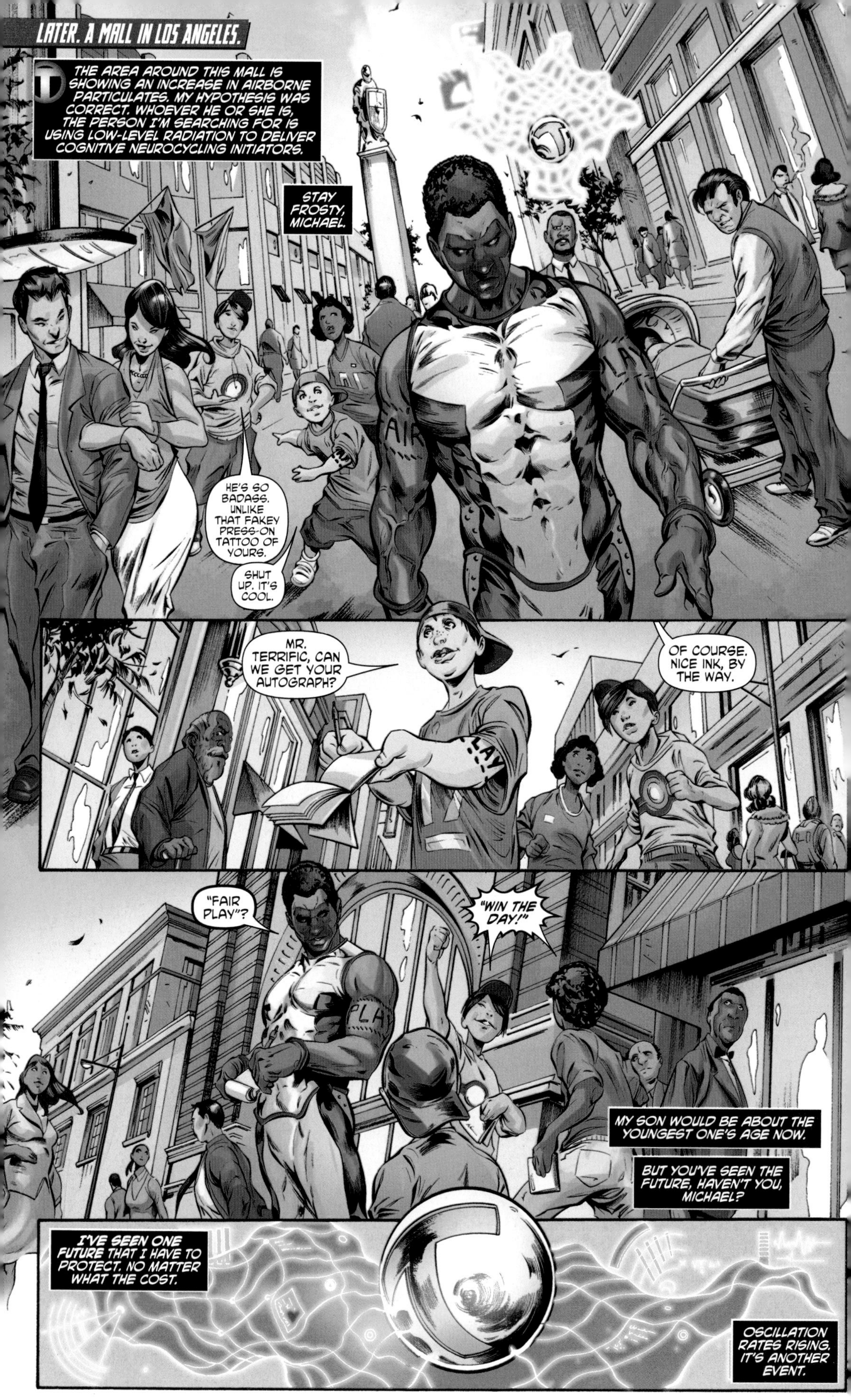
LATER. A MALL IN LOS ANGELES.
THE AREA AROUND THIS MALL IS SHOWING AN INCREASE IN AIRBORNE PARTICULATES. MY HYPOTHESIS WAS CORRECT. WHOEVER HE OR SHE IS, THE PERSON I'M SEARCHING FOR IS USING LOW-LEVEL RADIATION TO DELIVER COGNITIVE NEUROCYCLING INITIATORS.
STAY FROSTY, MICHAEL.
HE'S SO BADASS. UNLIKE THAT FAKEY PRESS-ON TATTOO OF YOURS.
SHUT UP. IT'S COOL.
MR. TERRIFIC, CAN WE GET YOUR AUTOGRAPH?
OF COURSE. NICE INK, BY THE WAY.
"FAIR PLAY"?
"WIN THE DAY!"
MY SON WOULD BE ABOUT THE YOUNGEST ONE'S AGE NOW.
BUT YOU'VE SEEN THE FUTURE, HAVEN'T YOU, MICHAEL?
I'VE SEEN ONE FUTURE THAT I HAVE TO PROTECT. NO MATTER WHAT THE COST.
OSCILLATION RATES RISING. IT'S ANOTHER EVENT.

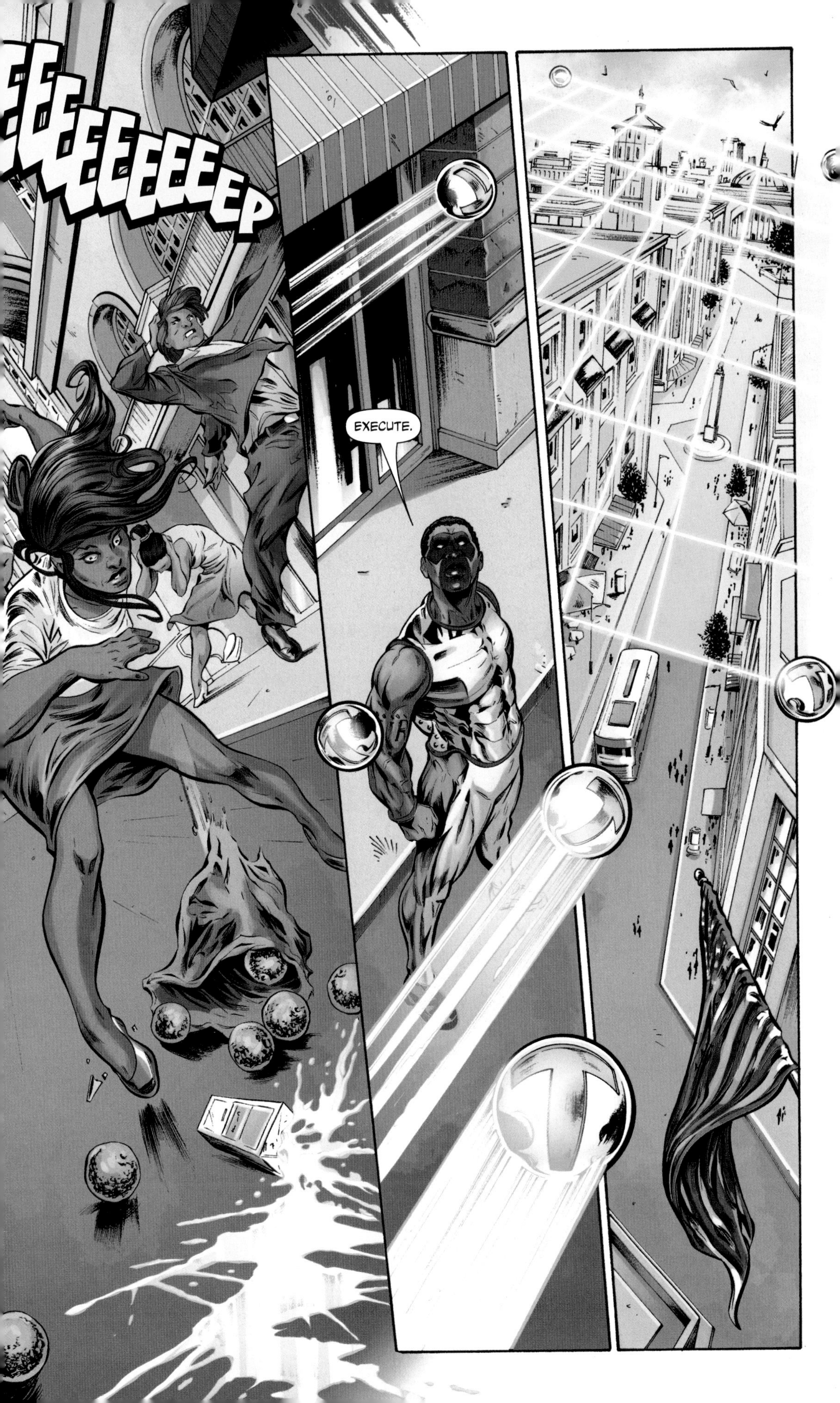
EEEEEEEEEEEP
EXECUTE.

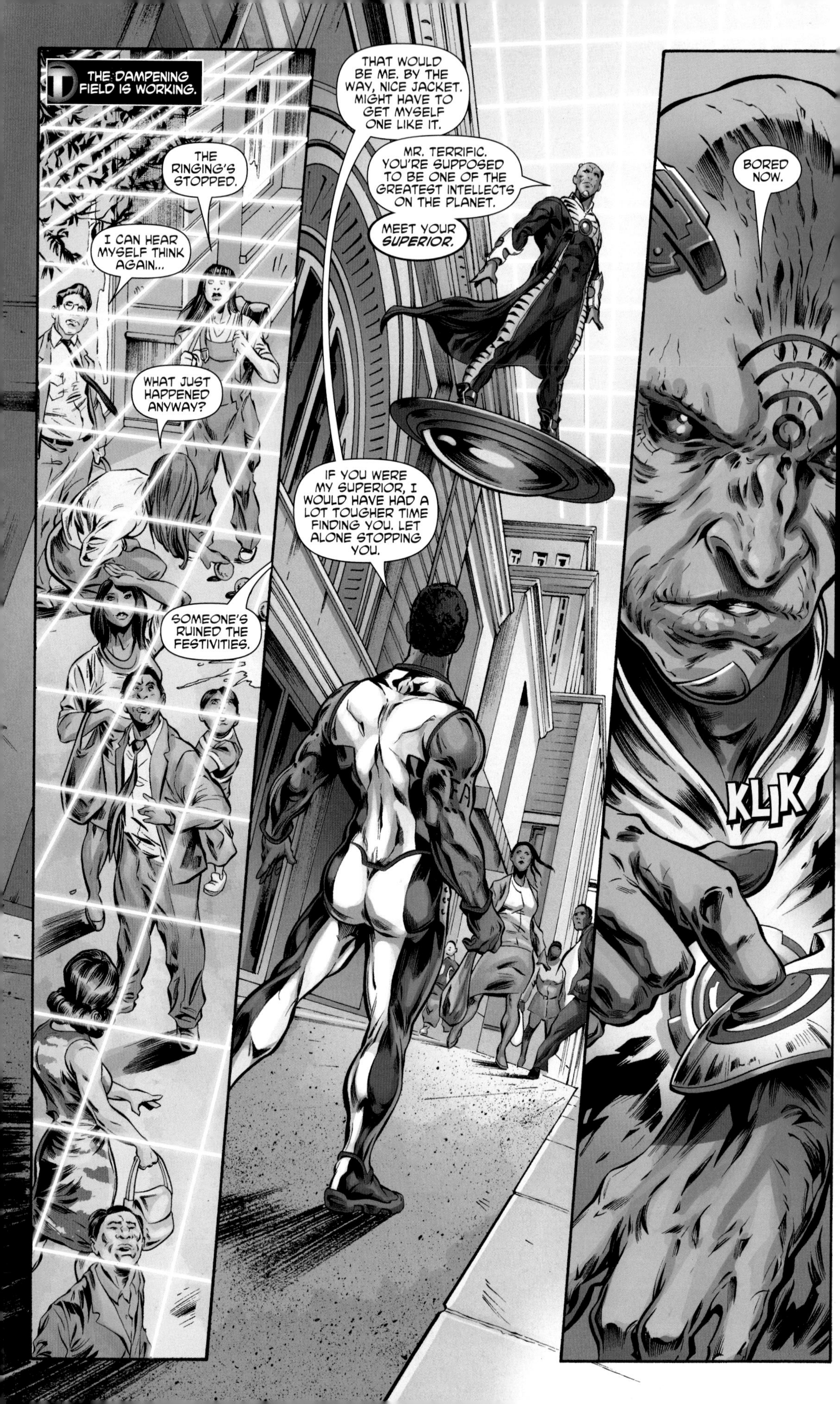
THE DAMPENING FIELD IS WORKING.
THE RINGING'S STOPPED.
I CAN HEAR MYSELF THINK AGAIN...
WHAT JUST HAPPENED ANYWAY?
SOMEONE'S RUINED THE FESTIVITIES.
THAT WOULD BE ME. BY THE WAY, NICE JACKET. MIGHT HAVE TO GET MYSELF ONE LIKE IT.
MR. TERRIFIC. YOU'RE SUPPOSED TO BE ONE OF THE GREATEST INTELLECTS ON THE PLANET.
MEET YOUR *SUPERIOR.*
IF YOU WERE MY SUPERIOR, I WOULD HAVE HAD A LOT TOUGHER TIME FINDING YOU. LET ALONE STOPPING YOU.
BORED NOW.
KLIK

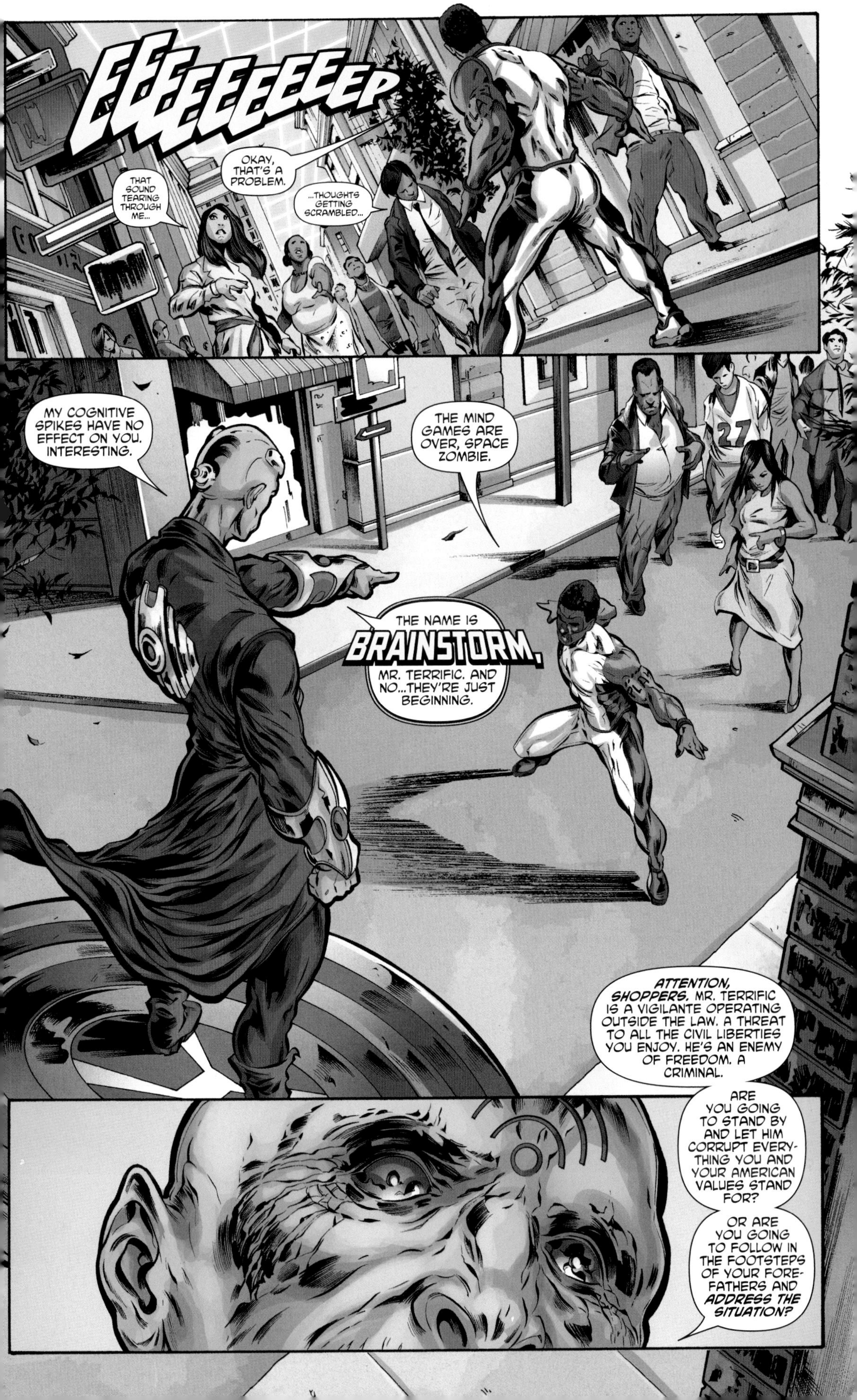
EEEEEEEEEEEP
THAT SOUND TEARING THROUGH ME...
OKAY, THAT'S A PROBLEM.
...THOUGHTS GETTING SCRAMBLED...
MY COGNITIVE SPIKES HAVE NO EFFECT ON YOU. INTERESTING.
THE MIND GAMES ARE OVER, SPACE ZOMBIE.
THE NAME IS BRAINSTORM, MR. TERRIFIC. AND NO...THEY'RE JUST BEGINNING.
ATTENTION, SHOPPERS. MR. TERRIFIC IS A VIGILANTE OPERATING OUTSIDE THE LAW. A THREAT TO ALL THE CIVIL LIBERTIES YOU ENJOY. HE'S AN ENEMY OF FREEDOM. A CRIMINAL.
ARE YOU GOING TO STAND BY AND LET HIM CORRUPT EVERY-THING YOU AND YOUR AMERICAN VALUES STAND FOR?
OR ARE YOU GOING TO FOLLOW IN THE FOOTSTEPS OF YOUR FORE-FATHERS AND ADDRESS THE SITUATION?

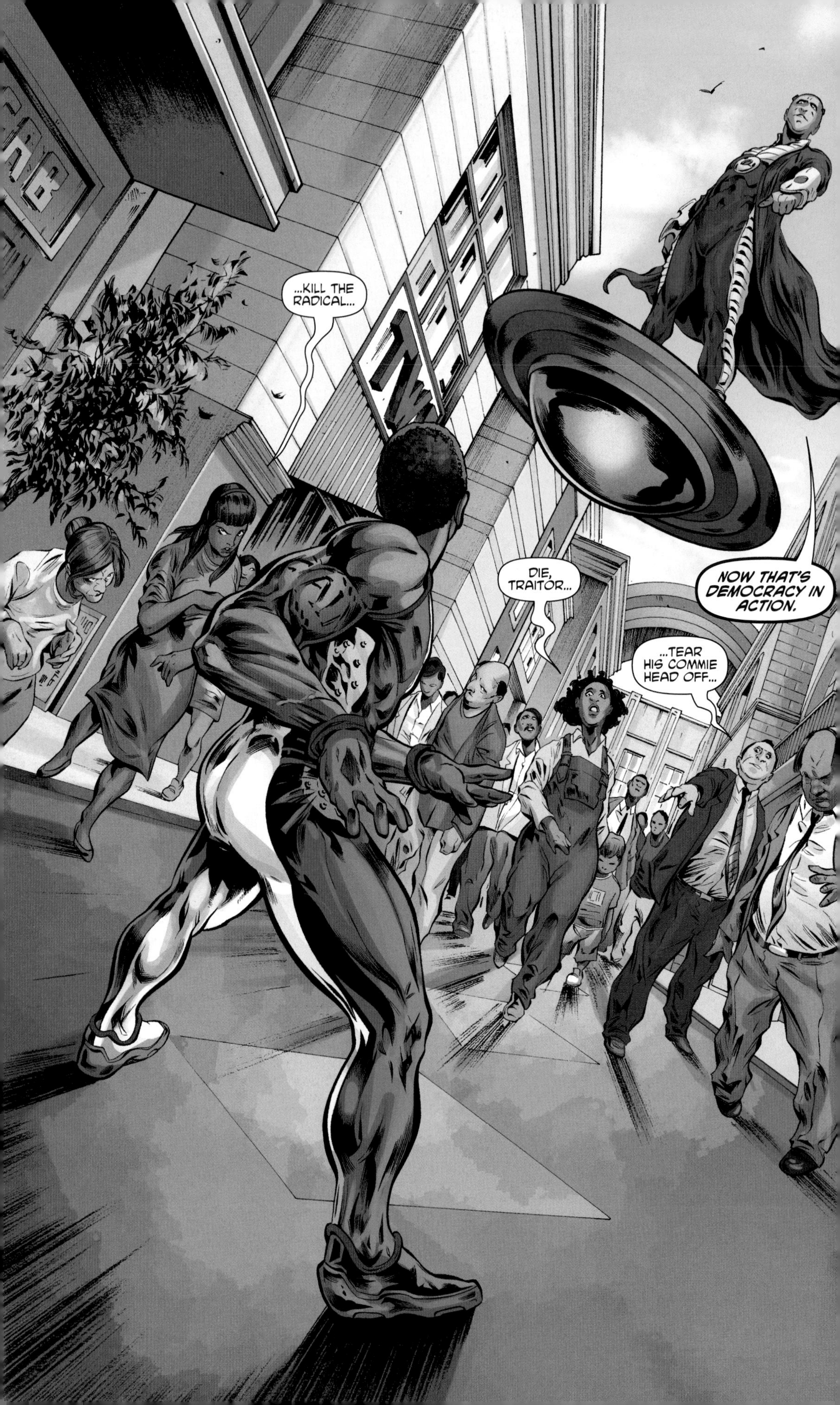

...KILL THE RADICAL...
NOW THAT'S DEMOCRACY IN ACTION.
DIE, TRAITOR...
...TEAR HIS COMMIE HEAD OFF...

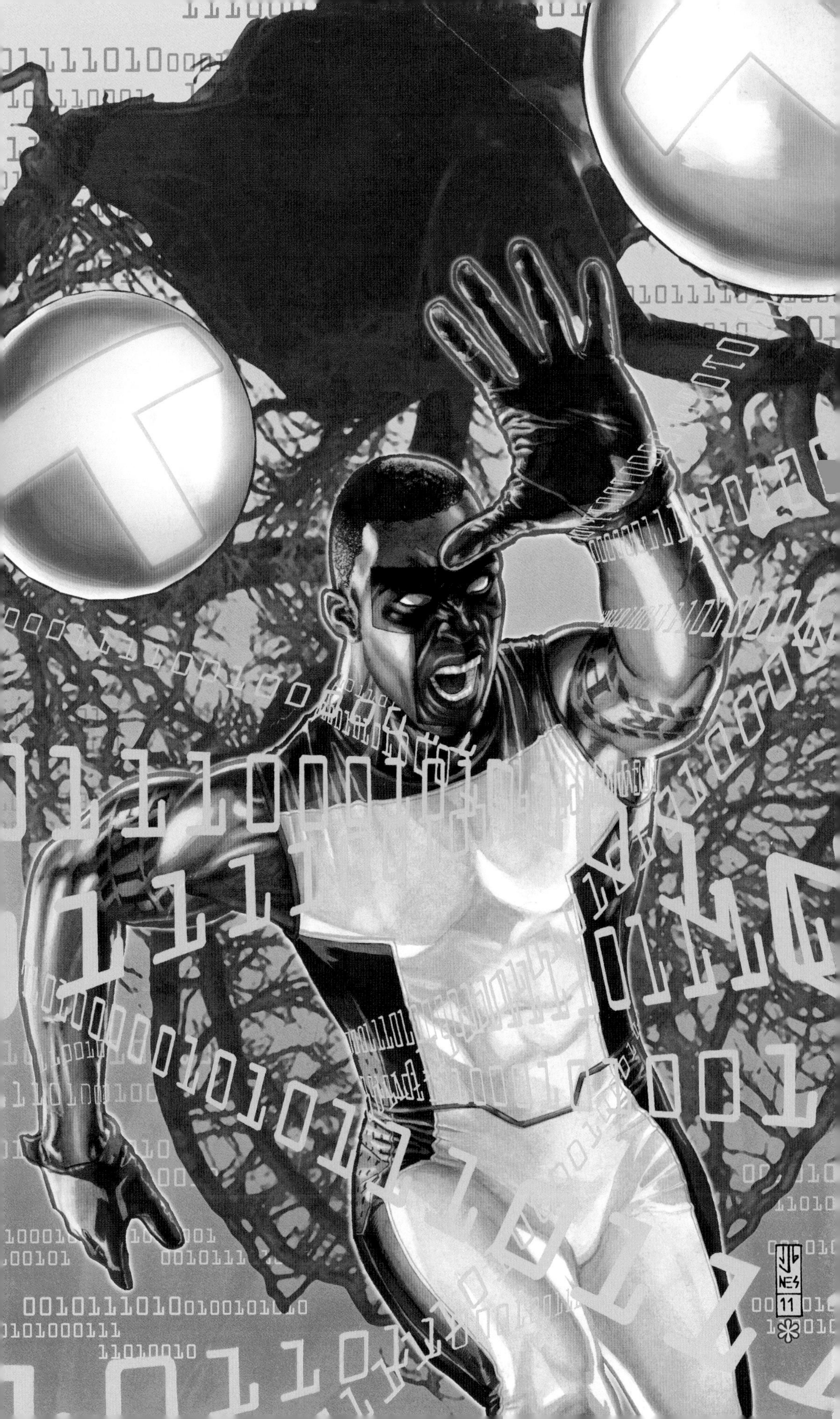

HAUNTED

ERIC WALLACE writer **SCOTT CLARK** penciller **DAVE BEATY** inker

cover art by **J.G. JONES** with colorist **HI-FI**

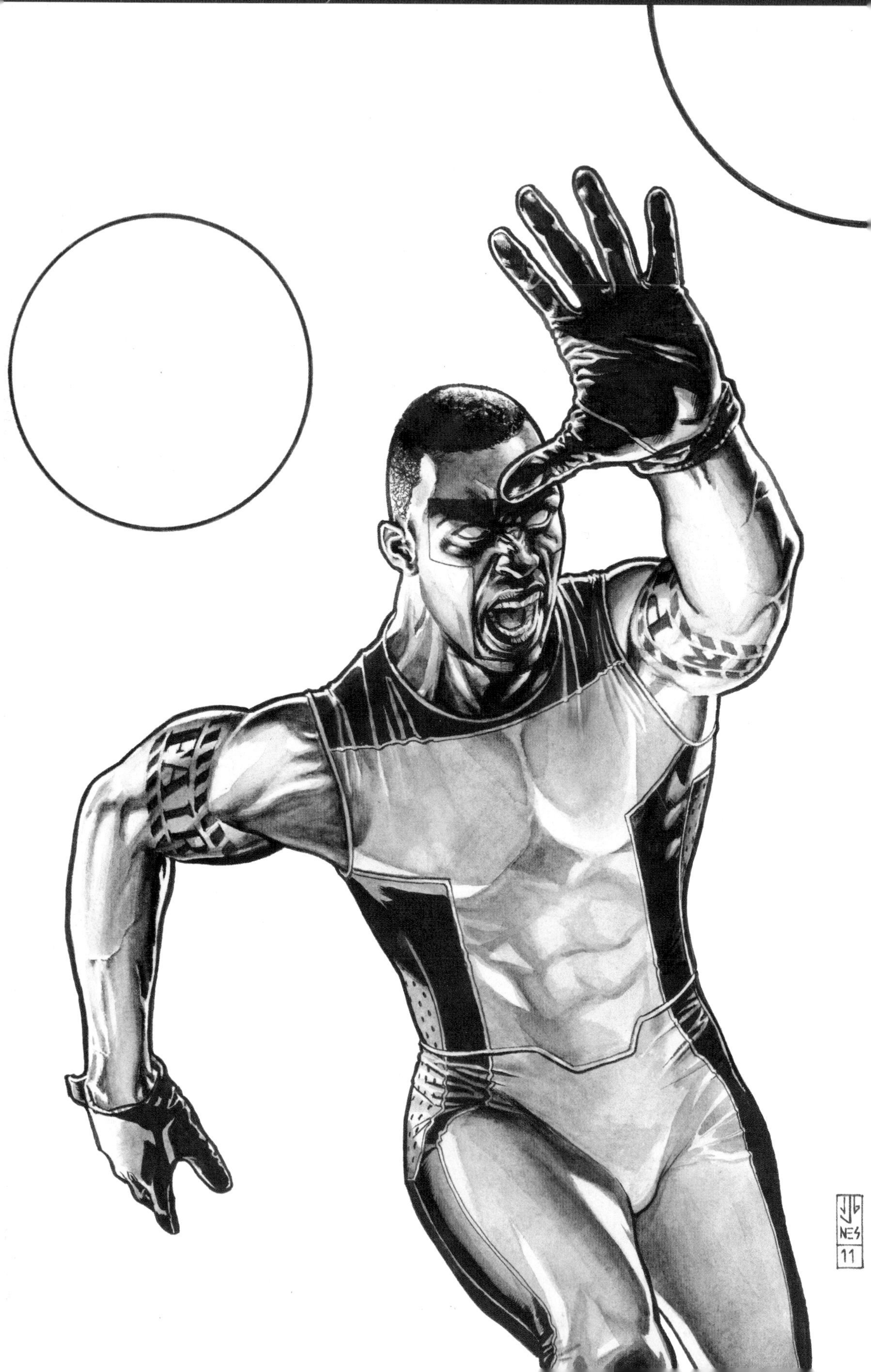
JG
JONES
11

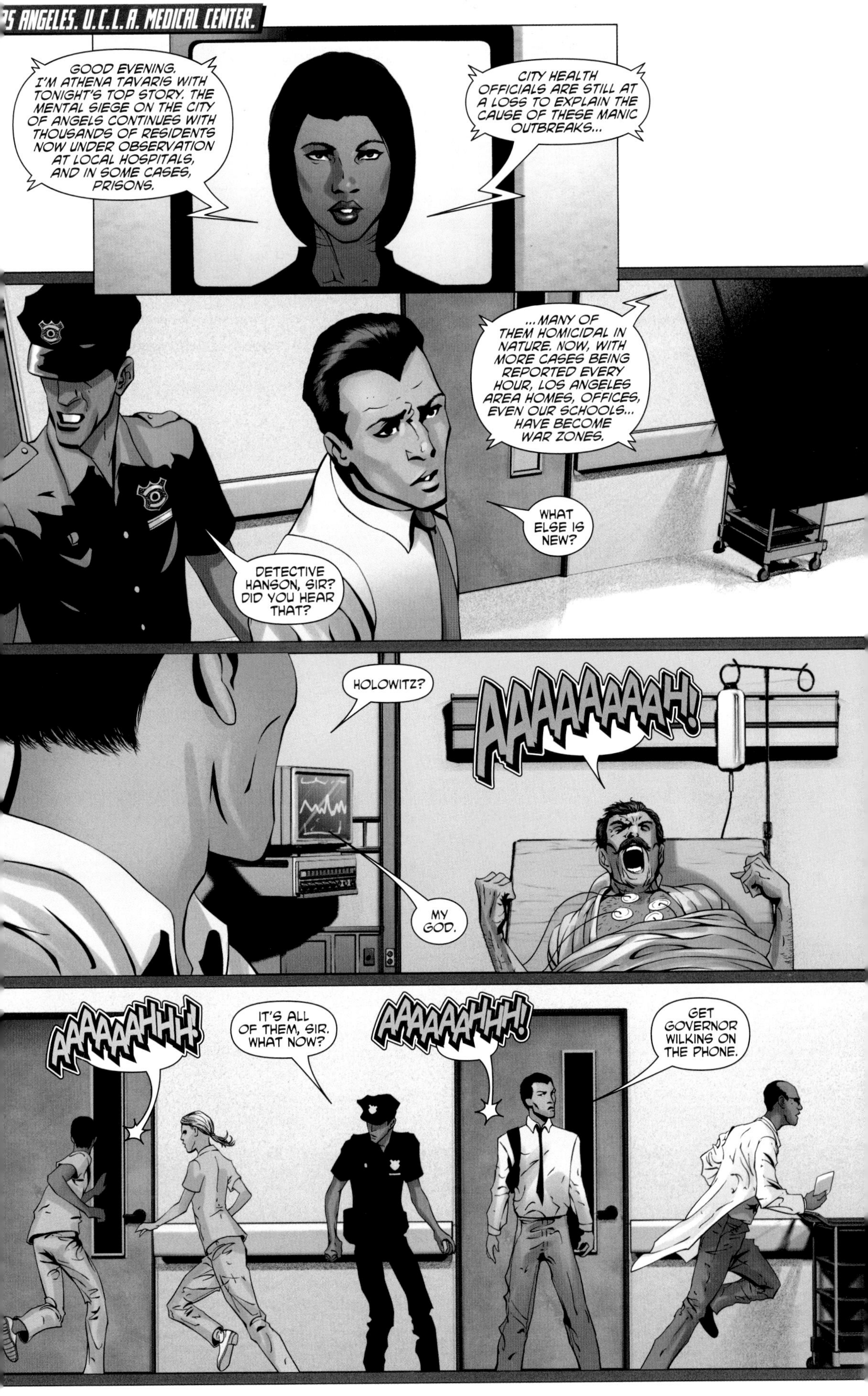

...S ANGELES. U.C.L.A. MEDICAL CENTER.
GOOD EVENING. I'M ATHENA TAVARIS WITH TONIGHT'S TOP STORY. THE MENTAL SIEGE ON THE CITY OF ANGELS CONTINUES WITH THOUSANDS OF RESIDENTS NOW UNDER OBSERVATION AT LOCAL HOSPITALS, AND IN SOME CASES, PRISONS.
CITY HEALTH OFFICIALS ARE STILL AT A LOSS TO EXPLAIN THE CAUSE OF THESE MANIC OUTBREAKS...
...MANY OF THEM HOMICIDAL IN NATURE. NOW, WITH MORE CASES BEING REPORTED EVERY HOUR, LOS ANGELES AREA HOMES, OFFICES, EVEN OUR SCHOOLS... HAVE BECOME WAR ZONES.
DETECTIVE HANSON, SIR? DID YOU HEAR THAT?
WHAT ELSE IS NEW?
HOLOWITZ?
AAAAAAAAH!
MY GOD.
AAAAAHHH!
IT'S ALL OF THEM, SIR. WHAT NOW?
AAAAAAHHH!
GET GOVERNOR WILKINS ON THE PHONE.

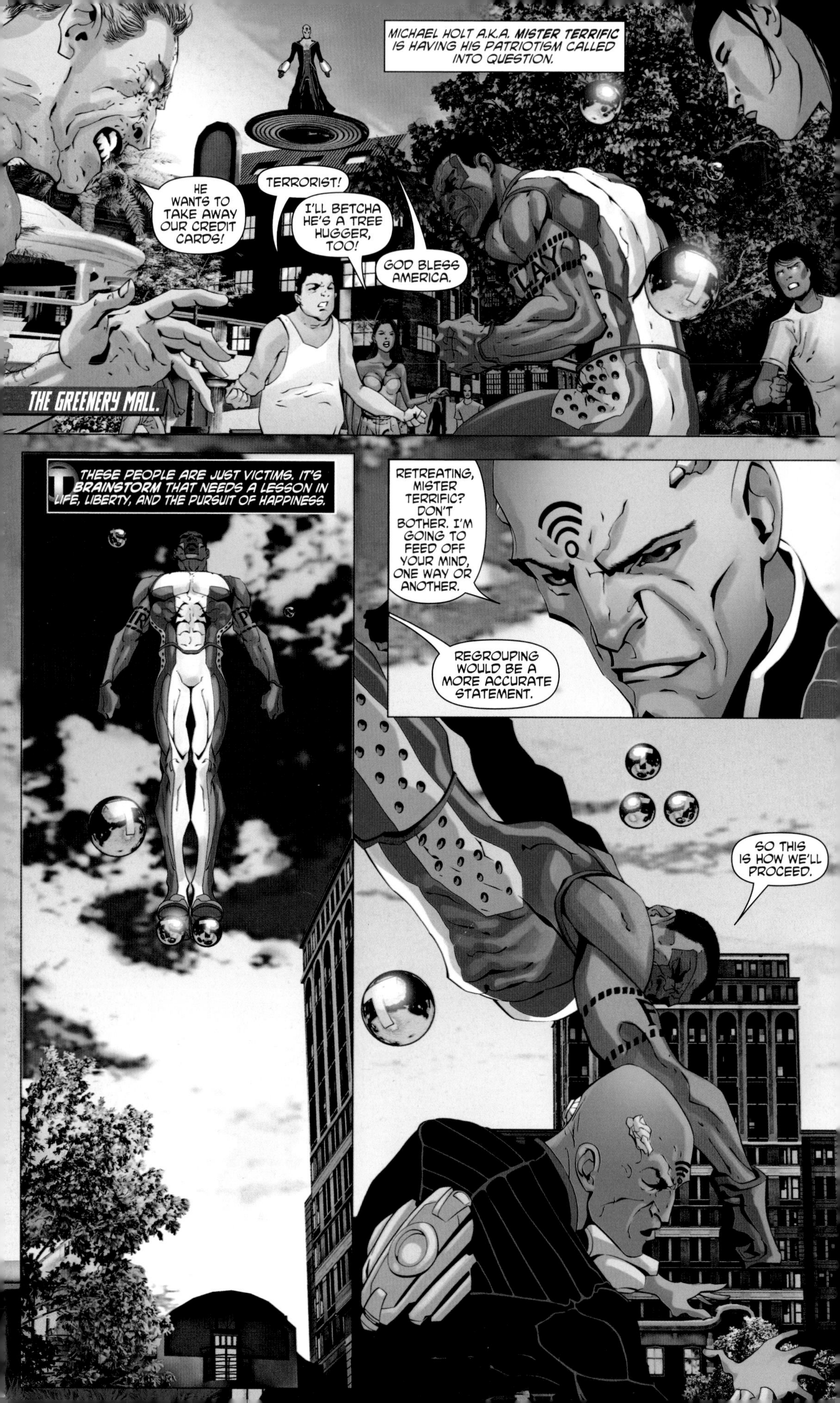
MICHAEL HOLT A.K.A. MISTER TERRIFIC IS HAVING HIS PATRIOTISM CALLED INTO QUESTION.
HE WANTS TO TAKE AWAY OUR CREDIT CARDS!
TERRORIST!
I'LL BETCHA HE'S A TREE HUGGER, TOO!
GOD BLESS AMERICA.
THE GREENERY MALL.
THESE PEOPLE ARE JUST VICTIMS. IT'S BRAINSTORM THAT NEEDS A LESSON IN LIFE, LIBERTY, AND THE PURSUIT OF HAPPINESS.
RETREATING, MISTER TERRIFIC? DON'T BOTHER. I'M GOING TO FEED OFF YOUR MIND, ONE WAY OR ANOTHER.
REGROUPING WOULD BE A MORE ACCURATE STATEMENT.
SO THIS IS HOW WE'LL PROCEED.

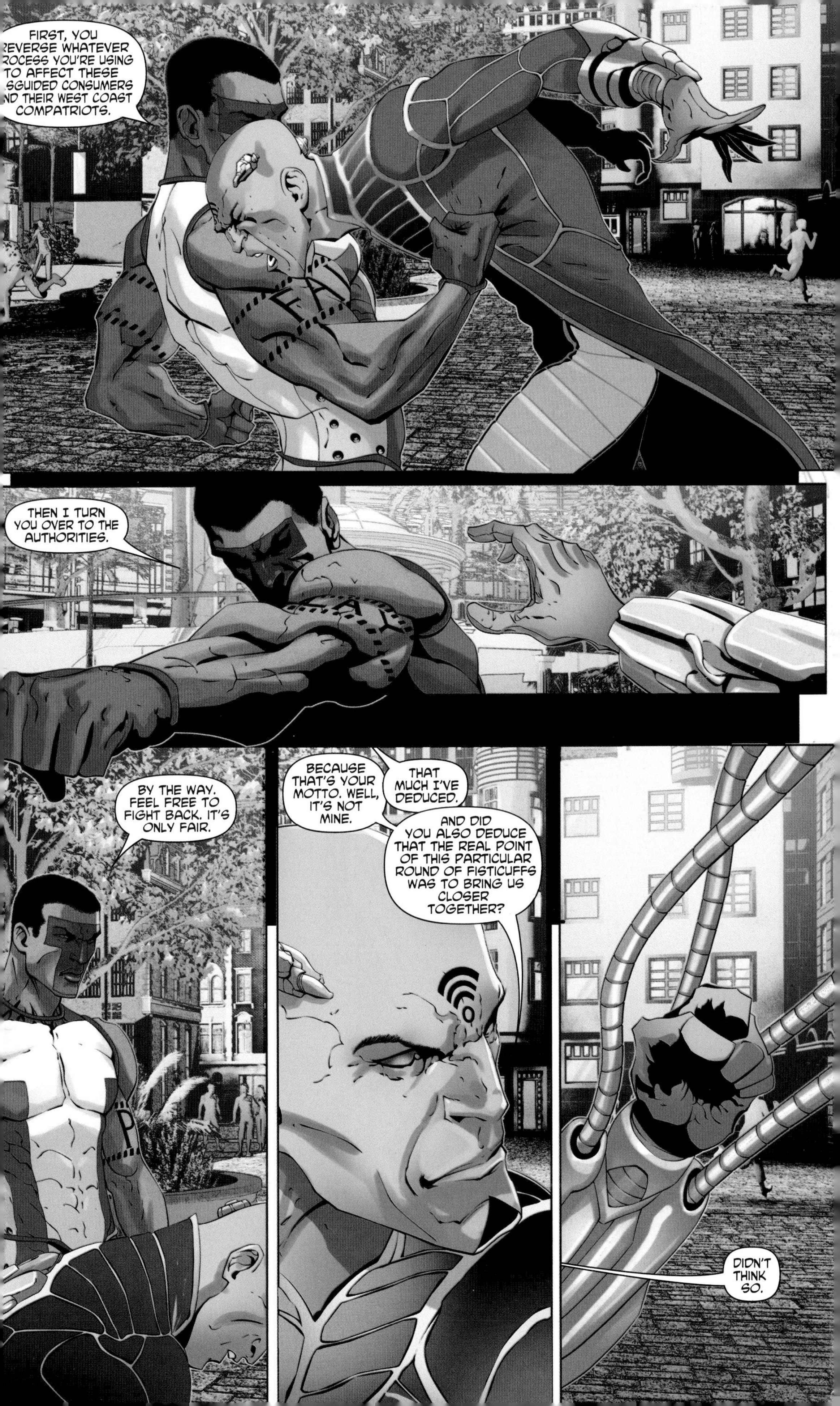
FIRST, YOU REVERSE WHATEVER PROCESS YOU'RE USING TO AFFECT THESE MISGUIDED CONSUMERS AND THEIR WEST COAST COMPATRIOTS.
THEN I TURN YOU OVER TO THE AUTHORITIES.
BY THE WAY. FEEL FREE TO FIGHT BACK. IT'S ONLY FAIR.
BECAUSE THAT'S YOUR MOTTO. WELL, IT'S NOT MINE.
THAT MUCH I'VE DEDUCED.
AND DID YOU ALSO DEDUCE THAT THE REAL POINT OF THIS PARTICULAR ROUND OF FISTICUFFS WAS TO BRING US CLOSER TOGETHER?
DIDN'T THINK SO.

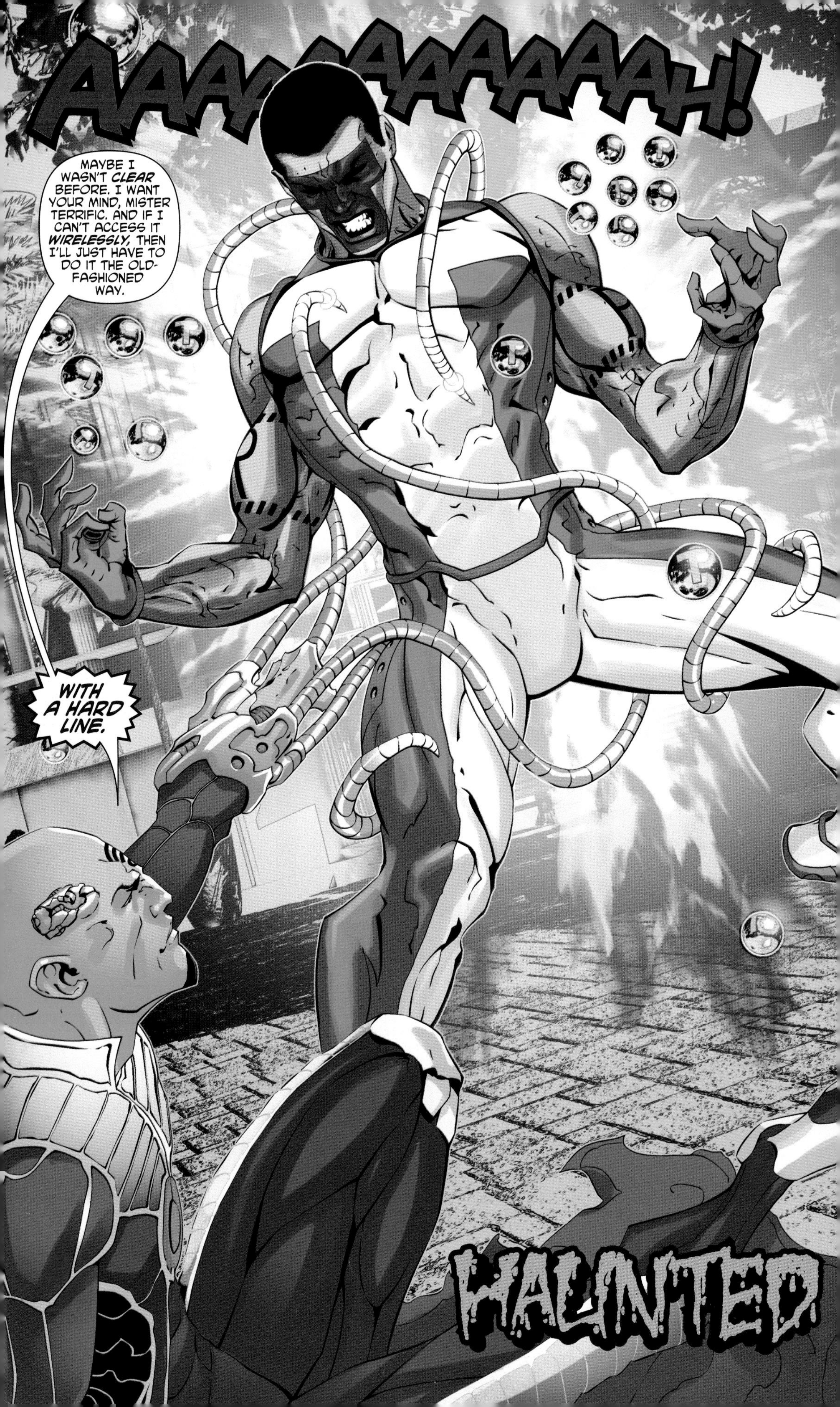
AAAAAAAAAAAAH!
MAYBE I WASN'T CLEAR BEFORE. I WANT YOUR MIND, MISTER TERRIFIC. AND IF I CAN'T ACCESS IT WIRELESSLY, THEN I'LL JUST HAVE TO DO IT THE OLD-FASHIONED WAY.
WITH A HARD LINE.
HAUNTED

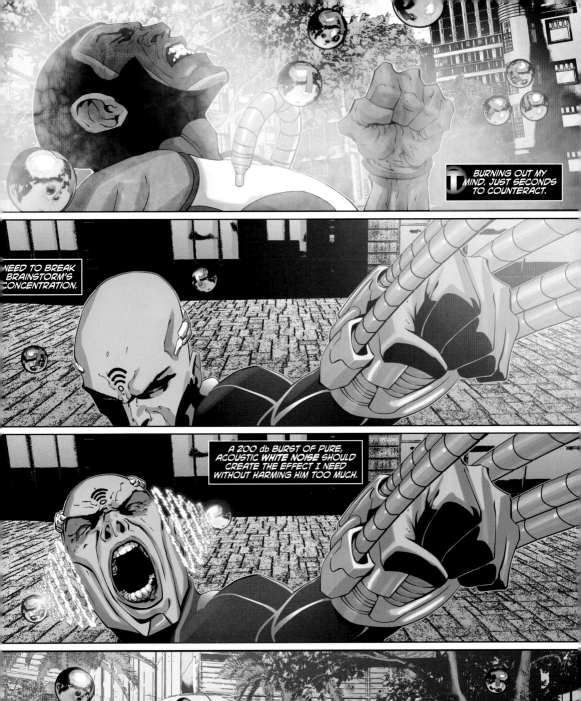

BURNING OUT MY MIND. JUST SECONDS TO COUNTERACT.

NEED TO BREAK BRAINSTORM'S CONCENTRATION.

A 200 db BURST OF PURE, ACOUSTIC *WHITE NOISE* SHOULD CREATE THE EFFECT I NEED WITHOUT HARMING HIM TOO MUCH.

ALSO, IT SHOULD PROVIDE ME A FEW SECONDS TO RECOVER.

YOU HAVE A BEAUTIFUL MIND, MISTER TERRIFIC.

OR NOT.

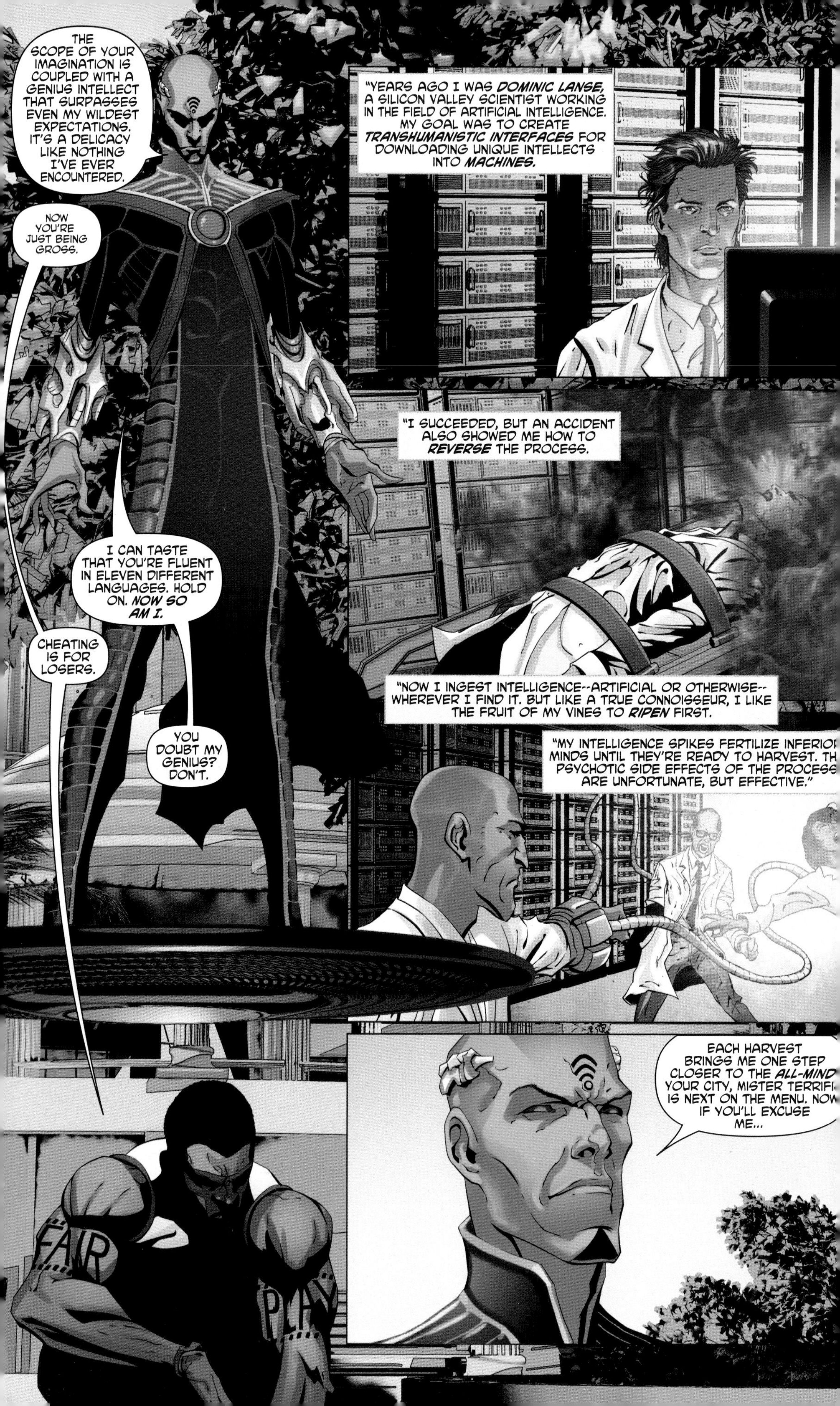

THE SCOPE OF YOUR IMAGINATION IS COUPLED WITH A GENIUS INTELLECT THAT SURPASSES EVEN MY WILDEST EXPECTATIONS. IT'S A DELICACY LIKE NOTHING I'VE EVER ENCOUNTERED.
NOW YOU'RE JUST BEING GROSS.
"YEARS AGO I WAS DOMINIC LANSE, A SILICON VALLEY SCIENTIST WORKING IN THE FIELD OF ARTIFICIAL INTELLIGENCE. MY GOAL WAS TO CREATE TRANSHUMANISTIC INTERFACES FOR DOWNLOADING UNIQUE INTELLECTS INTO MACHINES.
"I SUCCEEDED, BUT AN ACCIDENT ALSO SHOWED ME HOW TO REVERSE THE PROCESS.
I CAN TASTE THAT YOU'RE FLUENT IN ELEVEN DIFFERENT LANGUAGES. HOLD ON. NOW SO AM I.
CHEATING IS FOR LOSERS.
YOU DOUBT MY GENIUS? DON'T.
"NOW I INGEST INTELLIGENCE--ARTIFICIAL OR OTHERWISE--WHEREVER I FIND IT. BUT LIKE A TRUE CONNOISSEUR, I LIKE THE FRUIT OF MY VINES TO RIPEN FIRST.
"MY INTELLIGENCE SPIKES FERTILIZE INFERIOR MINDS UNTIL THEY'RE READY TO HARVEST. TH PSYCHOTIC SIDE EFFECTS OF THE PROCESS ARE UNFORTUNATE, BUT EFFECTIVE."
EACH HARVEST BRINGS ME ONE STEP CLOSER TO THE ALL-MIND. YOUR CITY, MISTER TERRIFI IS NEXT ON THE MENU. NOW IF YOU'LL EXCUSE ME...
FAIR
PLAY

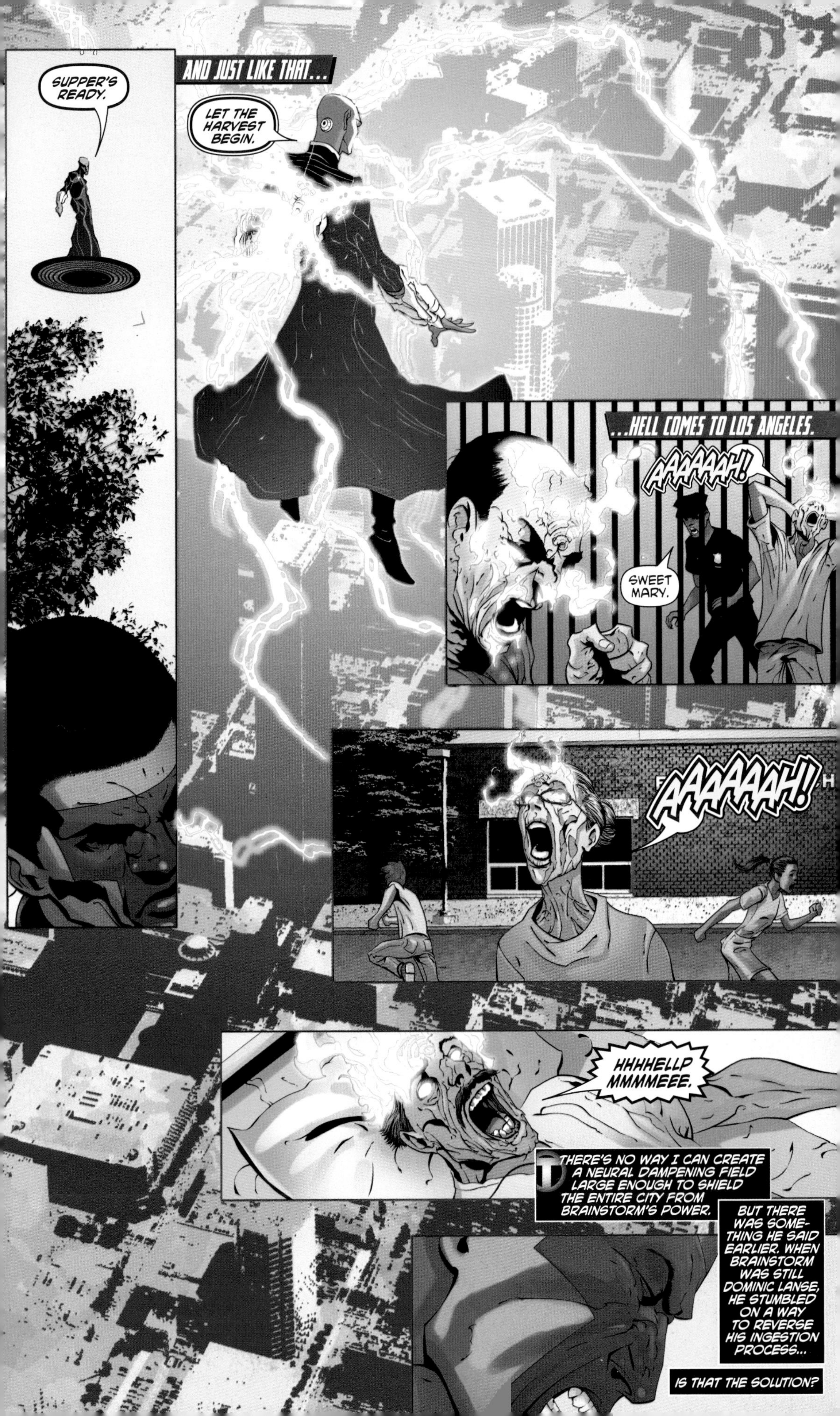
SUPPER'S READY.
AND JUST LIKE THAT...
LET THE HARVEST BEGIN.
...HELL COMES TO LOS ANGELES.
AAAAAAH!
SWEET MARY.
AAAAAAH!
HHHHELLP MMMMEEE.
THERE'S NO WAY I CAN CREATE A NEURAL DAMPENING FIELD LARGE ENOUGH TO SHIELD THE ENTIRE CITY FROM BRAINSTORM'S POWER.
BUT THERE WAS SOMETHING HE SAID EARLIER. WHEN BRAINSTORM WAS STILL DOMINIC LANSE, HE STUMBLED ON A WAY TO REVERSE HIS INGESTION PROCESS...
IS THAT THE SOLUTION?

BRAINSTORM'S CAUGHT UP IN HIS CEREBRAL GLUTTONY. GOOD. THEN HE WON'T NOTICE THIS.

REMOTE.

THE T-SANCTUARY, MISTER TERRIFIC'S HIDDEN SANCTUM.

SEEK.

AT MY COMMAND, THOUSANDS OF T-SPHERES BEGIN THE JOURNEY ACROSS DIMENSIONAL SPACE.

TARGET.

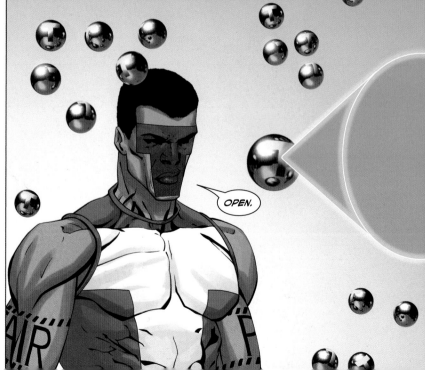

OPEN.

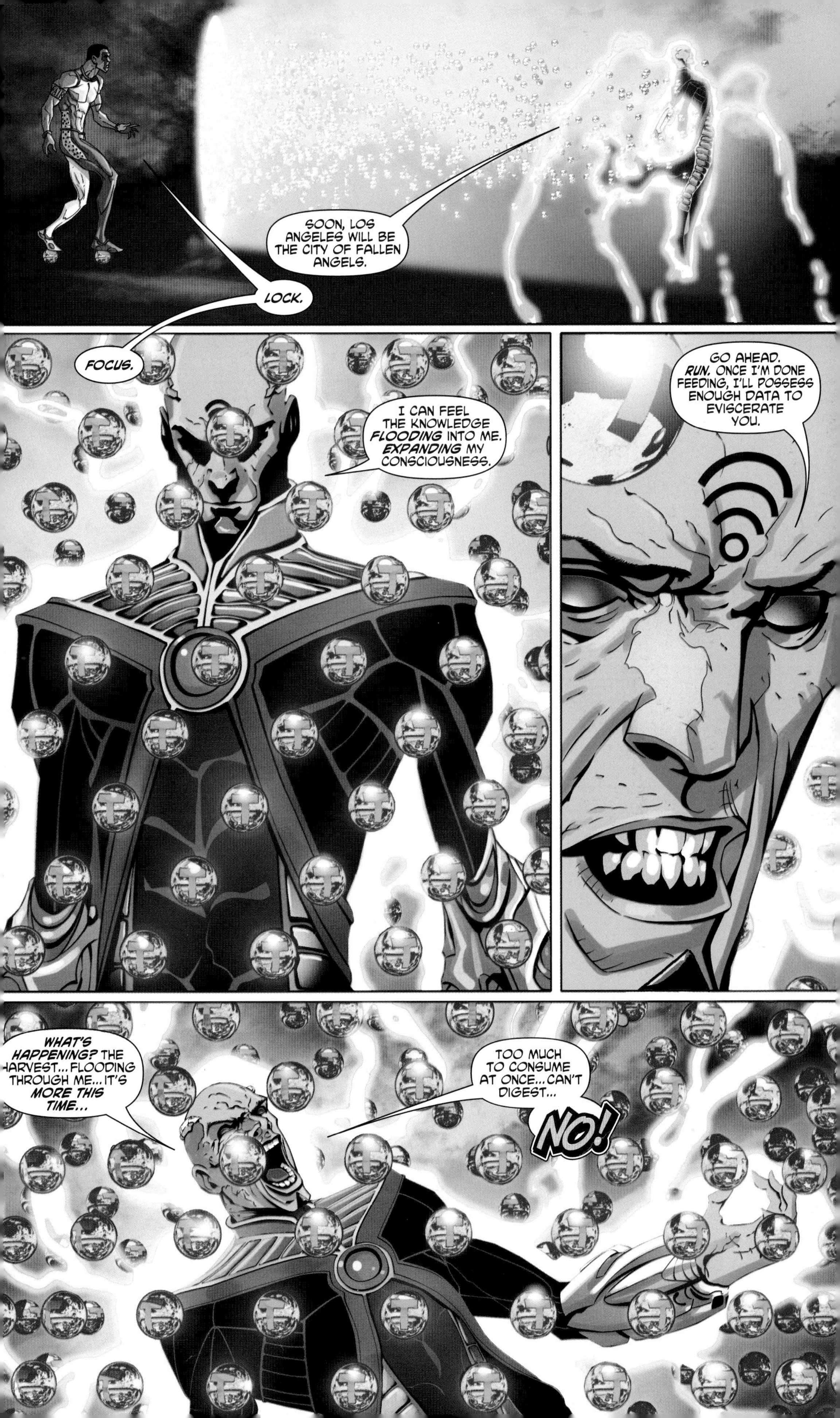
SOON, LOS ANGELES WILL BE THE CITY OF FALLEN ANGELS.
LOCK.
FOCUS.
I CAN FEEL THE KNOWLEDGE FLOODING INTO ME. EXPANDING MY CONSCIOUSNESS.
GO AHEAD. RUN. ONCE I'M DONE FEEDING, I'LL POSSESS ENOUGH DATA TO EVISCERATE YOU.
WHAT'S HAPPENING? THE HARVEST... FLOODING THROUGH ME... IT'S MORE THIS TIME...
TOO MUCH TO CONSUME AT ONCE... CAN'T DIGEST...
NO!

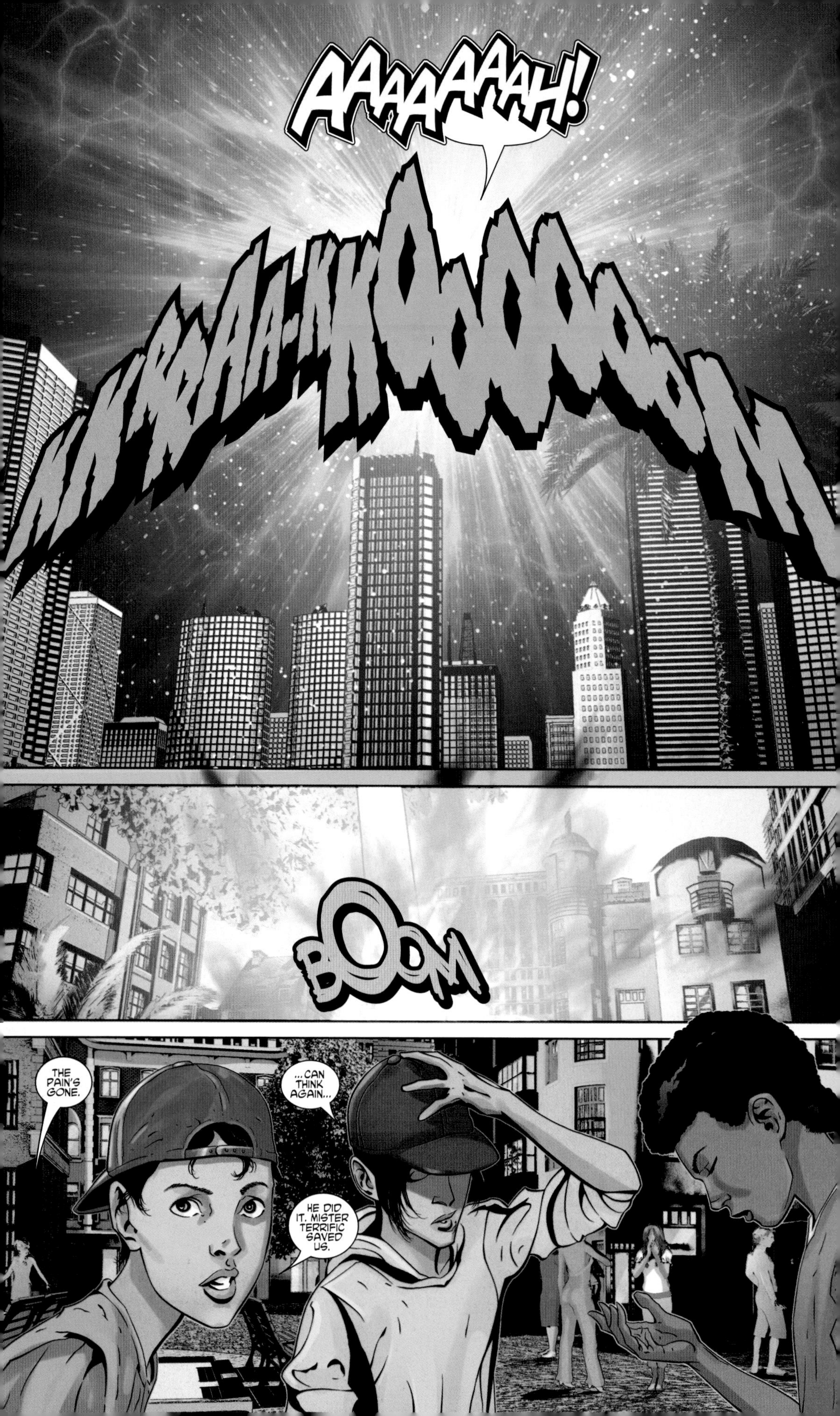
AAAAAAAH!
K-KRAA-KOOOOOM
BOOM
THE PAIN'S GONE.
...CAN THINK AGAIN...
HE DID IT. MISTER TERRIFIC SAVED US.

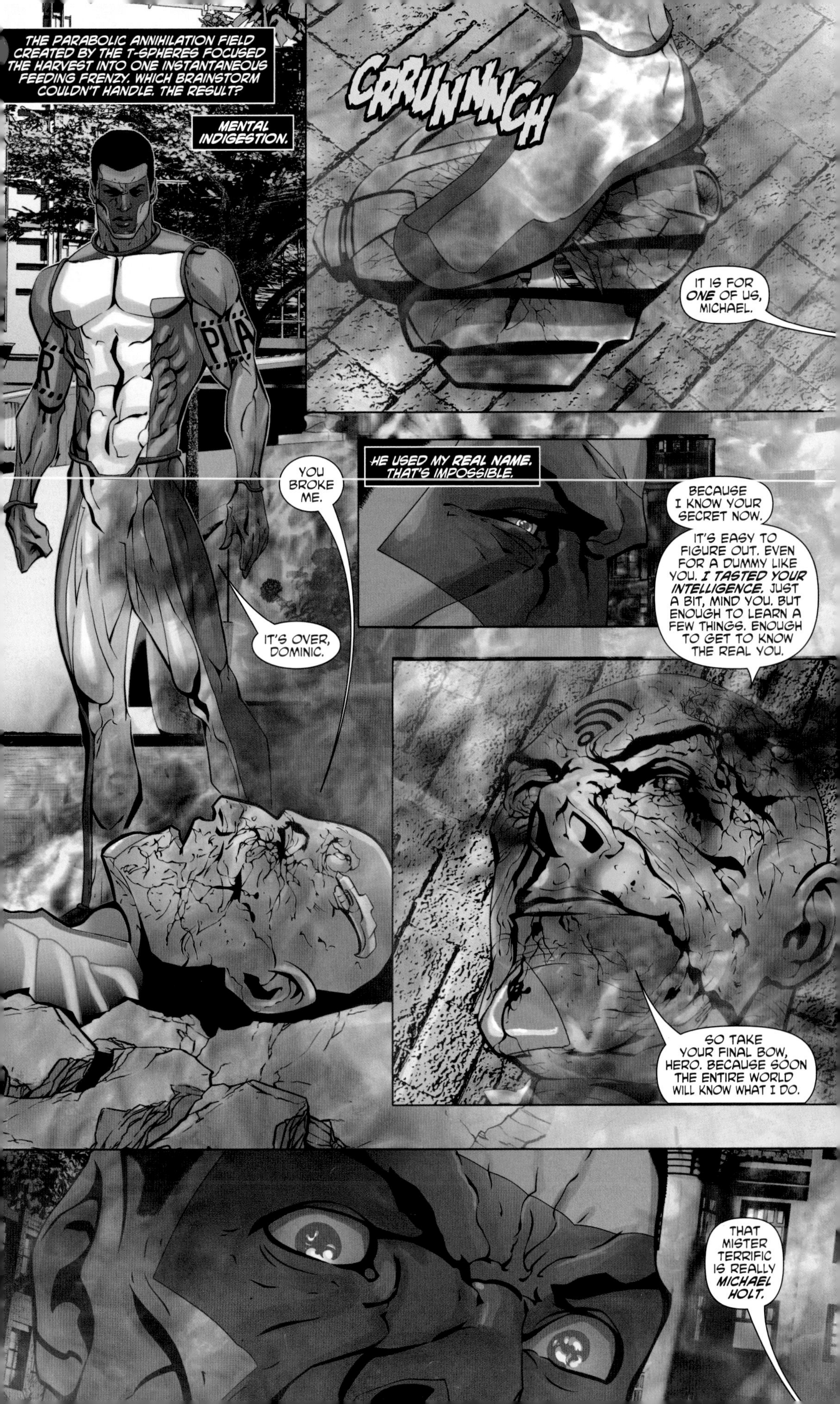
THE PARABOLIC ANNIHILATION FIELD CREATED BY THE T-SPHERES FOCUSED THE HARVEST INTO ONE INSTANTANEOUS FEEDING FRENZY. WHICH BRAINSTORM COULDN'T HANDLE. THE RESULT?
MENTAL INDIGESTION.
CRRUNNNCH
IT IS FOR ONE OF US, MICHAEL.
HE USED MY REAL NAME. THAT'S IMPOSSIBLE.
YOU BROKE ME.
IT'S OVER, DOMINIC.
BECAUSE I KNOW YOUR SECRET NOW.
IT'S EASY TO FIGURE OUT. EVEN FOR A DUMMY LIKE YOU. I TASTED YOUR INTELLIGENCE. JUST A BIT, MIND YOU. BUT ENOUGH TO LEARN A FEW THINGS. ENOUGH TO GET TO KNOW THE REAL YOU.
SO TAKE YOUR FINAL BOW, HERO. BECAUSE SOON THE ENTIRE WORLD WILL KNOW WHAT I DO.
THAT MISTER TERRIFIC IS REALLY MICHAEL HOLT.

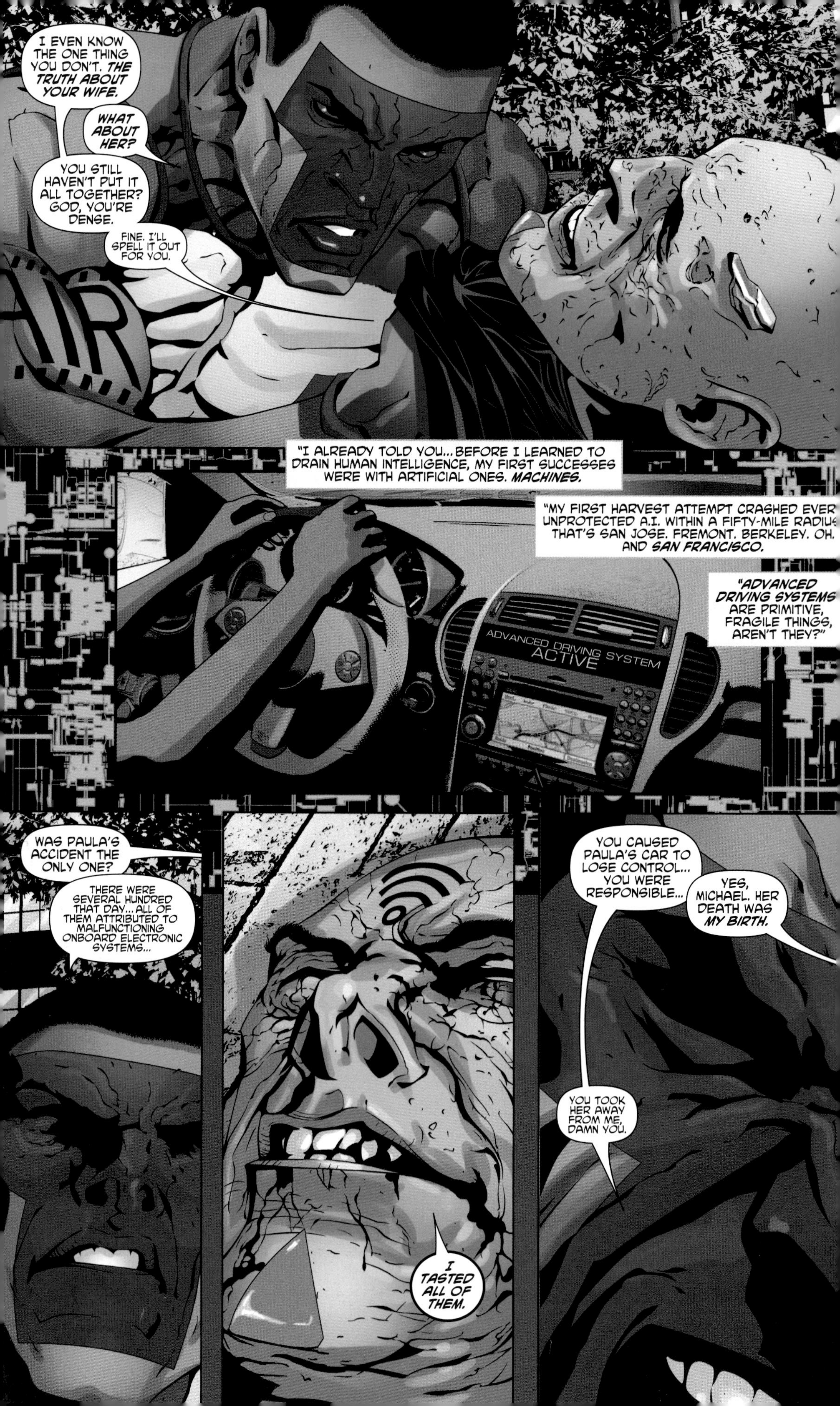

I EVEN KNOW THE ONE THING YOU DON'T. THE TRUTH ABOUT YOUR WIFE.
WHAT ABOUT HER?
YOU STILL HAVEN'T PUT IT ALL TOGETHER? GOD, YOU'RE DENSE.
FINE. I'LL SPELL IT OUT FOR YOU.
"I ALREADY TOLD YOU... BEFORE I LEARNED TO DRAIN HUMAN INTELLIGENCE, MY FIRST SUCCESSES WERE WITH ARTIFICIAL ONES. MACHINES.
"MY FIRST HARVEST ATTEMPT CRASHED EVER UNPROTECTED A.I. WITHIN A FIFTY-MILE RADIU THAT'S SAN JOSE. FREMONT. BERKELEY. OH. AND SAN FRANCISCO.
"ADVANCED DRIVING SYSTEMS ARE PRIMITIVE, FRAGILE THINGS, AREN'T THEY?"
ADVANCED DRIVING SYSTEM ACTIVE
WAS PAULA'S ACCIDENT THE ONLY ONE?
THERE WERE SEVERAL HUNDRED THAT DAY... ALL OF THEM ATTRIBUTED TO MALFUNCTIONING ONBOARD ELECTRONIC SYSTEMS...
I TASTED ALL OF THEM.
YOU CAUSED PAULA'S CAR TO LOSE CONTROL... YOU WERE RESPONSIBLE...
YES, MICHAEL. HER DEATH WAS MY BIRTH.
YOU TOOK HER AWAY FROM ME, DAMN YOU.

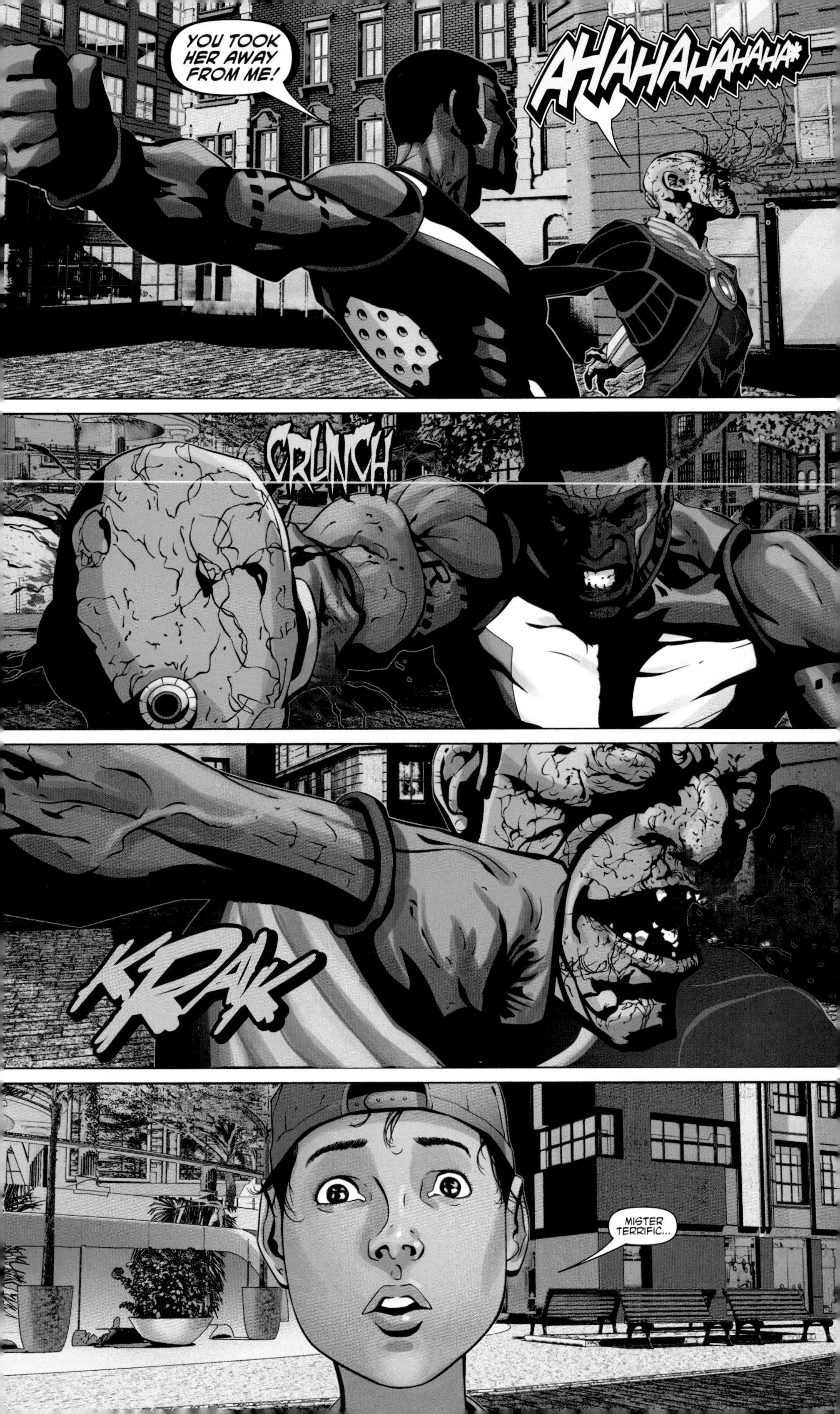
YOU TOOK HER AWAY FROM ME!
AHAHAHAHAHAHA!
CRUNCH
KRAK
MISTER TERRIFIC...

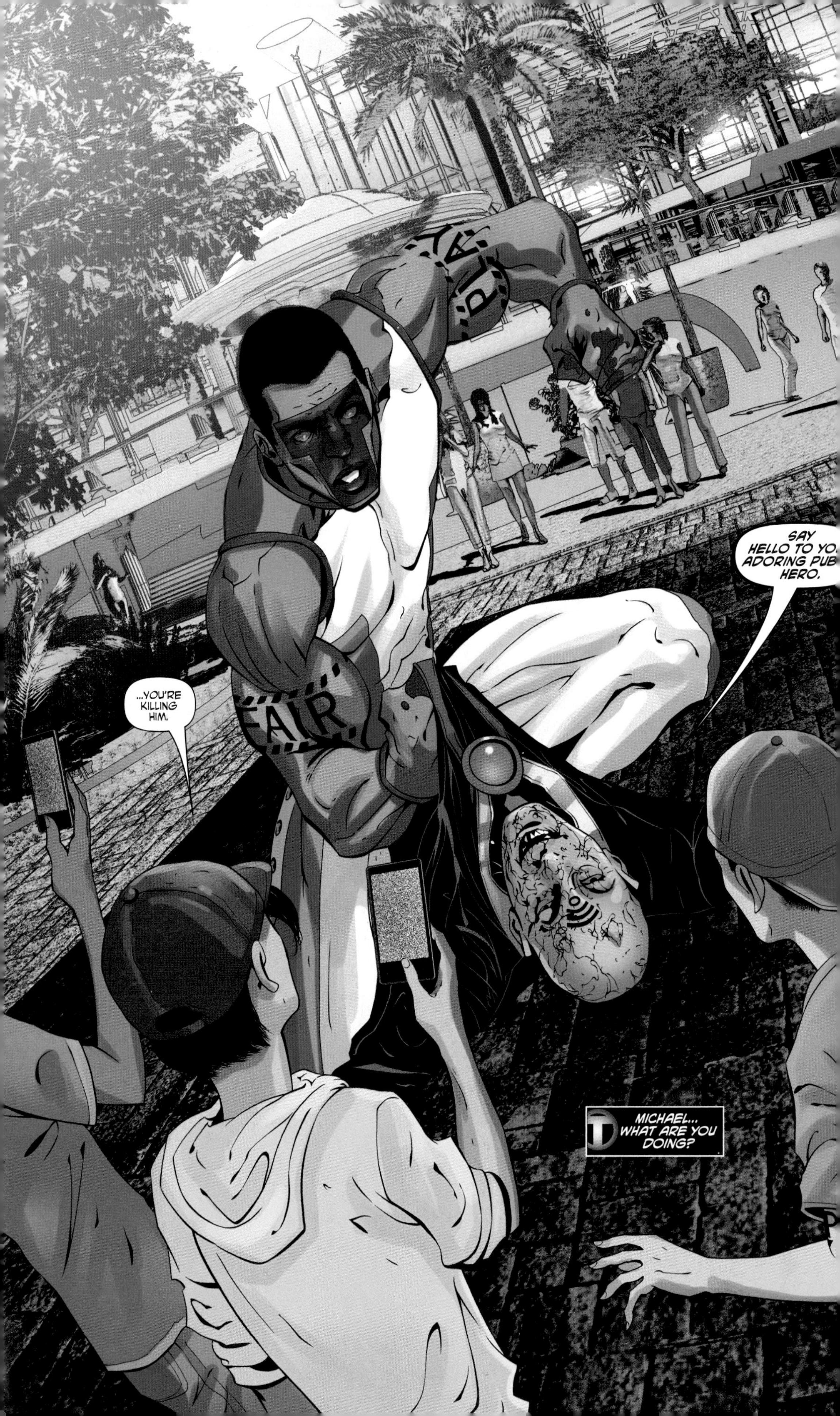

PLA
...YOU'RE KILLING HIM.
SAY HELLO TO YO ADORING PUB HERO.
FAIR
MICHAEL... WHAT ARE YOU DOING?

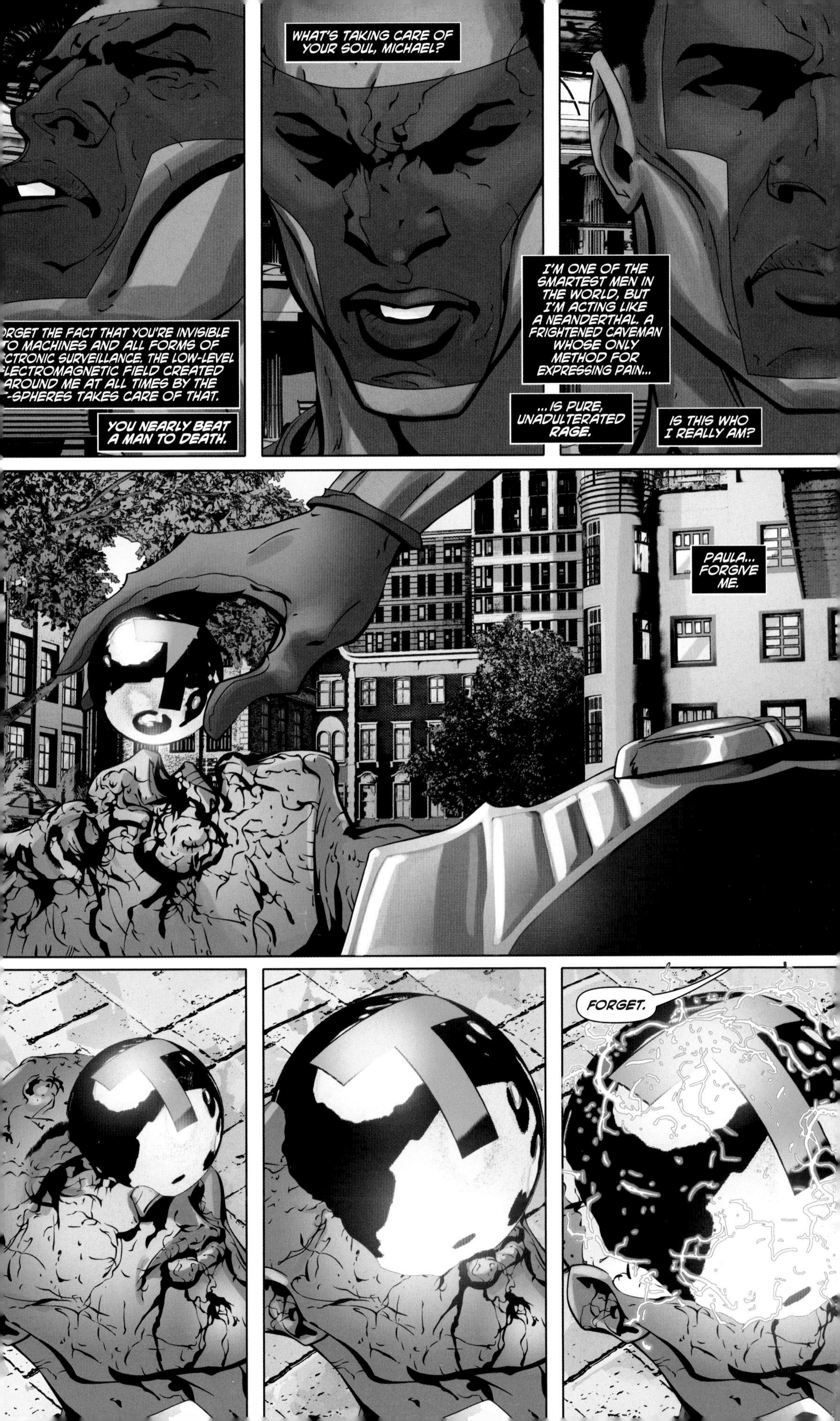
ORGET THE FACT THAT YOU'RE INVISIBLE TO MACHINES AND ALL FORMS OF CTRONIC SURVEILLANCE. THE LOW-LEVEL LECTROMAGNETIC FIELD CREATED AROUND ME AT ALL TIMES BY THE -SPHERES TAKES CARE OF THAT.
YOU NEARLY BEAT A MAN TO DEATH.
WHAT'S TAKING CARE OF YOUR SOUL, MICHAEL?
I'M ONE OF THE SMARTEST MEN IN THE WORLD, BUT I'M ACTING LIKE A NEANDERTHAL. A FRIGHTENED CAVEMAN WHOSE ONLY METHOD FOR EXPRESSING PAIN...
...IS PURE, UNADULTERATED RAGE.
IS THIS WHO I REALLY AM?
PAULA... FORGIVE ME.
FORGET.

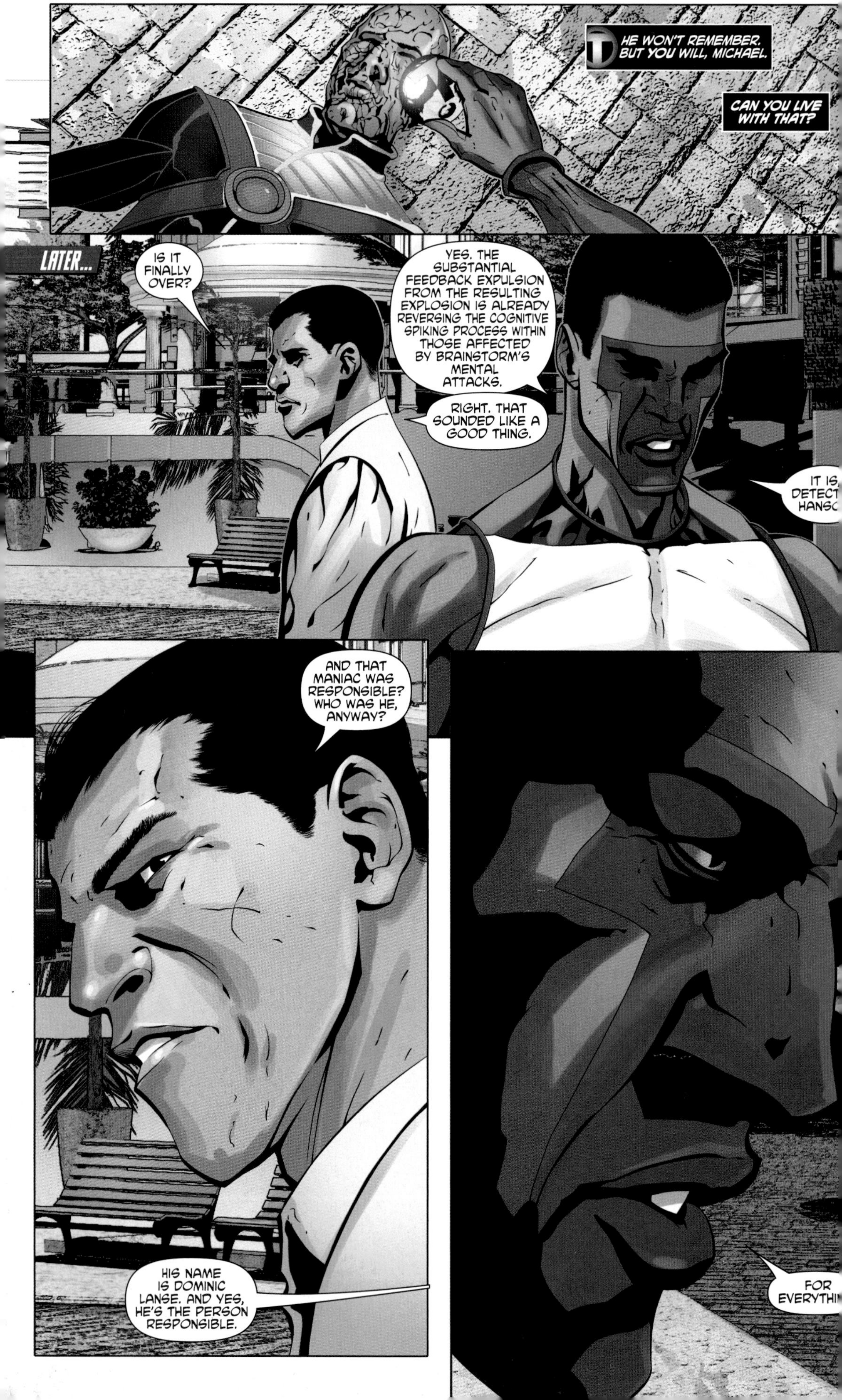
HE WON'T REMEMBER. BUT YOU WILL, MICHAEL.
CAN YOU LIVE WITH THAT?
LATER...
IS IT FINALLY OVER?
YES. THE SUBSTANTIAL FEEDBACK EXPULSION FROM THE RESULTING EXPLOSION IS ALREADY REVERSING THE COGNITIVE SPIKING PROCESS WITHIN THOSE AFFECTED BY BRAINSTORM'S MENTAL ATTACKS.
RIGHT. THAT SOUNDED LIKE A GOOD THING.
AND THAT MANIAC WAS RESPONSIBLE? WHO WAS HE, ANYWAY?
HIS NAME IS DOMINIC LANSE. AND YES, HE'S THE PERSON RESPONSIBLE.

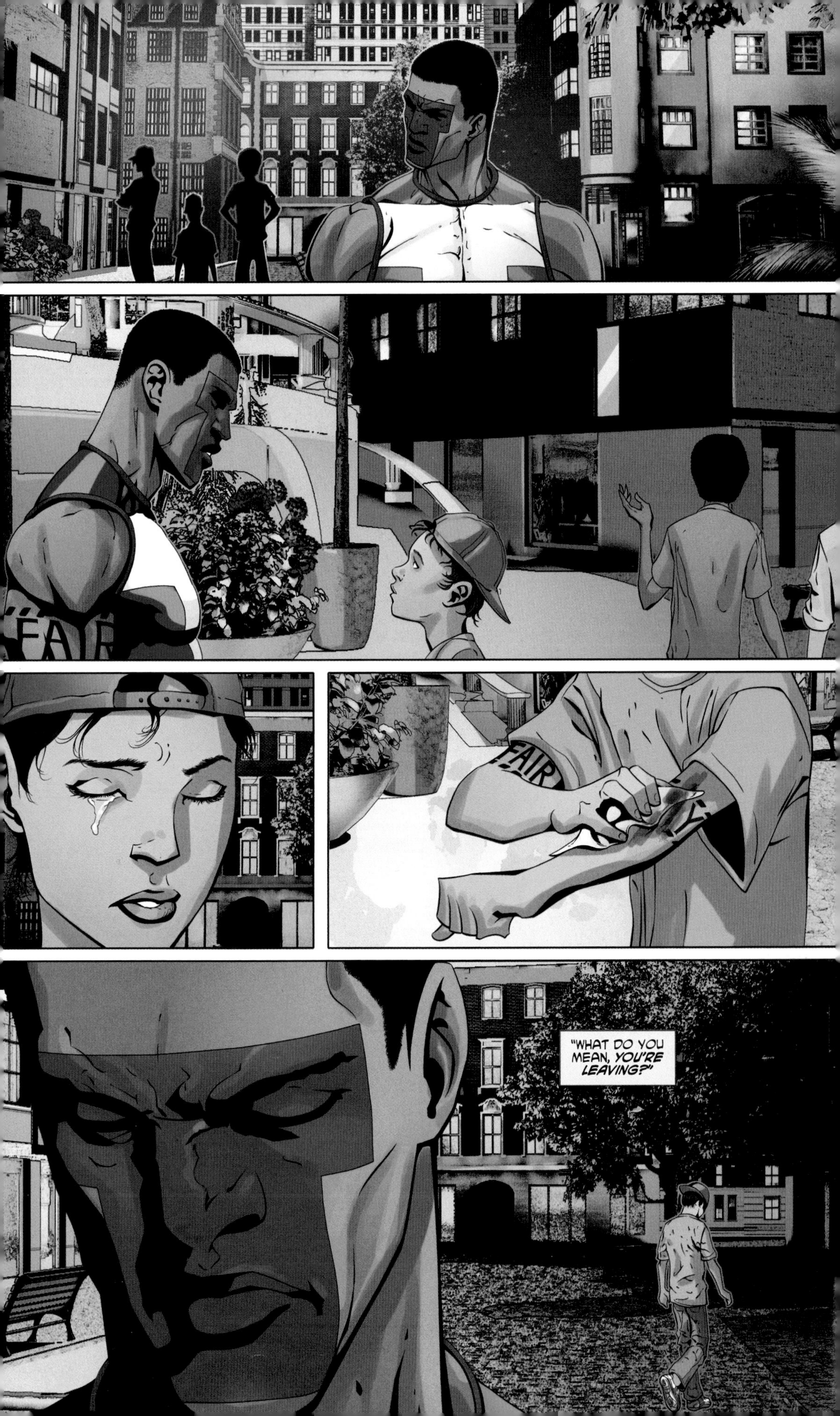
"WHAT DO YOU MEAN, *YOU'RE LEAVING?*"

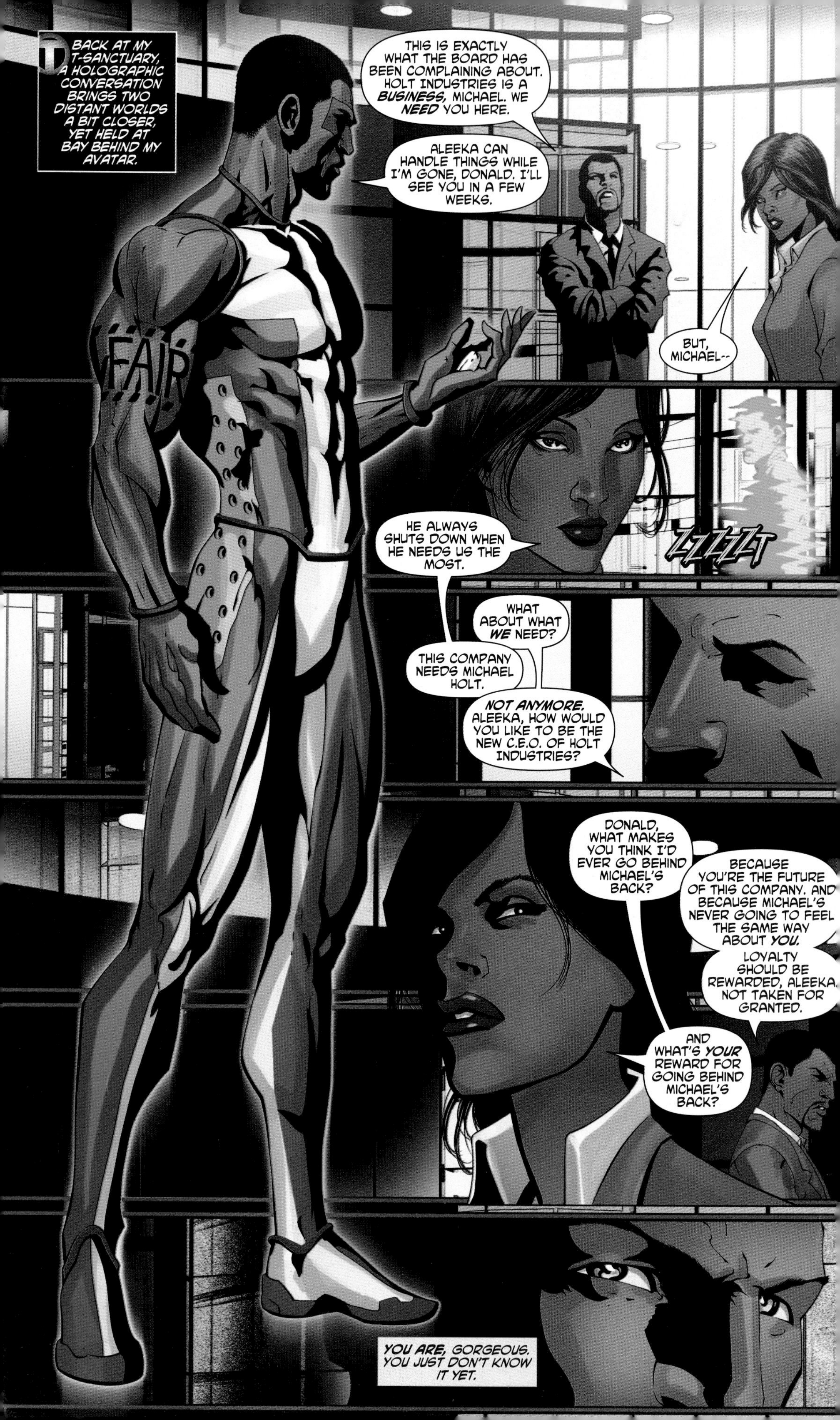

BACK AT MY T-SANCTUARY, A HOLOGRAPHIC CONVERSATION BRINGS TWO DISTANT WORLDS A BIT CLOSER, YET HELD AT BAY BEHIND MY AVATAR.
THIS IS EXACTLY WHAT THE BOARD HAS BEEN COMPLAINING ABOUT. HOLT INDUSTRIES IS A BUSINESS, MICHAEL. WE NEED YOU HERE.
ALEEKA CAN HANDLE THINGS WHILE I'M GONE, DONALD. I'LL SEE YOU IN A FEW WEEKS.
BUT, MICHAEL--
FAIR
ZZZZZT
HE ALWAYS SHUTS DOWN WHEN HE NEEDS US THE MOST.
THIS COMPANY NEEDS MICHAEL HOLT.
WHAT ABOUT WHAT WE NEED?
NOT ANYMORE. ALEEKA, HOW WOULD YOU LIKE TO BE THE NEW C.E.O. OF HOLT INDUSTRIES?
DONALD, WHAT MAKES YOU THINK I'D EVER GO BEHIND MICHAEL'S BACK?
BECAUSE YOU'RE THE FUTURE OF THIS COMPANY. AND BECAUSE MICHAEL'S NEVER GOING TO FEEL THE SAME WAY ABOUT YOU.
LOYALTY SHOULD BE REWARDED, ALEEKA, NOT TAKEN FOR GRANTED.
AND WHAT'S YOUR REWARD FOR GOING BEHIND MICHAEL'S BACK?
YOU ARE, GORGEOUS. YOU JUST DON'T KNOW IT YET.

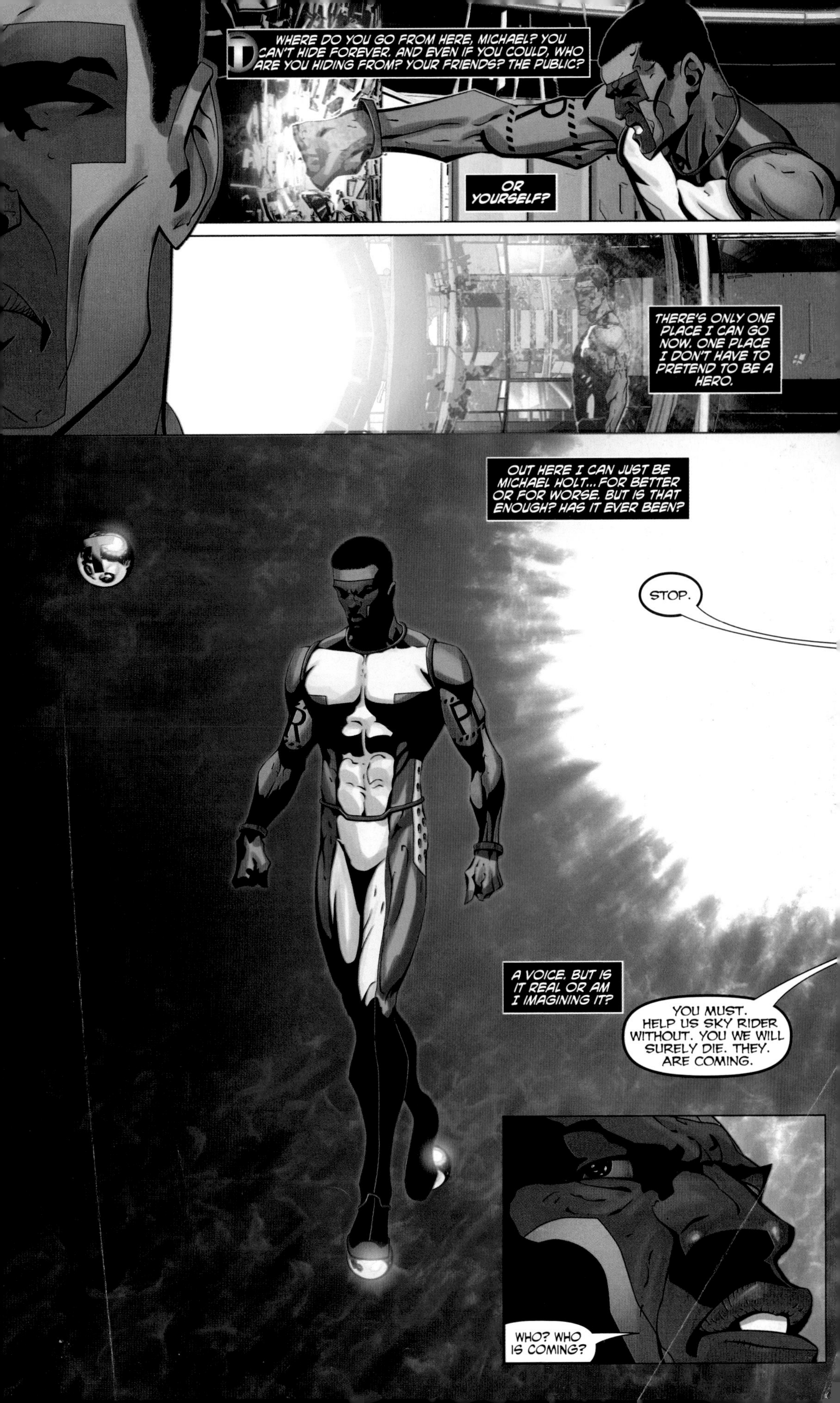
WHERE DO YOU GO FROM HERE, MICHAEL? YOU CAN'T HIDE FOREVER. AND EVEN IF YOU COULD, WHO ARE YOU HIDING FROM? YOUR FRIENDS? THE PUBLIC?
OR YOURSELF?
THERE'S ONLY ONE PLACE I CAN GO NOW. ONE PLACE I DON'T HAVE TO PRETEND TO BE A HERO.
OUT HERE I CAN JUST BE MICHAEL HOLT... FOR BETTER OR FOR WORSE. BUT IS THAT ENOUGH? HAS IT EVER BEEN?
STOP.
A VOICE. BUT IS IT REAL OR AM I IMAGINING IT?
YOU MUST. HELP US SKY RIDER WITHOUT. YOU WE WILL SURELY DIE. THEY. ARE COMING.
WHO? WHO IS COMING?

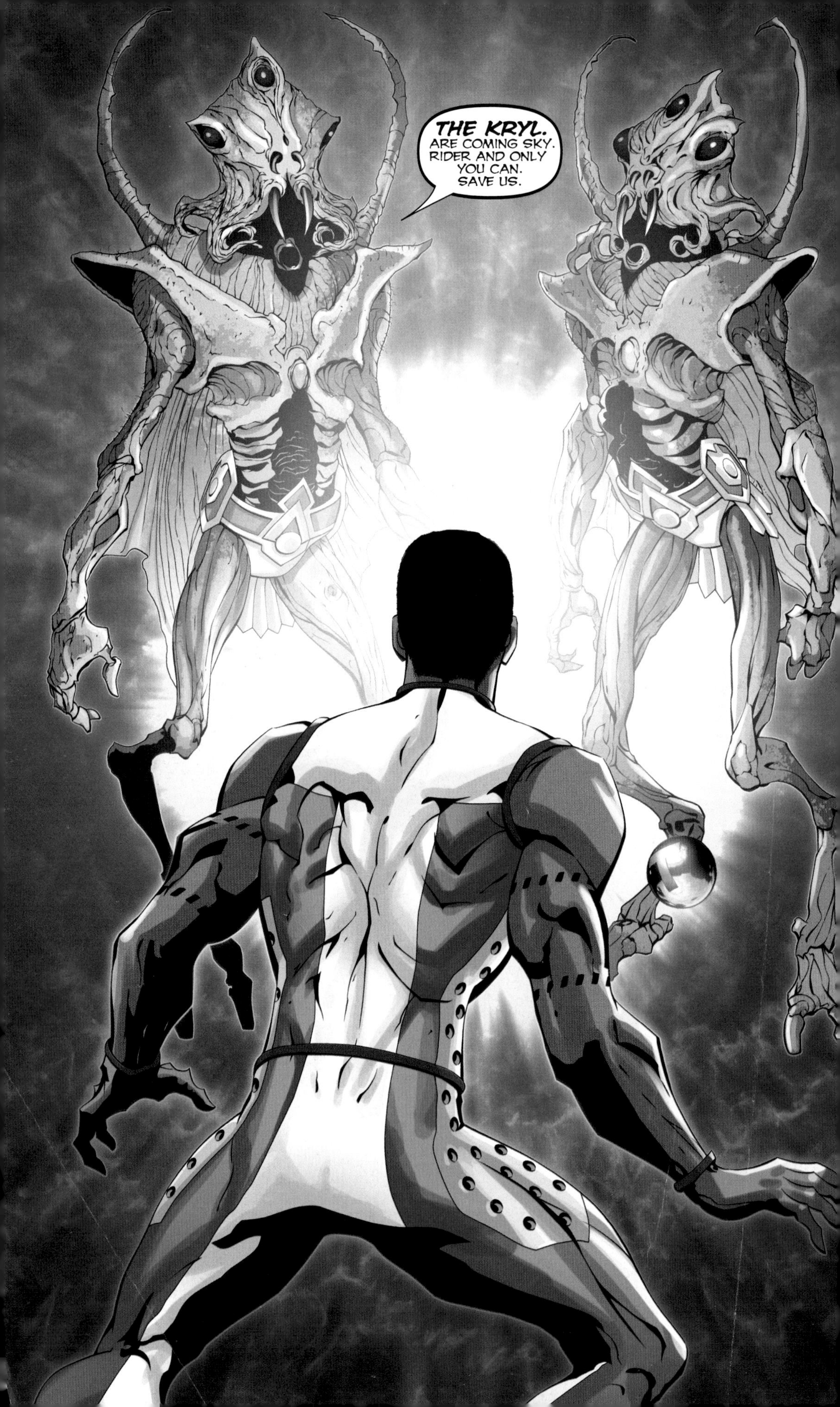
THE KRYL.
ARE COMING SKY. RIDER AND ONLY YOU CAN. SAVE US.

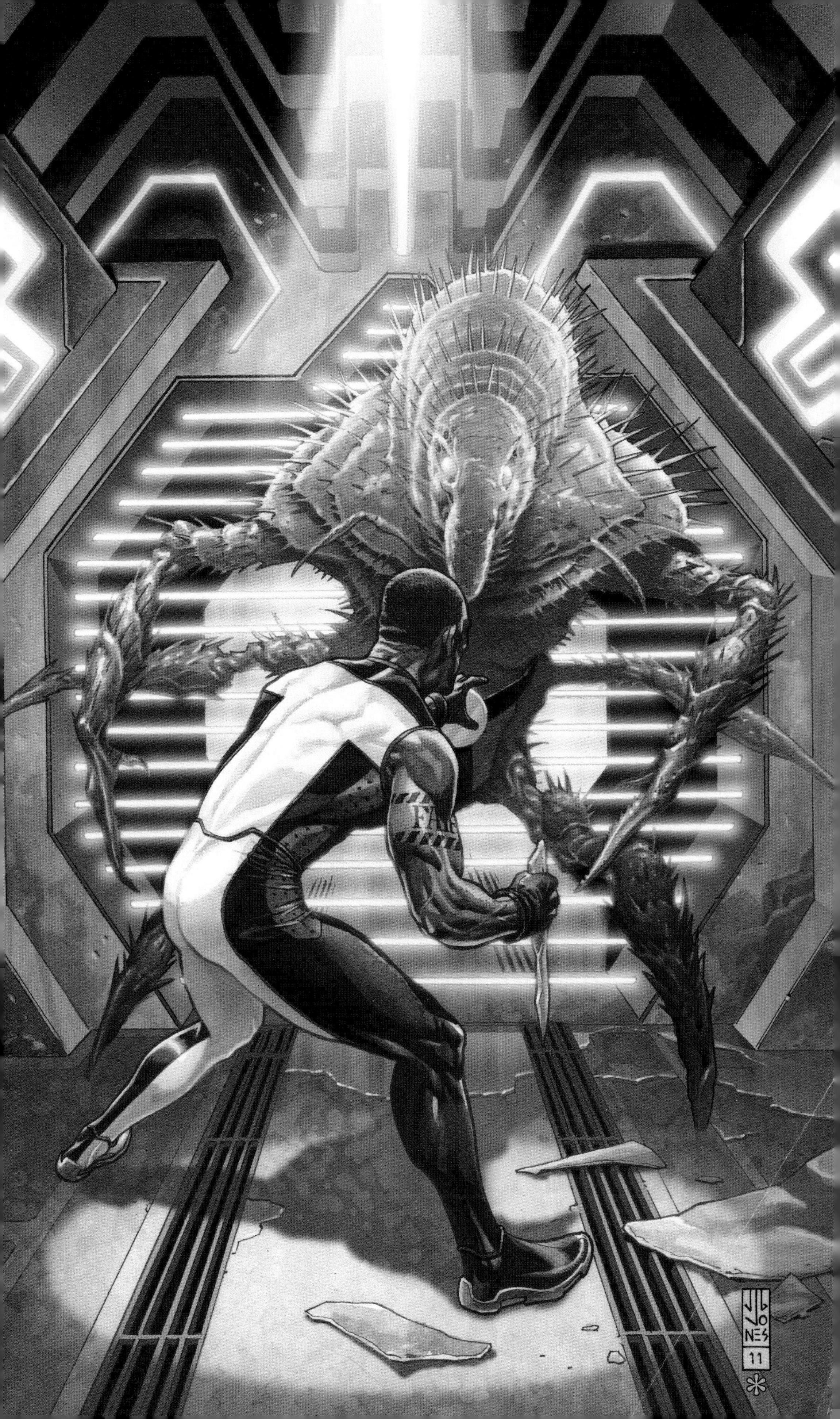

EXPOSED

ERIC WALLACE writer **GIANLUCA GUGLIOTTA** penciller **WAYNE FAUCHER** inker
cover art by **J.G. JONES** with colorist **HI-FI**

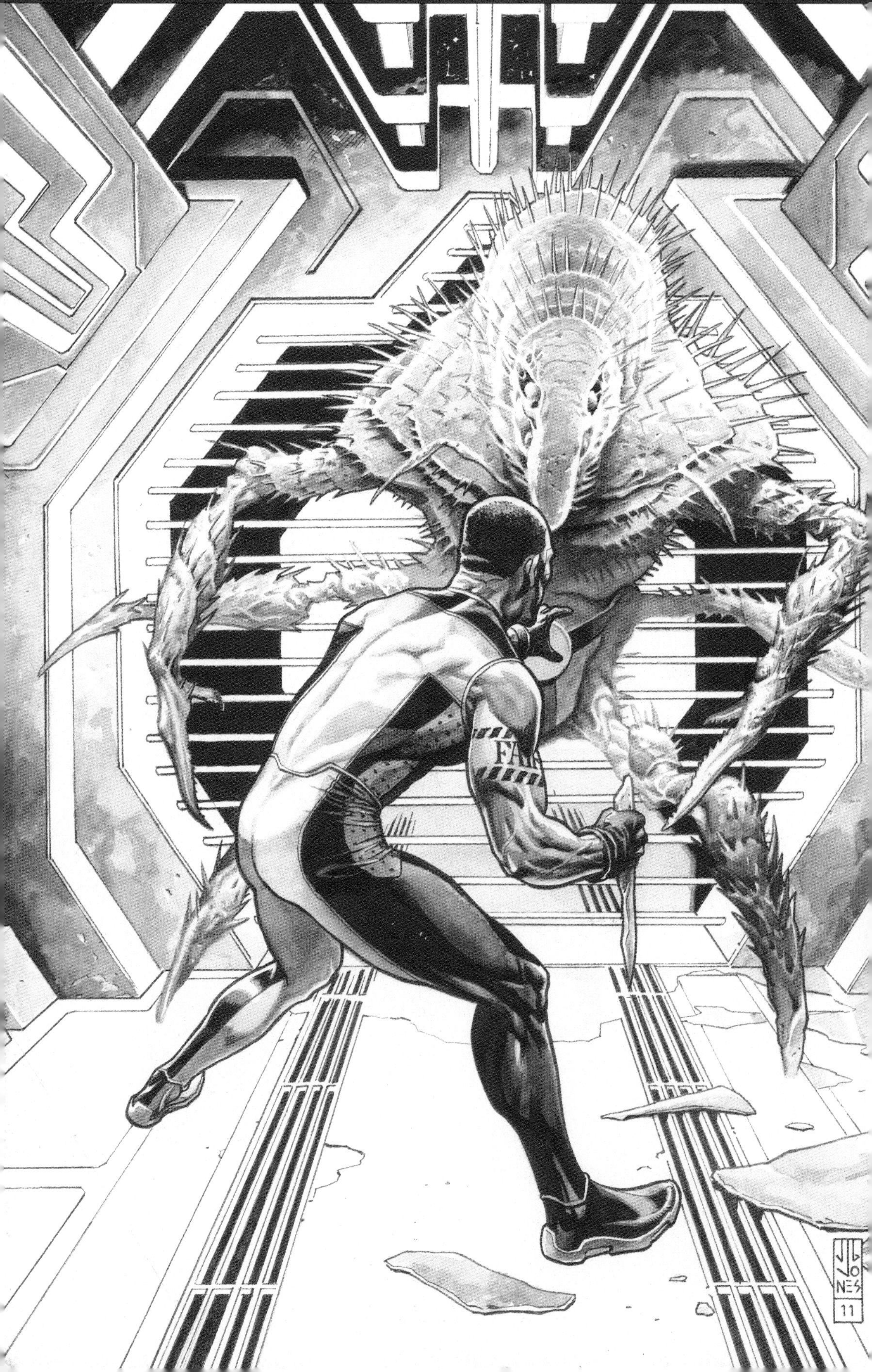

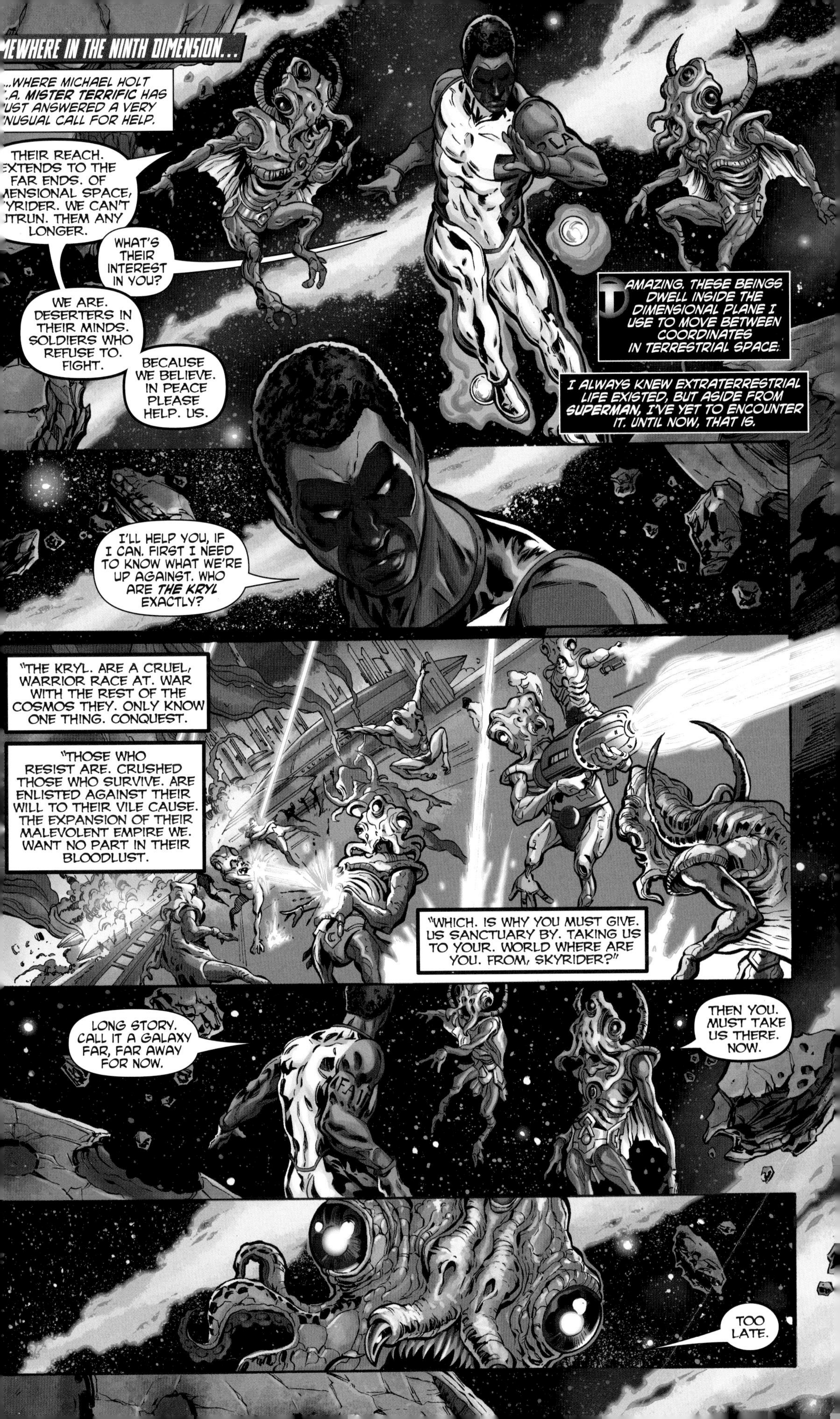
MEWHERE IN THE NINTH DIMENSION...
...WHERE MICHAEL HOLT A.A. MISTER TERRIFIC HAS JUST ANSWERED A VERY NUSUAL CALL FOR HELP.
THEIR REACH. EXTENDS TO THE FAR ENDS. OF MENSIONAL SPACE, YRIDER. WE CAN'T UTRUN. THEM ANY LONGER.
WHAT'S THEIR INTEREST IN YOU?
WE ARE. DESERTERS IN THEIR MINDS. SOLDIERS WHO REFUSE TO. FIGHT.
BECAUSE WE BELIEVE. IN PEACE PLEASE HELP. US.
AMAZING. THESE BEINGS DWELL INSIDE THE DIMENSIONAL PLANE I USE TO MOVE BETWEEN COORDINATES IN TERRESTRIAL SPACE.
I ALWAYS KNEW EXTRATERRESTRIAL LIFE EXISTED, BUT ASIDE FROM SUPERMAN, I'VE YET TO ENCOUNTER IT. UNTIL NOW, THAT IS.
I'LL HELP YOU, IF I CAN. FIRST I NEED TO KNOW WHAT WE'RE UP AGAINST. WHO ARE THE KRYL EXACTLY?
"THE KRYL. ARE A CRUEL, WARRIOR RACE AT. WAR WITH THE REST OF THE COSMOS THEY. ONLY KNOW ONE THING. CONQUEST.
"THOSE WHO RESIST ARE. CRUSHED THOSE WHO SURVIVE. ARE ENLISTED AGAINST THEIR WILL TO THEIR VILE CAUSE. THE EXPANSION OF THEIR MALEVOLENT EMPIRE WE. WANT NO PART IN THEIR BLOODLUST.
"WHICH. IS WHY YOU MUST GIVE. US SANCTUARY BY. TAKING US TO YOUR. WORLD WHERE ARE YOU. FROM, SKYRIDER?"
LONG STORY. CALL IT A GALAXY FAR, FAR AWAY FOR NOW.
THEN YOU. MUST TAKE US THERE. NOW.
TOO LATE.

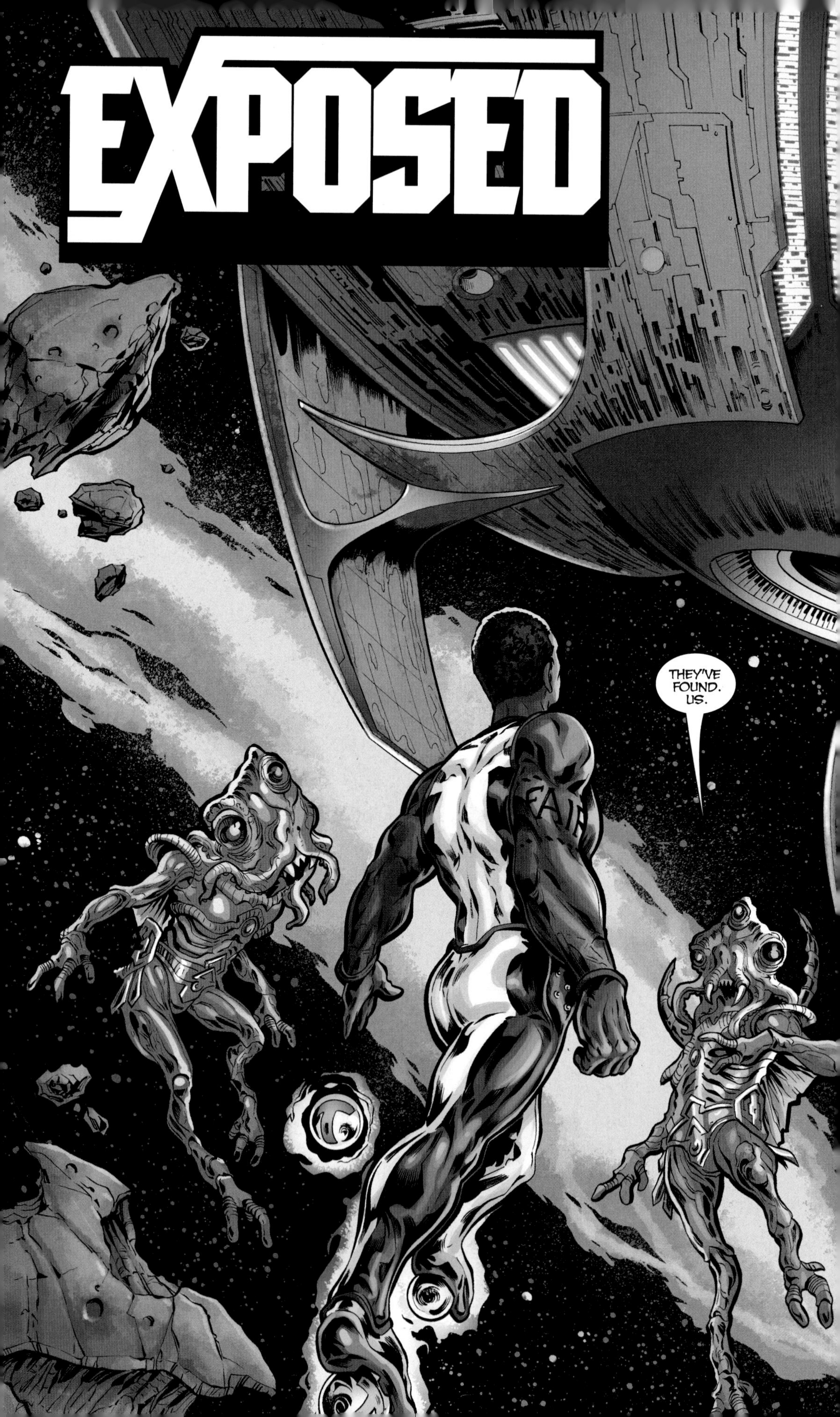
EXPOSED
THEY'VE FOUND. US.
FAITH

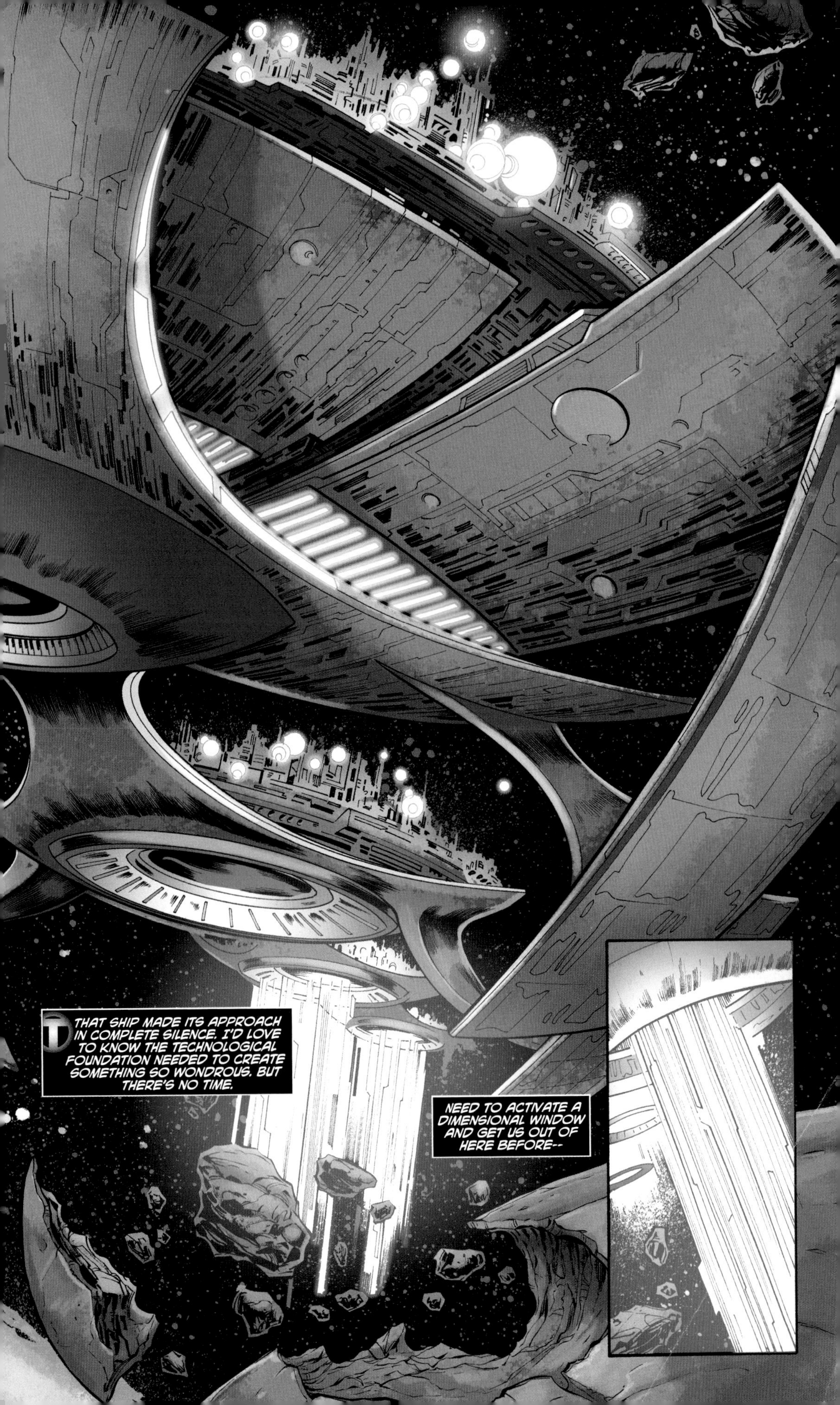
THAT SHIP MADE ITS APPROACH IN COMPLETE SILENCE. I'D LOVE TO KNOW THE TECHNOLOGICAL FOUNDATION NEEDED TO CREATE SOMETHING SO WONDROUS. BUT THERE'S NO TIME.
NEED TO ACTIVATE A DIMENSIONAL WINDOW AND GET US OUT OF HERE BEFORE--

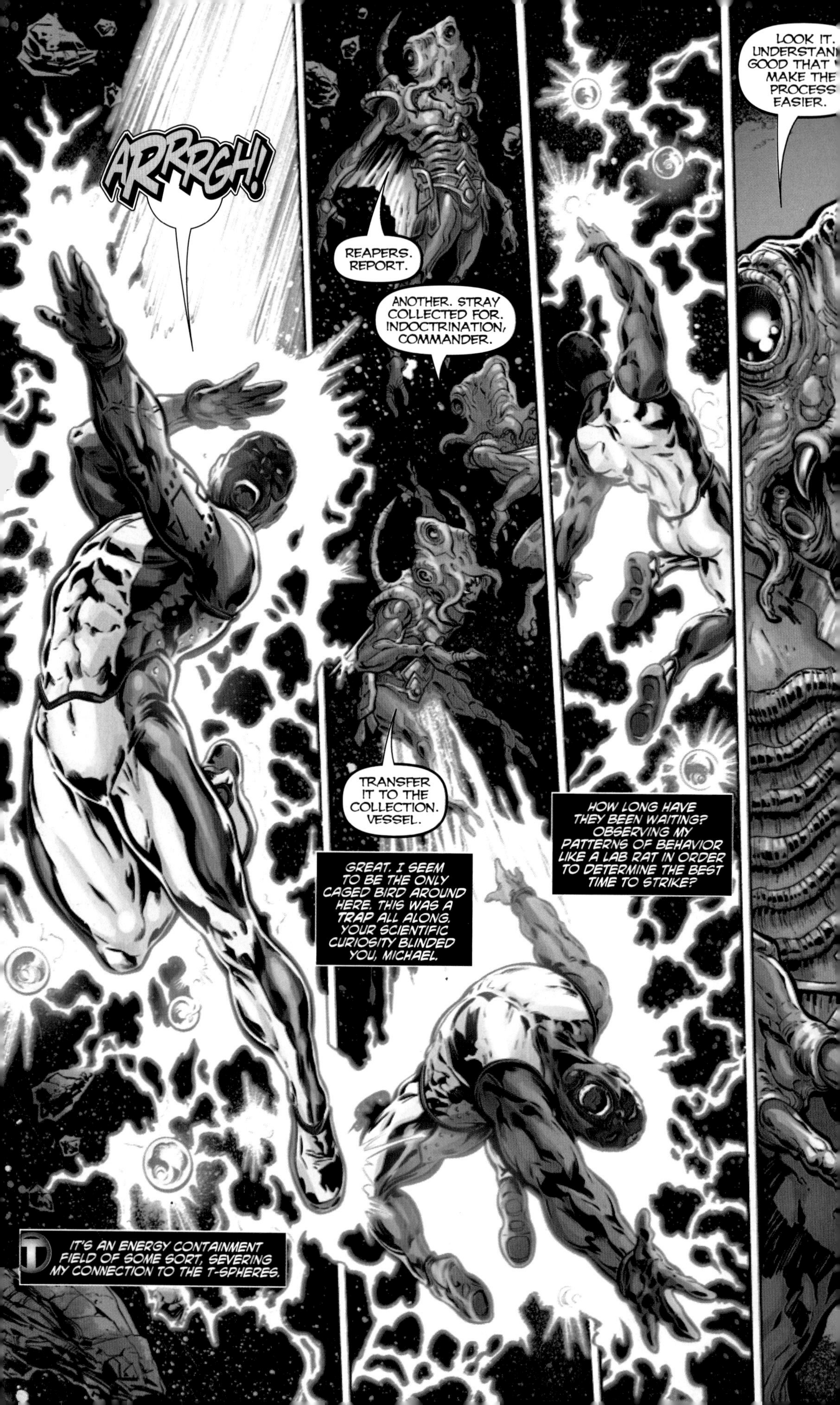

ARRRGH!
IT'S AN ENERGY CONTAINMENT FIELD OF SOME SORT, SEVERING MY CONNECTION TO THE T-SPHERES.
REAPERS. REPORT.
ANOTHER. STRAY COLLECTED FOR. INDOCTRINATION, COMMANDER.
TRANSFER IT TO THE COLLECTION. VESSEL.
GREAT. I SEEM TO BE THE ONLY CAGED BIRD AROUND HERE. THIS WAS A TRAP ALL ALONG. YOUR SCIENTIFIC CURIOSITY BLINDED YOU, MICHAEL.
HOW LONG HAVE THEY BEEN WAITING? OBSERVING MY PATTERNS OF BEHAVIOR LIKE A LAB RAT IN ORDER TO DETERMINE THE BEST TIME TO STRIKE?
LOOK IT. UNDERSTAN GOOD THAT MAKE THE PROCESS EASIER.

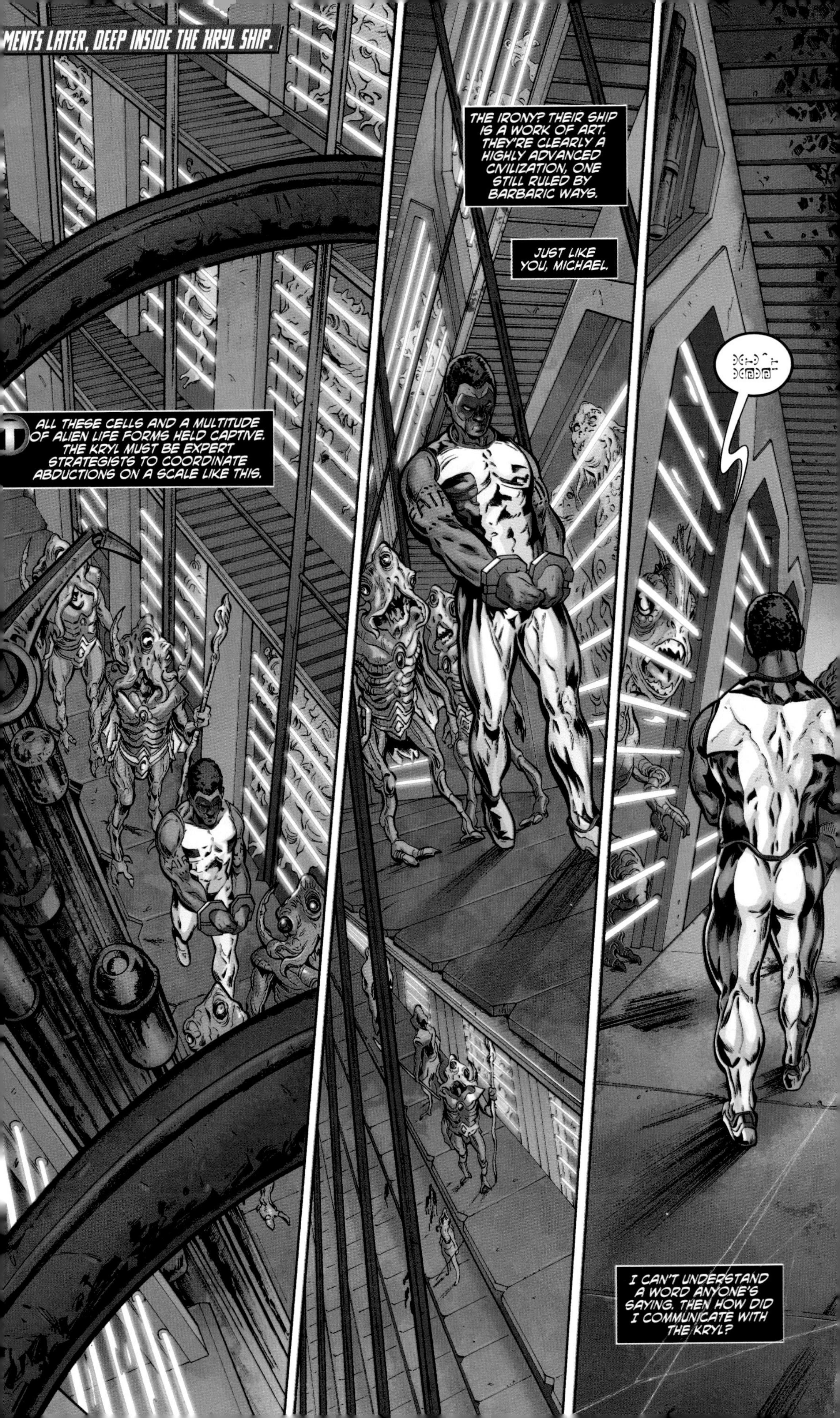
MENTS LATER, DEEP INSIDE THE KRYL SHIP.
ALL THESE CELLS AND A MULTITUDE OF ALIEN LIFE FORMS HELD CAPTIVE. THE KRYL MUST BE EXPERT STRATEGISTS TO COORDINATE ABDUCTIONS ON A SCALE LIKE THIS.
THE IRONY? THEIR SHIP IS A WORK OF ART. THEY'RE CLEARLY A HIGHLY ADVANCED CIVILIZATION, ONE STILL RULED BY BARBARIC WAYS.
JUST LIKE YOU, MICHAEL.
I CAN'T UNDERSTAND A WORD ANYONE'S SAYING. THEN HOW DID I COMMUNICATE WITH THE KRYL?

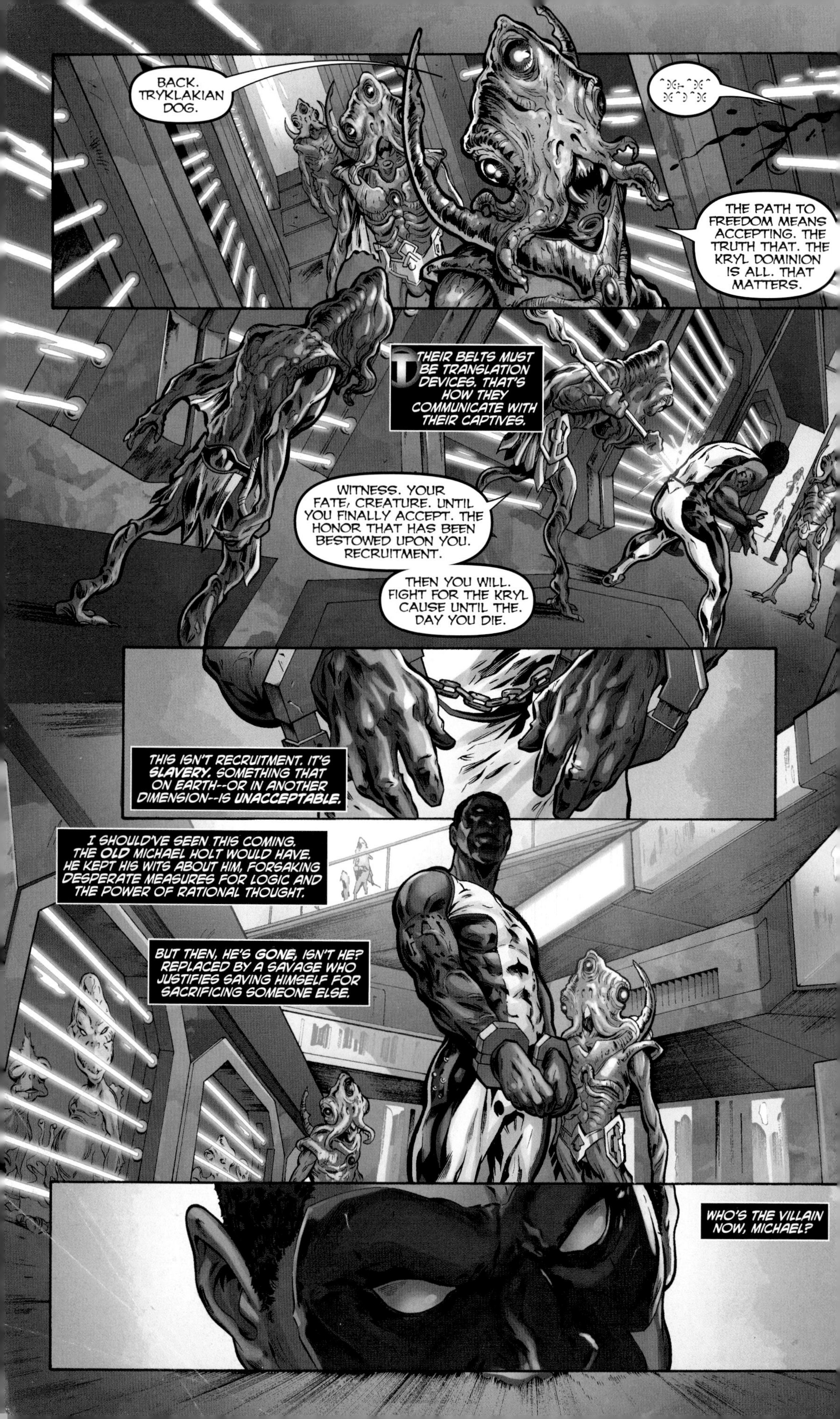
BACK. TRYKLAKIAN DOG.
THE PATH TO FREEDOM MEANS ACCEPTING. THE TRUTH THAT. THE KRYL DOMINION IS ALL. THAT MATTERS.
THEIR BELTS MUST BE TRANSLATION DEVICES. THAT'S HOW THEY COMMUNICATE WITH THEIR CAPTIVES.
WITNESS. YOUR FATE, CREATURE. UNTIL YOU FINALLY ACCEPT. THE HONOR THAT HAS BEEN BESTOWED UPON YOU. RECRUITMENT.
THEN YOU WILL. FIGHT FOR THE KRYL CAUSE UNTIL THE. DAY YOU DIE.
THIS ISN'T RECRUITMENT. IT'S SLAVERY. SOMETHING THAT ON EARTH--OR IN ANOTHER DIMENSION--IS UNACCEPTABLE.
I SHOULD'VE SEEN THIS COMING. THE OLD MICHAEL HOLT WOULD HAVE. HE KEPT HIS WITS ABOUT HIM, FORSAKING DESPERATE MEASURES FOR LOGIC AND THE POWER OF RATIONAL THOUGHT.
BUT THEN, HE'S GONE, ISN'T HE? REPLACED BY A SAVAGE WHO JUSTIFIES SAVING HIMSELF FOR SACRIFICING SOMEONE ELSE.
WHO'S THE VILLAIN NOW, MICHAEL?

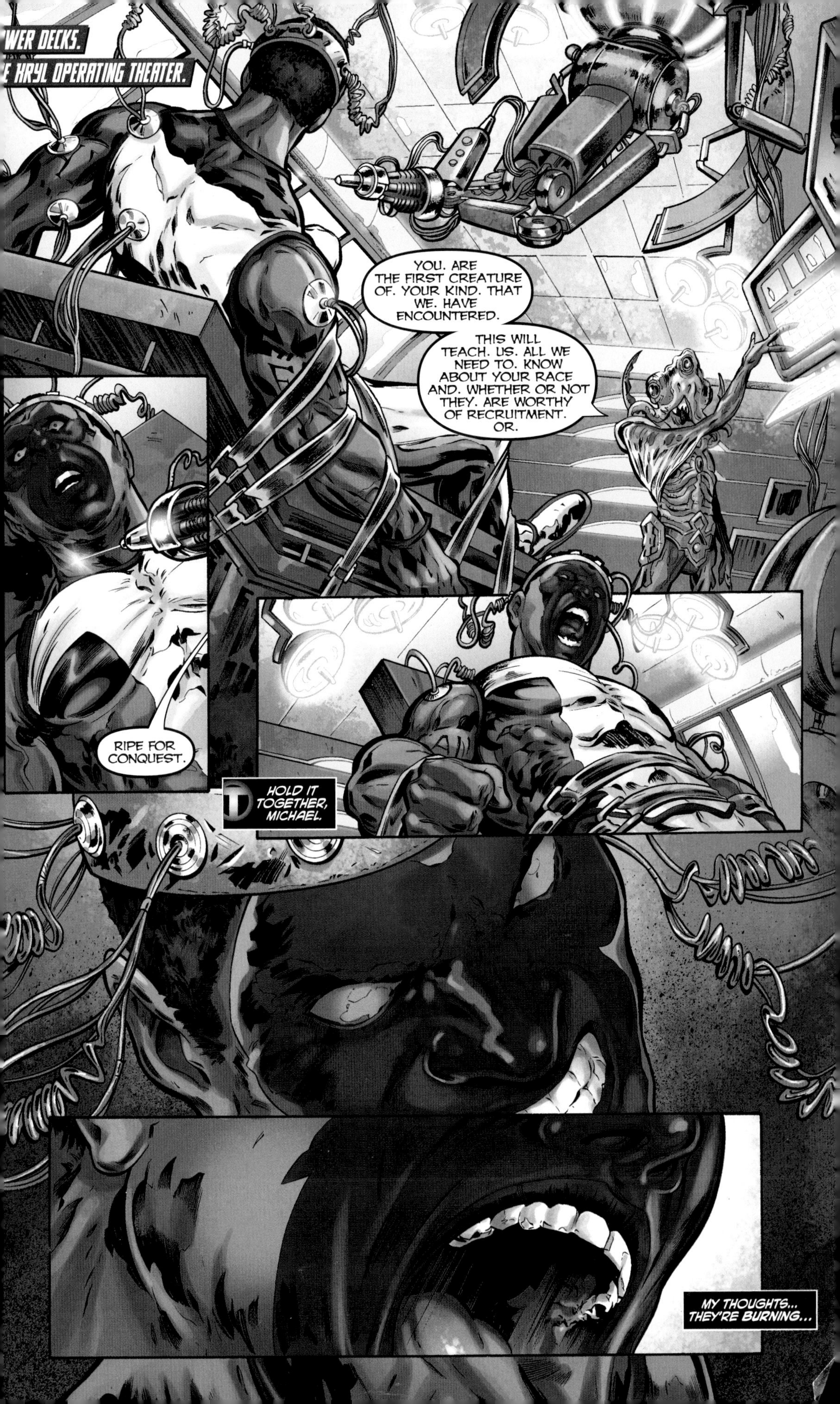
WER DECKS.
E XRYL OPERATING THEATER.
YOU. ARE THE FIRST CREATURE OF. YOUR KIND. THAT WE. HAVE ENCOUNTERED.
THIS WILL TEACH. US. ALL WE NEED TO. KNOW ABOUT YOUR RACE AND. WHETHER OR NOT THEY. ARE WORTHY OF RECRUITMENT. OR.
RIPE FOR CONQUEST.
HOLD IT TOGETHER, MICHAEL.
MY THOUGHTS... THEY'RE BURNING...

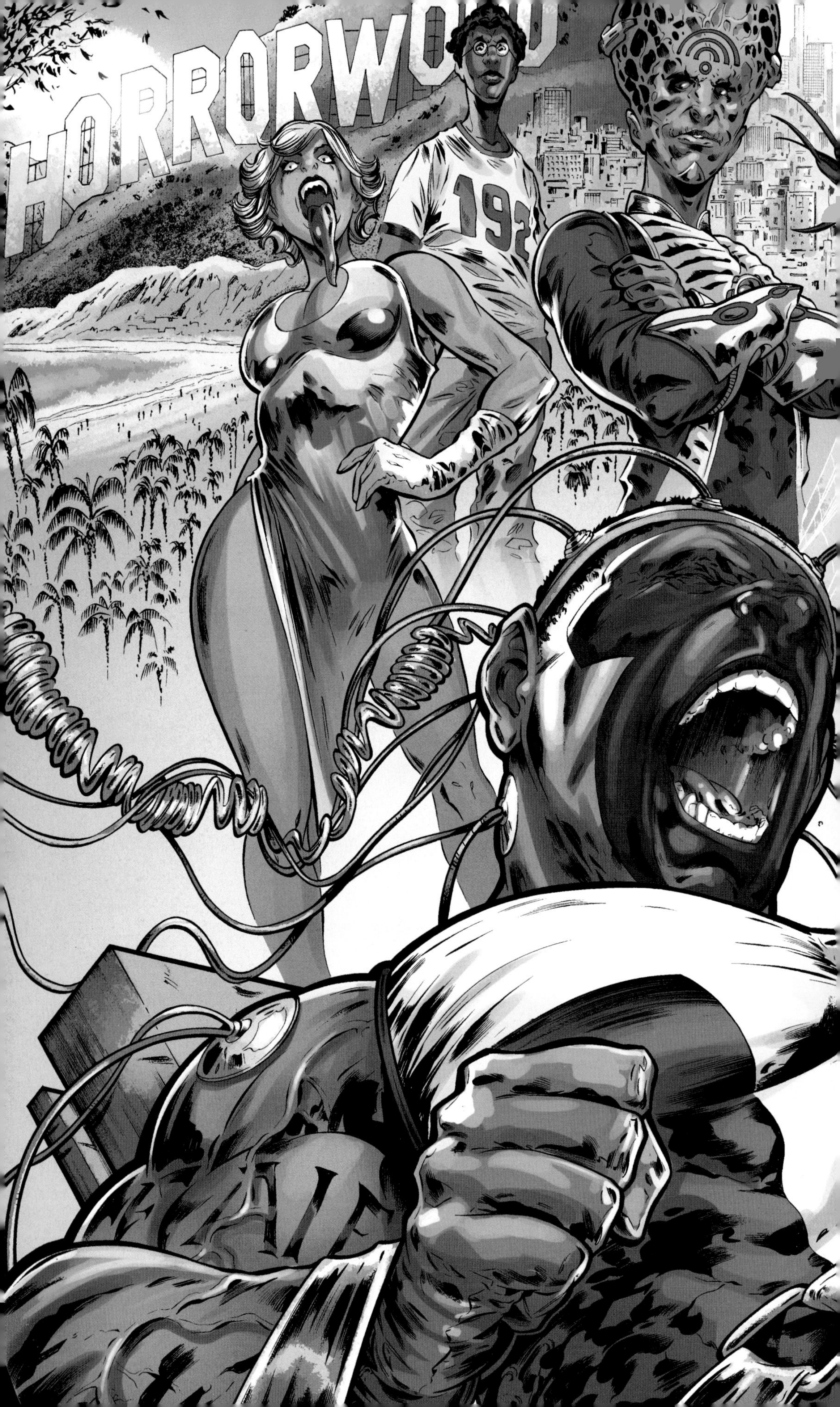

HORRORWO
192

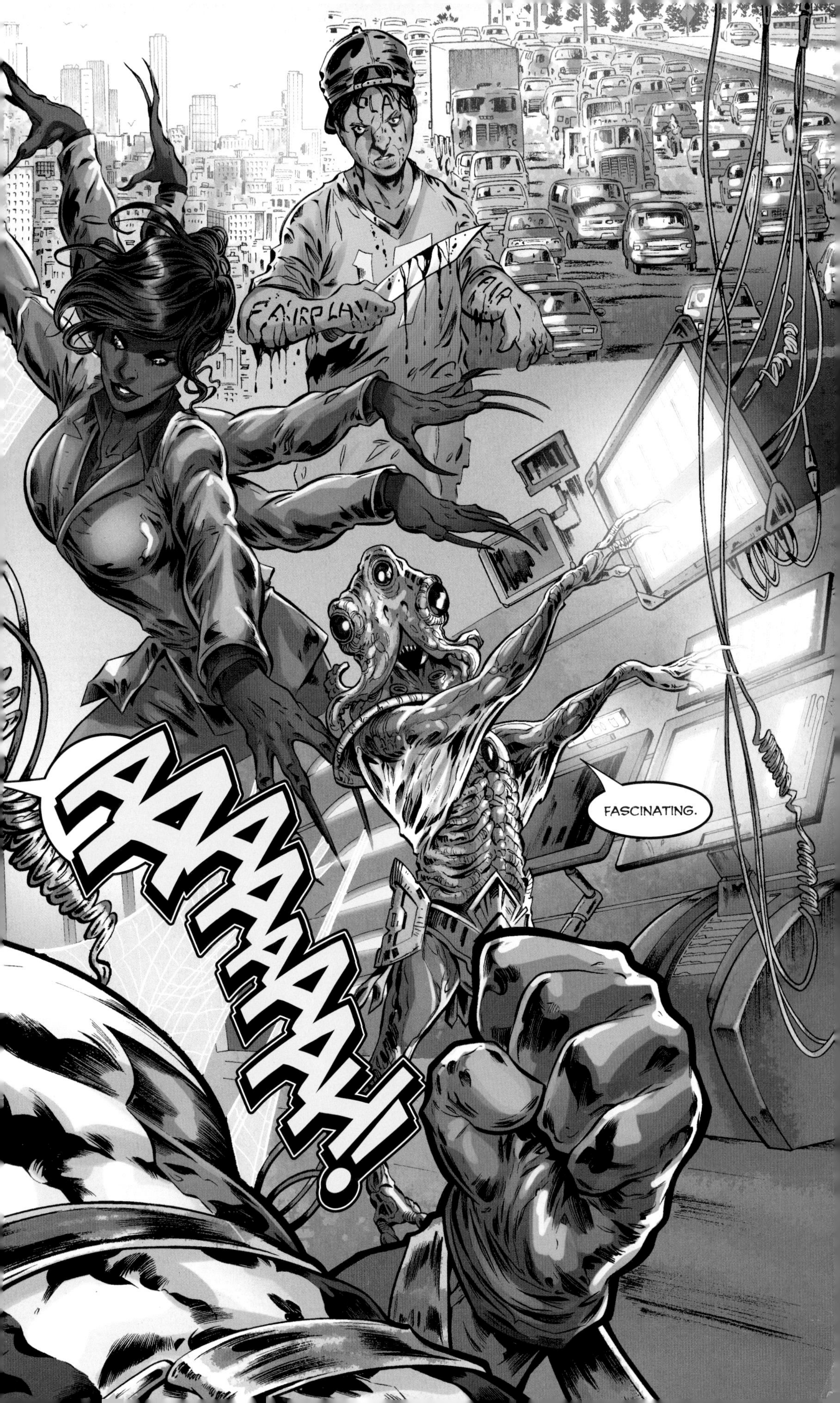
AAAAAAH!!
FASCINATING.

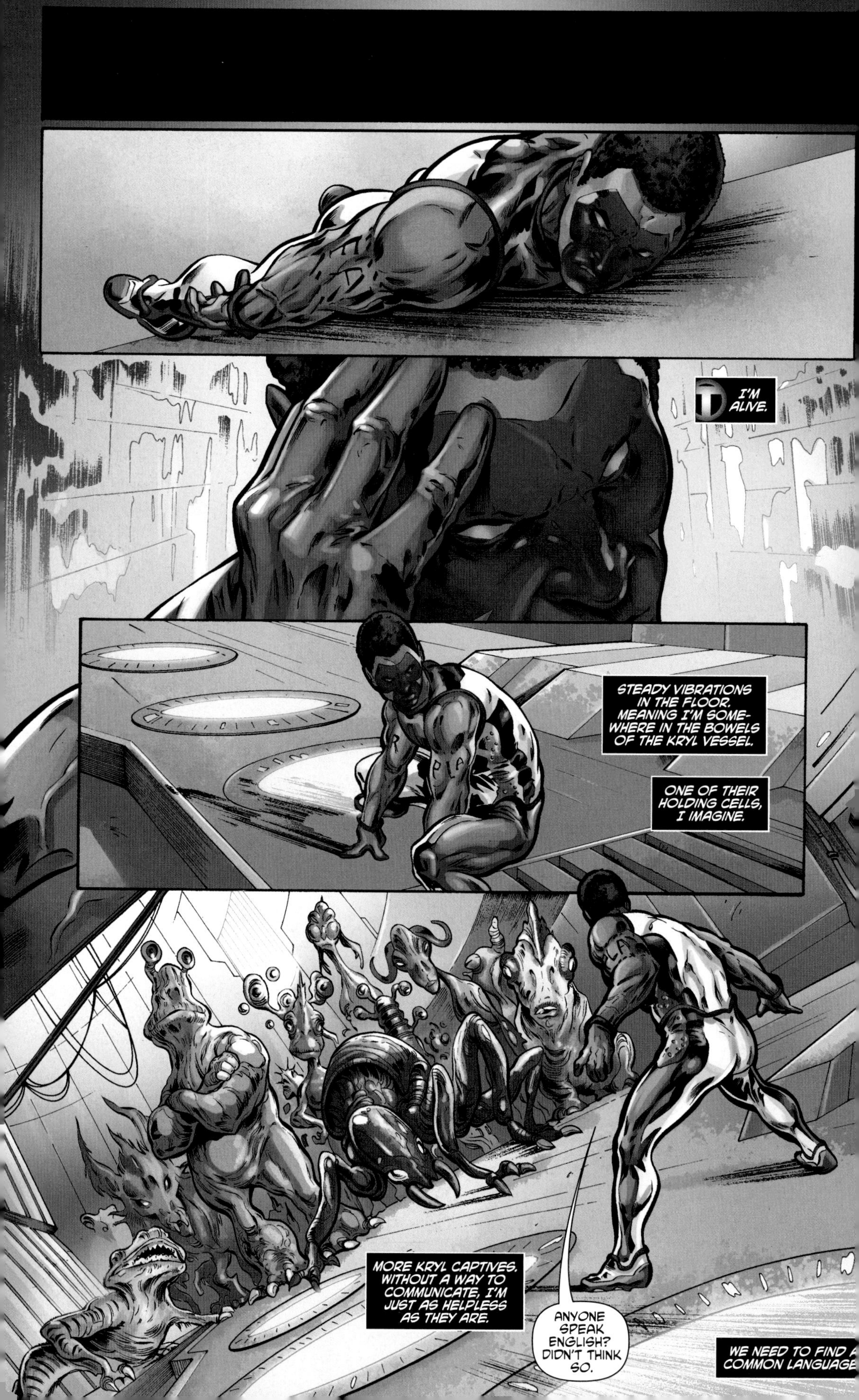
I'M ALIVE.
STEADY VIBRATIONS IN THE FLOOR. MEANING I'M SOME-WHERE IN THE BOWELS OF THE KRYL VESSEL.
ONE OF THEIR HOLDING CELLS, I IMAGINE.
MORE KRYL CAPTIVES. WITHOUT A WAY TO COMMUNICATE, I'M JUST AS HELPLESS AS THEY ARE.
ANYONE SPEAK ENGLISH? DIDN'T THINK SO.
WE NEED TO FIND A COMMON LANGUAGE

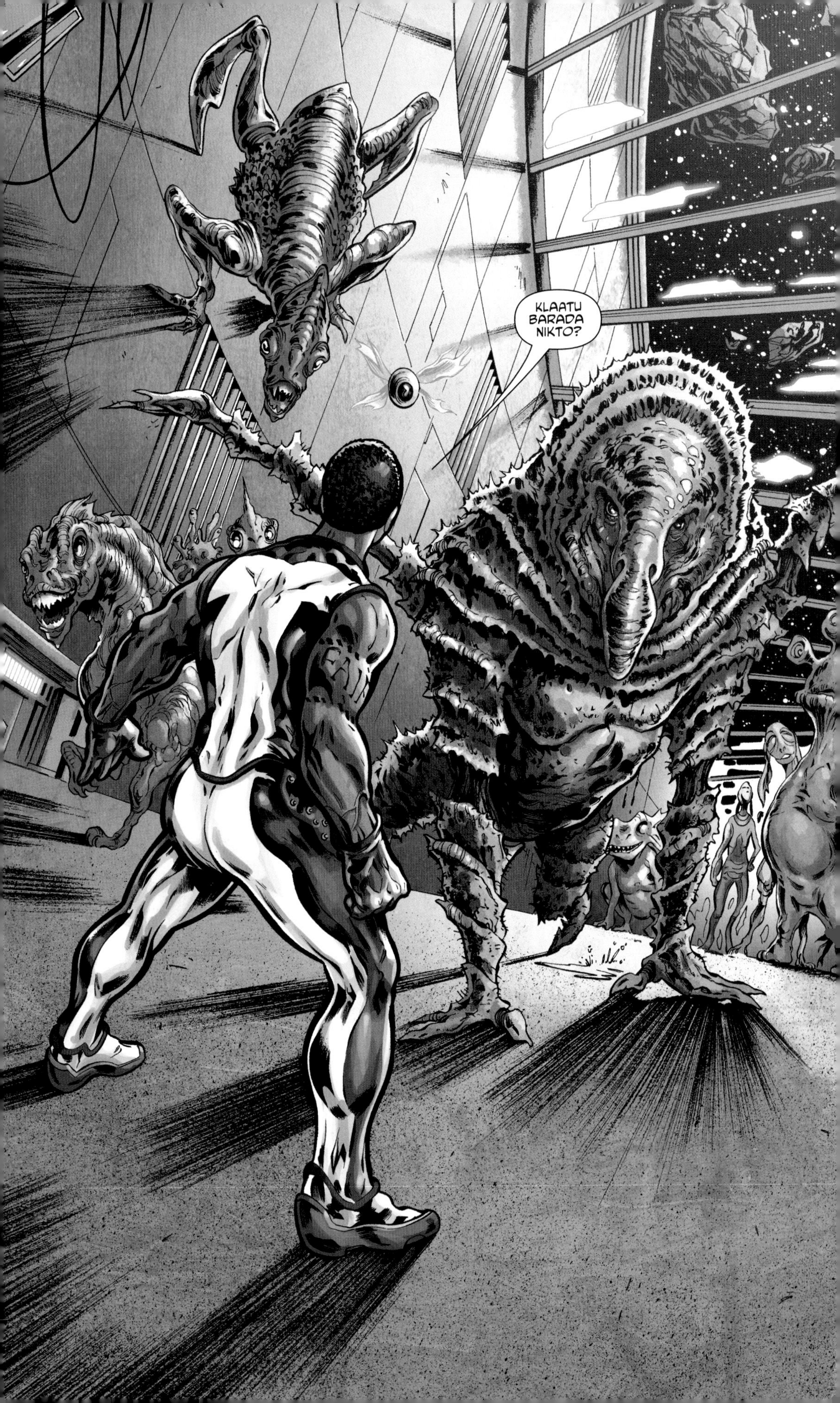
KLAATU BARADA NIKTO?

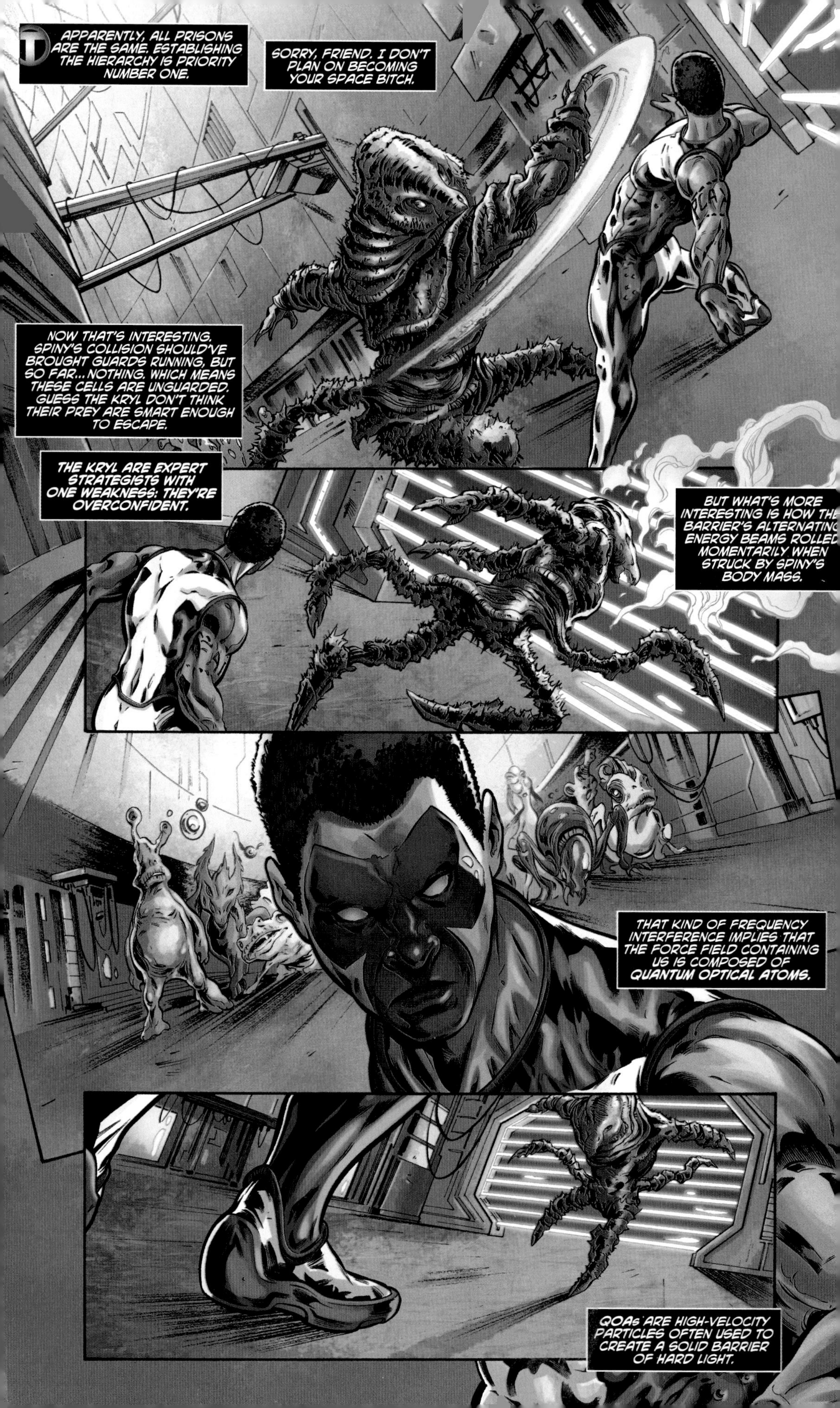

APPARENTLY, ALL PRISONS ARE THE SAME. ESTABLISHING THE HIERARCHY IS PRIORITY NUMBER ONE.
SORRY, FRIEND. I DON'T PLAN ON BECOMING YOUR SPACE BITCH.
NOW THAT'S INTERESTING. SPINY'S COLLISION SHOULD'VE BROUGHT GUARDS RUNNING, BUT SO FAR...NOTHING. WHICH MEANS THESE CELLS ARE UNGUARDED. GUESS THE KRYL DON'T THINK THEIR PREY ARE SMART ENOUGH TO ESCAPE.
THE KRYL ARE EXPERT STRATEGISTS WITH ONE WEAKNESS: THEY'RE OVERCONFIDENT.
BUT WHAT'S MORE INTERESTING IS HOW THE BARRIER'S ALTERNATING ENERGY BEAMS ROLLED MOMENTARILY WHEN STRUCK BY SPINY'S BODY MASS.
THAT KIND OF FREQUENCY INTERFERENCE IMPLIES THAT THE FORCE FIELD CONTAINING US IS COMPOSED OF QUANTUM OPTICAL ATOMS.
QOAs ARE HIGH-VELOCITY PARTICLES OFTEN USED TO CREATE A SOLID BARRIER OF HARD LIGHT.

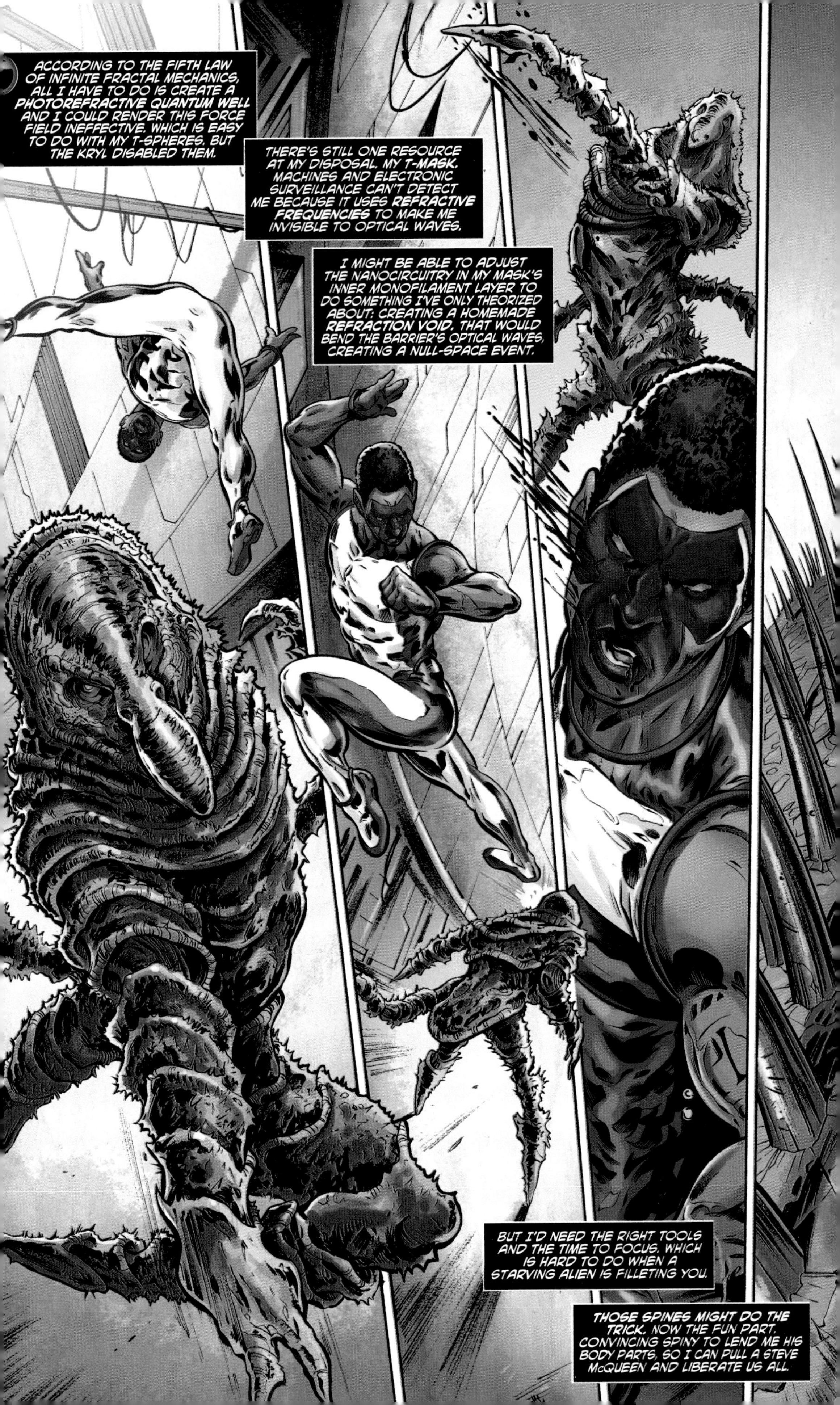

ACCORDING TO THE FIFTH LAW OF INFINITE FRACTAL MECHANICS, ALL I HAVE TO DO IS CREATE A **PHOTOREFRACTIVE QUANTUM WELL** AND I COULD RENDER THIS FORCE FIELD INEFFECTIVE. WHICH IS EASY TO DO WITH MY T-SPHERES. BUT THE KRYL DISABLED THEM.
THERE'S STILL ONE RESOURCE AT MY DISPOSAL. MY **T-MASK**. MACHINES AND ELECTRONIC SURVEILLANCE CAN'T DETECT ME BECAUSE IT USES **REFRACTIVE FREQUENCIES** TO MAKE ME INVISIBLE TO OPTICAL WAVES.
I MIGHT BE ABLE TO ADJUST THE NANOCIRCUITRY IN MY MASK'S INNER MONOFILAMENT LAYER TO DO SOMETHING I'VE ONLY THEORIZED ABOUT: CREATING A HOMEMADE **REFRACTION VOID**. THAT WOULD BEND THE BARRIER'S OPTICAL WAVES, CREATING A NULL-SPACE EVENT.
BUT I'D NEED THE RIGHT TOOLS AND THE TIME TO FOCUS. WHICH IS HARD TO DO WHEN A STARVING ALIEN IS FILLETING YOU.
THOSE SPINES MIGHT DO THE TRICK. NOW THE FUN PART. CONVINCING SPINY TO LEND ME HIS BODY PARTS, SO I CAN PULL A STEVE McQUEEN AND LIBERATE US ALL.

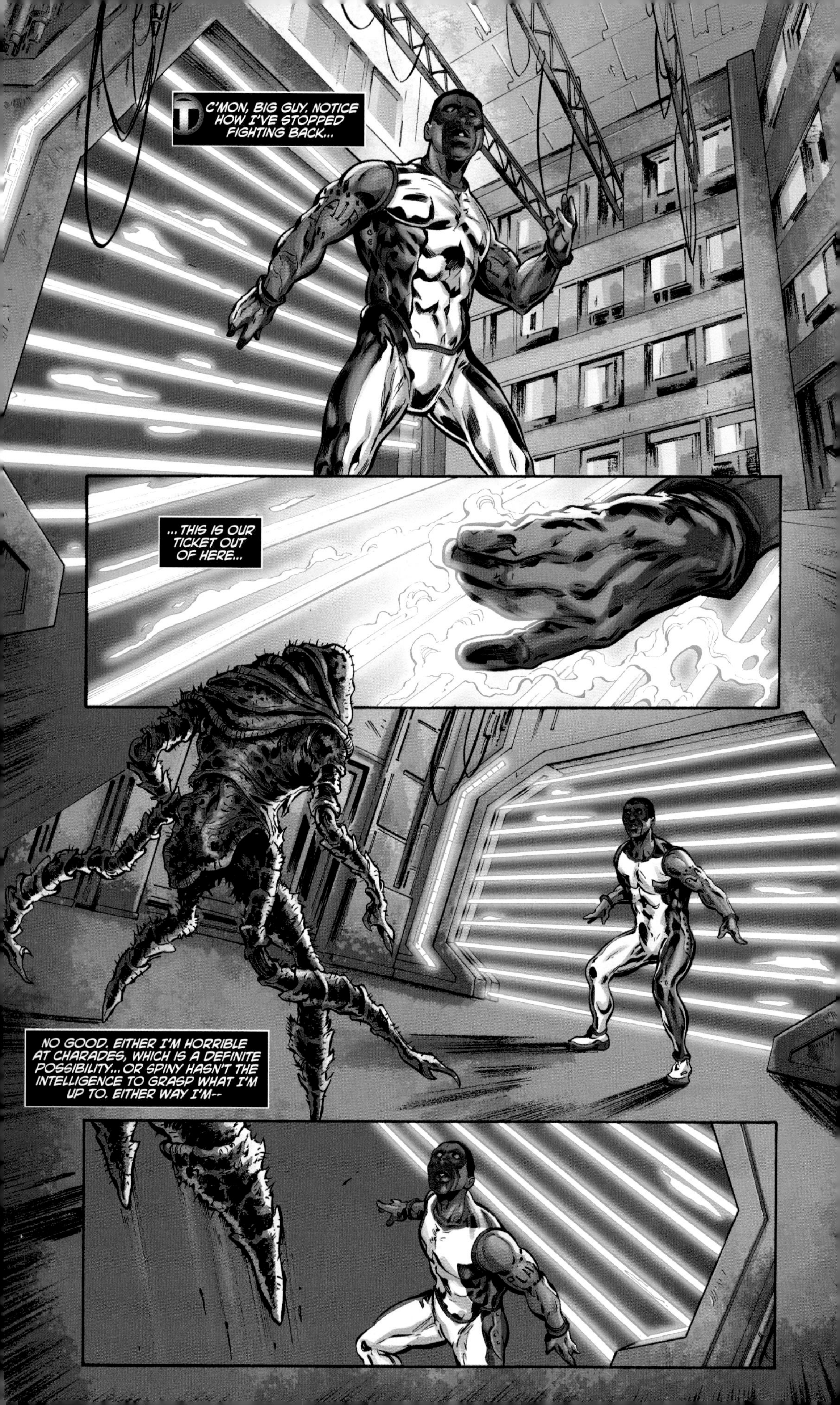
C'MON, BIG GUY. NOTICE HOW I'VE STOPPED FIGHTING BACK...
...THIS IS OUR TICKET OUT OF HERE...
NO GOOD. EITHER I'M HORRIBLE AT CHARADES, WHICH IS A DEFINITE POSSIBILITY...OR SPINY HASN'T THE INTELLIGENCE TO GRASP WHAT I'M UP TO. EITHER WAY I'M--

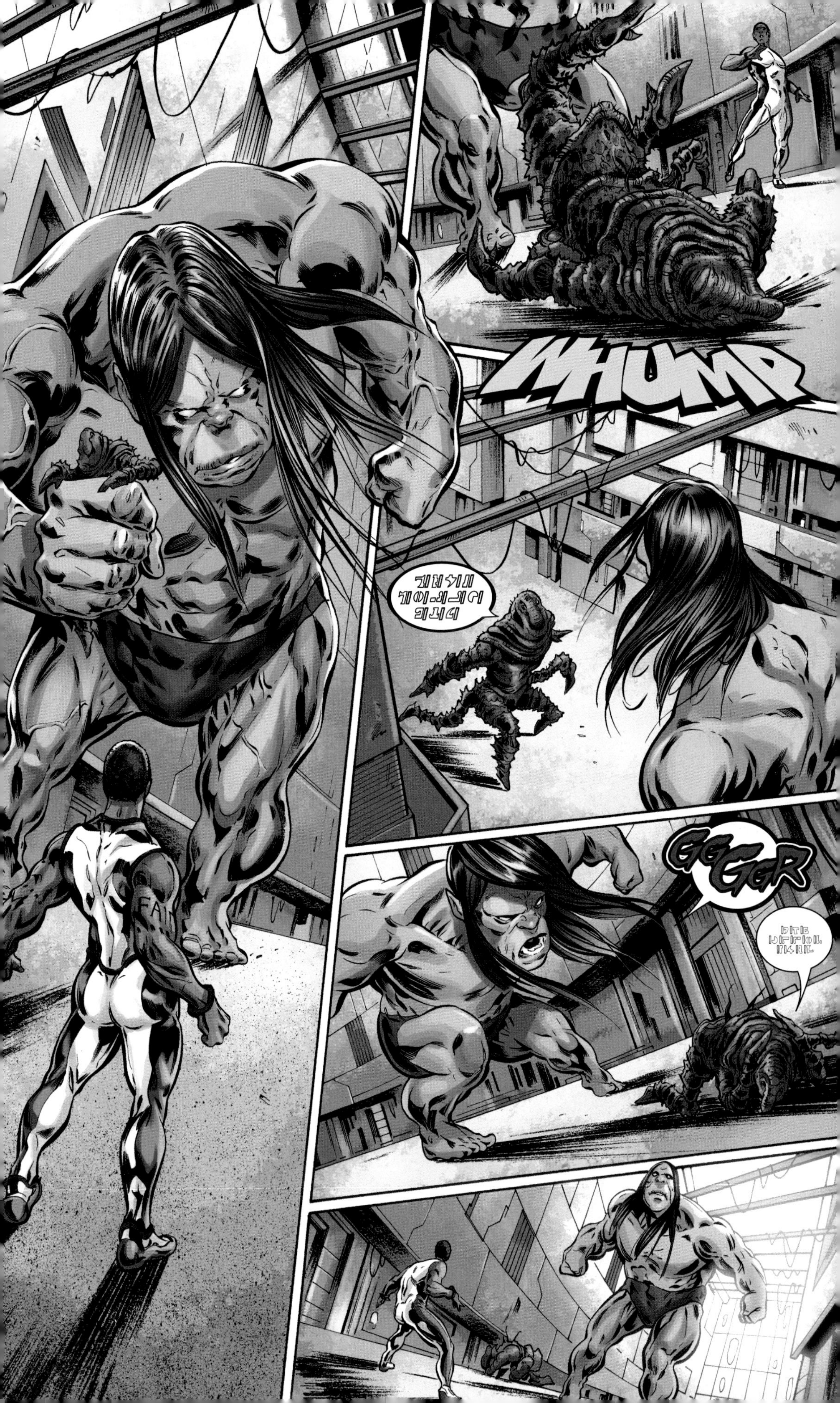
WHUMP
GGGGR

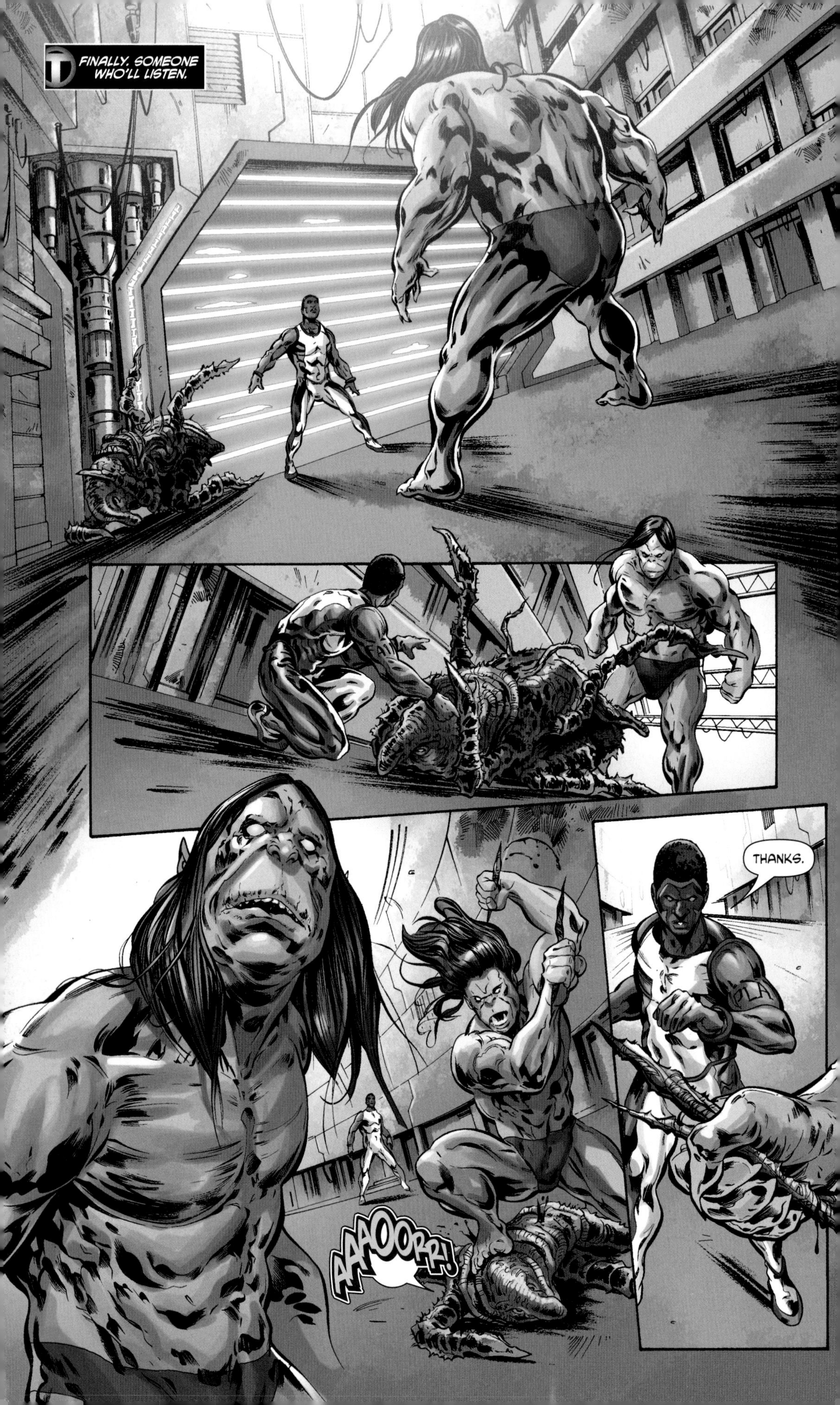
FINALLY, SOMEONE WHO'LL LISTEN.
THANKS.
AAAOORR!

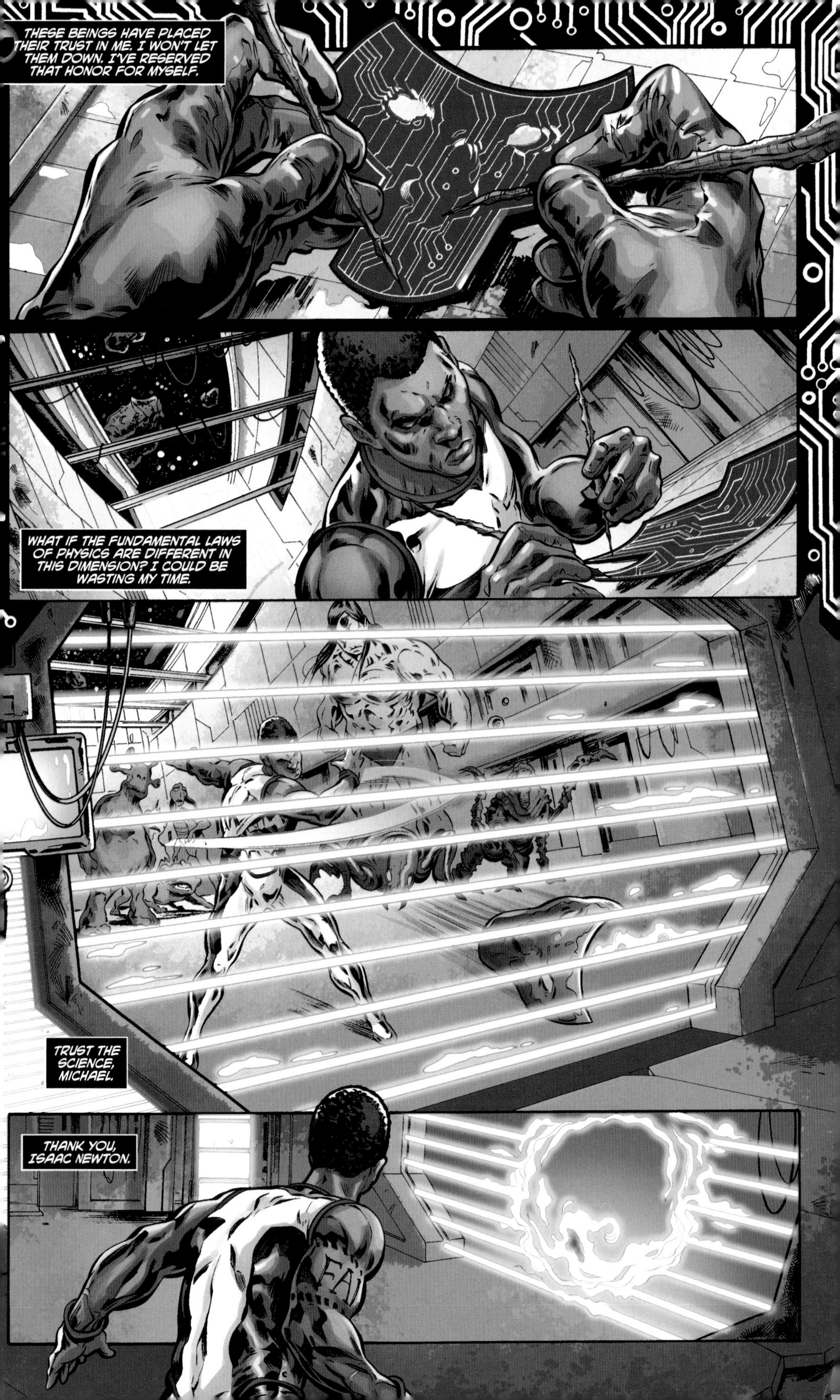
THESE BEINGS HAVE PLACED THEIR TRUST IN ME. I WON'T LET THEM DOWN. I'VE RESERVED THAT HONOR FOR MYSELF.
WHAT IF THE FUNDAMENTAL LAWS OF PHYSICS ARE DIFFERENT IN THIS DIMENSION? I COULD BE WASTING MY TIME.
TRUST THE SCIENCE, MICHAEL.
THANK YOU, ISAAC NEWTON.

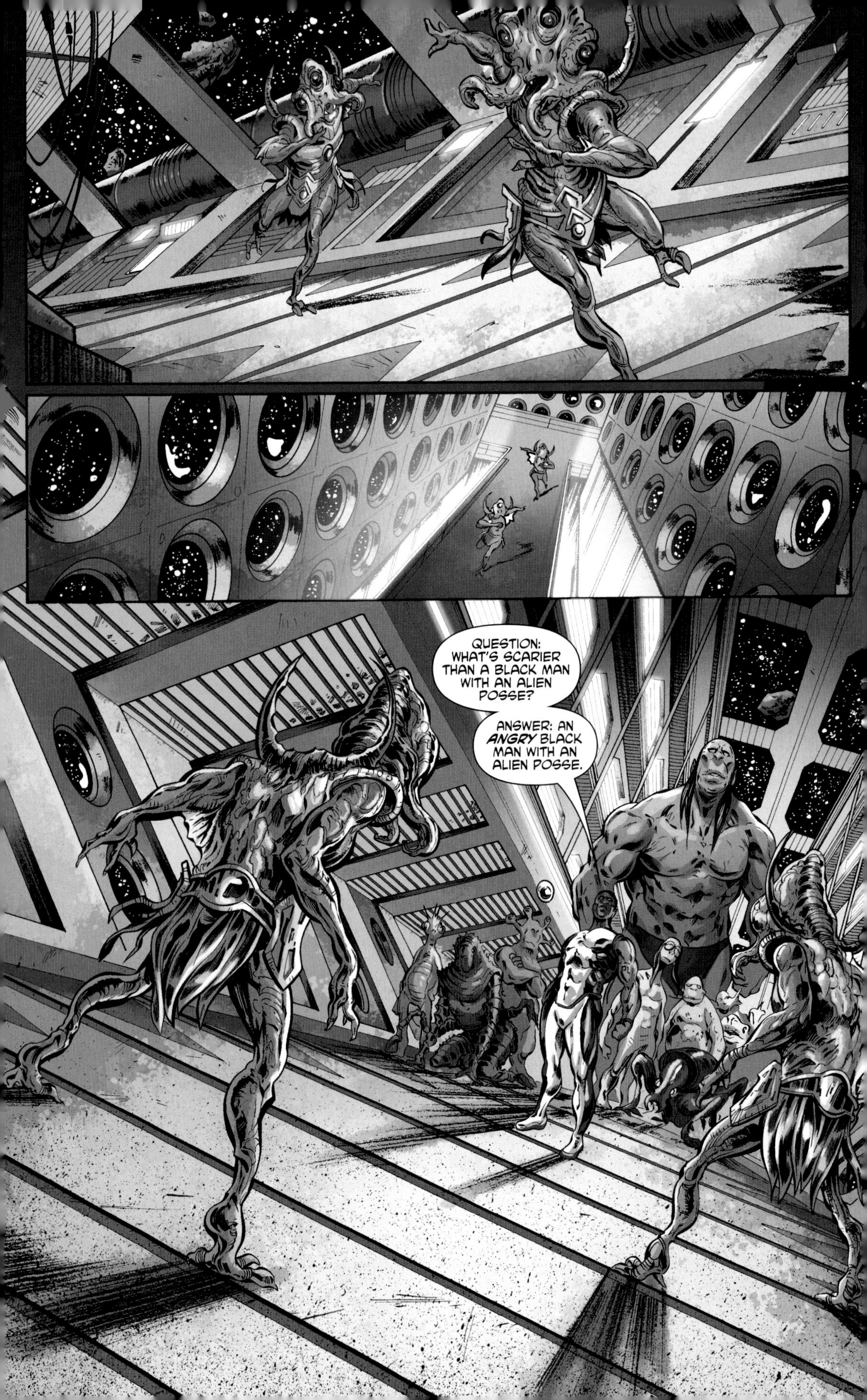
QUESTION: WHAT'S SCARIER THAN A BLACK MAN WITH AN ALIEN POSSE?
ANSWER: AN *ANGRY* BLACK MAN WITH AN ALIEN POSSE.

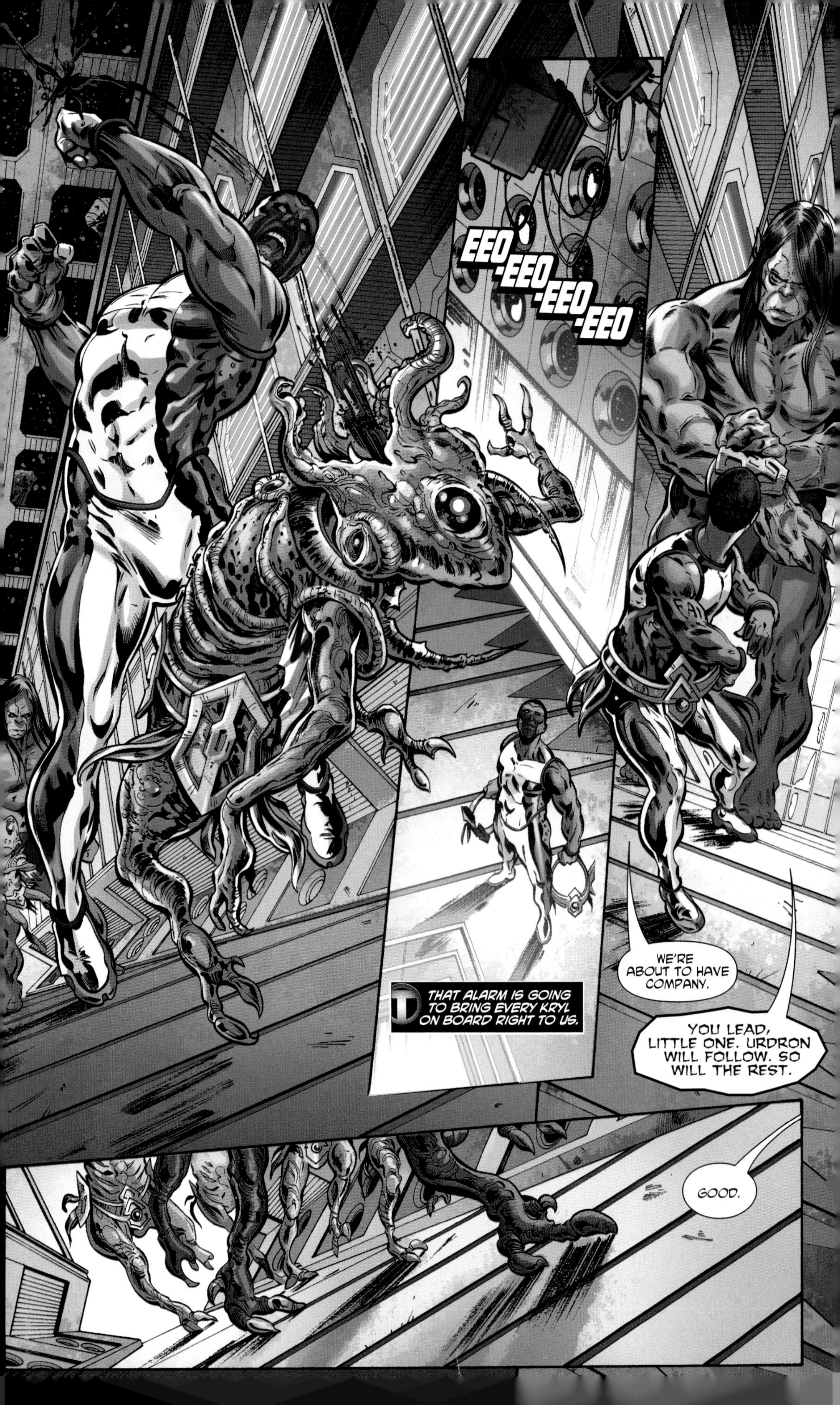
EEO-EEO-EEO-EEO
THAT ALARM IS GOING TO BRING EVERY KRYL ON BOARD RIGHT TO US.
WE'RE ABOUT TO HAVE COMPANY.
YOU LEAD, LITTLE ONE. URDRON WILL FOLLOW. SO WILL THE REST.
GOOD.

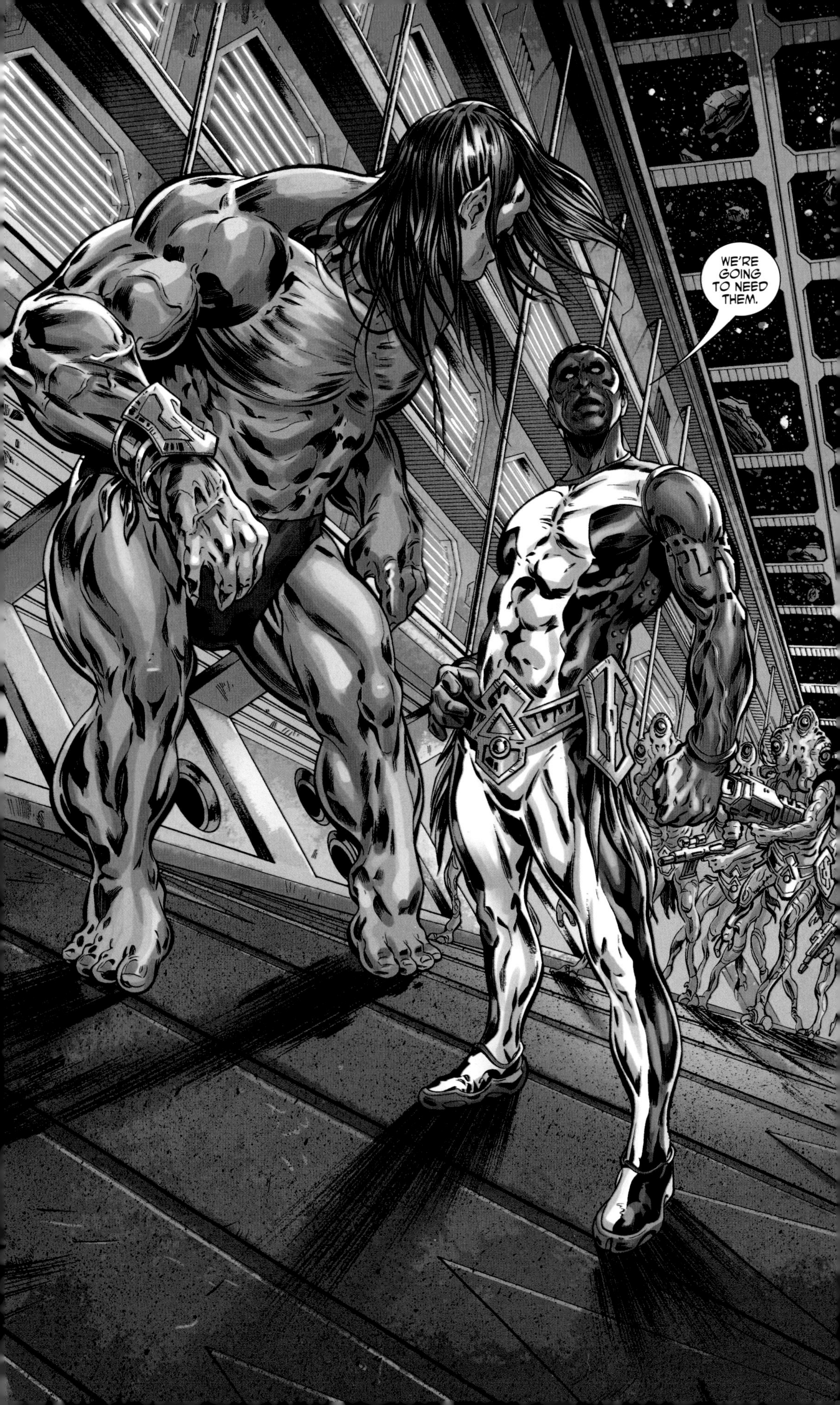
WE'RE GOING TO NEED THEM.

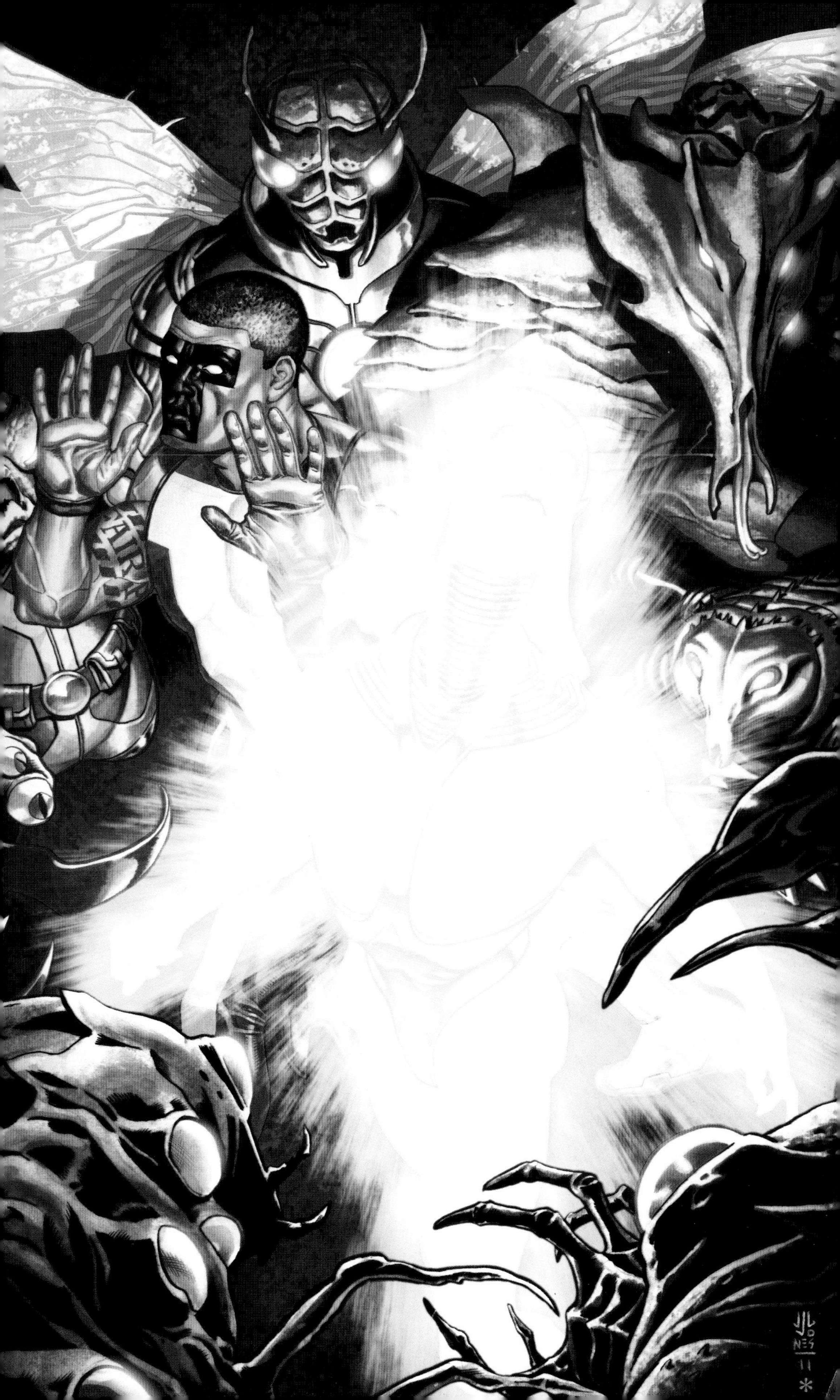

IN VERITAS

ERIC WALLACE writer **GIANLUCA GUGLIOTTA** penciller **WAYNE FAUCHER** inker
cover art by **J.G. JONES** with colorist **HI-FI**

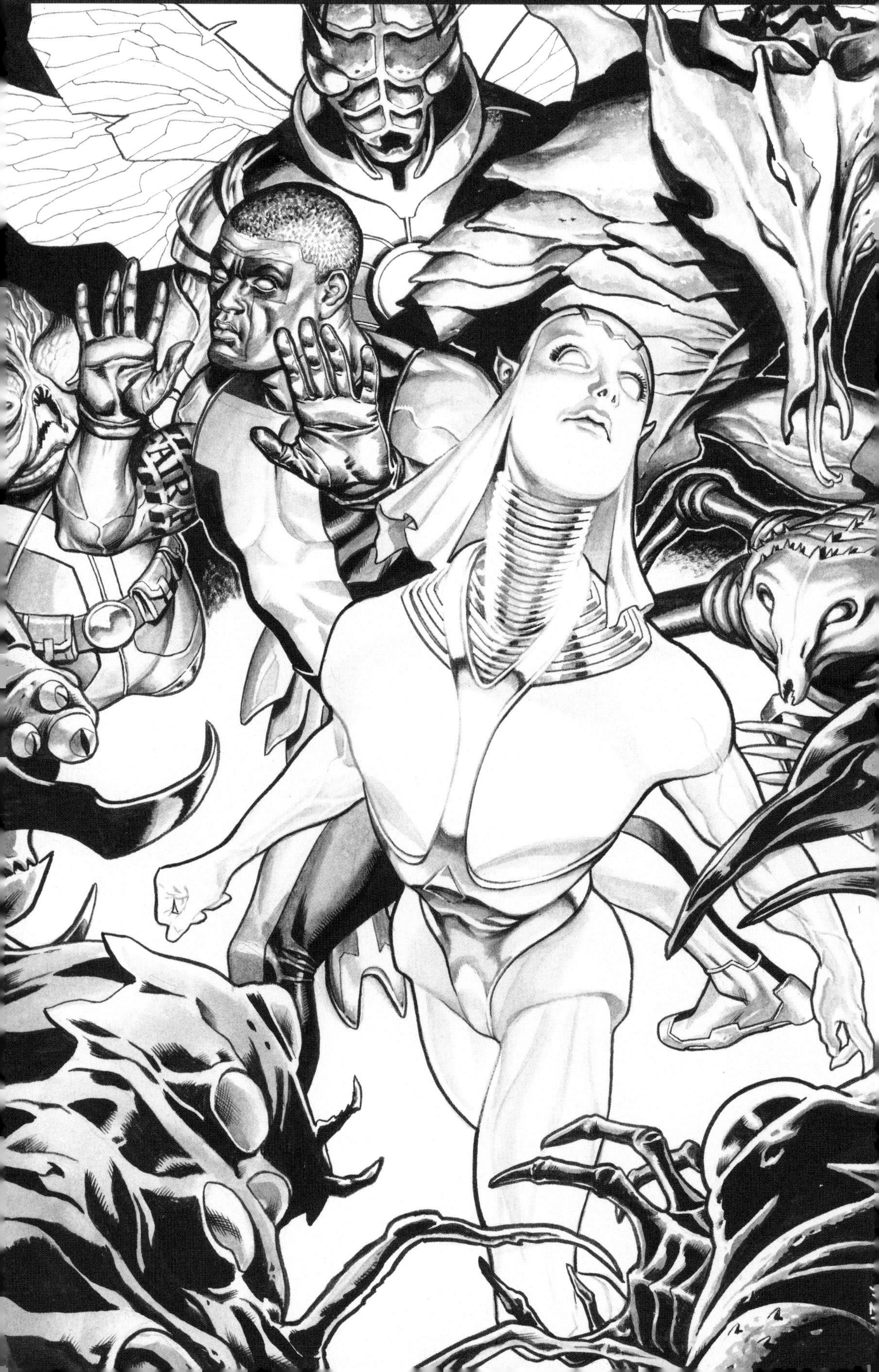

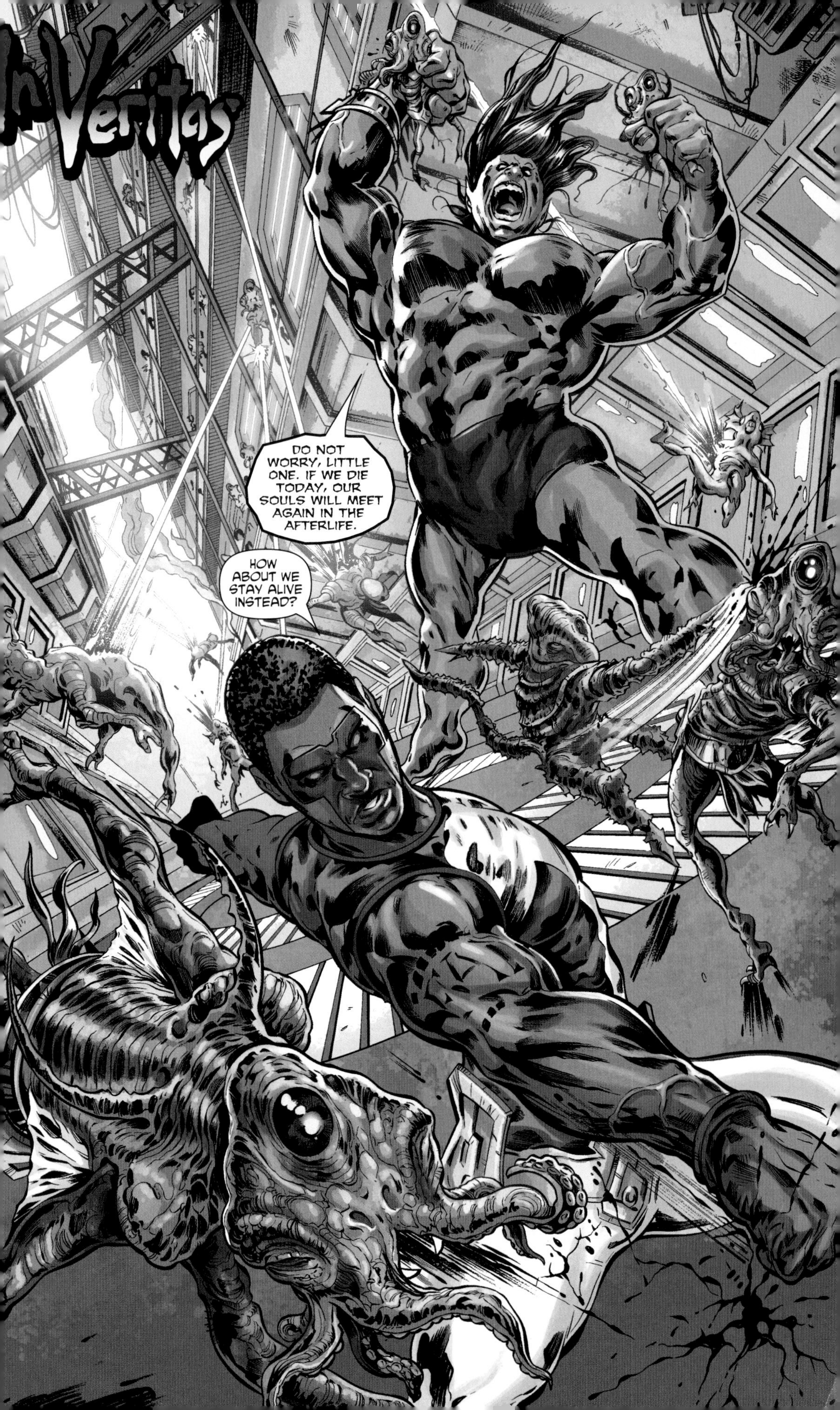
In Veritas
DO NOT WORRY, LITTLE ONE. IF WE DIE TODAY, OUR SOULS WILL MEET AGAIN IN THE AFTERLIFE.
HOW ABOUT WE STAY ALIVE INSTEAD?

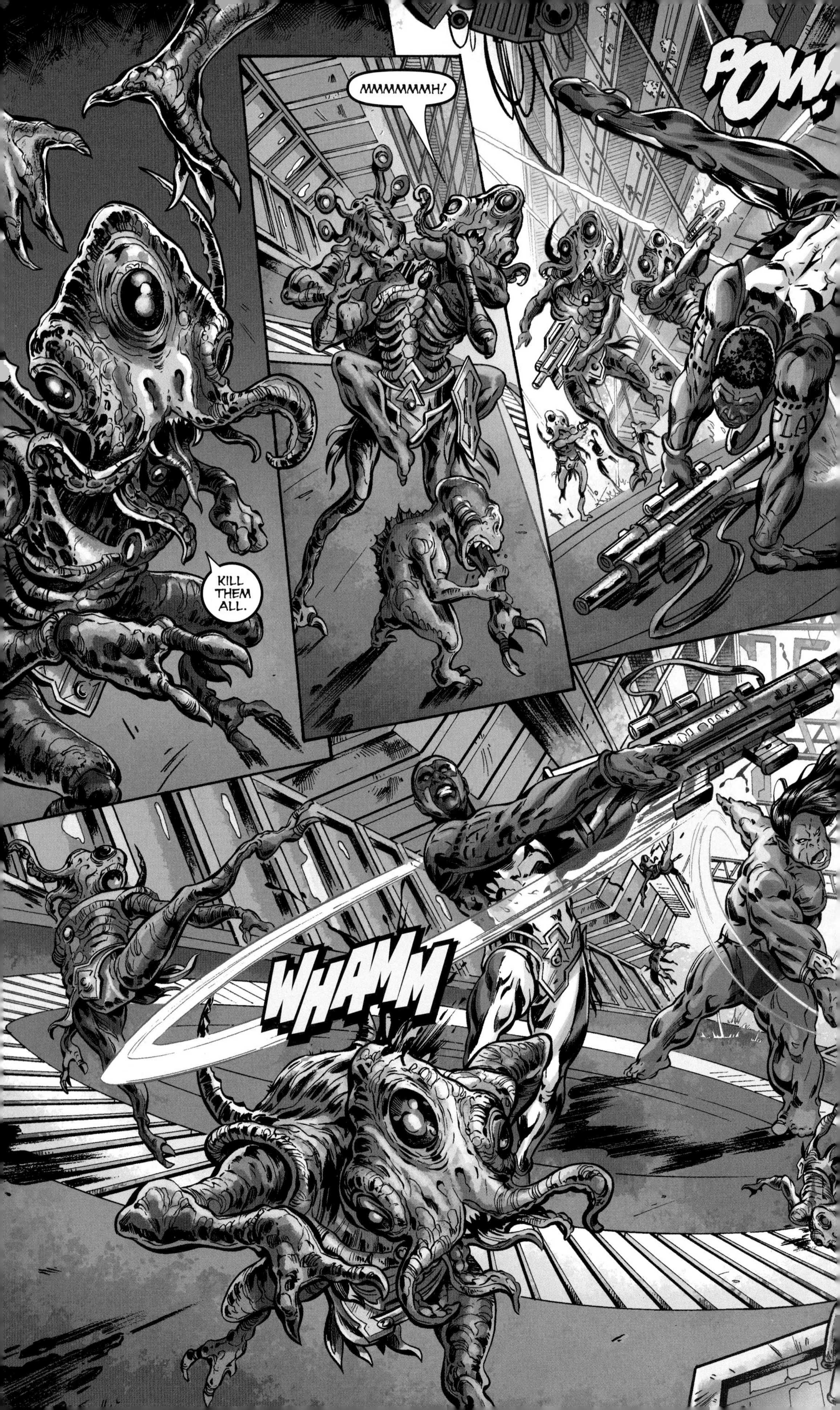
POW
MMMMMMMH!
KILL THEM ALL.
WHAMM

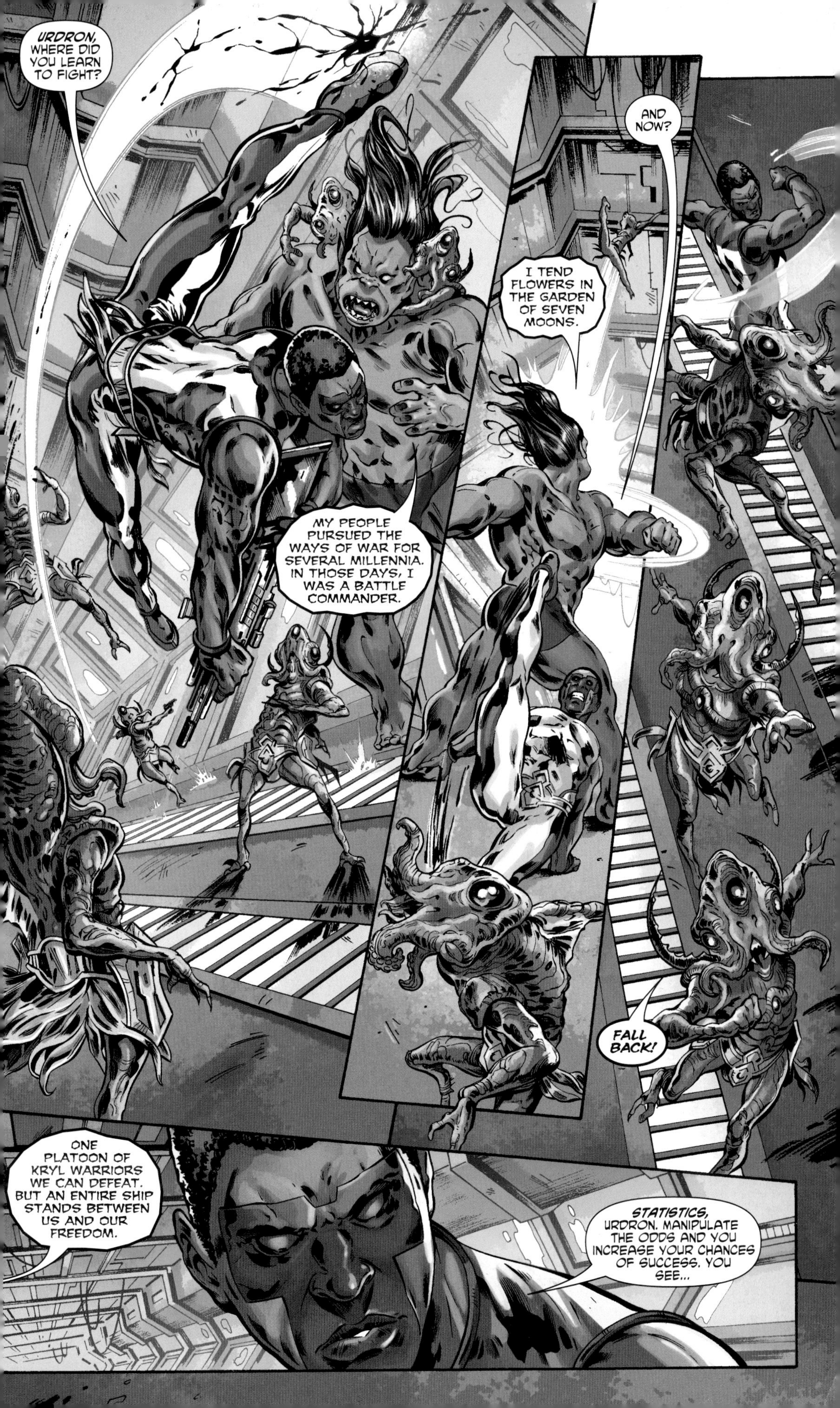
URDRON, WHERE DID YOU LEARN TO FIGHT?
MY PEOPLE PURSUED THE WAYS OF WAR FOR SEVERAL MILLENNIA. IN THOSE DAYS, I WAS A BATTLE COMMANDER.
AND NOW?
I TEND FLOWERS IN THE GARDEN OF SEVEN MOONS.
FALL BACK!
ONE PLATOON OF KRYL WARRIORS WE CAN DEFEAT. BUT AN ENTIRE SHIP STANDS BETWEEN US AND OUR FREEDOM.
STATISTICS, URDRON. MANIPULATE THE ODDS AND YOU INCREASE YOUR CHANCES OF SUCCESS. YOU SEE...

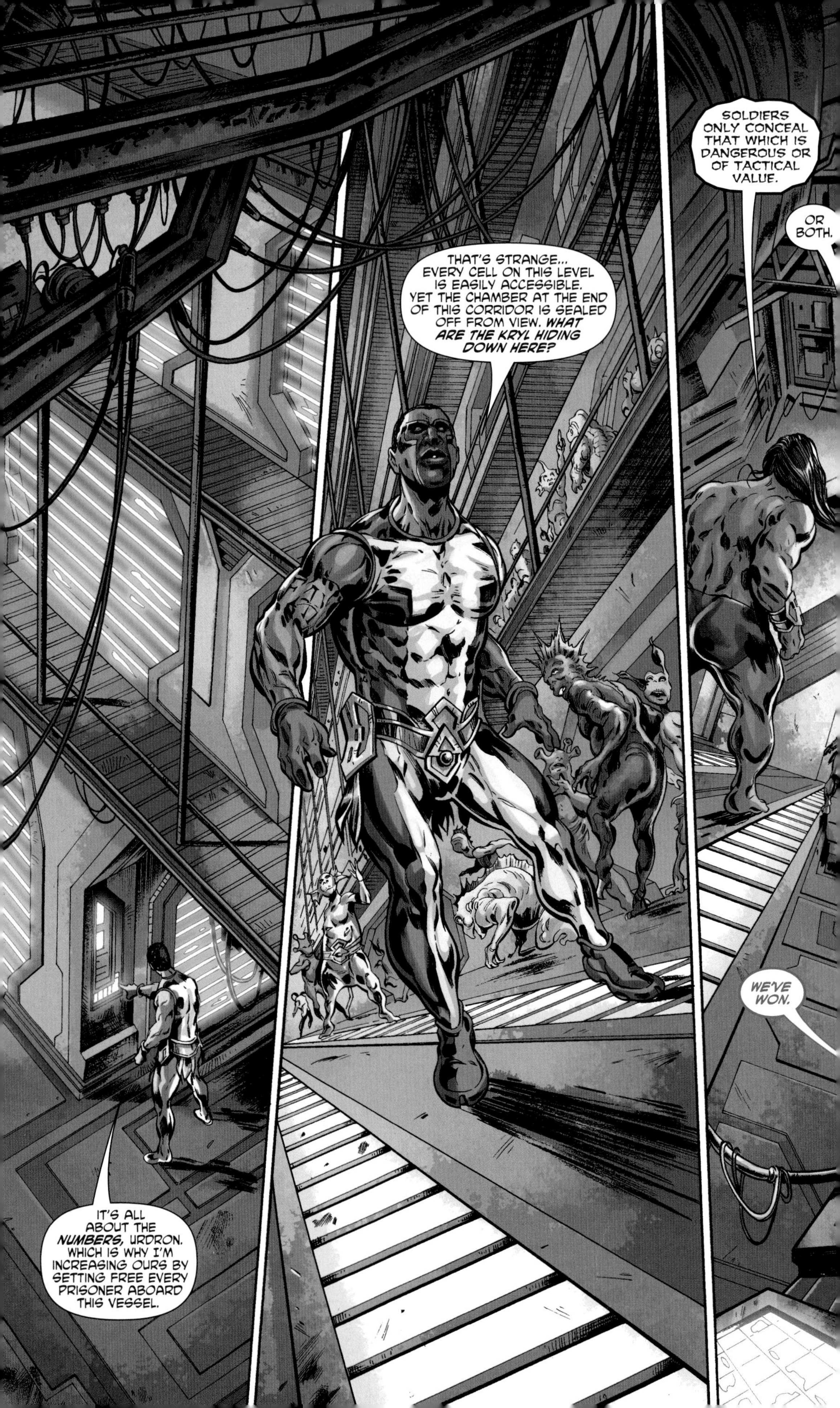

SOLDIERS ONLY CONCEAL THAT WHICH IS DANGEROUS OR OF TACTICAL VALUE.
OR BOTH.
THAT'S STRANGE... EVERY CELL ON THIS LEVEL IS EASILY ACCESSIBLE. YET THE CHAMBER AT THE END OF THIS CORRIDOR IS SEALED OFF FROM VIEW. WHAT ARE THE KRYL HIDING DOWN HERE?
WE'VE WON.
IT'S ALL ABOUT THE NUMBERS, URDRON. WHICH IS WHY I'M INCREASING OURS BY SETTING FREE EVERY PRISONER ABOARD THIS VESSEL.

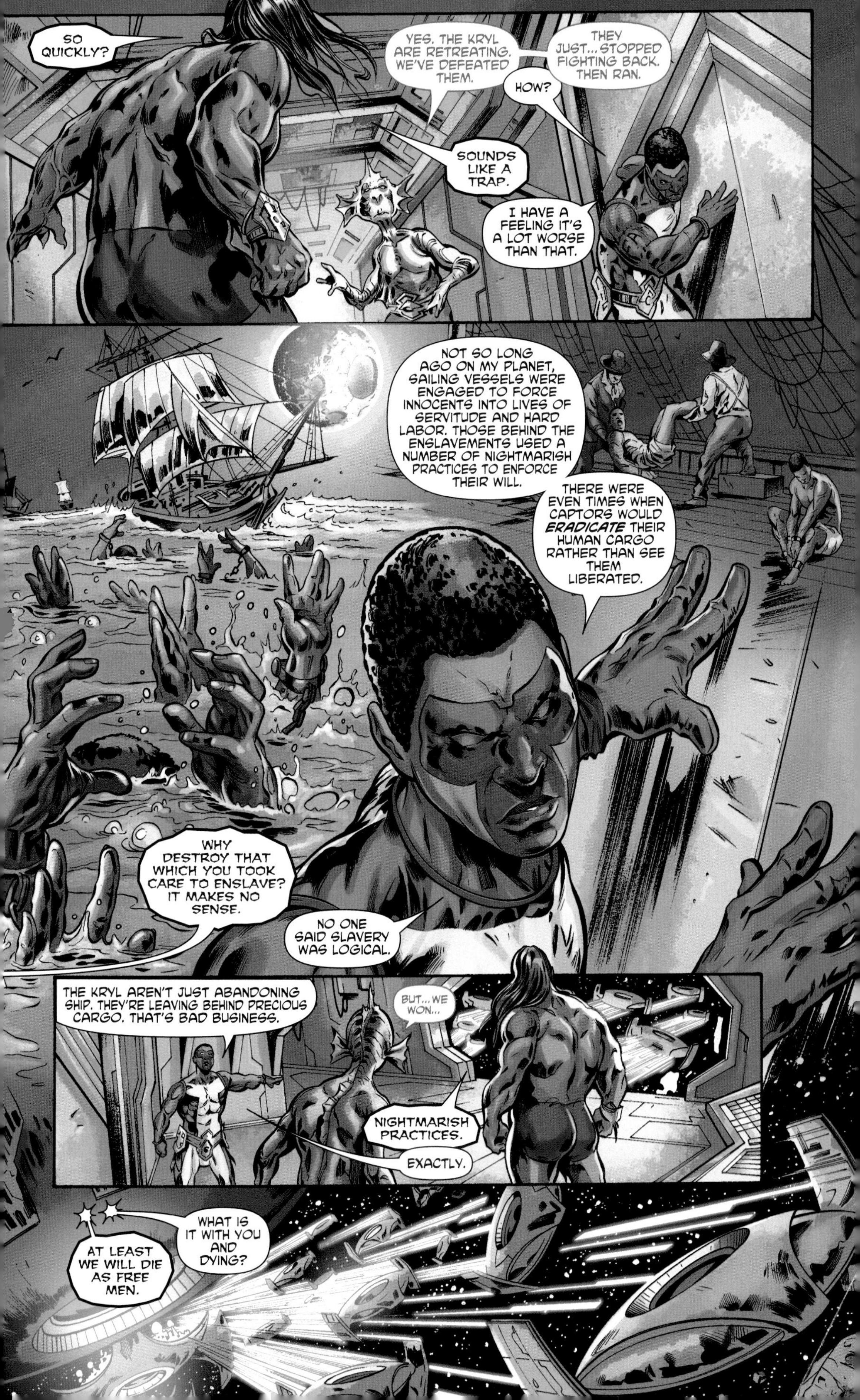

SO QUICKLY?
YES. THE KRYL ARE RETREATING. WE'VE DEFEATED THEM.
THEY JUST... STOPPED FIGHTING BACK. THEN RAN.
HOW?
SOUNDS LIKE A TRAP.
I HAVE A FEELING IT'S A LOT WORSE THAN THAT.
NOT SO LONG AGO ON MY PLANET, SAILING VESSELS WERE ENGAGED TO FORCE INNOCENTS INTO LIVES OF SERVITUDE AND HARD LABOR. THOSE BEHIND THE ENSLAVEMENTS USED A NUMBER OF NIGHTMARISH PRACTICES TO ENFORCE THEIR WILL.
THERE WERE EVEN TIMES WHEN CAPTORS WOULD *ERADICATE* THEIR HUMAN CARGO RATHER THAN SEE THEM LIBERATED.
WHY DESTROY THAT WHICH YOU TOOK CARE TO ENSLAVE? IT MAKES NO SENSE.
NO ONE SAID SLAVERY WAS LOGICAL.
THE KRYL AREN'T JUST ABANDONING SHIP. THEY'RE LEAVING BEHIND PRECIOUS CARGO. THAT'S BAD BUSINESS.
BUT... WE WON...
NIGHTMARISH PRACTICES.
EXACTLY.
AT LEAST WE WILL DIE AS FREE MEN.
WHAT IS IT WITH YOU AND DYING?

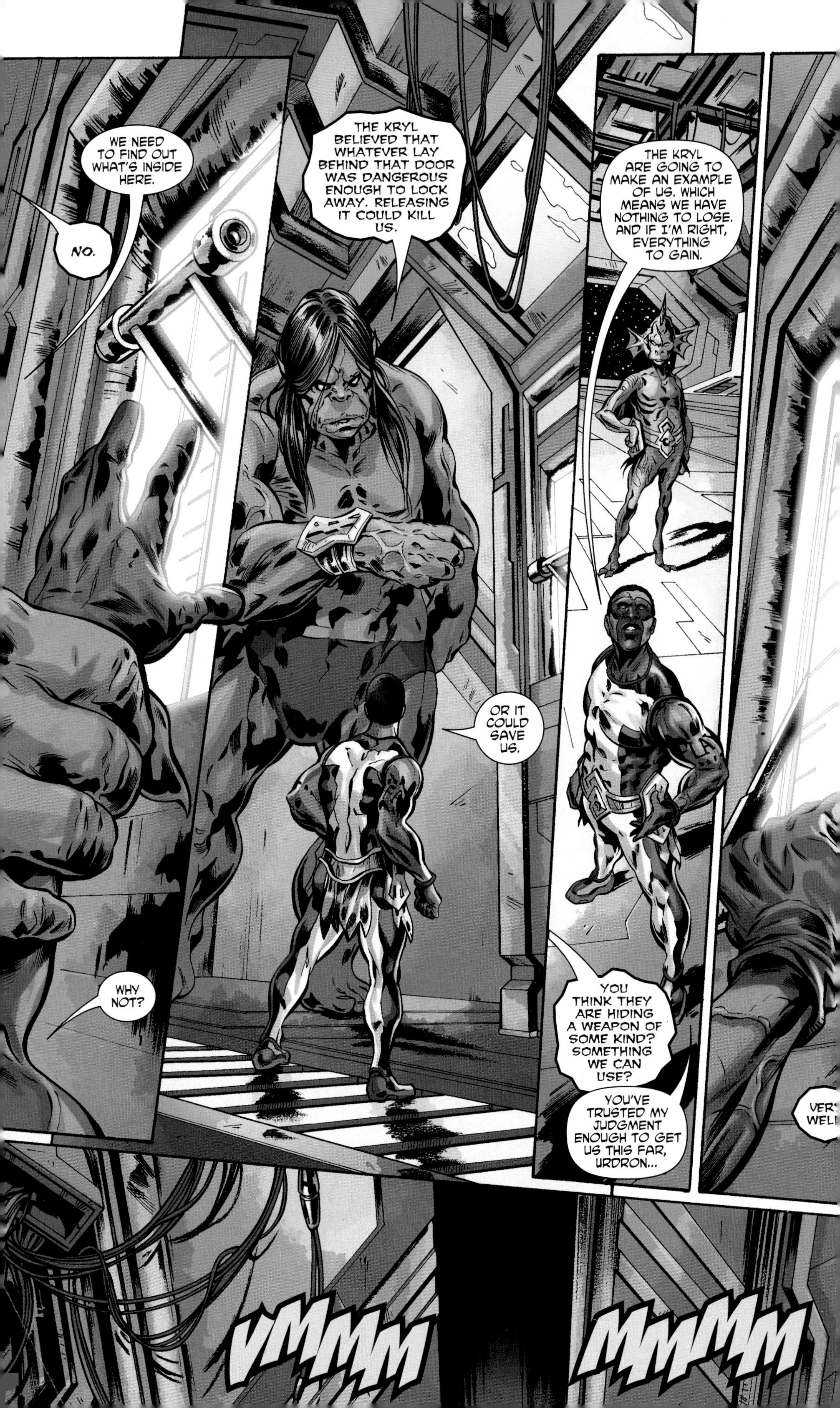
WE NEED TO FIND OUT WHAT'S INSIDE HERE.
NO.
THE KRYL BELIEVED THAT WHATEVER LAY BEHIND THAT DOOR WAS DANGEROUS ENOUGH TO LOCK AWAY. RELEASING IT COULD KILL US.
WHY NOT?
OR IT COULD SAVE US.
THE KRYL ARE GOING TO MAKE AN EXAMPLE OF US. WHICH MEANS WE HAVE NOTHING TO LOSE. AND IF I'M RIGHT, EVERYTHING TO GAIN.
YOU THINK THEY ARE HIDING A WEAPON OF SOME KIND? SOMETHING WE CAN USE?
YOU'VE TRUSTED MY JUDGMENT ENOUGH TO GET US THIS FAR, URDRON...
VMMMM
MMMMM

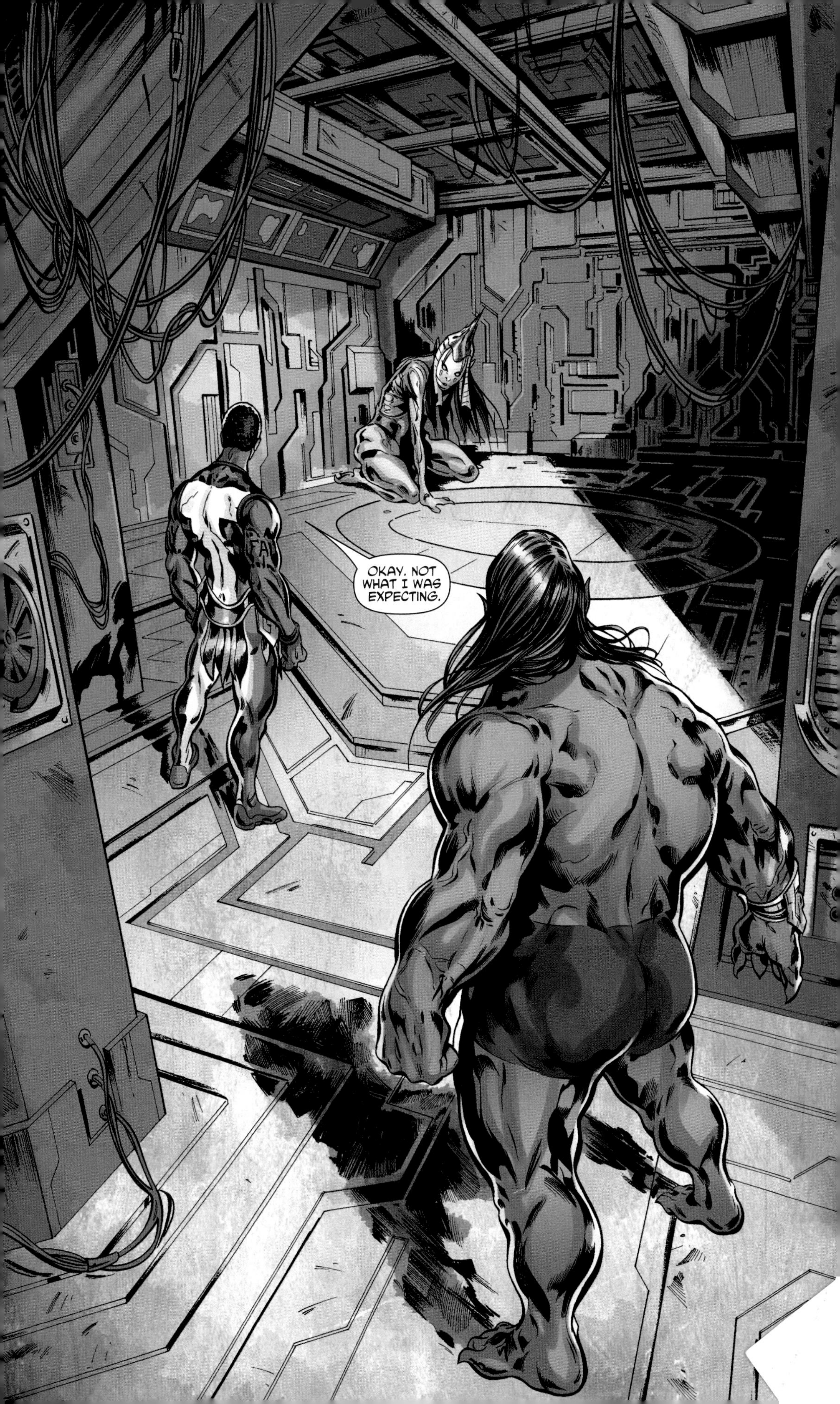
OKAY. NOT WHAT I WAS EXPECTING.

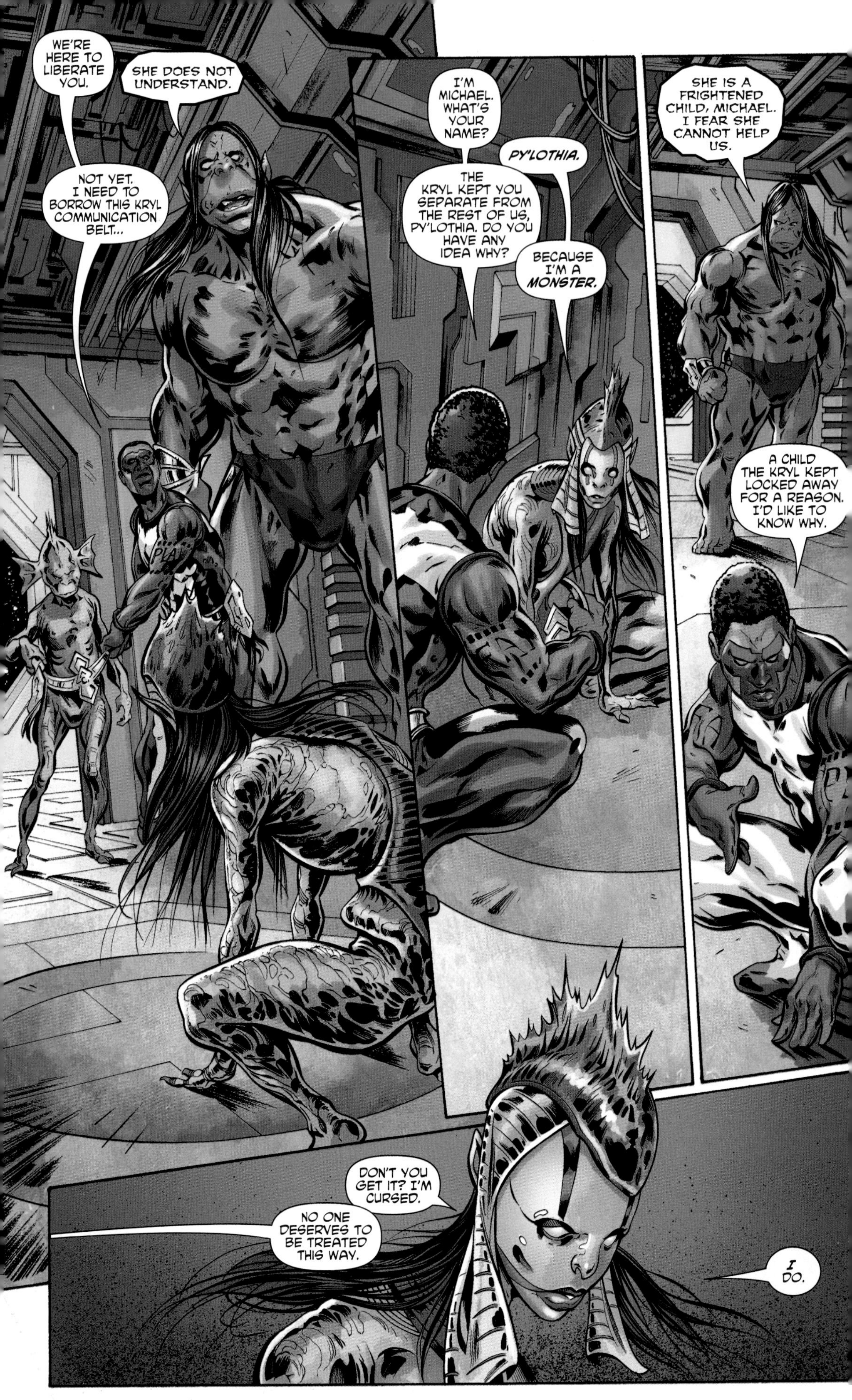
WE'RE HERE TO LIBERATE YOU.
SHE DOES NOT UNDERSTAND.
NOT YET. I NEED TO BORROW THIS KRYL COMMUNICATION BELT...
I'M MICHAEL. WHAT'S YOUR NAME?
PY'LOTHIA.
THE KRYL KEPT YOU SEPARATE FROM THE REST OF US, PY'LOTHIA. DO YOU HAVE ANY IDEA WHY?
BECAUSE I'M A MONSTER.
SHE IS A FRIGHTENED CHILD, MICHAEL. I FEAR SHE CANNOT HELP US.
A CHILD THE KRYL KEPT LOCKED AWAY FOR A REASON. I'D LIKE TO KNOW WHY.
DON'T YOU GET IT? I'M CURSED.
NO ONE DESERVES TO BE TREATED THIS WAY.
I DO.

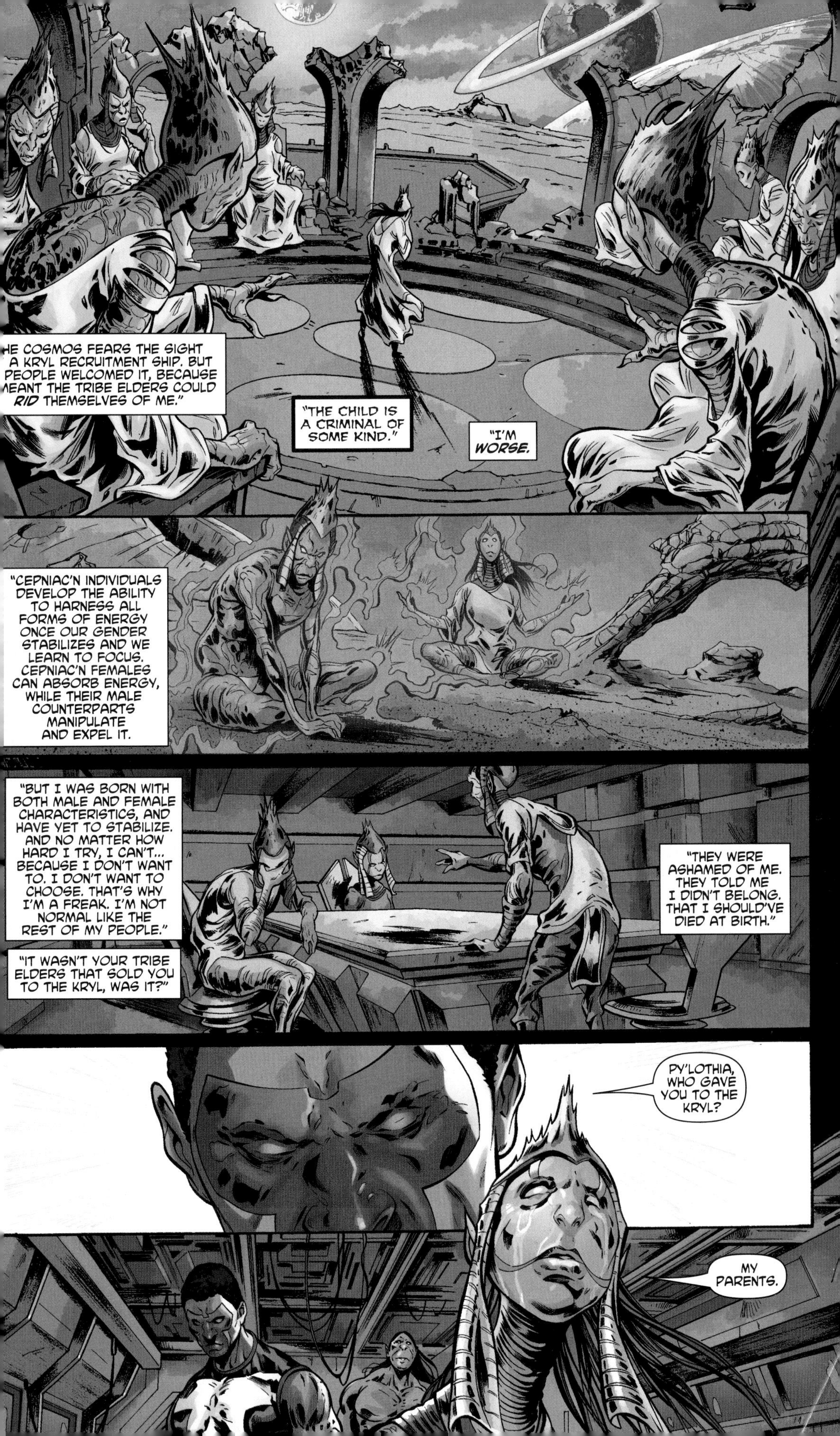
HE COSMOS FEARS THE SIGHT A KRYL RECRUITMENT SHIP. BUT PEOPLE WELCOMED IT, BECAUSE MEANT THE TRIBE ELDERS COULD RID THEMSELVES OF ME."
"THE CHILD IS A CRIMINAL OF SOME KIND."
"I'M WORSE.
"CEPNIAC'N INDIVIDUALS DEVELOP THE ABILITY TO HARNESS ALL FORMS OF ENERGY ONCE OUR GENDER STABILIZES AND WE LEARN TO FOCUS. CEPNIAC'N FEMALES CAN ABSORB ENERGY, WHILE THEIR MALE COUNTERPARTS MANIPULATE AND EXPEL IT.
"BUT I WAS BORN WITH BOTH MALE AND FEMALE CHARACTERISTICS, AND HAVE YET TO STABILIZE. AND NO MATTER HOW HARD I TRY, I CAN'T... BECAUSE I DON'T WANT TO. I DON'T WANT TO CHOOSE. THAT'S WHY I'M A FREAK. I'M NOT NORMAL LIKE THE REST OF MY PEOPLE."
"THEY WERE ASHAMED OF ME. THEY TOLD ME I DIDN'T BELONG. THAT I SHOULD'VE DIED AT BIRTH."
"IT WASN'T YOUR TRIBE ELDERS THAT SOLD YOU TO THE KRYL, WAS IT?"
PY'LOTHIA, WHO GAVE YOU TO THE KRYL?
MY PARENTS.

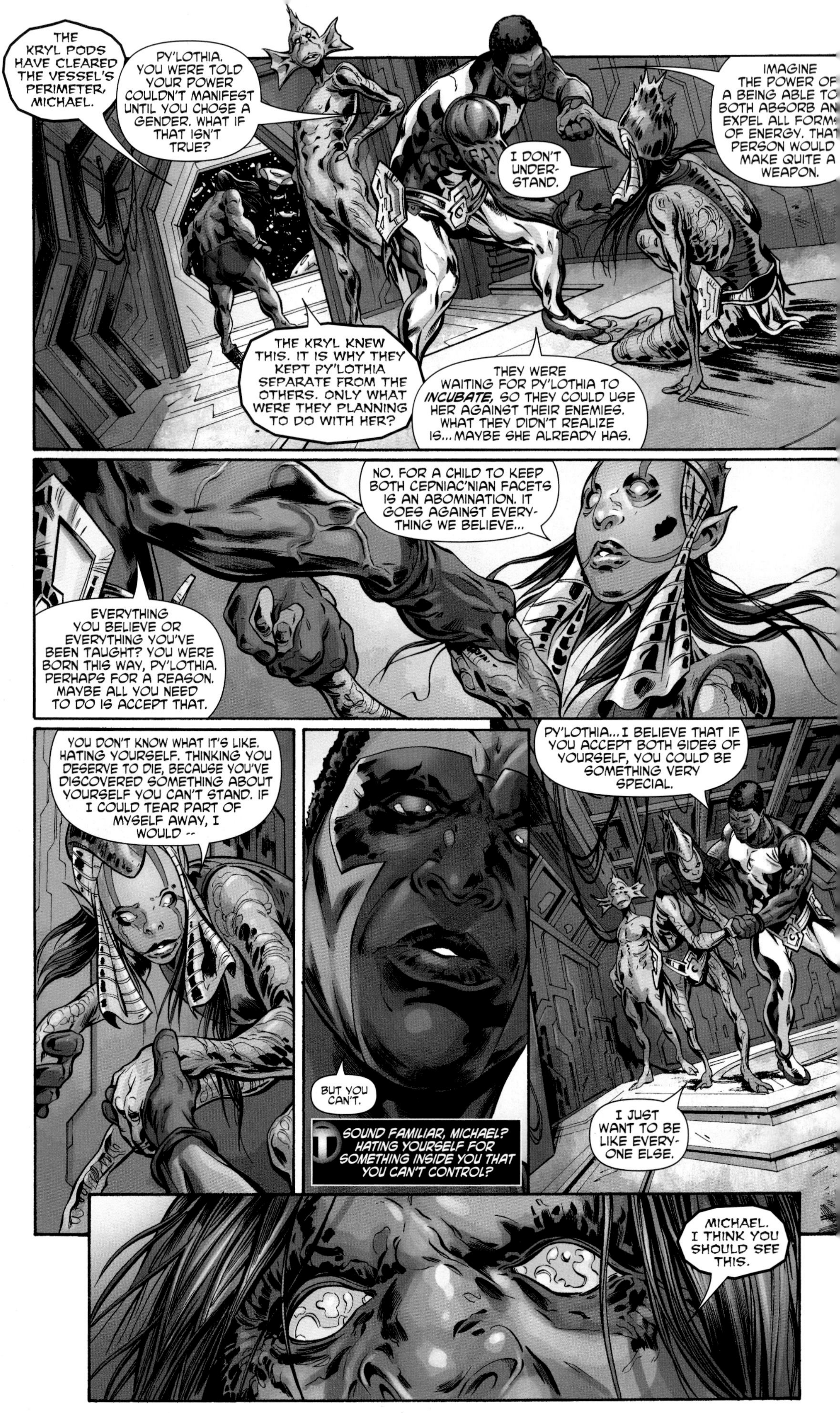
THE KRYL PODS HAVE CLEARED THE VESSEL'S PERIMETER, MICHAEL.
PY'LOTHIA. YOU WERE TOLD YOUR POWER COULDN'T MANIFEST UNTIL YOU CHOSE A GENDER. WHAT IF THAT ISN'T TRUE?
I DON'T UNDER-STAND.
IMAGINE THE POWER OF A BEING ABLE TO BOTH ABSORB AN EXPEL ALL FORMS OF ENERGY. THAT PERSON WOULD MAKE QUITE A WEAPON.
THE KRYL KNEW THIS. IT IS WHY THEY KEPT PY'LOTHIA SEPARATE FROM THE OTHERS. ONLY WHAT WERE THEY PLANNING TO DO WITH HER?
THEY WERE WAITING FOR PY'LOTHIA TO *INCUBATE,* SO THEY COULD USE HER AGAINST THEIR ENEMIES. WHAT THEY DIDN'T REALIZE IS... MAYBE SHE ALREADY HAS.
NO. FOR A CHILD TO KEEP BOTH CEPNIAC'NIAN FACETS IS AN ABOMINATION. IT GOES AGAINST EVERY-THING WE BELIEVE...
EVERYTHING YOU BELIEVE OR EVERYTHING YOU'VE BEEN TAUGHT? YOU WERE BORN THIS WAY, PY'LOTHIA. PERHAPS FOR A REASON. MAYBE ALL YOU NEED TO DO IS ACCEPT THAT.
YOU DON'T KNOW WHAT IT'S LIKE. HATING YOURSELF. THINKING YOU DESERVE TO DIE, BECAUSE YOU'VE DISCOVERED SOMETHING ABOUT YOURSELF YOU CAN'T STAND. IF I COULD TEAR PART OF MYSELF AWAY, I WOULD --
BUT YOU CAN'T.
SOUND FAMILIAR, MICHAEL? HATING YOURSELF FOR SOMETHING INSIDE YOU THAT YOU CAN'T CONTROL?
PY'LOTHIA... I BELIEVE THAT IF YOU ACCEPT BOTH SIDES OF YOURSELF, YOU COULD BE SOMETHING VERY SPECIAL.
I JUST WANT TO BE LIKE EVERY-ONE ELSE.
MICHAEL. I THINK YOU SHOULD SEE THIS.

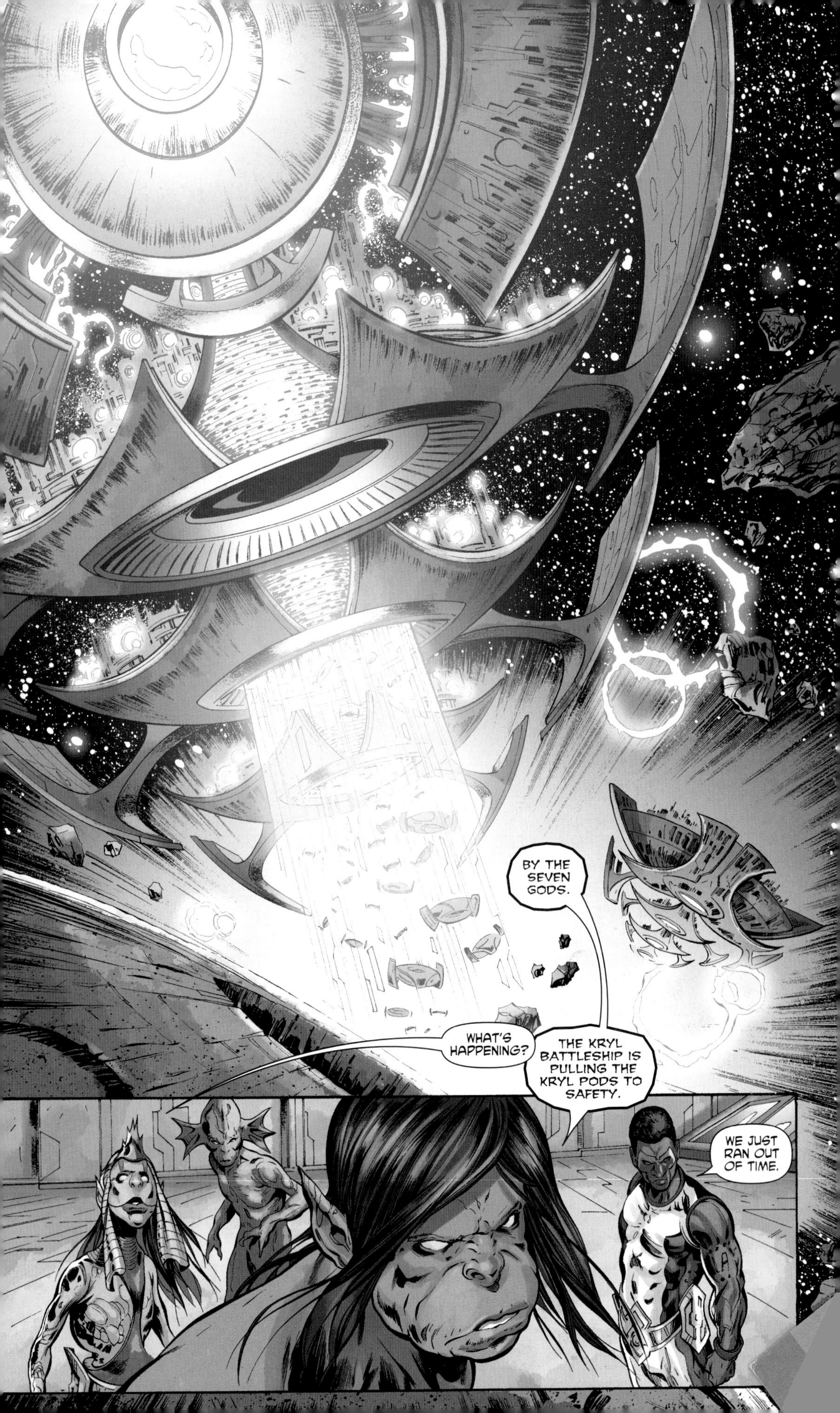
BY THE SEVEN GODS.
WHAT'S HAPPENING?
THE KRYL BATTLESHIP IS PULLING THE KRYL PODS TO SAFETY.
WE JUST RAN OUT OF TIME.

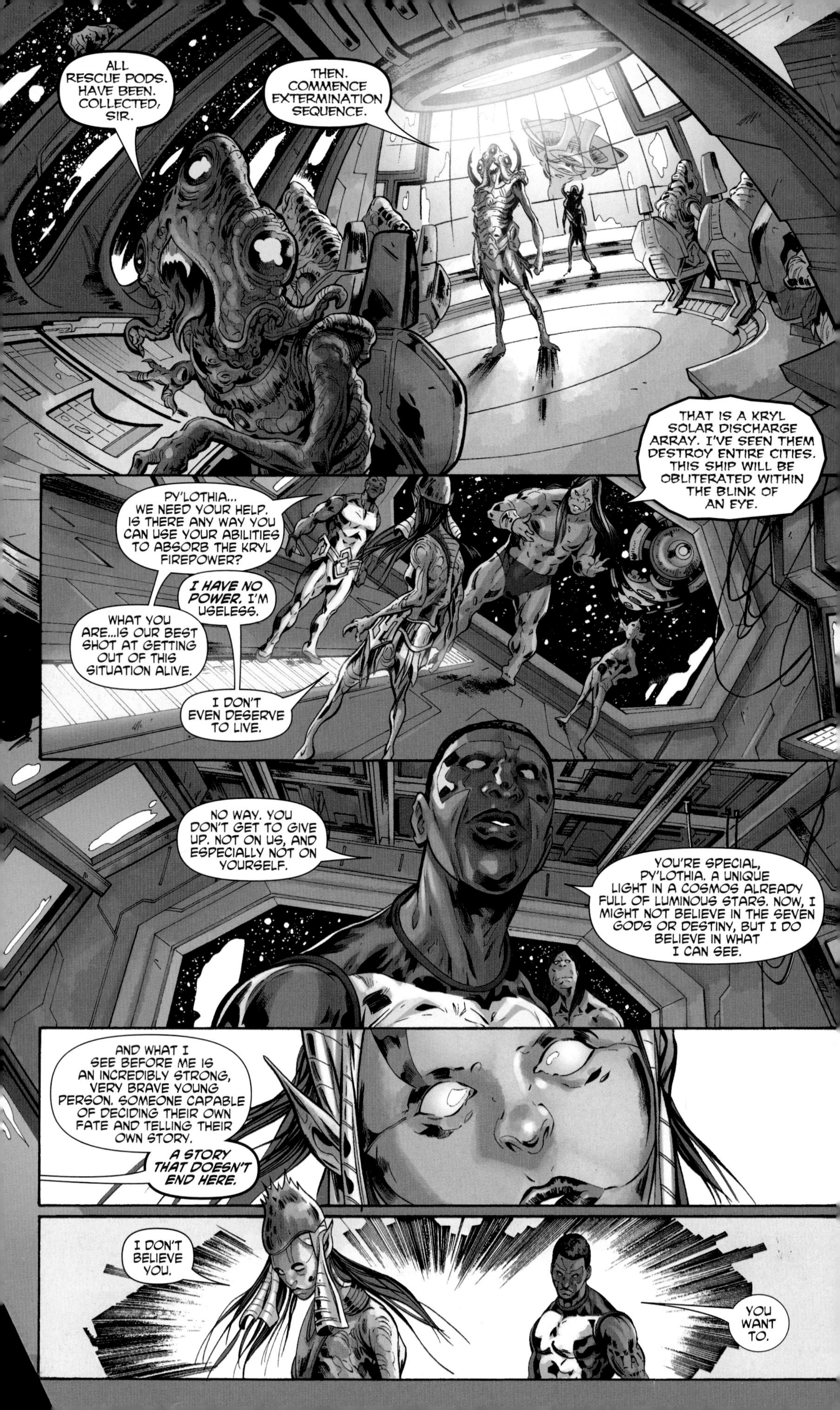

ALL RESCUE PODS. HAVE BEEN. COLLECTED, SIR.
THEN. COMMENCE EXTERMINATION SEQUENCE.
THAT IS A KRYL SOLAR DISCHARGE ARRAY. I'VE SEEN THEM DESTROY ENTIRE CITIES. THIS SHIP WILL BE OBLITERATED WITHIN THE BLINK OF AN EYE.
PY'LOTHIA... WE NEED YOUR HELP. IS THERE ANY WAY YOU CAN USE YOUR ABILITIES TO ABSORB THE KRYL FIREPOWER?
I HAVE NO POWER. I'M USELESS.
WHAT YOU ARE...IS OUR BEST SHOT AT GETTING OUT OF THIS SITUATION ALIVE.
I DON'T EVEN DESERVE TO LIVE.
NO WAY. YOU DON'T GET TO GIVE UP. NOT ON US, AND ESPECIALLY NOT ON YOURSELF.
YOU'RE SPECIAL, PY'LOTHIA. A UNIQUE LIGHT IN A COSMOS ALREADY FULL OF LUMINOUS STARS. NOW, I MIGHT NOT BELIEVE IN THE SEVEN GODS OR DESTINY, BUT I DO BELIEVE IN WHAT I CAN SEE.
AND WHAT I SEE BEFORE ME IS AN INCREDIBLY STRONG, VERY BRAVE YOUNG PERSON. SOMEONE CAPABLE OF DECIDING THEIR OWN FATE AND TELLING THEIR OWN STORY.
A STORY THAT DOESN'T END HERE.
I DON'T BELIEVE YOU.
YOU WANT TO.

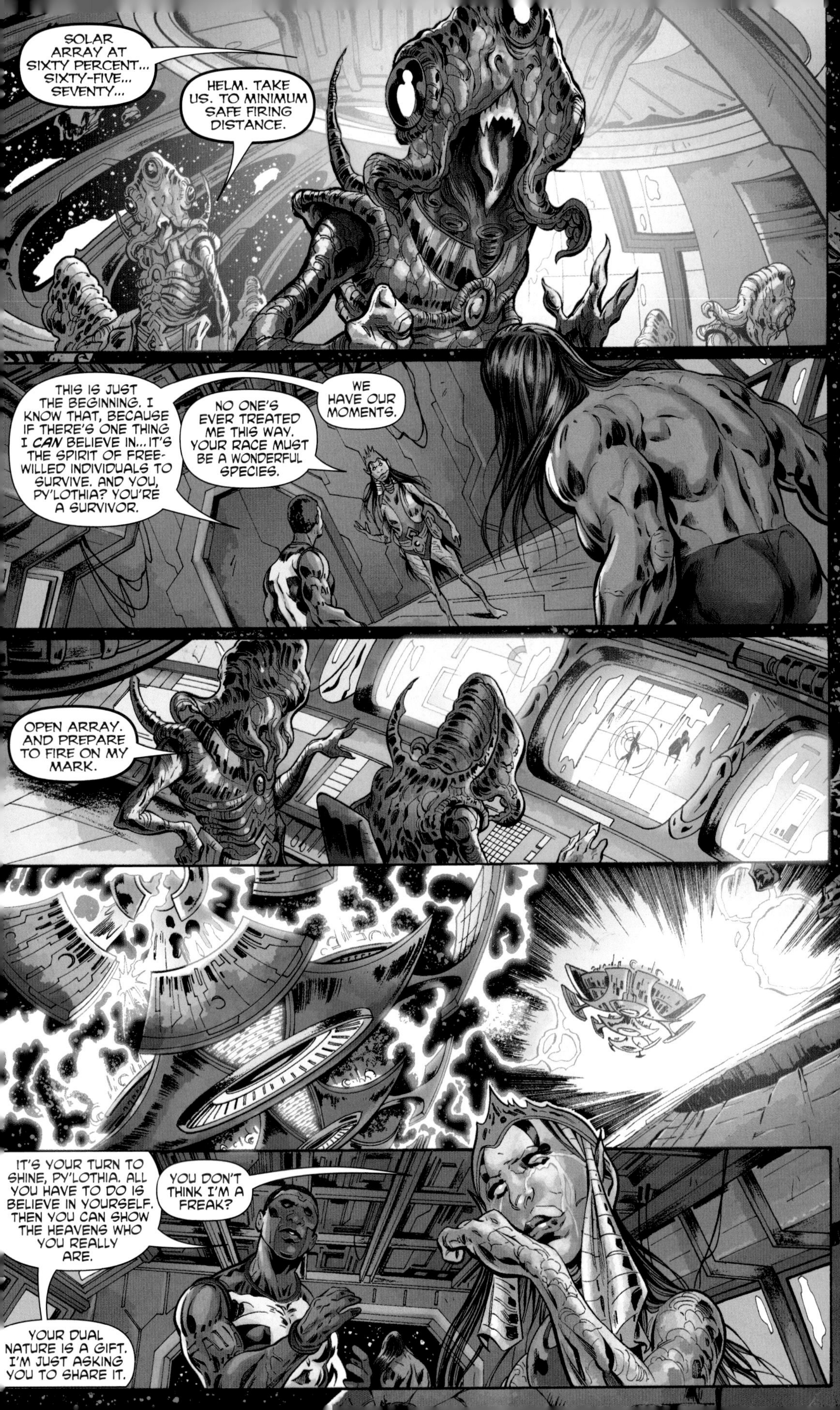
SOLAR ARRAY AT SIXTY PERCENT... SIXTY-FIVE... SEVENTY...
HELM. TAKE US. TO MINIMUM SAFE FIRING DISTANCE.
THIS IS JUST THE BEGINNING. I KNOW THAT, BECAUSE IF THERE'S ONE THING I *CAN* BELIEVE IN... IT'S THE SPIRIT OF FREE-WILLED INDIVIDUALS TO SURVIVE. AND YOU, PY'LOTHIA? YOU'RE A SURVIVOR.
NO ONE'S EVER TREATED ME THIS WAY. YOUR RACE MUST BE A WONDERFUL SPECIES.
WE HAVE OUR MOMENTS.
OPEN ARRAY. AND PREPARE TO FIRE ON MY MARK.
IT'S YOUR TURN TO SHINE, PY'LOTHIA. ALL YOU HAVE TO DO IS BELIEVE IN YOURSELF. THEN YOU CAN SHOW THE HEAVENS WHO YOU REALLY ARE.
YOU DON'T THINK I'M A FREAK?
YOUR DUAL NATURE IS A GIFT. I'M JUST ASKING YOU TO SHARE IT.

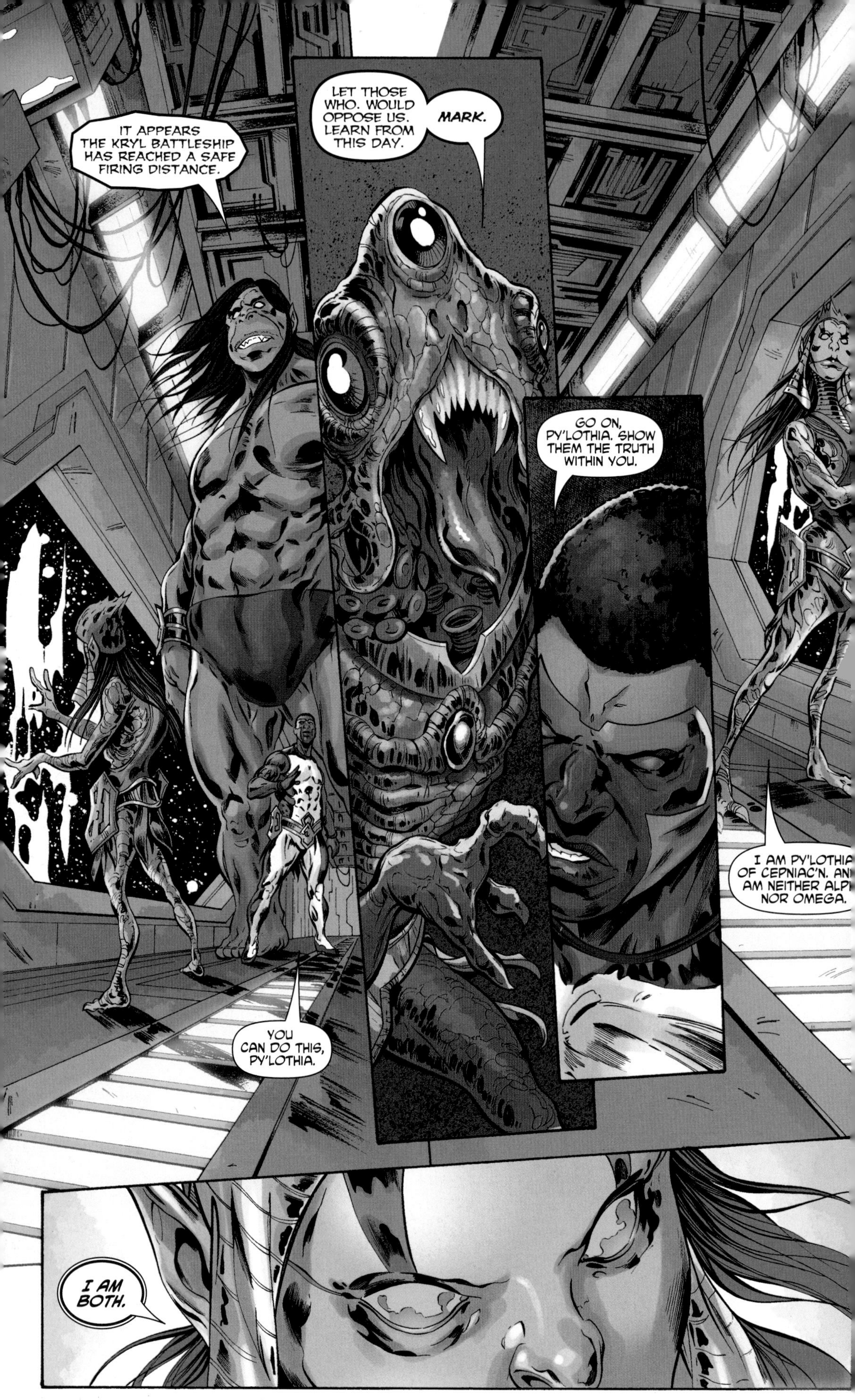
IT APPEARS THE KRYL BATTLESHIP HAS REACHED A SAFE FIRING DISTANCE.
LET THOSE WHO. WOULD OPPOSE US. LEARN FROM THIS DAY.
MARK.
GO ON, PY'LOTHIA. SHOW THEM THE TRUTH WITHIN YOU.
YOU CAN DO THIS, PY'LOTHIA.
I AM PY'LOTHIA OF CEPNIAC'N. AN AM NEITHER ALP NOR OMEGA.
I AM BOTH.

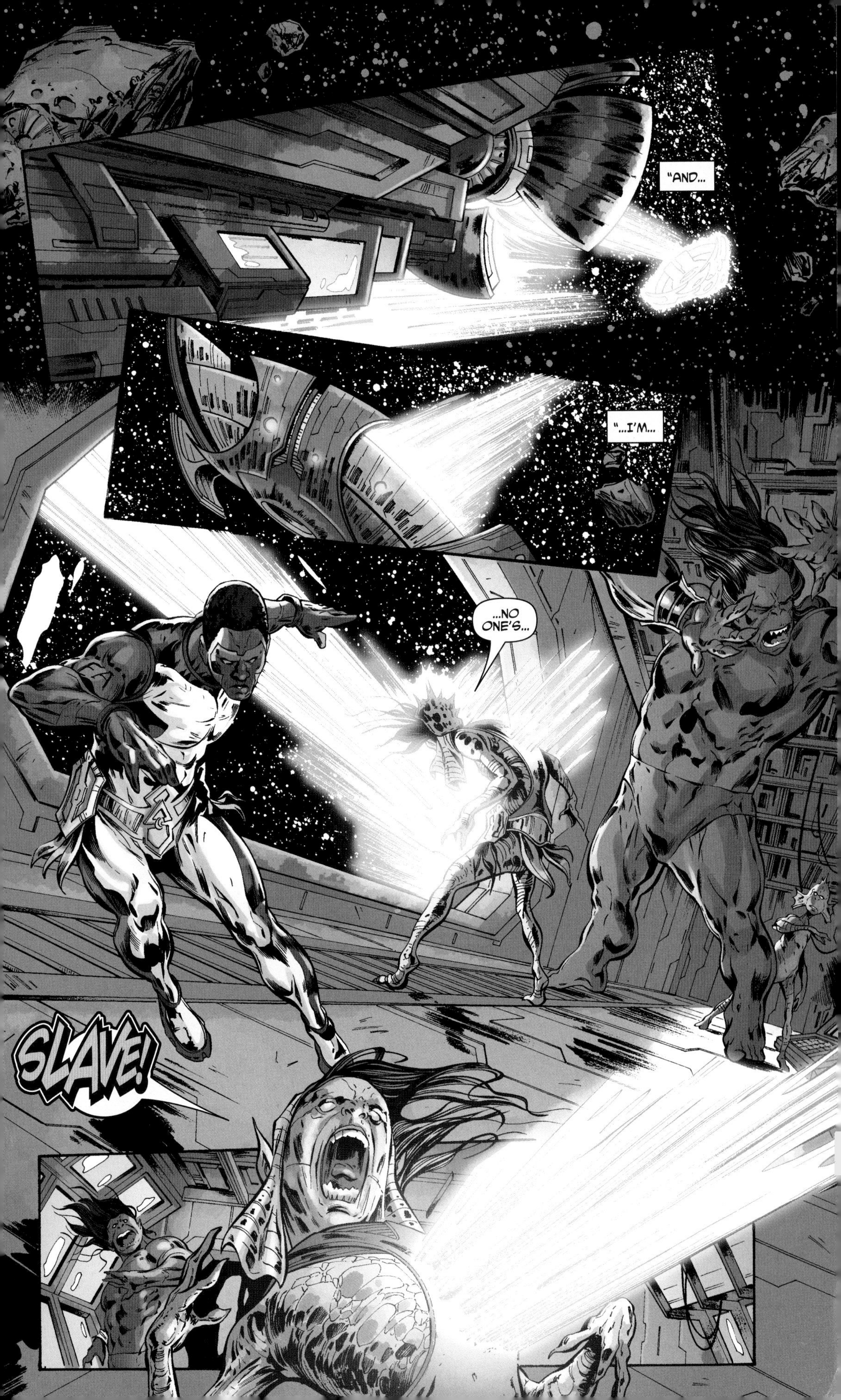
"AND...
"...I'M...
...NO ONE'S...
SLAVE!

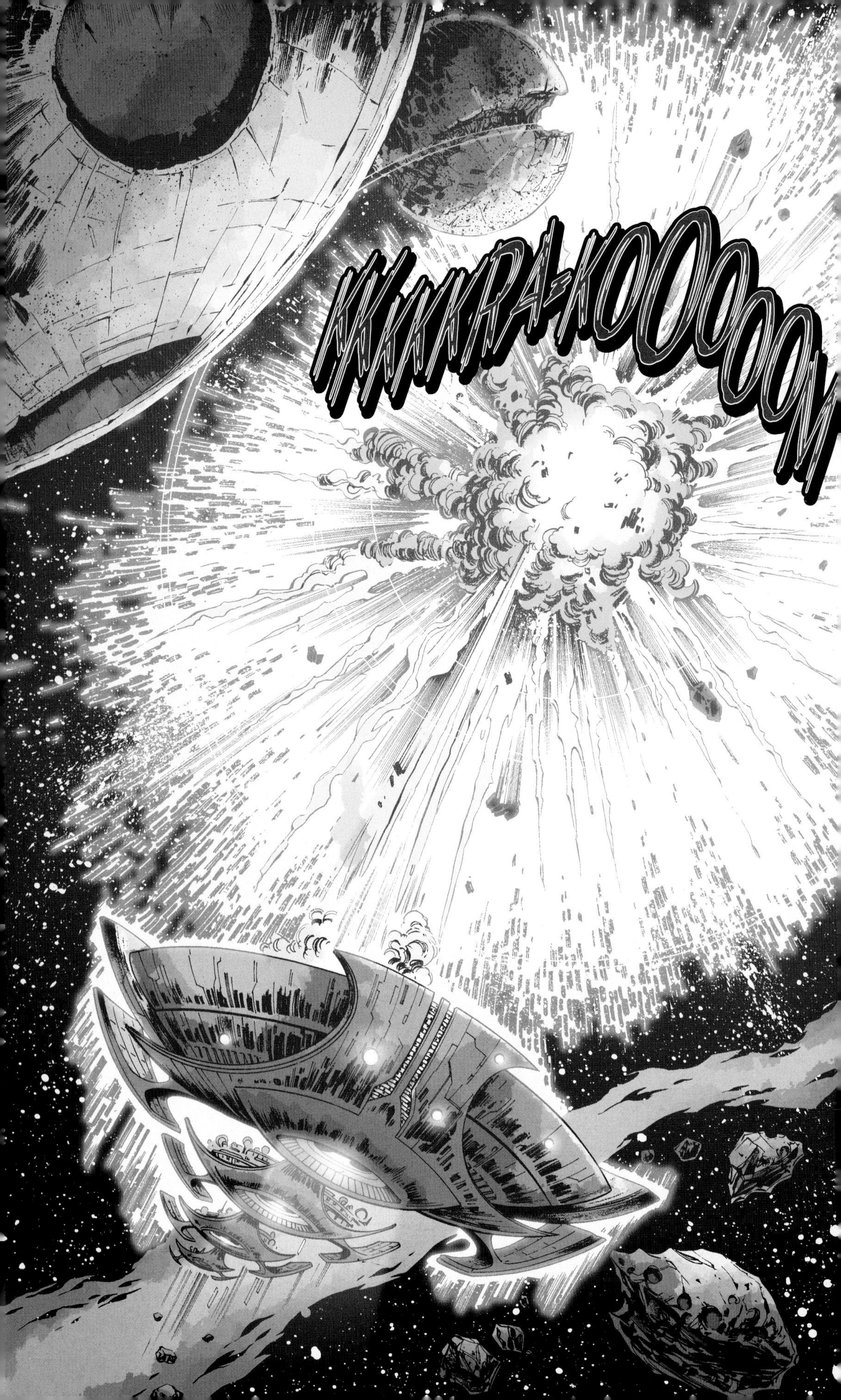
KKKKKRA-KOOOOOM

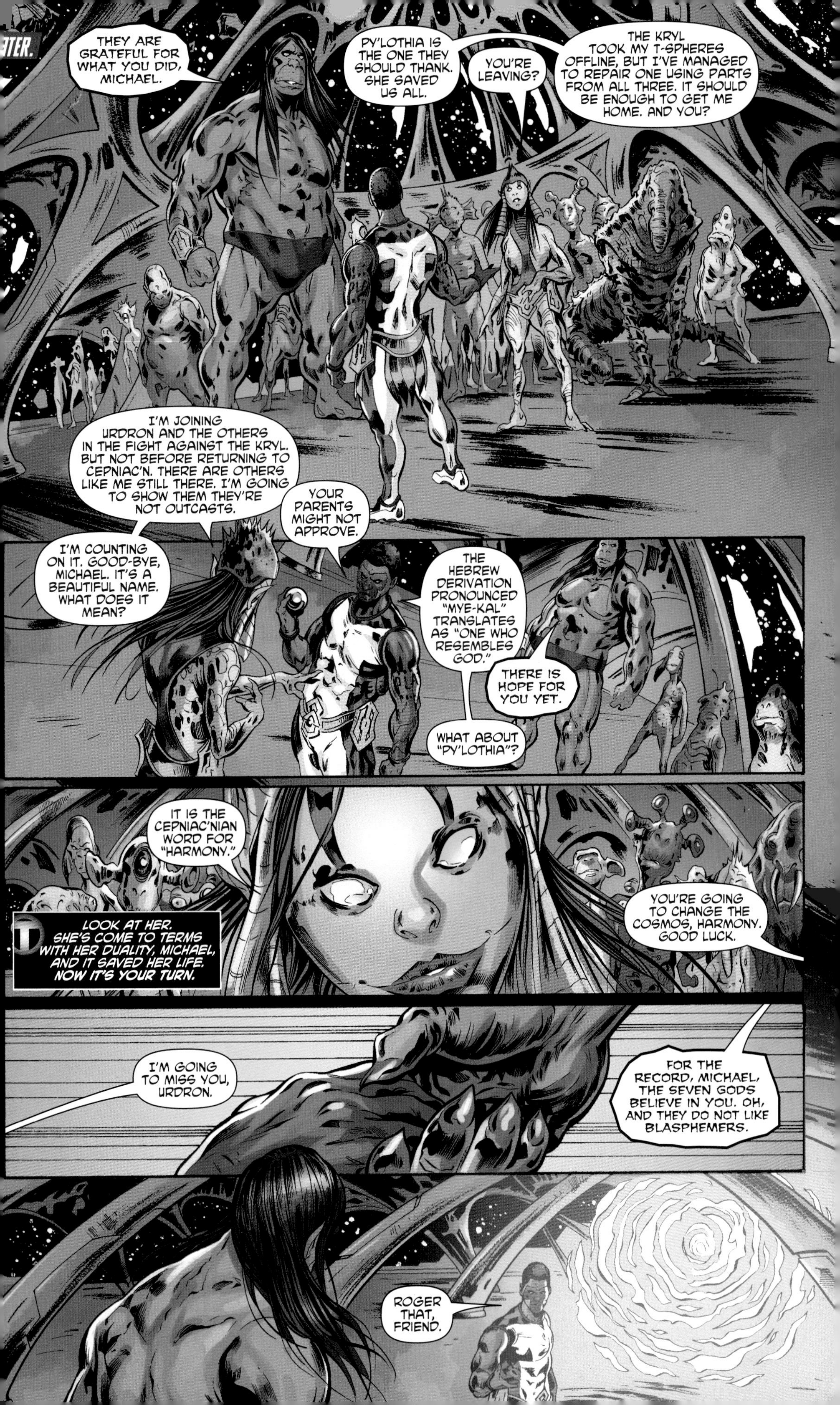

ATER.
THEY ARE GRATEFUL FOR WHAT YOU DID, MICHAEL.
PY'LOTHIA IS THE ONE THEY SHOULD THANK. SHE SAVED US ALL.
YOU'RE LEAVING?
THE KRYL TOOK MY T-SPHERES OFFLINE, BUT I'VE MANAGED TO REPAIR ONE USING PARTS FROM ALL THREE. IT SHOULD BE ENOUGH TO GET ME HOME. AND YOU?
I'M JOINING URDRON AND THE OTHERS IN THE FIGHT AGAINST THE KRYL. BUT NOT BEFORE RETURNING TO CEPNIAC'N. THERE ARE OTHERS LIKE ME STILL THERE. I'M GOING TO SHOW THEM THEY'RE NOT OUTCASTS.
YOUR PARENTS MIGHT NOT APPROVE.
I'M COUNTING ON IT. GOOD-BYE, MICHAEL. IT'S A BEAUTIFUL NAME. WHAT DOES IT MEAN?
THE HEBREW DERIVATION PRONOUNCED "MYE-KAL" TRANSLATES AS "ONE WHO RESEMBLES GOD."
THERE IS HOPE FOR YOU YET.
WHAT ABOUT "PY'LOTHIA"?
IT IS THE CEPNIAC'NIAN WORD FOR "HARMONY."
LOOK AT HER. SHE'S COME TO TERMS WITH HER DUALITY, MICHAEL, AND IT SAVED HER LIFE. NOW IT'S YOUR TURN.
YOU'RE GOING TO CHANGE THE COSMOS, HARMONY. GOOD LUCK.
I'M GOING TO MISS YOU, URDRON.
FOR THE RECORD, MICHAEL, THE SEVEN GODS BELIEVE IN YOU. OH, AND THEY DO NOT LIKE BLASPHEMERS.
ROGER THAT, FRIEND.

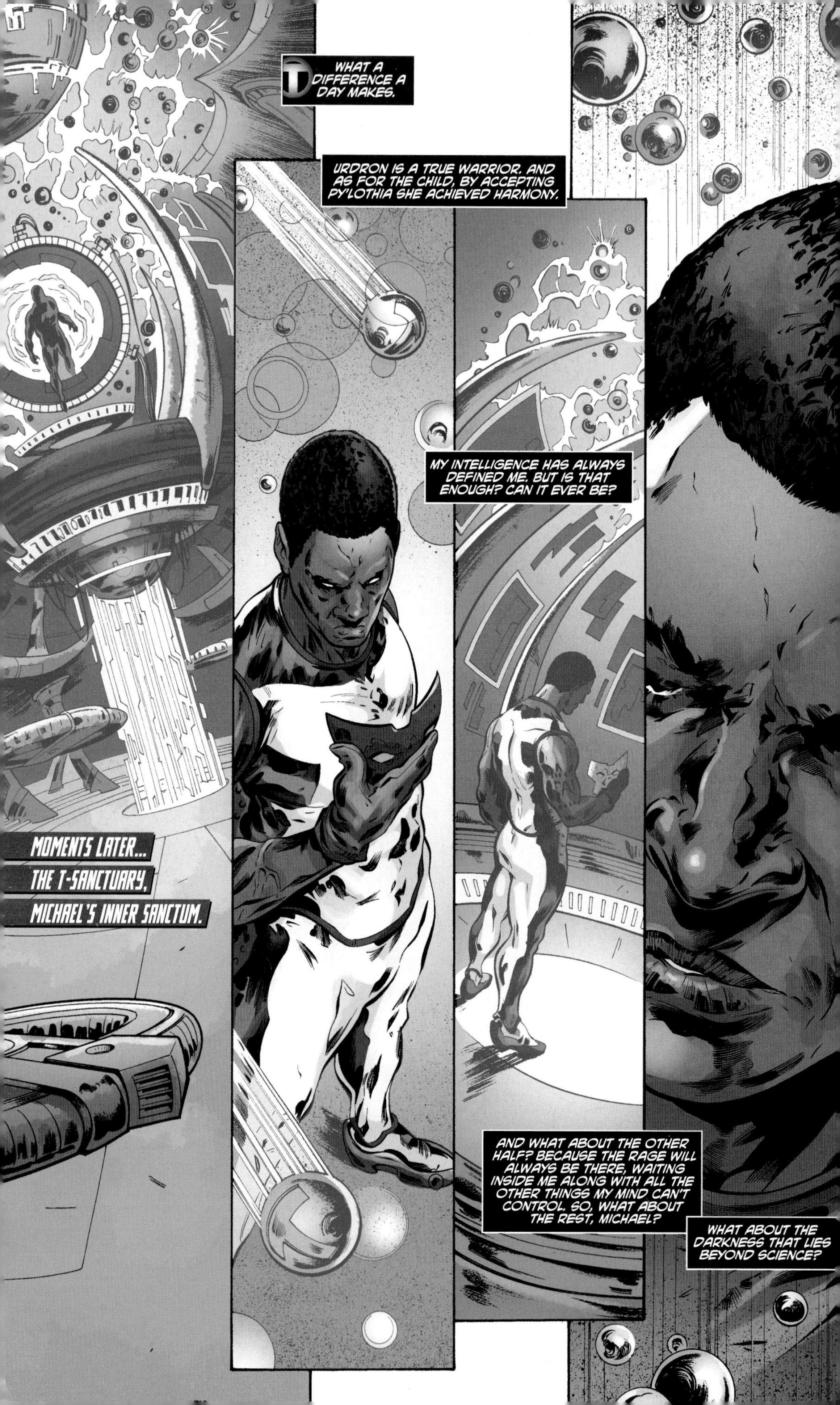

WHAT A DIFFERENCE A DAY MAKES.
URDRON IS A TRUE WARRIOR. AND AS FOR THE CHILD, BY ACCEPTING PY'LOTHIA SHE ACHIEVED HARMONY.
MOMENTS LATER...
THE T-SANCTUARY,
MICHAEL'S INNER SANCTUM.
MY INTELLIGENCE HAS ALWAYS DEFINED ME. BUT IS THAT ENOUGH? CAN IT EVER BE?
AND WHAT ABOUT THE OTHER HALF? BECAUSE THE RAGE WILL ALWAYS BE THERE, WAITING INSIDE ME ALONG WITH ALL THE OTHER THINGS MY MIND CAN'T CONTROL. SO, WHAT ABOUT THE REST, MICHAEL?
WHAT ABOUT THE DARKNESS THAT LIES BEYOND SCIENCE?

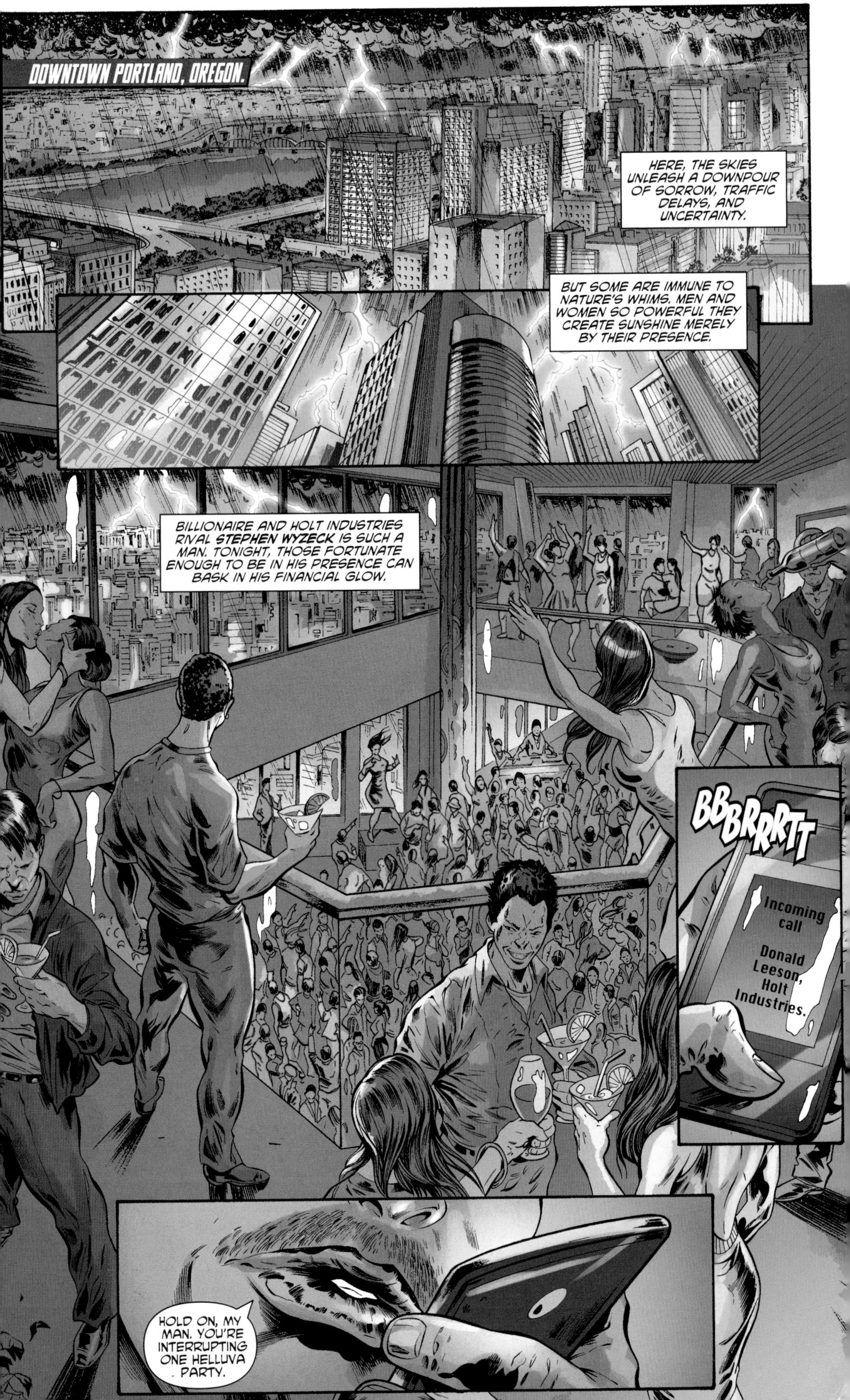
DOWNTOWN PORTLAND, OREGON.
HERE, THE SKIES UNLEASH A DOWNPOUR OF SORROW, TRAFFIC DELAYS, AND UNCERTAINTY.
BUT SOME ARE IMMUNE TO NATURE'S WHIMS. MEN AND WOMEN SO POWERFUL THEY CREATE SUNSHINE MERELY BY THEIR PRESENCE.
BILLIONAIRE AND HOLT INDUSTRIES RIVAL STEPHEN WYZECK IS SUCH A MAN. TONIGHT, THOSE FORTUNATE ENOUGH TO BE IN HIS PRESENCE CAN BASK IN HIS FINANCIAL GLOW.
BBBRRRTT
Incoming call
Donald Leeson, Holt Industries.
HOLD ON, MY MAN. YOU'RE INTERRUPTING ONE HELLUVA PARTY.

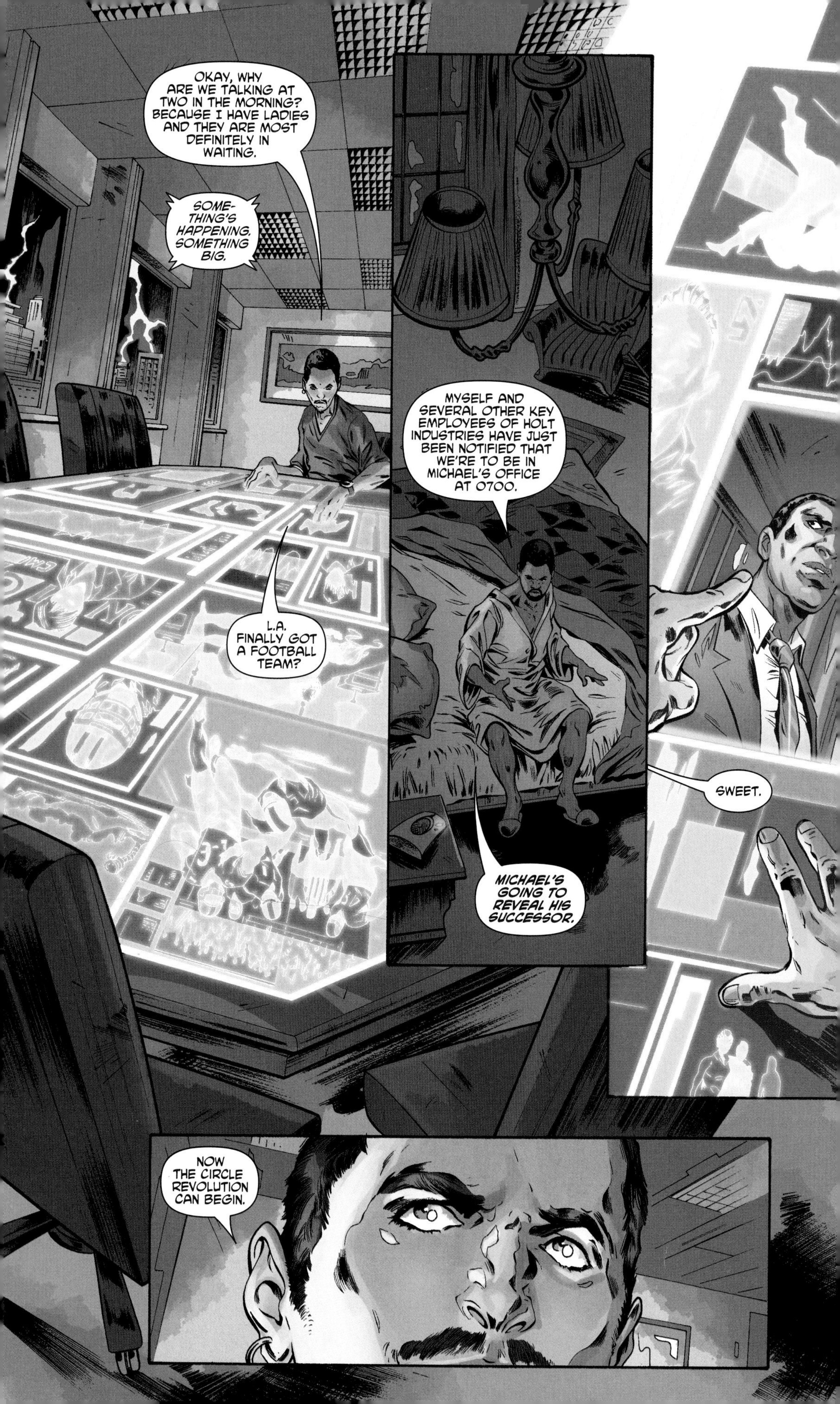
OKAY, WHY ARE WE TALKING AT TWO IN THE MORNING? BECAUSE I HAVE LADIES AND THEY ARE MOST DEFINITELY IN WAITING.
SOME-THING'S HAPPENING. SOMETHING BIG.
L.A. FINALLY GOT A FOOTBALL TEAM?
MYSELF AND SEVERAL OTHER KEY EMPLOYEES OF HOLT INDUSTRIES HAVE JUST BEEN NOTIFIED THAT WE'RE TO BE IN MICHAEL'S OFFICE AT 0700.
MICHAEL'S GOING TO REVEAL HIS SUCCESSOR.
SWEET.
NOW THE CIRCLE REVOLUTION CAN BEGIN.

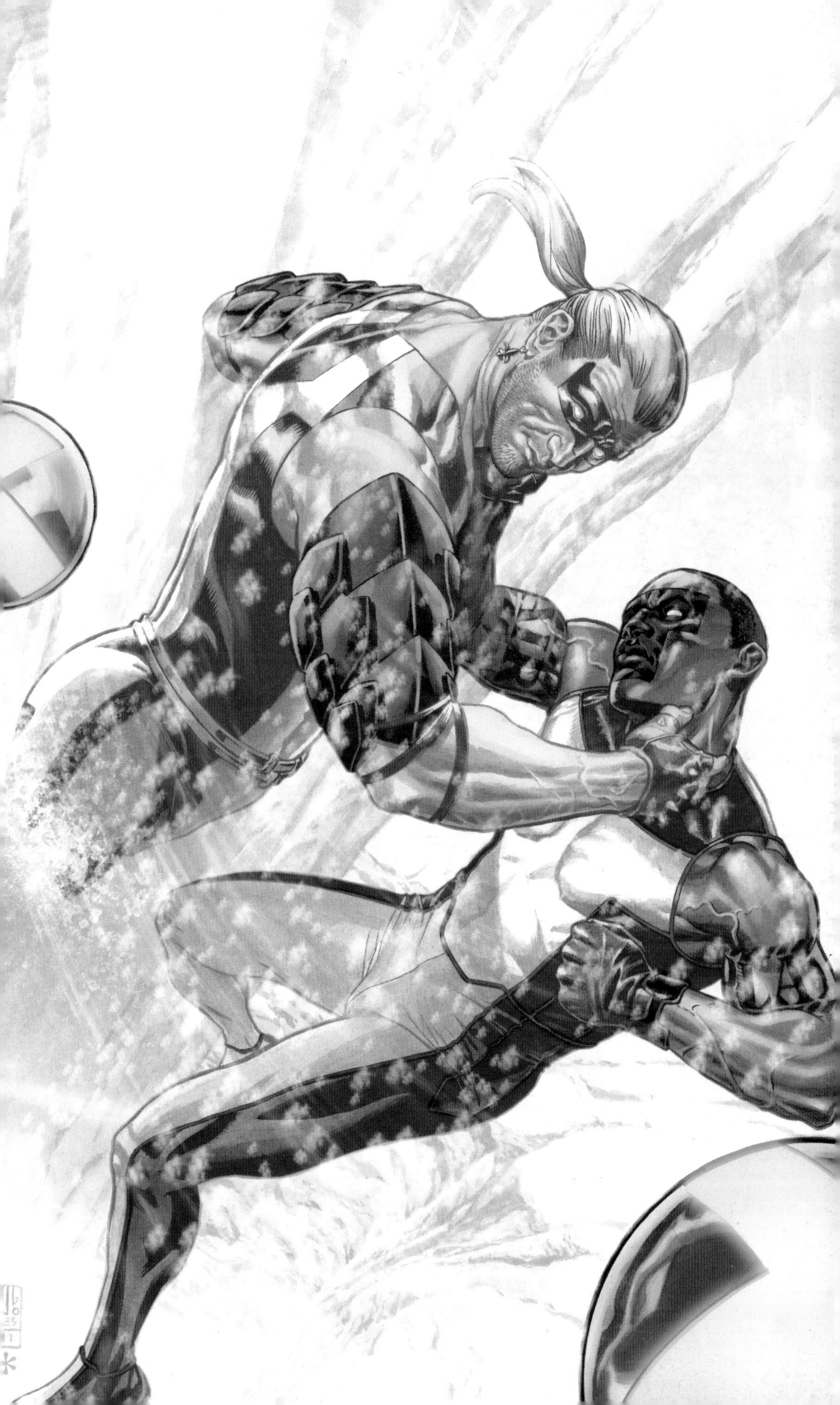

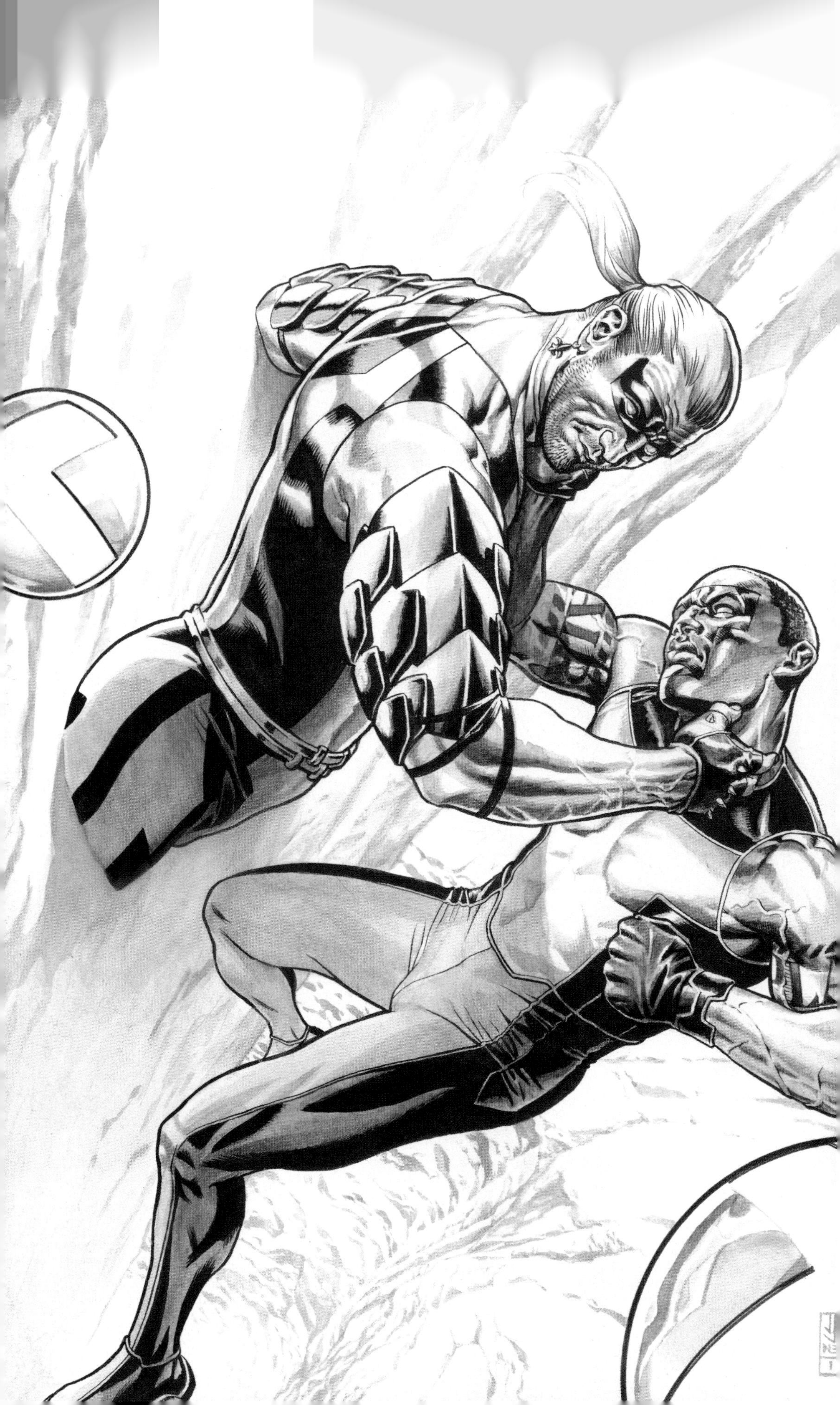

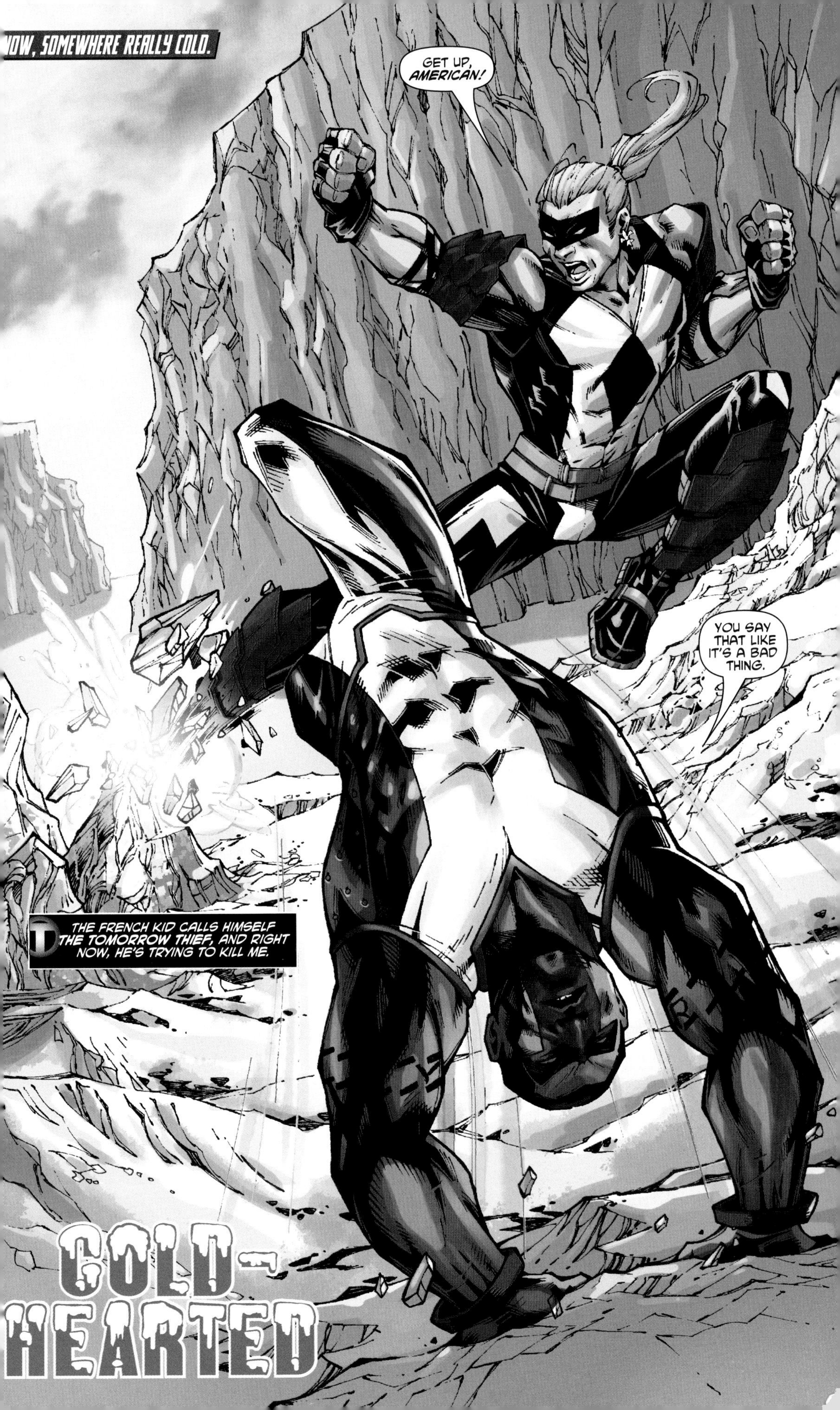
NOW, SOMEWHERE REALLY COLD.
GET UP, AMERICAN!
YOU SAY THAT LIKE IT'S A BAD THING.
THE FRENCH KID CALLS HIMSELF THE TOMORROW THIEF, AND RIGHT NOW, HE'S TRYING TO KILL ME.
COLD-HEARTED

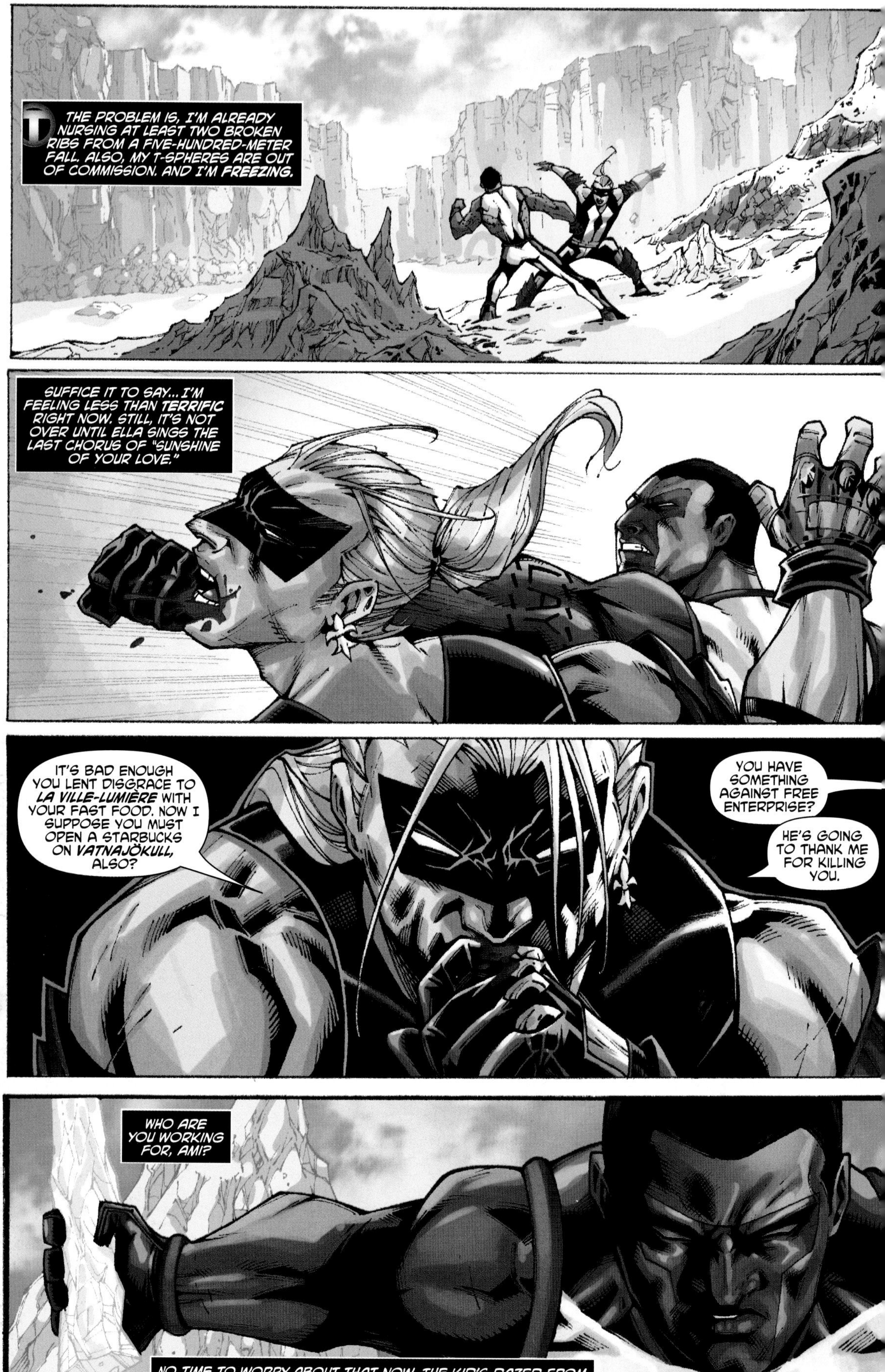
THE PROBLEM IS, I'M ALREADY NURSING AT LEAST TWO BROKEN RIBS FROM A FIVE-HUNDRED-METER FALL. ALSO, MY T-SPHERES ARE OUT OF COMMISSION. AND I'M FREEZING.
SUFFICE IT TO SAY... I'M FEELING LESS THAN TERRIFIC RIGHT NOW. STILL, IT'S NOT OVER UNTIL ELLA SINGS THE LAST CHORUS OF "SUNSHINE OF YOUR LOVE."
IT'S BAD ENOUGH YOU LENT DISGRACE TO LA VILLE-LUMIÈRE WITH YOUR FAST FOOD. NOW I SUPPOSE YOU MUST OPEN A STARBUCKS ON VATNAJÖKULL, ALSO?
YOU HAVE SOMETHING AGAINST FREE ENTERPRISE?
HE'S GOING TO THANK ME FOR KILLING YOU.
WHO ARE YOU WORKING FOR, AMI?
NO TIME TO WORRY ABOUT THAT NOW. THE KID'S DAZED FROM THAT LAST RIGHT HOOK. MAYBE... IF I MOVE FAST ENOUGH...

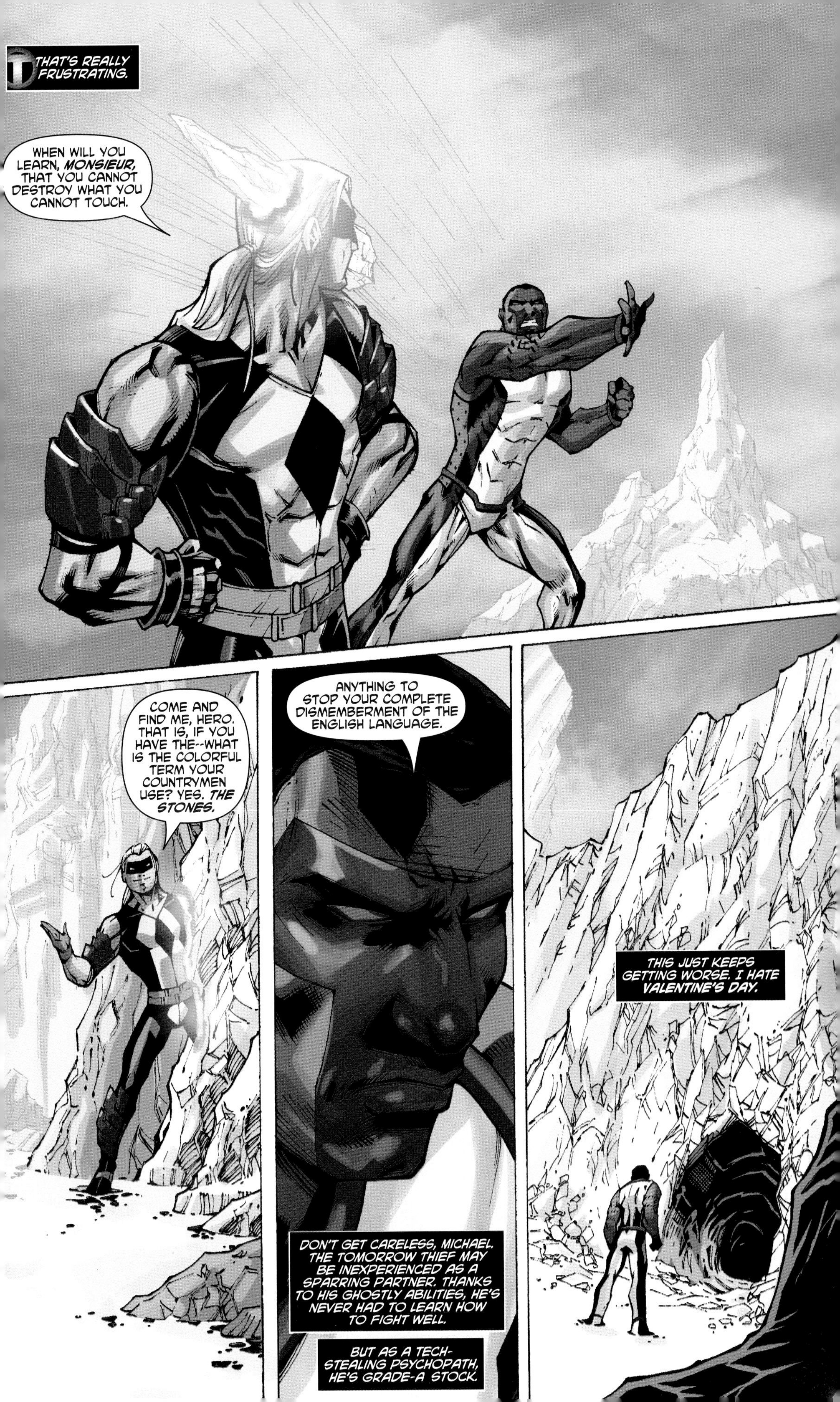
THAT'S REALLY FRUSTRATING.
WHEN WILL YOU LEARN, MONSIEUR, THAT YOU CANNOT DESTROY WHAT YOU CANNOT TOUCH.
COME AND FIND ME, HERO. THAT IS, IF YOU HAVE THE--WHAT IS THE COLORFUL TERM YOUR COUNTRYMEN USE? YES. THE STONES.
ANYTHING TO STOP YOUR COMPLETE DISMEMBERMENT OF THE ENGLISH LANGUAGE.
DON'T GET CARELESS, MICHAEL. THE TOMORROW THIEF MAY BE INEXPERIENCED AS A SPARRING PARTNER. THANKS TO HIS GHOSTLY ABILITIES, HE'S NEVER HAD TO LEARN HOW TO FIGHT WELL.
BUT AS A TECH-STEALING PSYCHOPATH, HE'S GRADE-A STOCK.
THIS JUST KEEPS GETTING WORSE. I HATE VALENTINE'S DAY.

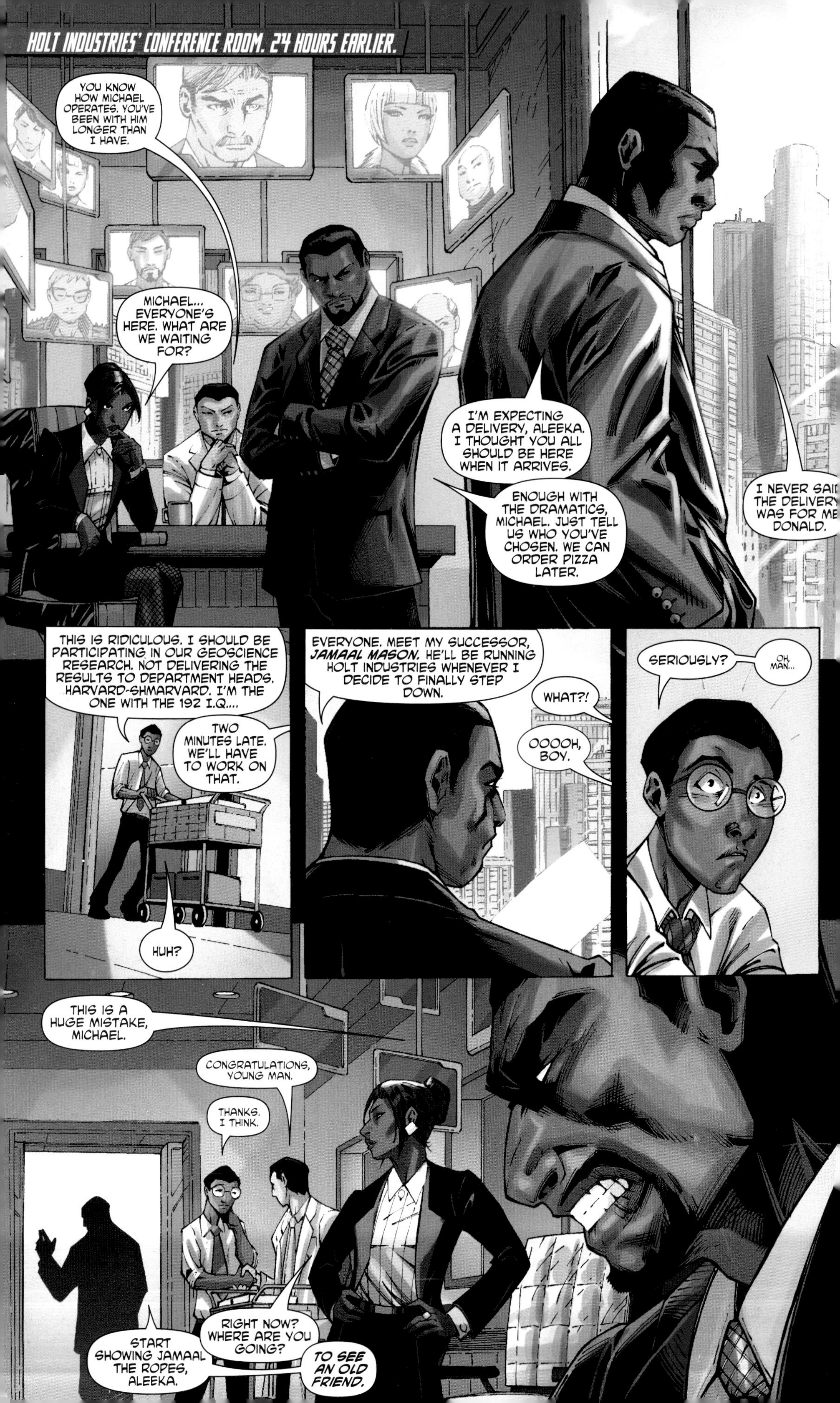

HOLT INDUSTRIES' CONFERENCE ROOM. 24 HOURS EARLIER.
YOU KNOW HOW MICHAEL OPERATES. YOU'VE BEEN WITH HIM LONGER THAN I HAVE.
MICHAEL... EVERYONE'S HERE. WHAT ARE WE WAITING FOR?
I'M EXPECTING A DELIVERY, ALEEKA. I THOUGHT YOU ALL SHOULD BE HERE WHEN IT ARRIVES.
ENOUGH WITH THE DRAMATICS, MICHAEL. JUST TELL US WHO YOU'VE CHOSEN. WE CAN ORDER PIZZA LATER.
I NEVER SAI THE DELIVERY WAS FOR ME DONALD.
THIS IS RIDICULOUS. I SHOULD BE PARTICIPATING IN OUR GEOSCIENCE RESEARCH. NOT DELIVERING THE RESULTS TO DEPARTMENT HEADS. HARVARD-SHMARVARD. I'M THE ONE WITH THE 192 I.Q....
TWO MINUTES LATE. WE'LL HAVE TO WORK ON THAT.
HUH?
EVERYONE. MEET MY SUCCESSOR, JAMAAL MASON. HE'LL BE RUNNING HOLT INDUSTRIES WHENEVER I DECIDE TO FINALLY STEP DOWN.
WHAT?!
OOOOH, BOY.
SERIOUSLY?
OH, MAN...
THIS IS A HUGE MISTAKE, MICHAEL.
CONGRATULATIONS, YOUNG MAN.
THANKS. I THINK.
START SHOWING JAMAAL THE ROPES, ALEEKA.
RIGHT NOW? WHERE ARE YOU GOING?
TO SEE AN OLD FRIEND.

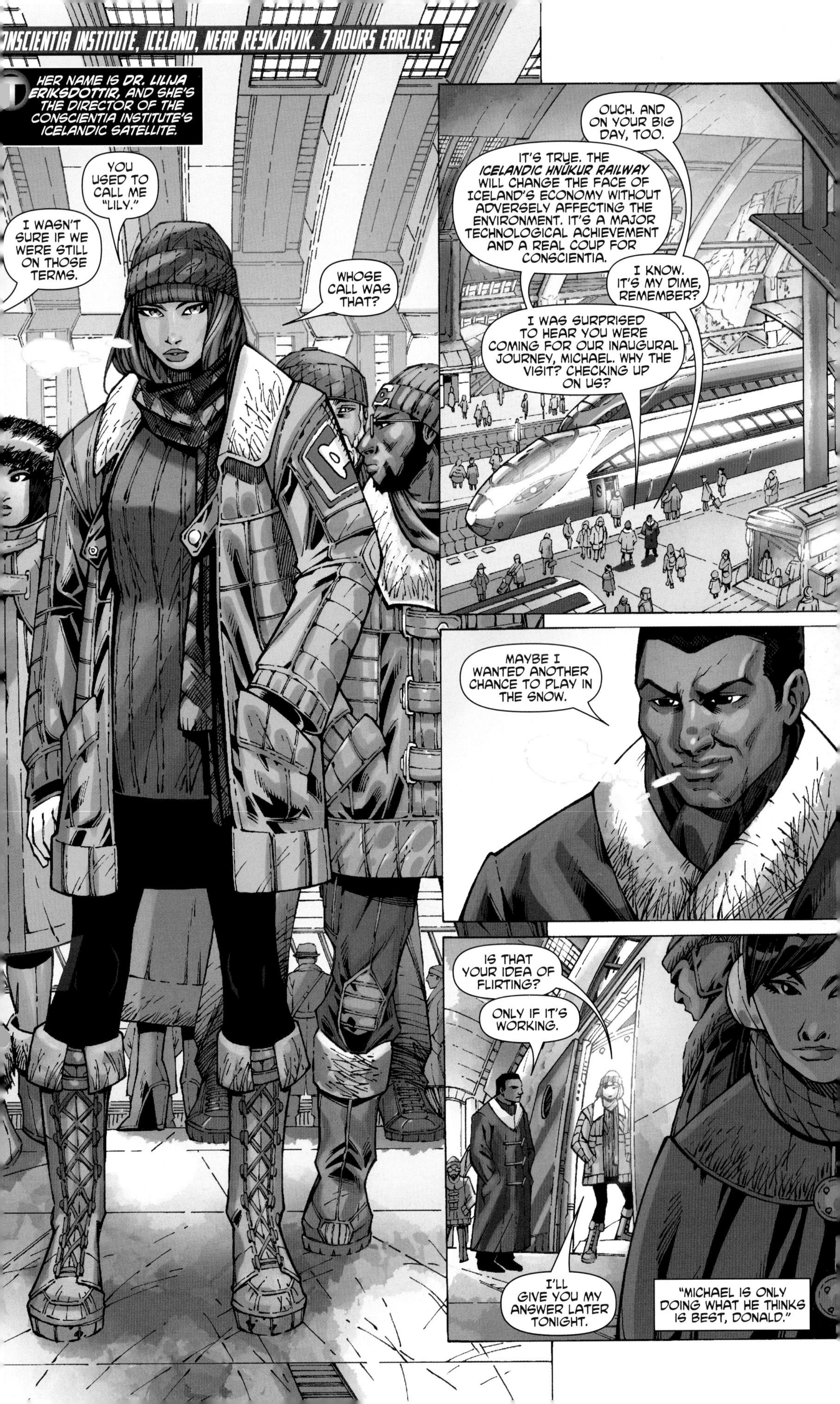
CONSCIENTIA INSTITUTE, ICELAND, NEAR REYKJAVIK. 7 HOURS EARLIER.
HER NAME IS DR. LILIJA ERIKSDOTTIR, AND SHE'S THE DIRECTOR OF THE CONSCIENTIA INSTITUTE'S ICELANDIC SATELLITE.
I WASN'T SURE IF WE WERE STILL ON THOSE TERMS.
YOU USED TO CALL ME "LILY."
WHOSE CALL WAS THAT?
OUCH. AND ON YOUR BIG DAY, TOO.
IT'S TRUE. THE ICELANDIC HNÚKUR RAILWAY WILL CHANGE THE FACE OF ICELAND'S ECONOMY WITHOUT ADVERSELY AFFECTING THE ENVIRONMENT. IT'S A MAJOR TECHNOLOGICAL ACHIEVEMENT AND A REAL COUP FOR CONSCIENTIA.
I KNOW. IT'S MY DIME, REMEMBER?
I WAS SURPRISED TO HEAR YOU WERE COMING FOR OUR INAUGURAL JOURNEY, MICHAEL. WHY THE VISIT? CHECKING UP ON US?
MAYBE I WANTED ANOTHER CHANCE TO PLAY IN THE SNOW.
IS THAT YOUR IDEA OF FLIRTING?
ONLY IF IT'S WORKING.
I'LL GIVE YOU MY ANSWER LATER TONIGHT.
"MICHAEL IS ONLY DOING WHAT HE THINKS IS BEST, DONALD."

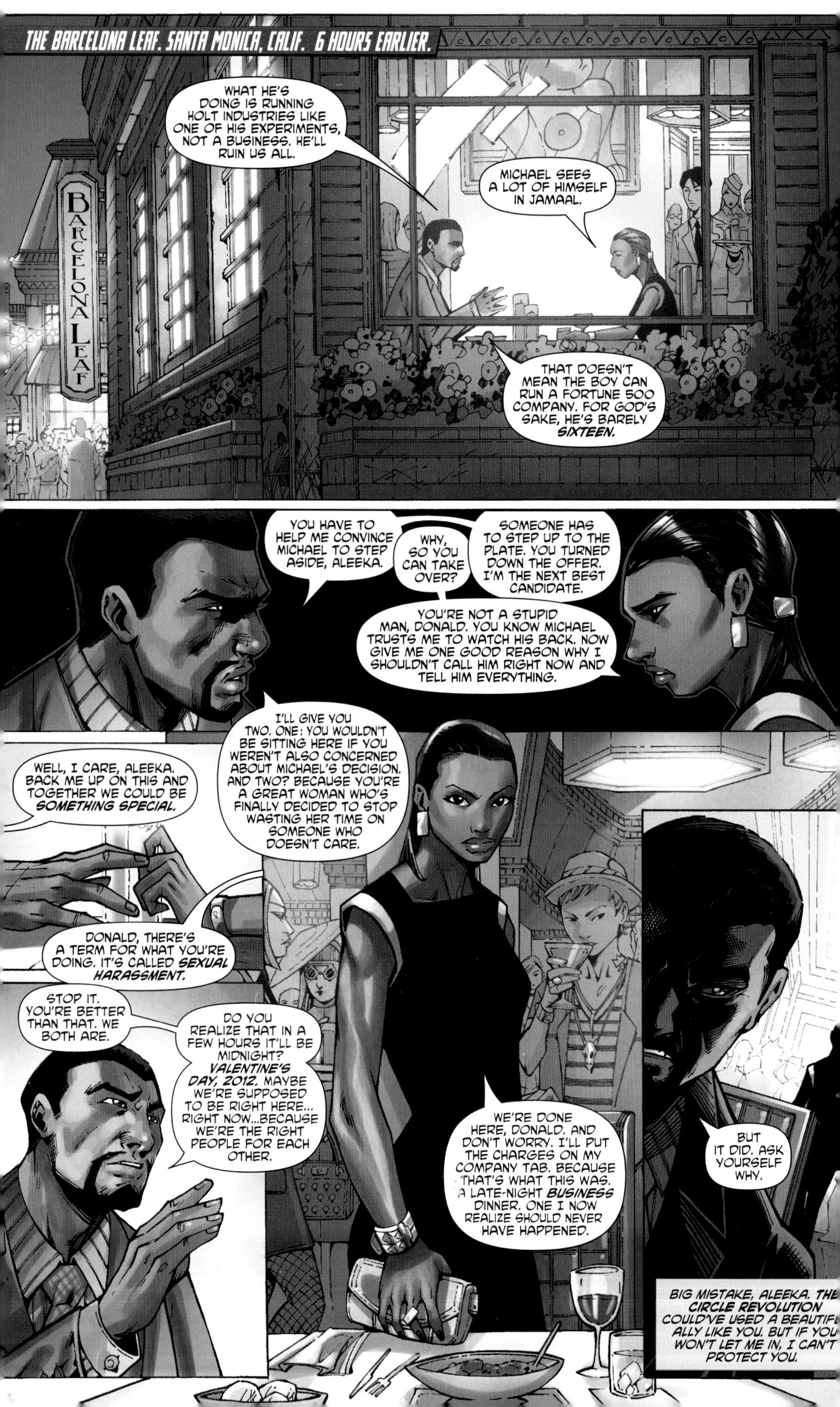
THE BARCELONA LEAF. SANTA MONICA, CALIF. 6 HOURS EARLIER.
BARCELONA LEAF
WHAT HE'S DOING IS RUNNING HOLT INDUSTRIES LIKE ONE OF HIS EXPERIMENTS, NOT A BUSINESS. HE'LL RUIN US ALL.
MICHAEL SEES A LOT OF HIMSELF IN JAMAAL.
THAT DOESN'T MEAN THE BOY CAN RUN A FORTUNE 500 COMPANY. FOR GOD'S SAKE, HE'S BARELY *SIXTEEN.*
YOU HAVE TO HELP ME CONVINCE MICHAEL TO STEP ASIDE, ALEEKA.
WHY, SO YOU CAN TAKE OVER?
SOMEONE HAS TO STEP UP TO THE PLATE. YOU TURNED DOWN THE OFFER. I'M THE NEXT BEST CANDIDATE.
YOU'RE NOT A STUPID MAN, DONALD. YOU KNOW MICHAEL TRUSTS ME TO WATCH HIS BACK. NOW GIVE ME ONE GOOD REASON WHY I SHOULDN'T CALL HIM RIGHT NOW AND TELL HIM EVERYTHING.
I'LL GIVE YOU TWO. ONE: YOU WOULDN'T BE SITTING HERE IF YOU WEREN'T ALSO CONCERNED ABOUT MICHAEL'S DECISION. AND TWO? BECAUSE YOU'RE A GREAT WOMAN WHO'S FINALLY DECIDED TO STOP WASTING HER TIME ON SOMEONE WHO DOESN'T CARE.
WELL, I CARE, ALEEKA. BACK ME UP ON THIS AND TOGETHER WE COULD BE *SOMETHING SPECIAL.*
DONALD, THERE'S A TERM FOR WHAT YOU'RE DOING. IT'S CALLED *SEXUAL HARASSMENT.*
STOP IT. YOU'RE BETTER THAN THAT. WE BOTH ARE.
DO YOU REALIZE THAT IN A FEW HOURS IT'LL BE MIDNIGHT? *VALENTINE'S DAY, 2012.* MAYBE WE'RE SUPPOSED TO BE RIGHT HERE... RIGHT NOW...BECAUSE WE'RE THE RIGHT PEOPLE FOR EACH OTHER.
WE'RE DONE HERE, DONALD. AND DON'T WORRY. I'LL PUT THE CHARGES ON MY COMPANY TAB. BECAUSE THAT'S WHAT THIS WAS. A LATE-NIGHT *BUSINESS* DINNER. ONE I NOW REALIZE SHOULD NEVER HAVE HAPPENED.
BUT IT DID. ASK YOURSELF WHY.
BIG MISTAKE, ALEEKA. THE *CIRCLE REVOLUTION* COULD'VE USED A BEAUTIF ALLY LIKE YOU. BUT IF YOU WON'T LET ME IN, I CAN'T PROTECT YOU.

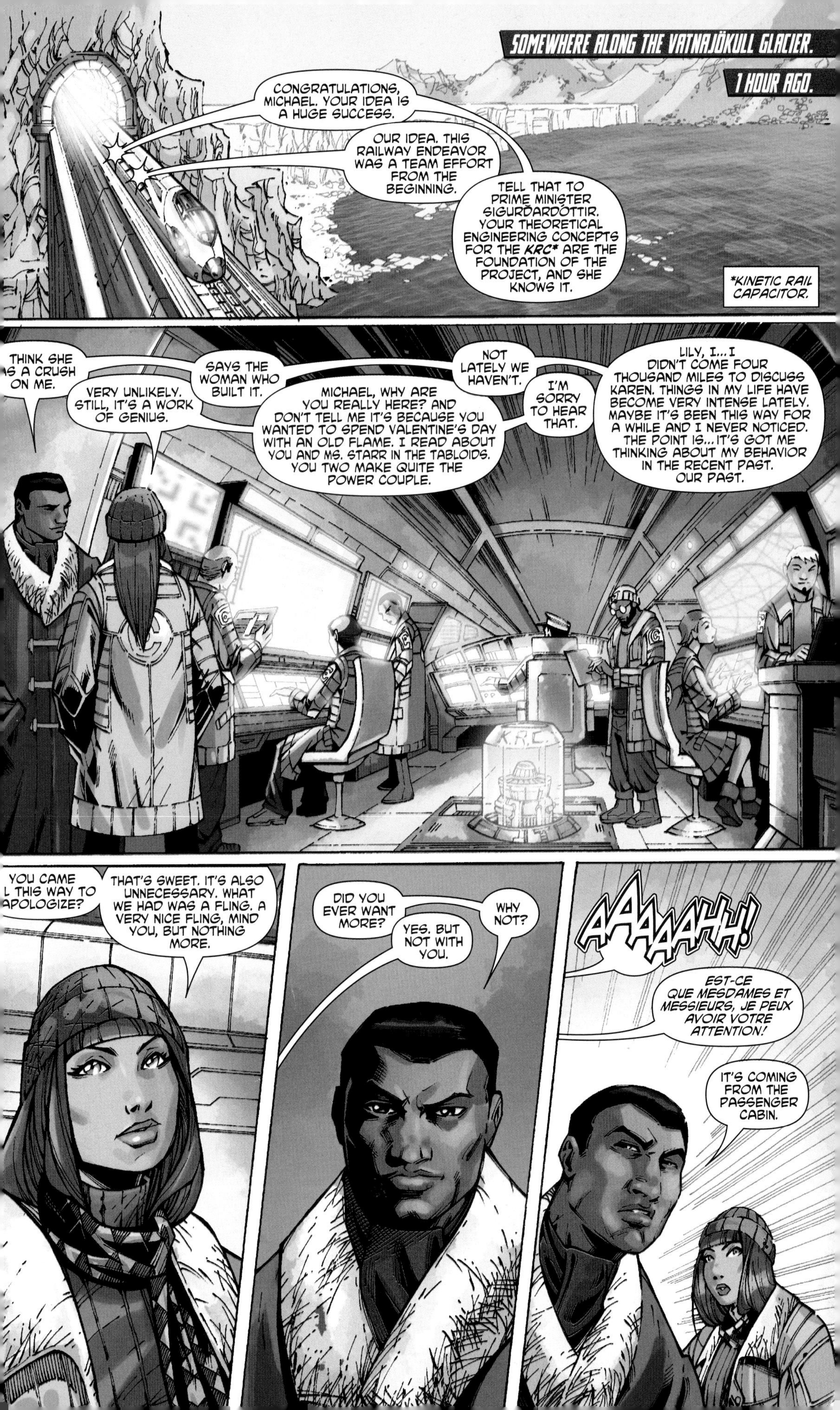
SOMEWHERE ALONG THE VATNAJÖKULL GLACIER.
1 HOUR AGO.
CONGRATULATIONS, MICHAEL. YOUR IDEA IS A HUGE SUCCESS.
OUR IDEA. THIS RAILWAY ENDEAVOR WAS A TEAM EFFORT FROM THE BEGINNING.
TELL THAT TO PRIME MINISTER SIGURÐARDÓTTIR. YOUR THEORETICAL ENGINEERING CONCEPTS FOR THE KRC* ARE THE FOUNDATION OF THE PROJECT, AND SHE KNOWS IT.
*KINETIC RAIL CAPACITOR.
THINK SHE AS A CRUSH ON ME.
VERY UNLIKELY. STILL, IT'S A WORK OF GENIUS.
SAYS THE WOMAN WHO BUILT IT.
MICHAEL, WHY ARE YOU REALLY HERE? AND DON'T TELL ME IT'S BECAUSE YOU WANTED TO SPEND VALENTINE'S DAY WITH AN OLD FLAME. I READ ABOUT YOU AND MS. STARR IN THE TABLOIDS. YOU TWO MAKE QUITE THE POWER COUPLE.
NOT LATELY WE HAVEN'T.
I'M SORRY TO HEAR THAT.
LILY, I... I DIDN'T COME FOUR THOUSAND MILES TO DISCUSS KAREN. THINGS IN MY LIFE HAVE BECOME VERY INTENSE LATELY. MAYBE IT'S BEEN THIS WAY FOR A WHILE AND I NEVER NOTICED. THE POINT IS... IT'S GOT ME THINKING ABOUT MY BEHAVIOR IN THE RECENT PAST. OUR PAST.
K.R.C.
YOU CAME L THIS WAY TO APOLOGIZE?
THAT'S SWEET. IT'S ALSO UNNECESSARY. WHAT WE HAD WAS A FLING. A VERY NICE FLING, MIND YOU, BUT NOTHING MORE.
DID YOU EVER WANT MORE?
YES. BUT NOT WITH YOU.
WHY NOT?
AAAAAHH!
EST-CE QUE MESDAMES ET MESSIEURS, JE PEUX AVOIR VOTRE ATTENTION!
IT'S COMING FROM THE PASSENGER CABIN.

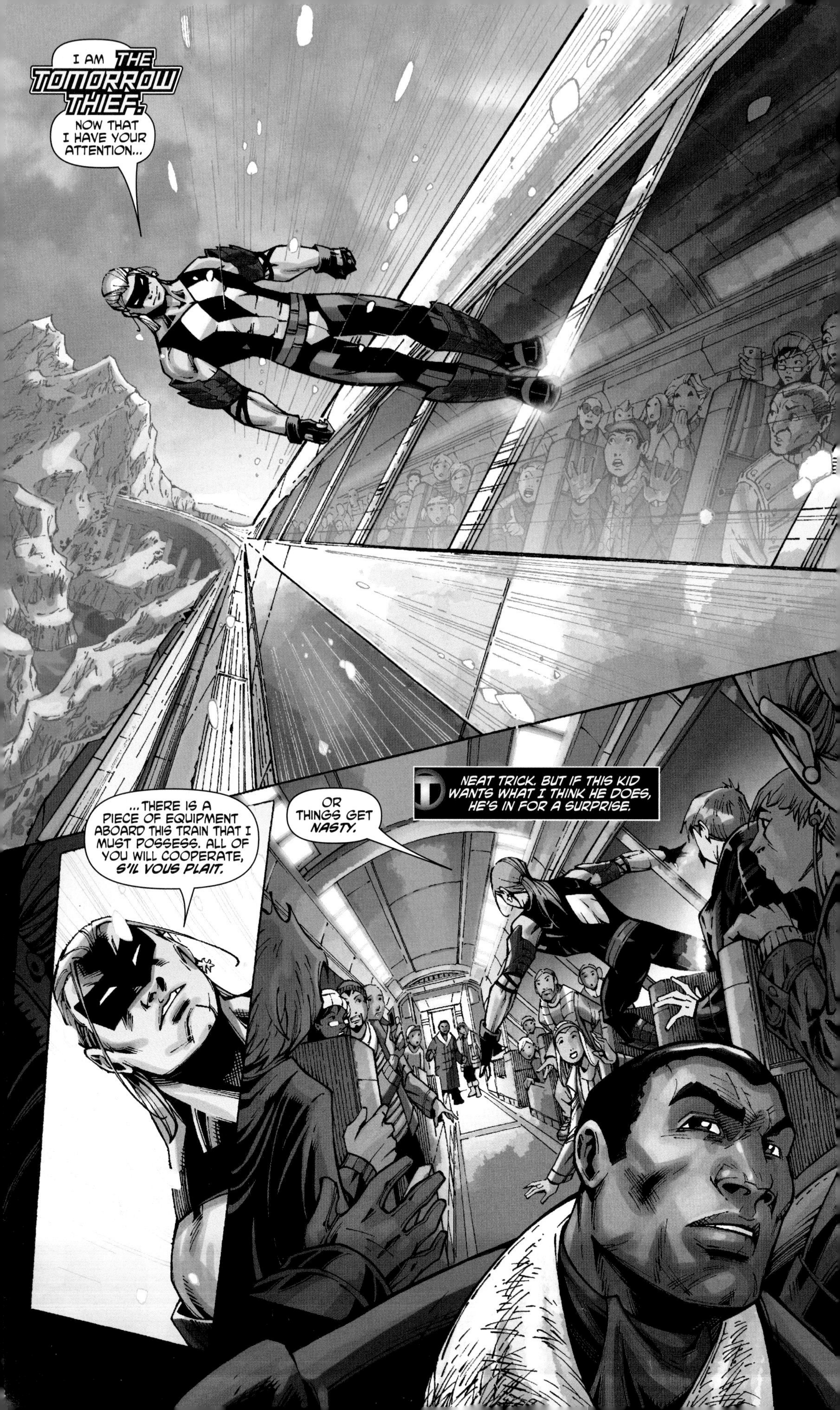
I AM THE TOMORROW THIEF.
NOW THAT I HAVE YOUR ATTENTION...
NEAT TRICK. BUT IF THIS KID WANTS WHAT I THINK HE DOES, HE'S IN FOR A SURPRISE.
...THERE IS A PIECE OF EQUIPMENT ABOARD THIS TRAIN THAT I MUST POSSESS. ALL OF YOU WILL COOPERATE, S'IL VOUS PLAIT.
OR THINGS GET NASTY.

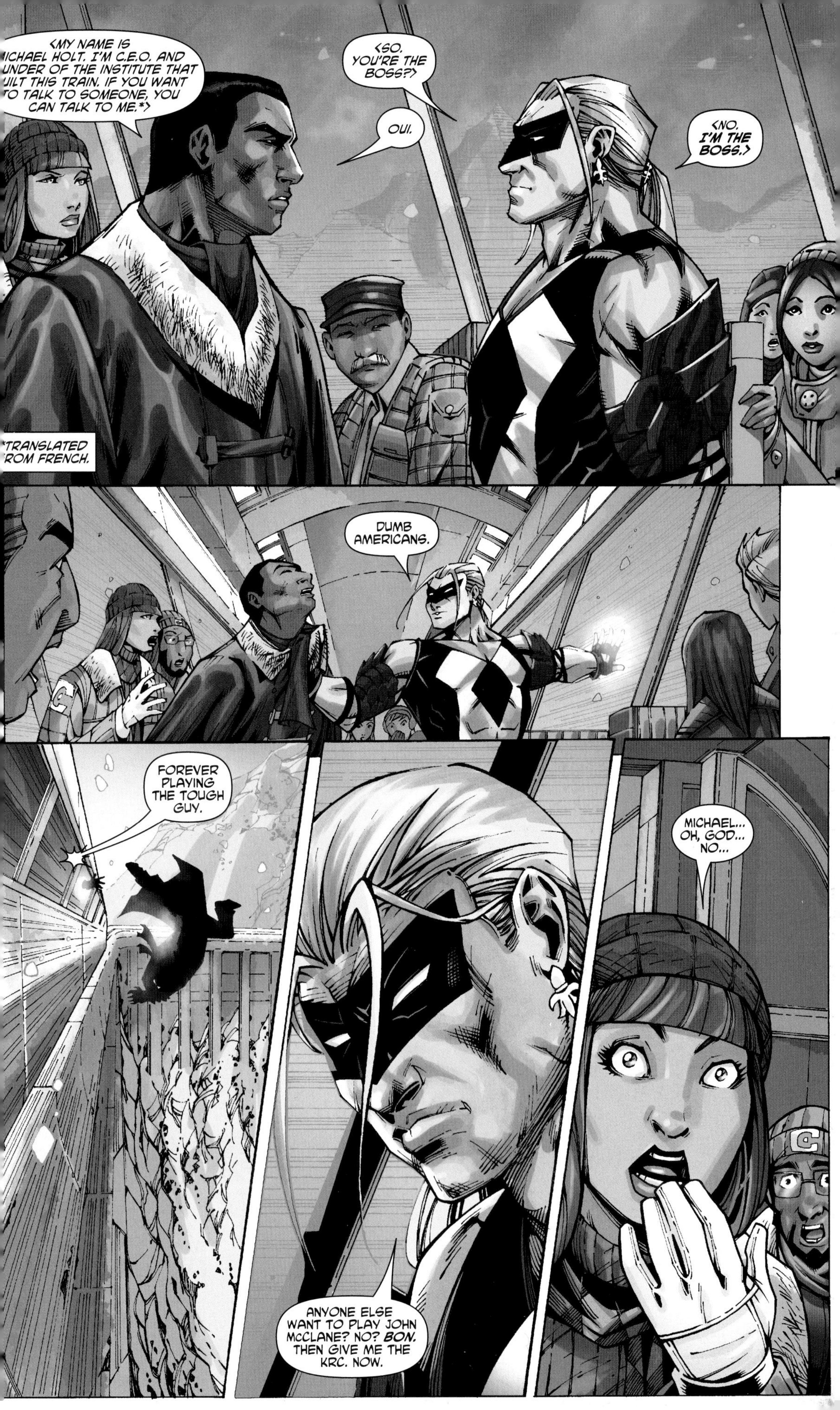
<MY NAME IS MICHAEL HOLT. I'M C.E.O. AND FOUNDER OF THE INSTITUTE THAT BUILT THIS TRAIN. IF YOU WANT TO TALK TO SOMEONE, YOU CAN TALK TO ME.*>
*TRANSLATED FROM FRENCH.
<SO, YOU'RE THE BOSS?>
OUI.
<NO, I'M THE BOSS.>
DUMB AMERICANS.
FOREVER PLAYING THE TOUGH GUY.
MICHAEL... OH, GOD... NO...
ANYONE ELSE WANT TO PLAY JOHN McCLANE? NO? BON. THEN GIVE ME THE KRC. NOW.

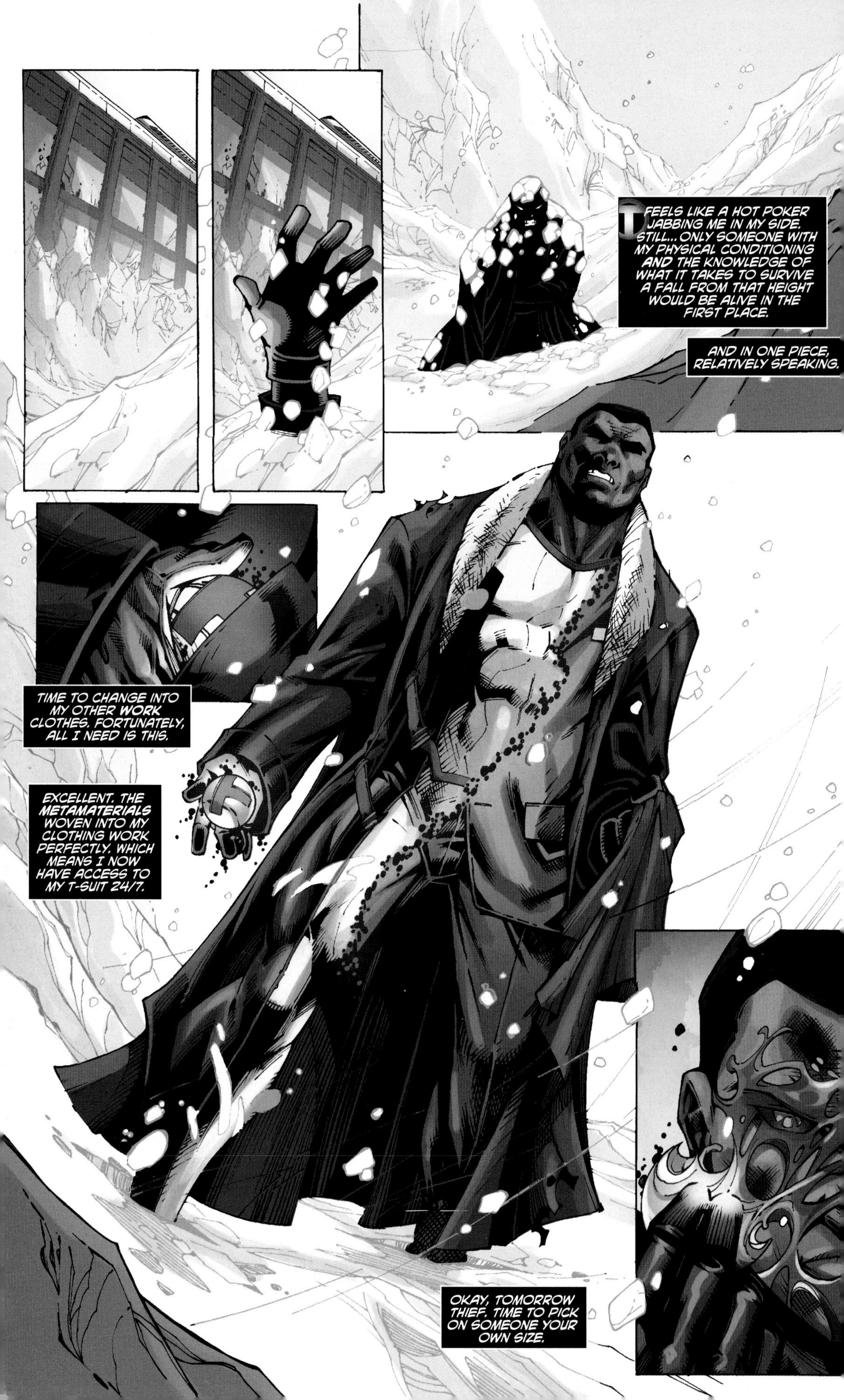
IT FEELS LIKE A HOT POKER JABBING ME IN MY SIDE. STILL...ONLY SOMEONE WITH MY PHYSICAL CONDITIONING AND THE KNOWLEDGE OF WHAT IT TAKES TO SURVIVE A FALL FROM THAT HEIGHT WOULD BE ALIVE IN THE FIRST PLACE.
AND IN ONE PIECE, RELATIVELY SPEAKING.
TIME TO CHANGE INTO MY OTHER WORK CLOTHES. FORTUNATELY, ALL I NEED IS THIS.
EXCELLENT. THE METAMATERIALS WOVEN INTO MY CLOTHING WORK PERFECTLY. WHICH MEANS I NOW HAVE ACCESS TO MY T-SUIT 24/7.
OKAY, TOMORROW THIEF. TIME TO PICK ON SOMEONE YOUR OWN SIZE.

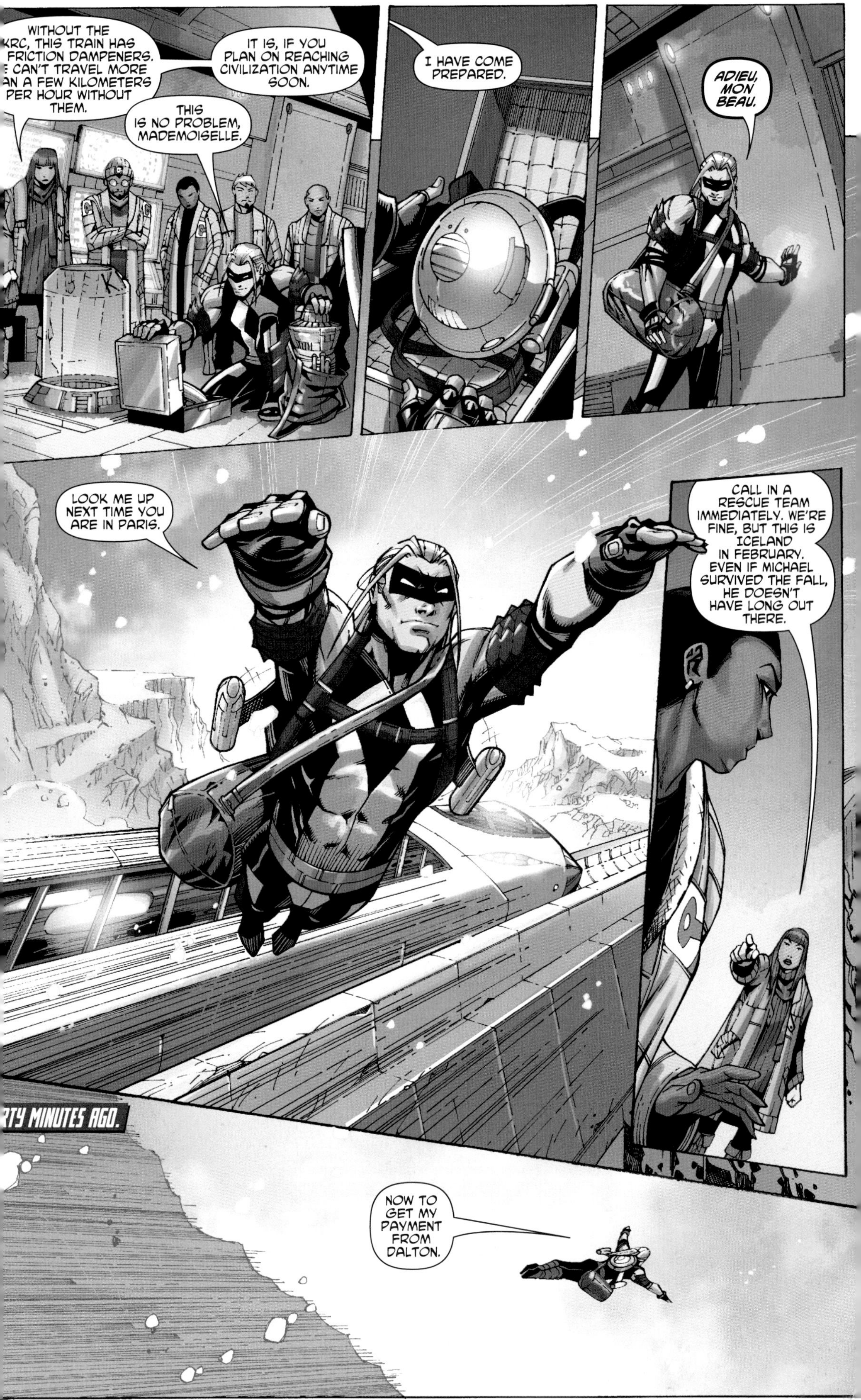
WITHOUT THE KRC, THIS TRAIN HAS FRICTION DAMPENERS. E CAN'T TRAVEL MORE AN A FEW KILOMETERS PER HOUR WITHOUT THEM.
THIS IS NO PROBLEM, MADEMOISELLE.
IT IS, IF YOU PLAN ON REACHING CIVILIZATION ANYTIME SOON.
I HAVE COME PREPARED.
ADIEU, MON BEAU.
LOOK ME UP NEXT TIME YOU ARE IN PARIS.
CALL IN A RESCUE TEAM IMMEDIATELY. WE'RE FINE, BUT THIS IS ICELAND IN FEBRUARY. EVEN IF MICHAEL SURVIVED THE FALL, HE DOESN'T HAVE LONG OUT THERE.
RTY MINUTES AGO.
NOW TO GET MY PAYMENT FROM DALTON.

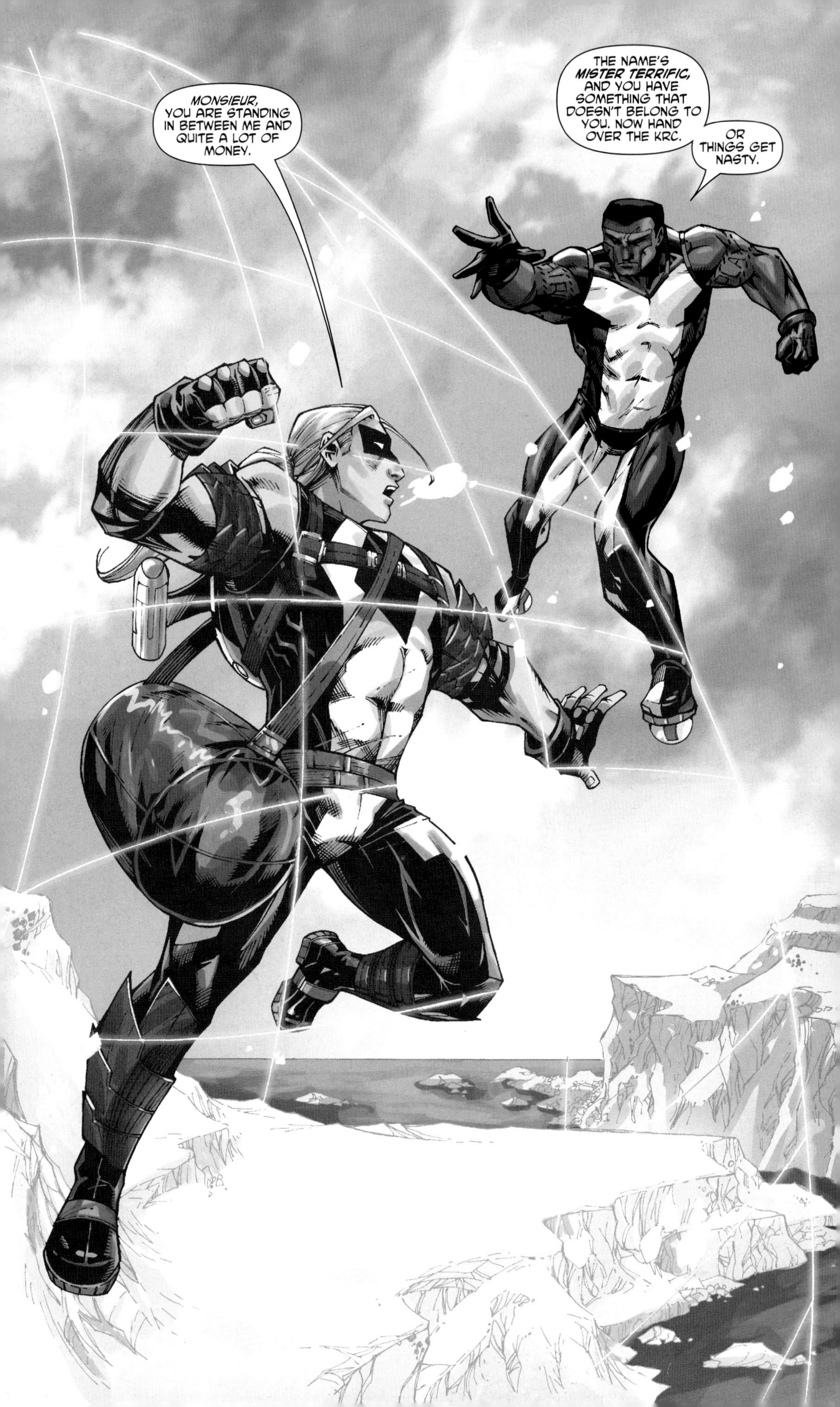
MONSIEUR, YOU ARE STANDING IN BETWEEN ME AND QUITE A LOT OF MONEY.
THE NAME'S MISTER TERRIFIC, AND YOU HAVE SOMETHING THAT DOESN'T BELONG TO YOU. NOW HAND OVER THE KRC.
OR THINGS GET NASTY.

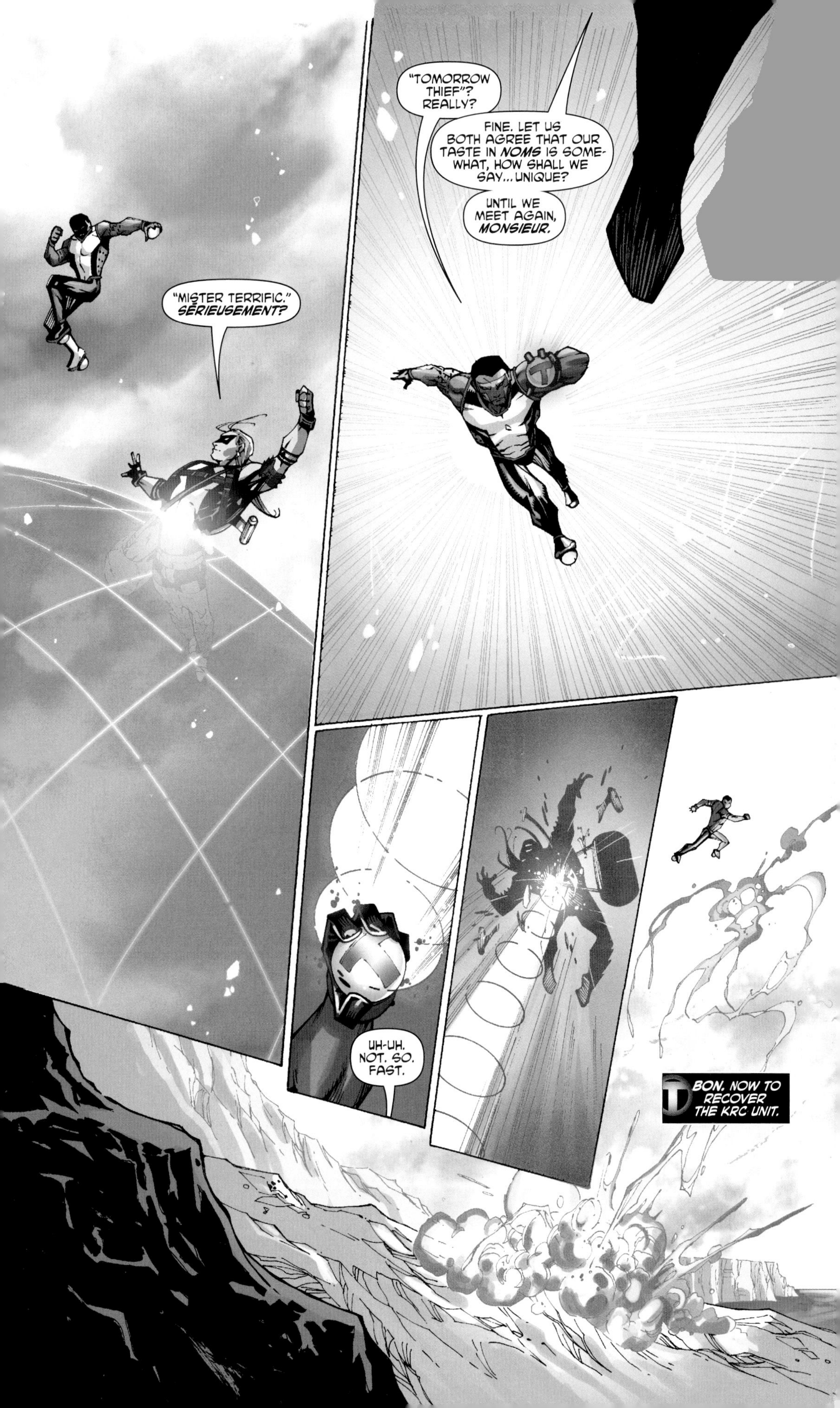
"MISTER TERRIFIC." SÉRIEUSEMENT?
"TOMORROW THIEF"? REALLY?
FINE. LET US BOTH AGREE THAT OUR TASTE IN NOMS IS SOMEWHAT, HOW SHALL WE SAY... UNIQUE?
UNTIL WE MEET AGAIN, MONSIEUR.
UH-UH. NOT. SO. FAST.
BON. NOW TO RECOVER THE KRC UNIT.

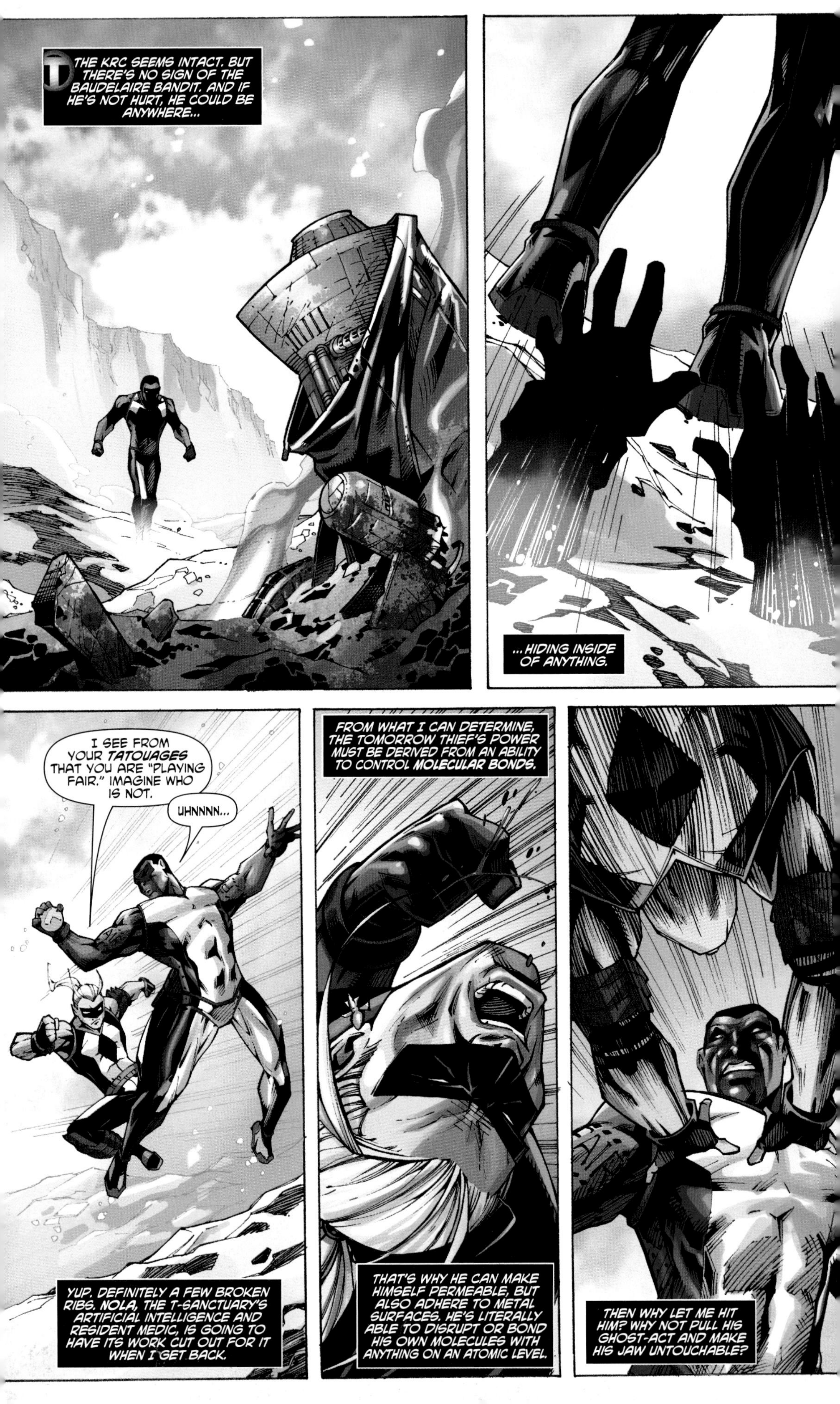
THE KRC SEEMS INTACT. BUT THERE'S NO SIGN OF THE BAUDELAIRE BANDIT. AND IF HE'S NOT HURT, HE COULD BE ANYWHERE...
...HIDING INSIDE OF ANYTHING.
I SEE FROM YOUR TATOUAGES THAT YOU ARE "PLAYING FAIR." IMAGINE WHO IS NOT.
UHNNNN...
YUP. DEFINITELY A FEW BROKEN RIBS. NOLA, THE T-SANCTUARY'S ARTIFICIAL INTELLIGENCE AND RESIDENT MEDIC, IS GOING TO HAVE ITS WORK CUT OUT FOR IT WHEN I GET BACK.
FROM WHAT I CAN DETERMINE, THE TOMORROW THIEF'S POWER MUST BE DERIVED FROM AN ABILITY TO CONTROL MOLECULAR BONDS.
THAT'S WHY HE CAN MAKE HIMSELF PERMEABLE, BUT ALSO ADHERE TO METAL SURFACES. HE'S LITERALLY ABLE TO DISRUPT OR BOND HIS OWN MOLECULES WITH ANYTHING ON AN ATOMIC LEVEL.
THEN WHY LET ME HIT HIM? WHY NOT PULL HIS GHOST-ACT AND MAKE HIS JAW UNTOUCHABLE?

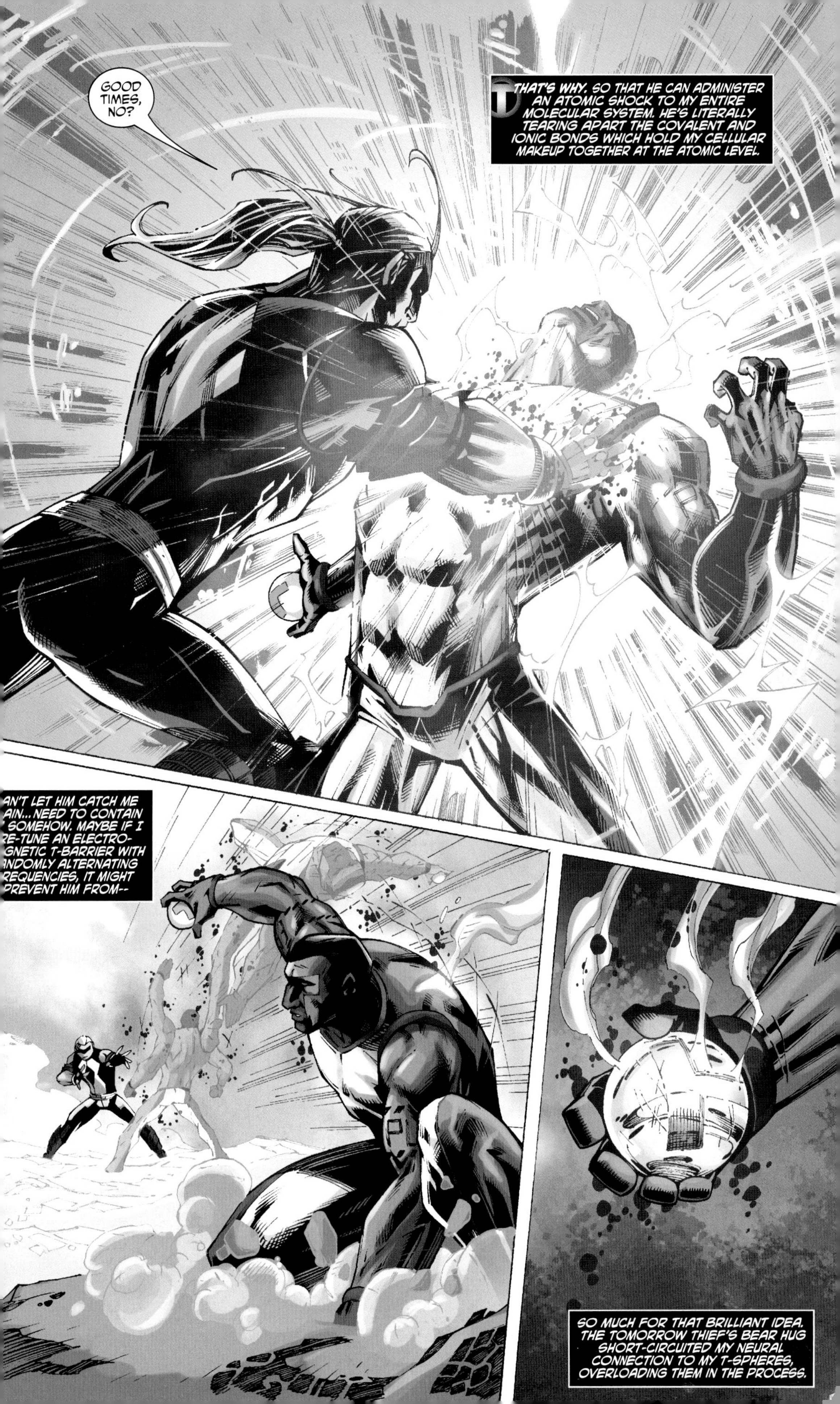
GOOD TIMES, NO?
THAT'S WHY. SO THAT HE CAN ADMINISTER AN ATOMIC SHOCK TO MY ENTIRE MOLECULAR SYSTEM. HE'S LITERALLY TEARING APART THE COVALENT AND IONIC BONDS WHICH HOLD MY CELLULAR MAKEUP TOGETHER AT THE ATOMIC LEVEL.
AN'T LET HIM CATCH ME AIN... NEED TO CONTAIN SOMEHOW. MAYBE IF I RE-TUNE AN ELECTRO-GNETIC T-BARRIER WITH NDOMLY ALTERNATING REQUENCIES, IT MIGHT PREVENT HIM FROM--
SO MUCH FOR THAT BRILLIANT IDEA. THE TOMORROW THIEF'S BEAR HUG SHORT-CIRCUITED MY NEURAL CONNECTION TO MY T-SPHERES, OVERLOADING THEM IN THE PROCESS.

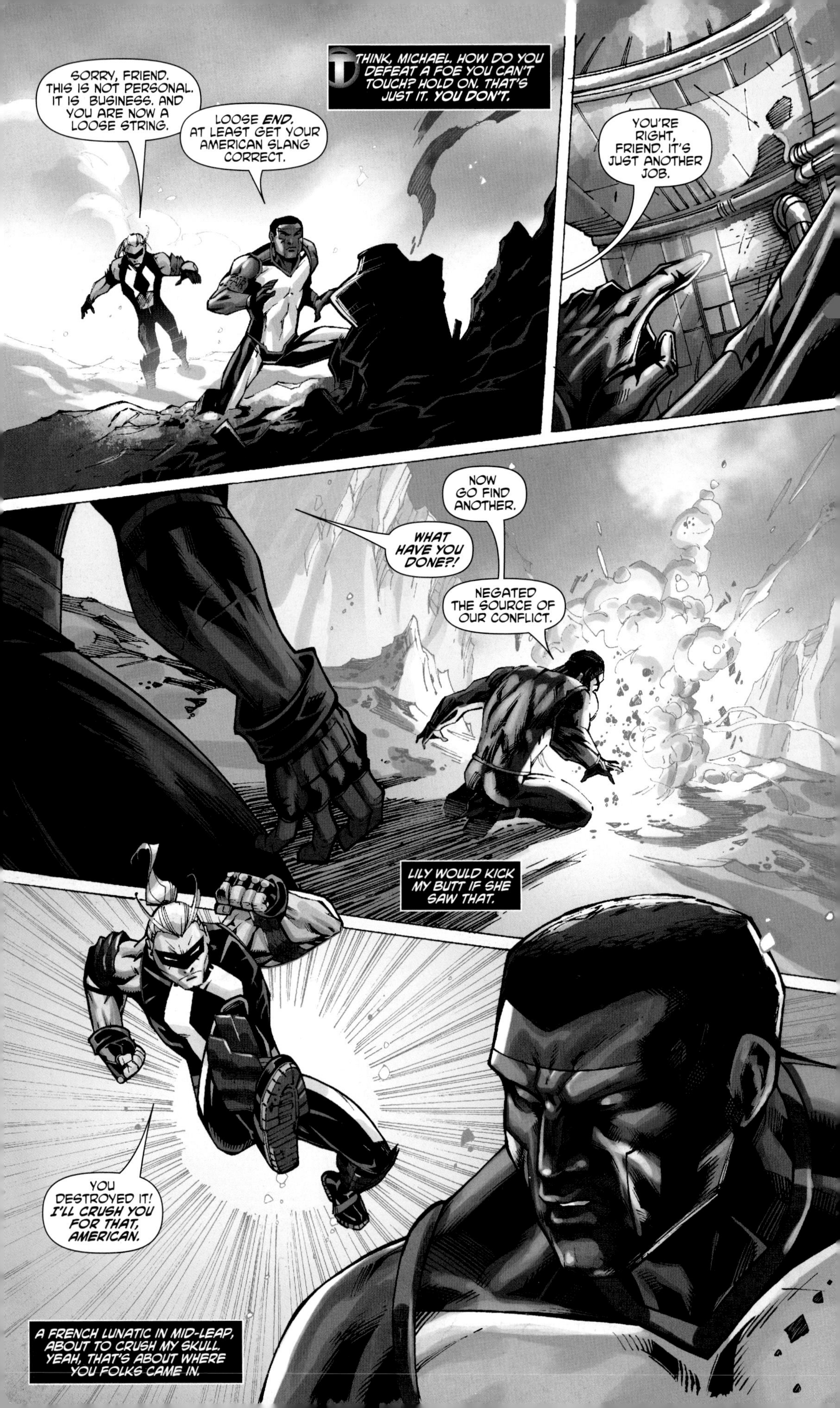

SORRY, FRIEND. THIS IS NOT PERSONAL. IT IS BUSINESS. AND YOU ARE NOW A LOOSE STRING.
LOOSE *END.* AT LEAST GET YOUR AMERICAN SLANG CORRECT.
THINK, MICHAEL. HOW DO YOU DEFEAT A FOE YOU CAN'T TOUCH? HOLD ON. THAT'S JUST IT. *YOU DON'T.*
YOU'RE RIGHT, FRIEND. IT'S JUST ANOTHER JOB.
NOW GO FIND ANOTHER.
WHAT HAVE YOU DONE?!
NEGATED THE SOURCE OF OUR CONFLICT.
LILY WOULD KICK MY BUTT IF SHE SAW THAT.
YOU DESTROYED IT! *I'LL CRUSH YOU FOR THAT, AMERICAN.*
A FRENCH LUNATIC IN MID-LEAP, ABOUT TO CRUSH MY SKULL. YEAH, THAT'S ABOUT WHERE YOU FOLKS CAME IN.

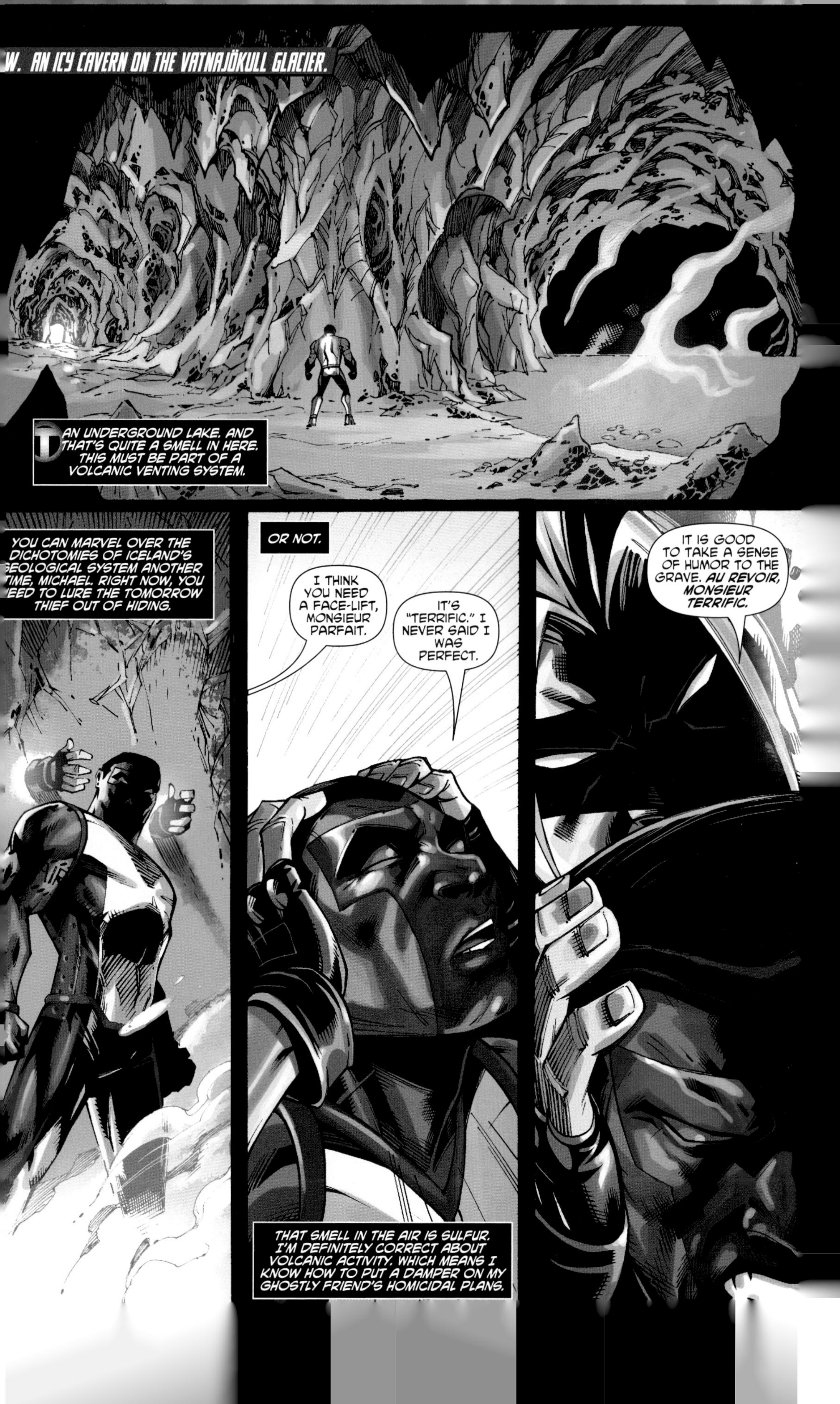
W. AN ICY CAVERN ON THE VATNAJÖKULL GLACIER.
AN UNDERGROUND LAKE. AND THAT'S QUITE A SMELL IN HERE. THIS MUST BE PART OF A VOLCANIC VENTING SYSTEM.
YOU CAN MARVEL OVER THE DICHOTOMIES OF ICELAND'S GEOLOGICAL SYSTEM ANOTHER TIME, MICHAEL. RIGHT NOW, YOU NEED TO LURE THE TOMORROW THIEF OUT OF HIDING.
OR NOT.
I THINK YOU NEED A FACE-LIFT, MONSIEUR PARFAIT.
IT'S "TERRIFIC." I NEVER SAID I WAS PERFECT.
THAT SMELL IN THE AIR IS SULFUR. I'M DEFINITELY CORRECT ABOUT VOLCANIC ACTIVITY. WHICH MEANS I KNOW HOW TO PUT A DAMPER ON MY GHOSTLY FRIEND'S HOMICIDAL PLANS.
IT IS GOOD TO TAKE A SENSE OF HUMOR TO THE GRAVE. AU REVOIR, MONSIEUR TERRIFIC.

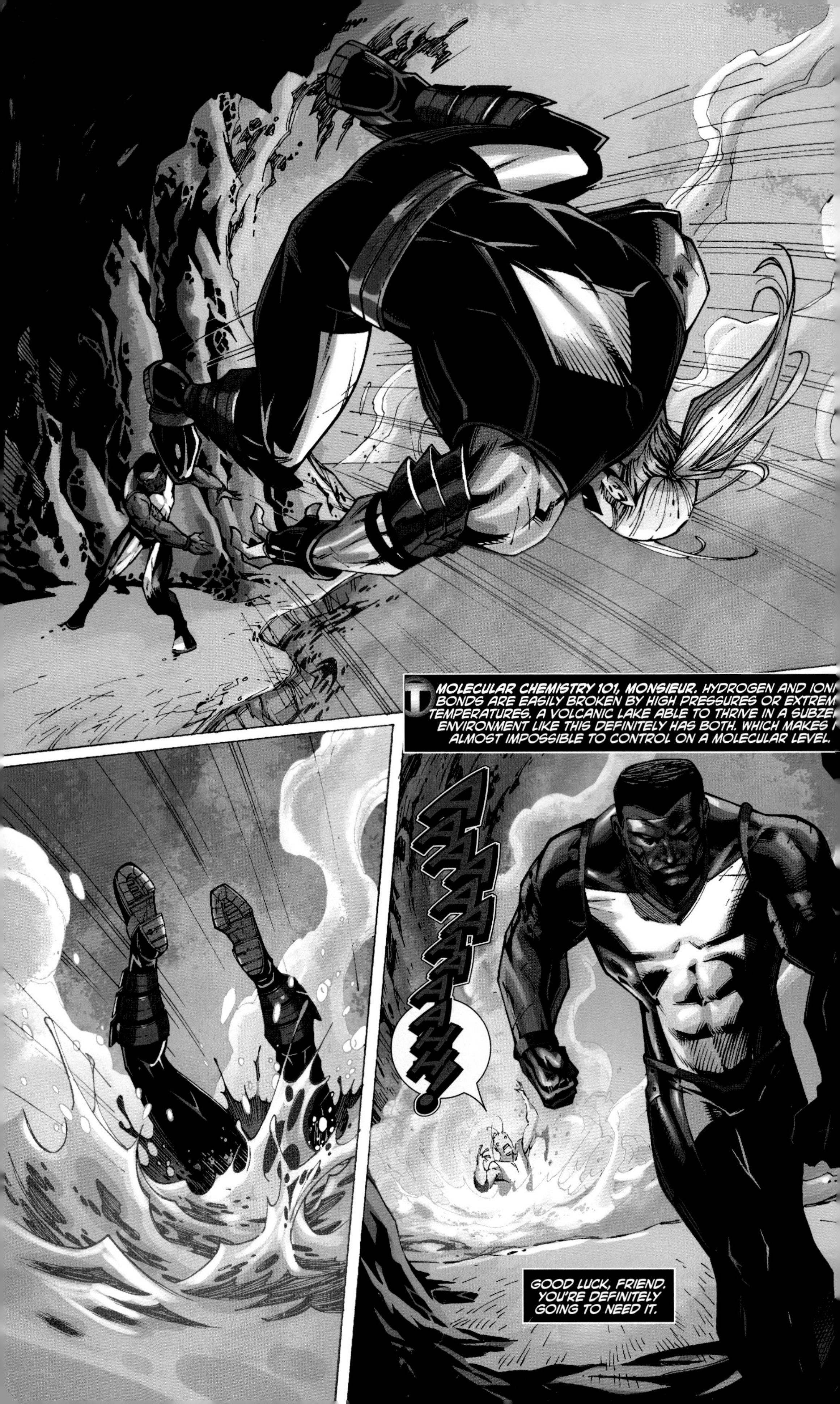
MOLECULAR CHEMISTRY 101, MONSIEUR. HYDROGEN AND IONI
BONDS ARE EASILY BROKEN BY HIGH PRESSURES OR EXTREM
TEMPERATURES. A VOLCANIC LAKE ABLE TO THRIVE IN A SUBZE
ENVIRONMENT LIKE THIS DEFINITELY HAS BOTH. WHICH MAKES I
ALMOST IMPOSSIBLE TO CONTROL ON A MOLECULAR LEVEL.
AAAAAAAAHH!
GOOD LUCK, FRIEND. YOU'RE DEFINITELY GOING TO NEED IT.

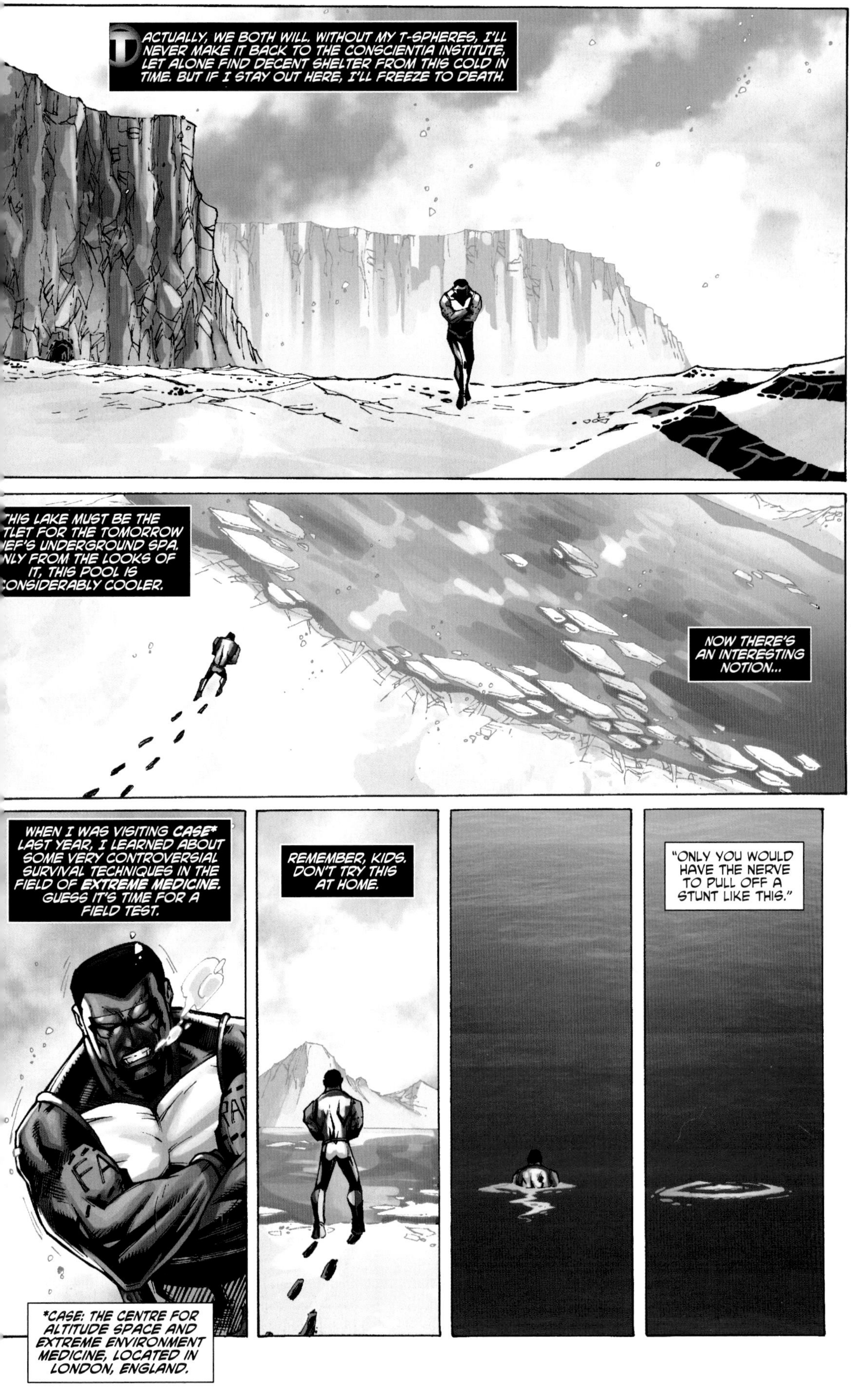
ACTUALLY, WE BOTH WILL. WITHOUT MY T-SPHERES, I'LL NEVER MAKE IT BACK TO THE CONSCIENTIA INSTITUTE, LET ALONE FIND DECENT SHELTER FROM THIS COLD IN TIME. BUT IF I STAY OUT HERE, I'LL FREEZE TO DEATH.
THIS LAKE MUST BE THE TLET FOR THE TOMORROW IEF'S UNDERGROUND SPA. NLY FROM THE LOOKS OF IT, THIS POOL IS CONSIDERABLY COOLER.
NOW THERE'S AN INTERESTING NOTION...
WHEN I WAS VISITING CASE* LAST YEAR, I LEARNED ABOUT SOME VERY CONTROVERSIAL SURVIVAL TECHNIQUES IN THE FIELD OF EXTREME MEDICINE. GUESS IT'S TIME FOR A FIELD TEST.
*CASE: THE CENTRE FOR ALTITUDE SPACE AND EXTREME ENVIRONMENT MEDICINE, LOCATED IN LONDON, ENGLAND.
REMEMBER, KIDS. DON'T TRY THIS AT HOME.
"ONLY YOU WOULD HAVE THE NERVE TO PULL OFF A STUNT LIKE THIS."

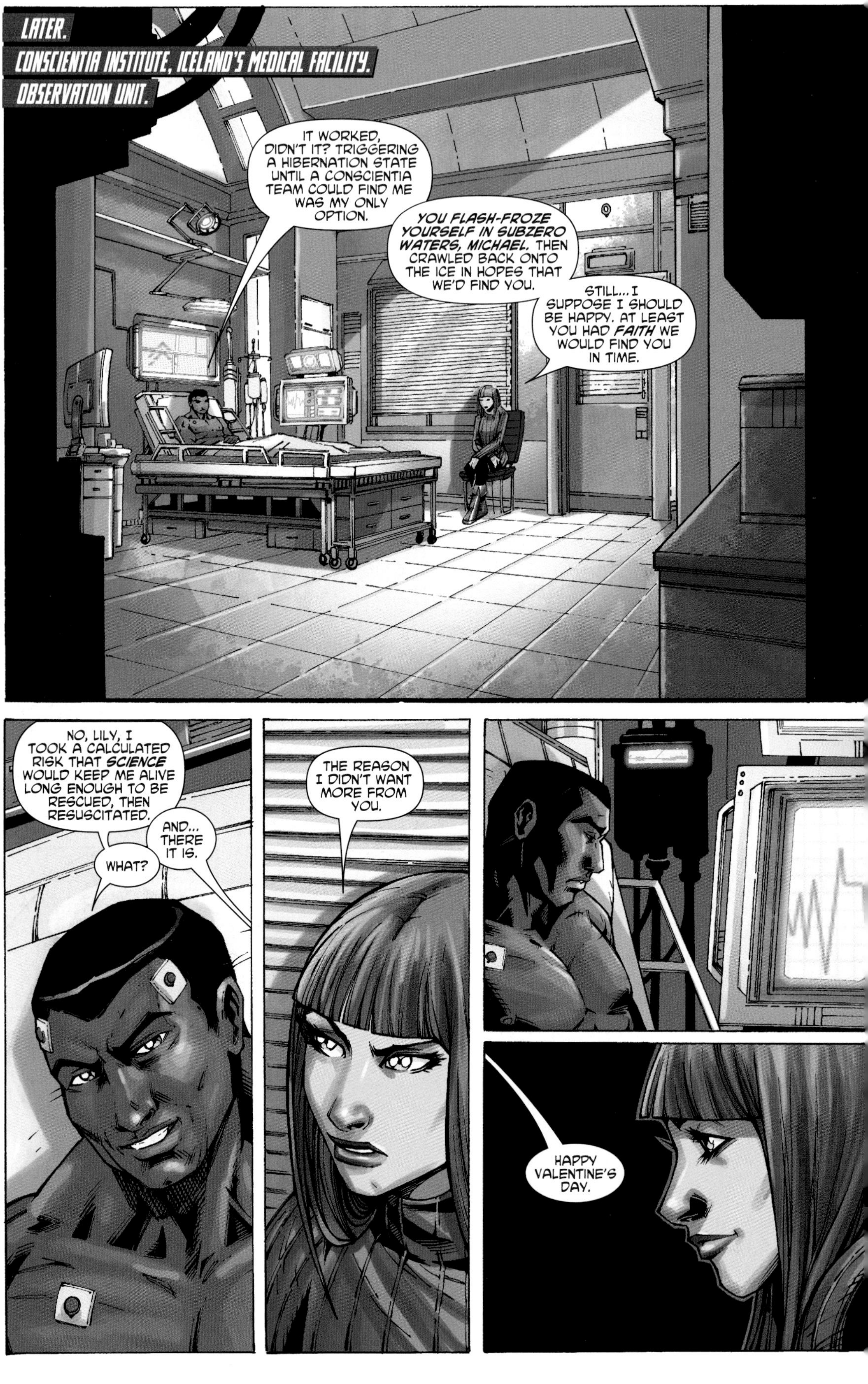
LATER.
CONSCIENTIA INSTITUTE, ICELAND'S MEDICAL FACILITY.
OBSERVATION UNIT.
IT WORKED, DIDN'T IT? TRIGGERING A HIBERNATION STATE UNTIL A CONSCIENTIA TEAM COULD FIND ME WAS MY ONLY OPTION.
YOU FLASH-FROZE YOURSELF IN SUBZERO WATERS, MICHAEL. THEN CRAWLED BACK ONTO THE ICE IN HOPES THAT WE'D FIND YOU.
STILL... I SUPPOSE I SHOULD BE HAPPY. AT LEAST YOU HAD FAITH WE WOULD FIND YOU IN TIME.
NO, LILY, I TOOK A CALCULATED RISK THAT SCIENCE WOULD KEEP ME ALIVE LONG ENOUGH TO BE RESCUED, THEN RESUSCITATED.
WHAT?
AND... THERE IT IS.
THE REASON I DIDN'T WANT MORE FROM YOU.
HAPPY VALENTINE'S DAY.

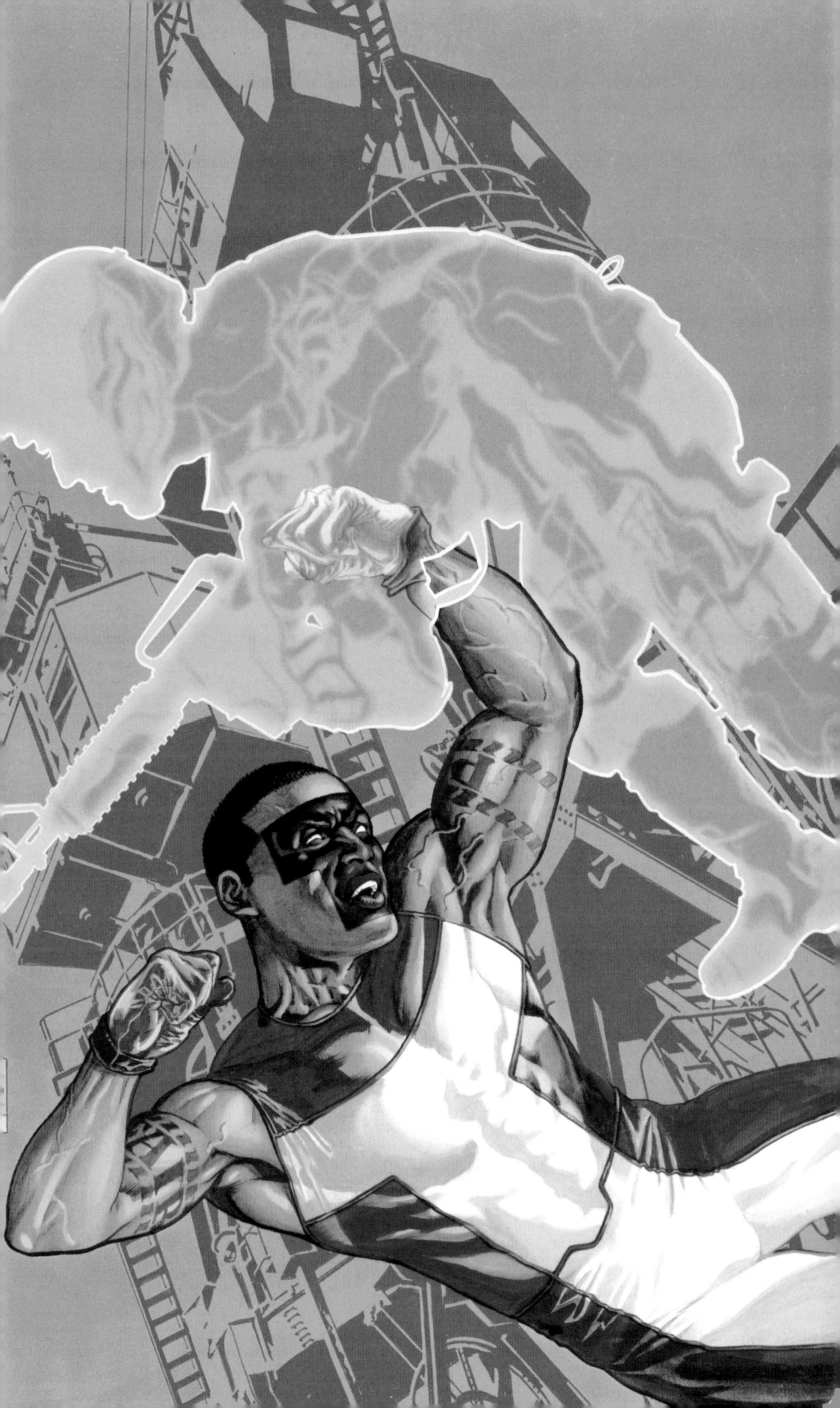

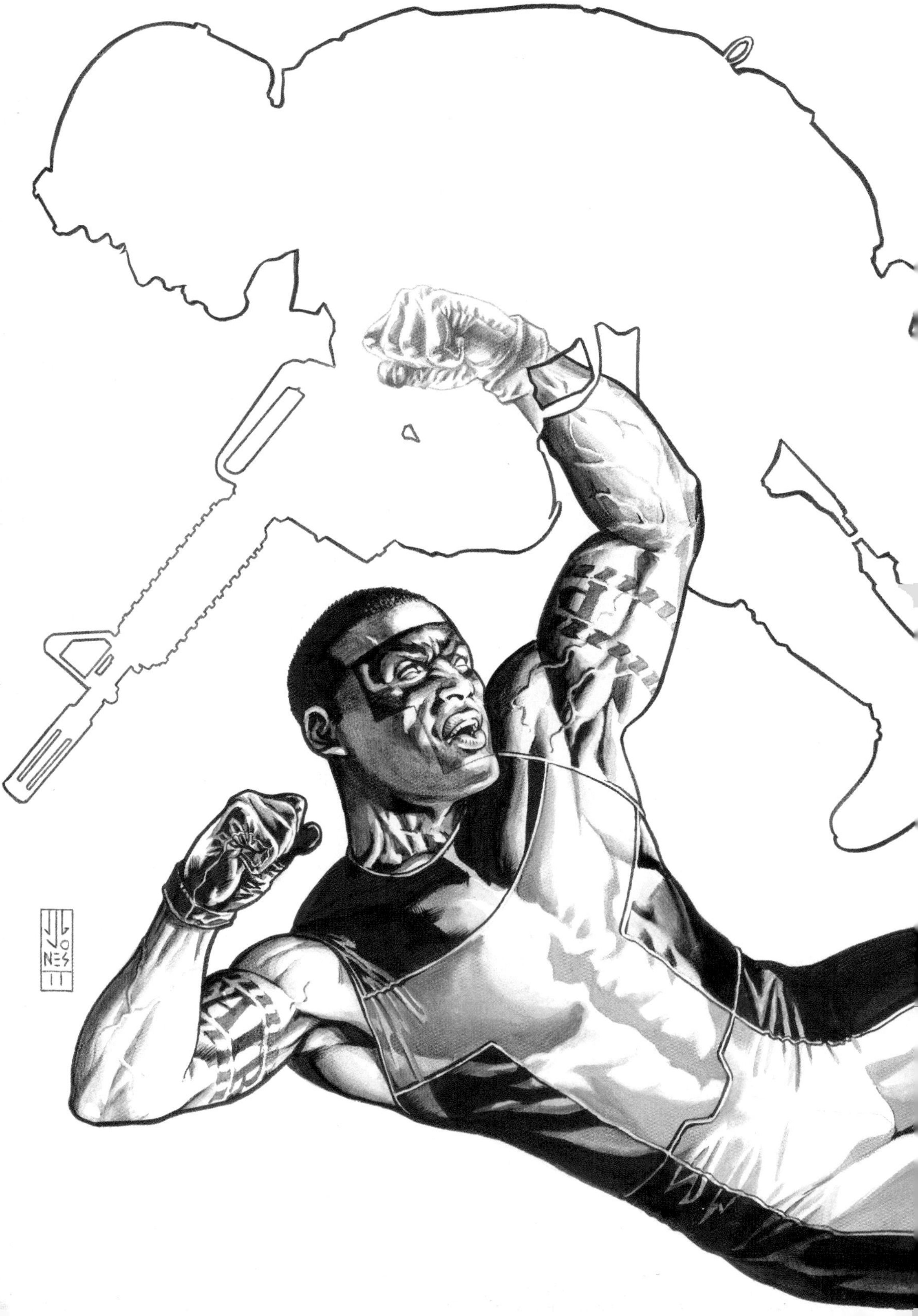
JG JONES 11

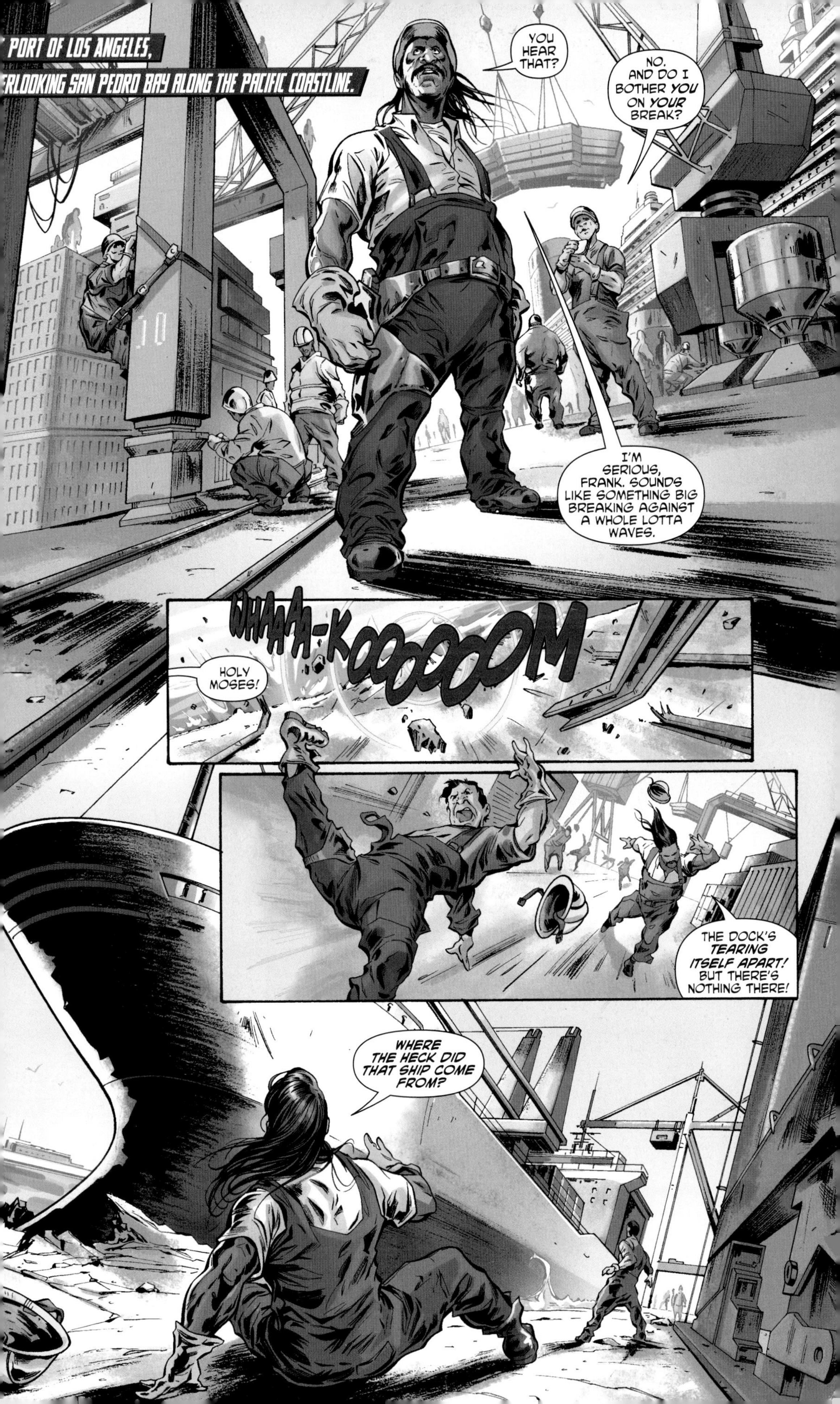
PORT OF LOS ANGELES,
RLOOKING SAN PEDRO BAY ALONG THE PACIFIC COASTLINE.
YOU HEAR THAT?
NO. AND DO I BOTHER YOU ON YOUR BREAK?
I'M SERIOUS, FRANK. SOUNDS LIKE SOMETHING BIG BREAKING AGAINST A WHOLE LOTTA WAVES.
WHAAAA-KOOOOOOM
HOLY MOSES!
THE DOCK'S TEARING ITSELF APART! BUT THERE'S NOTHING THERE!
WHERE THE HECK DID THAT SHIP COME FROM?

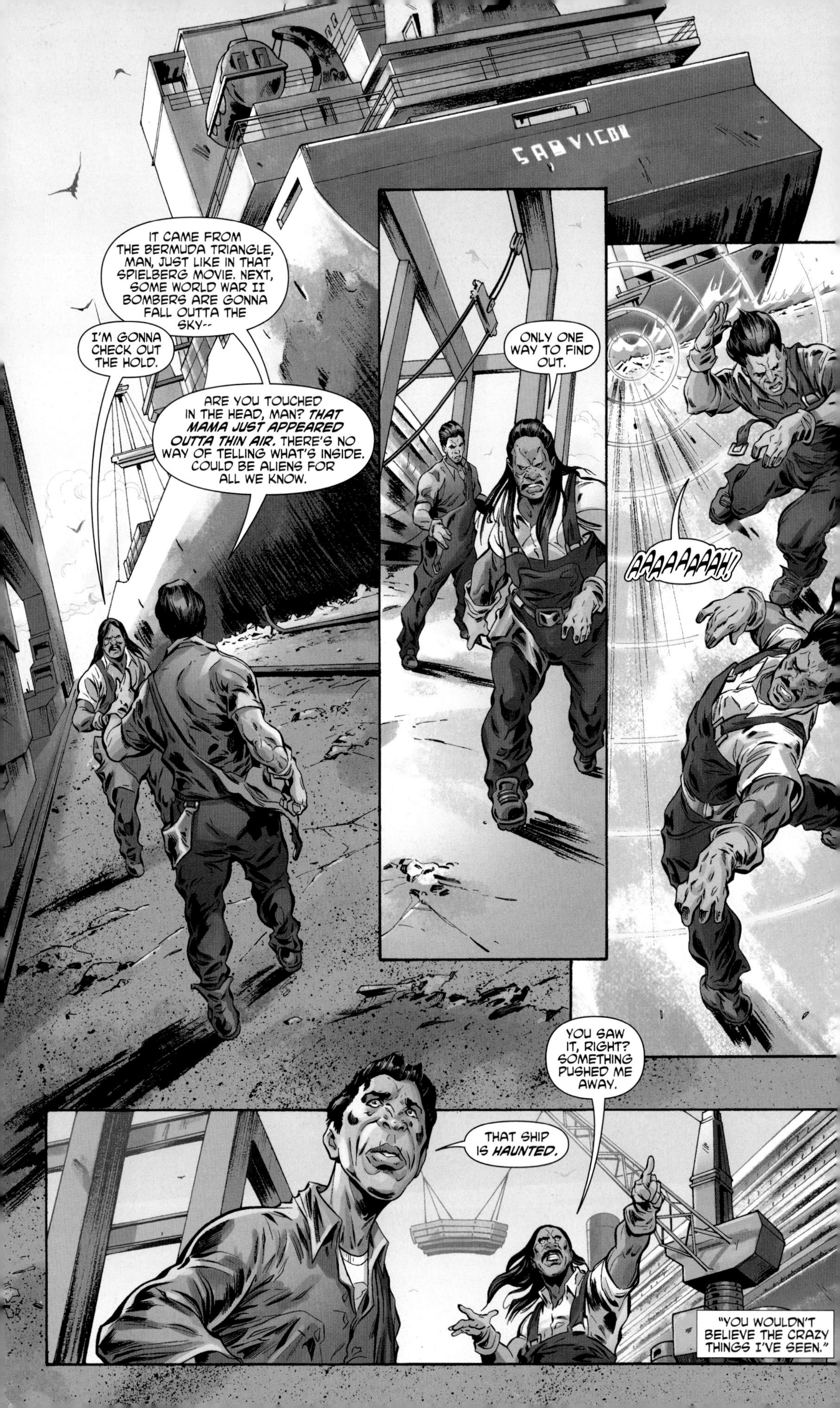
SABVICON
IT CAME FROM THE BERMUDA TRIANGLE, MAN, JUST LIKE IN THAT SPIELBERG MOVIE. NEXT, SOME WORLD WAR II BOMBERS ARE GONNA FALL OUTTA THE SKY--
I'M GONNA CHECK OUT THE HOLD.
ARE YOU TOUCHED IN THE HEAD, MAN? THAT MAMA JUST APPEARED OUTTA THIN AIR. THERE'S NO WAY OF TELLING WHAT'S INSIDE. COULD BE ALIENS FOR ALL WE KNOW.
ONLY ONE WAY TO FIND OUT.
AAAAAAAAH!
YOU SAW IT, RIGHT? SOMETHING PUSHED ME AWAY.
THAT SHIP IS HAUNTED.
"YOU WOULDN'T BELIEVE THE CRAZY THINGS I'VE SEEN."

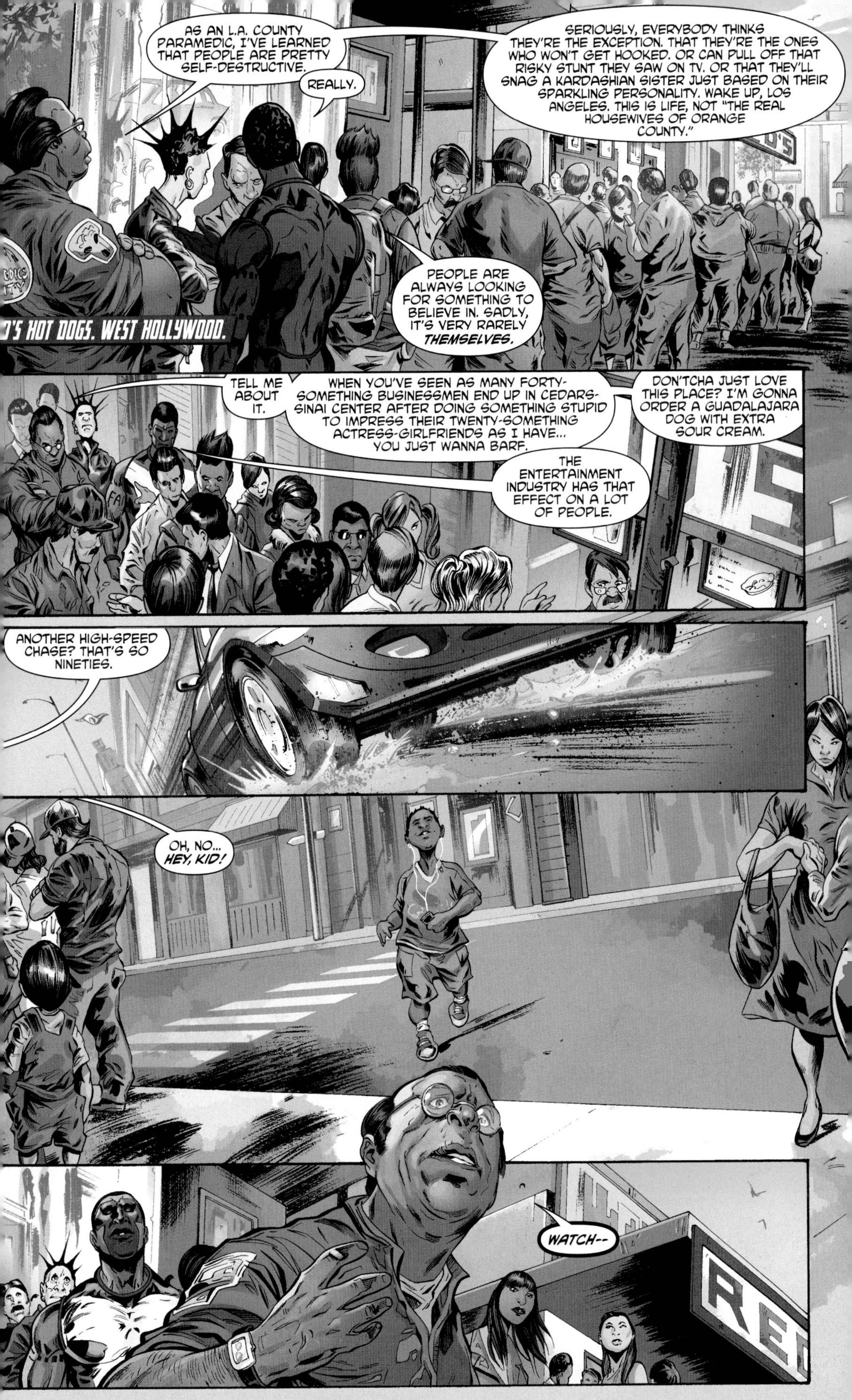
AS AN L.A. COUNTY PARAMEDIC, I'VE LEARNED THAT PEOPLE ARE PRETTY SELF-DESTRUCTIVE.
REALLY.
SERIOUSLY, EVERYBODY THINKS THEY'RE THE EXCEPTION. THAT THEY'RE THE ONES WHO WON'T GET HOOKED. OR CAN PULL OFF THAT RISKY STUNT THEY SAW ON TV. OR THAT THEY'LL SNAG A KARDASHIAN SISTER JUST BASED ON THEIR SPARKLING PERSONALITY. WAKE UP, LOS ANGELES. THIS IS LIFE, NOT "THE REAL HOUSEWIVES OF ORANGE COUNTY."
'S HOT DOGS. WEST HOLLYWOOD.
PEOPLE ARE ALWAYS LOOKING FOR SOMETHING TO BELIEVE IN. SADLY, IT'S VERY RARELY *THEMSELVES.*
TELL ME ABOUT IT.
WHEN YOU'VE SEEN AS MANY FORTY-SOMETHING BUSINESSMEN END UP IN CEDARS-SINAI CENTER AFTER DOING SOMETHING STUPID TO IMPRESS THEIR TWENTY-SOMETHING ACTRESS-GIRLFRIENDS AS I HAVE... YOU JUST WANNA BARF.
DON'TCHA JUST LOVE THIS PLACE? I'M GONNA ORDER A GUADALAJARA DOG WITH EXTRA SOUR CREAM.
THE ENTERTAINMENT INDUSTRY HAS THAT EFFECT ON A LOT OF PEOPLE.
ANOTHER HIGH-SPEED CHASE? THAT'S SO NINETIES.
OH, NO... *HEY, KID!*
WATCH--

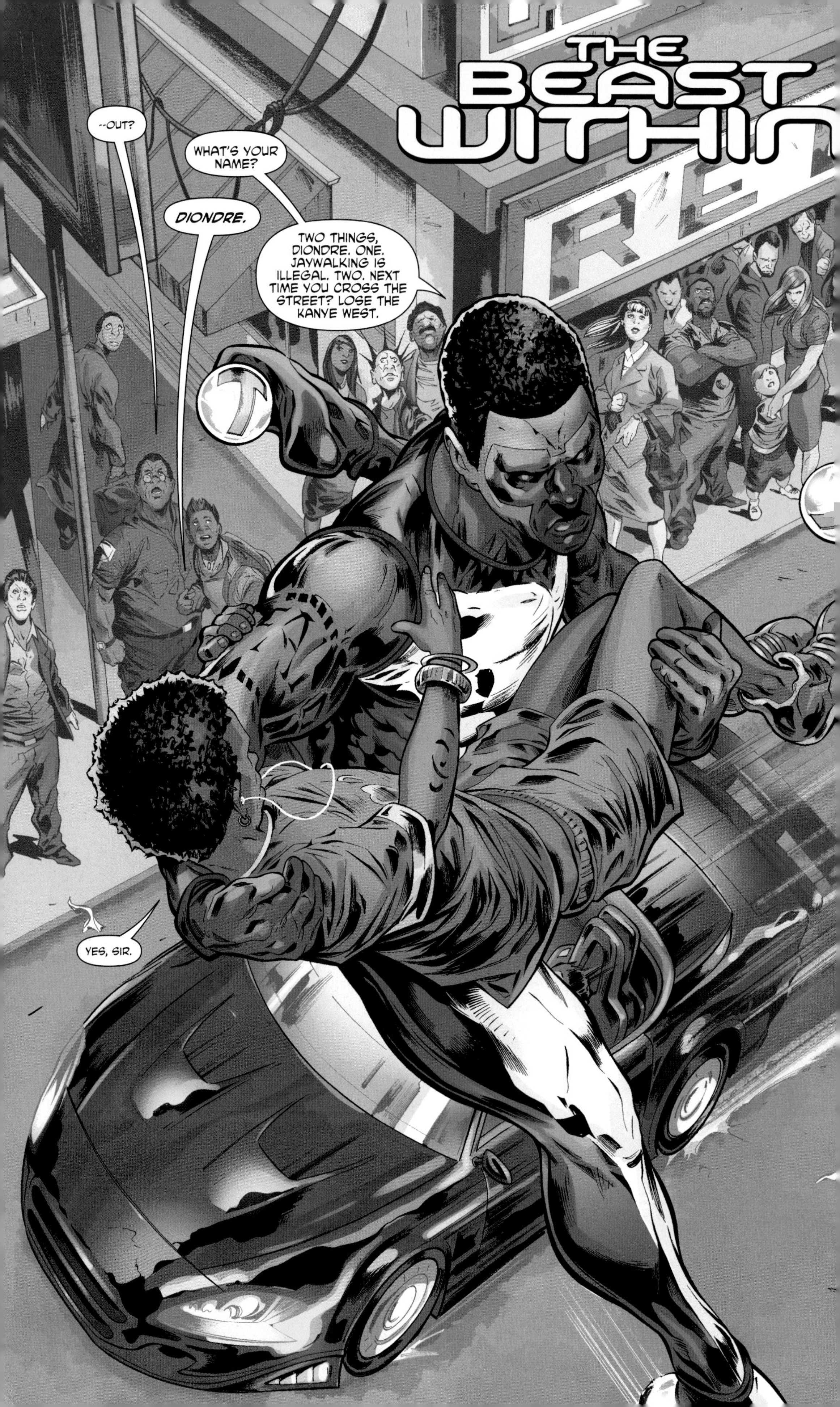
THE BEAST WITHIN
--OUT?
WHAT'S YOUR NAME?
DIONDRE.
TWO THINGS, DIONDRE. ONE. JAYWALKING IS ILLEGAL. TWO. NEXT TIME YOU CROSS THE STREET? LOSE THE KANYE WEST.
YES, SIR.

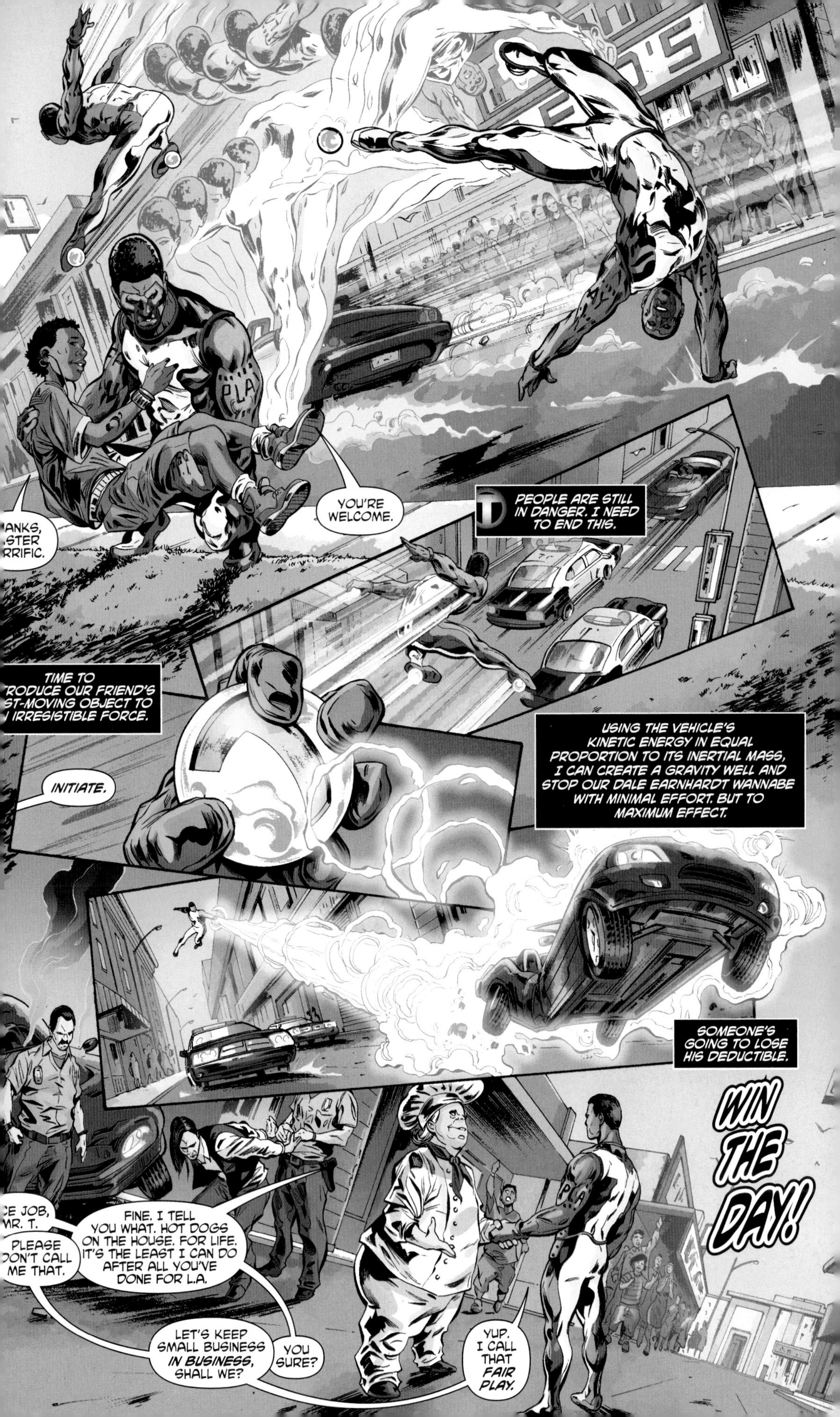
ANKS,
STER
RRIFIC.
YOU'RE WELCOME.
PEOPLE ARE STILL IN DANGER. I NEED TO END THIS.
TIME TO
RODUCE OUR FRIEND'S
ST-MOVING OBJECT TO
IRRESISTIBLE FORCE.
INITIATE.
USING THE VEHICLE'S KINETIC ENERGY IN EQUAL PROPORTION TO ITS INERTIAL MASS, I CAN CREATE A GRAVITY WELL AND STOP OUR DALE EARNHARDT WANNABE WITH MINIMAL EFFORT. BUT TO MAXIMUM EFFECT.
SOMEONE'S GOING TO LOSE HIS DEDUCTIBLE.
WIN THE DAY!
E JOB,
MR. T.
PLEASE
ON'T CALL
ME THAT.
FINE. I TELL YOU WHAT. HOT DOGS ON THE HOUSE. FOR LIFE. IT'S THE LEAST I CAN DO AFTER ALL YOU'VE DONE FOR L.A.
LET'S KEEP SMALL BUSINESS *IN BUSINESS*, SHALL WE?
YOU SURE?
YUP. I CALL THAT *FAIR PLAY*.

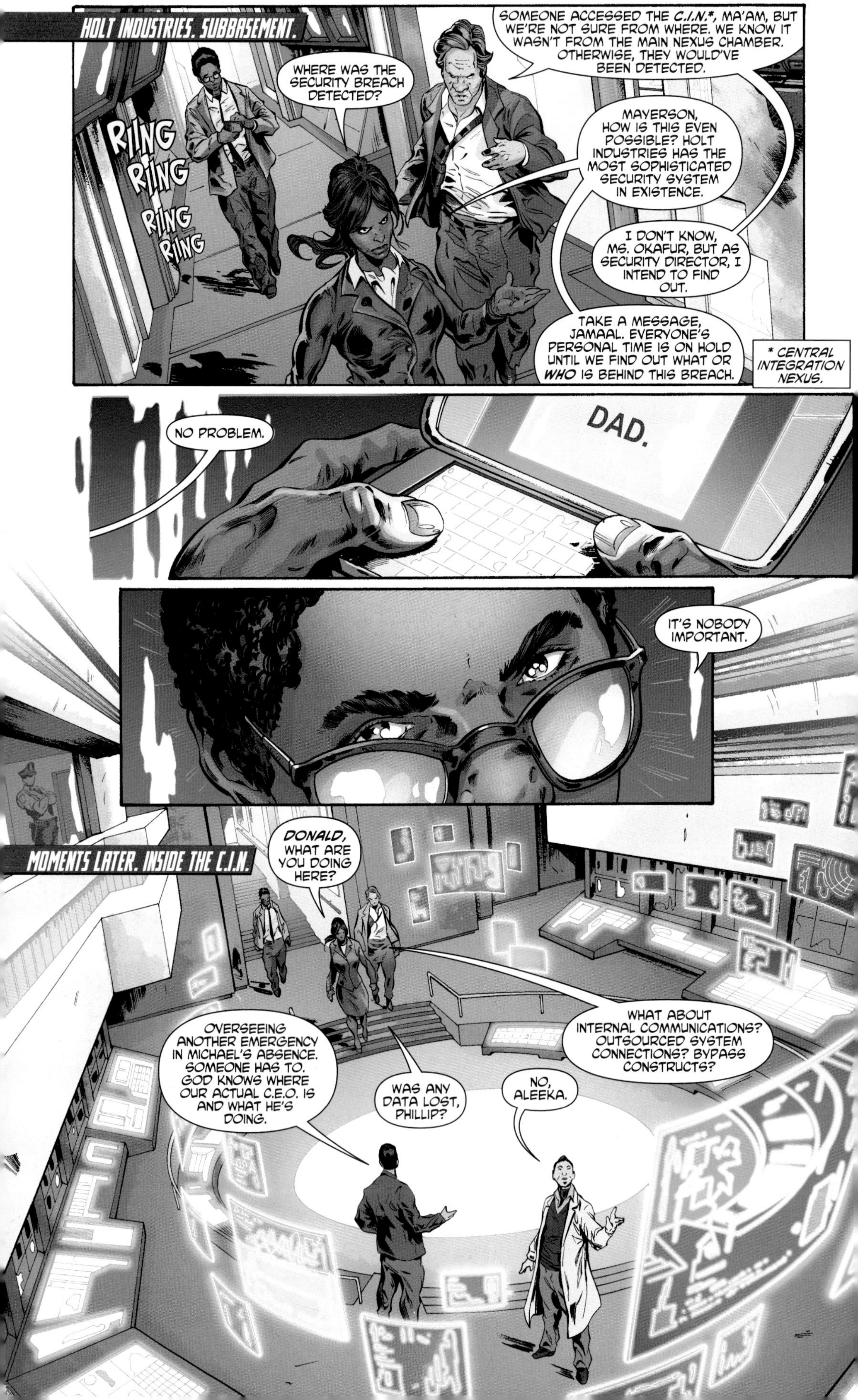
HOLT INDUSTRIES. SUBBASEMENT.
RING RING RING RING
WHERE WAS THE SECURITY BREACH DETECTED?
SOMEONE ACCESSED THE C.I.N.*, MA'AM, BUT WE'RE NOT SURE FROM WHERE. WE KNOW IT WASN'T FROM THE MAIN NEXUS CHAMBER. OTHERWISE, THEY WOULD'VE BEEN DETECTED.
MAYERSON, HOW IS THIS EVEN POSSIBLE? HOLT INDUSTRIES HAS THE MOST SOPHISTICATED SECURITY SYSTEM IN EXISTENCE.
I DON'T KNOW, MS. OKAFUR, BUT AS SECURITY DIRECTOR, I INTEND TO FIND OUT.
TAKE A MESSAGE, JAMAAL. EVERYONE'S PERSONAL TIME IS ON HOLD UNTIL WE FIND OUT WHAT OR WHO IS BEHIND THIS BREACH.
* CENTRAL INTEGRATION NEXUS.
DAD.
NO PROBLEM.
IT'S NOBODY IMPORTANT.
MOMENTS LATER. INSIDE THE C.I.N.
DONALD, WHAT ARE YOU DOING HERE?
OVERSEEING ANOTHER EMERGENCY IN MICHAEL'S ABSENCE. SOMEONE HAS TO. GOD KNOWS WHERE OUR ACTUAL C.E.O. IS AND WHAT HE'S DOING.
WAS ANY DATA LOST, PHILLIP?
NO, ALEEKA.
WHAT ABOUT INTERNAL COMMUNICATIONS? OUTSOURCED SYSTEM CONNECTIONS? BYPASS CONSTRUCTS?

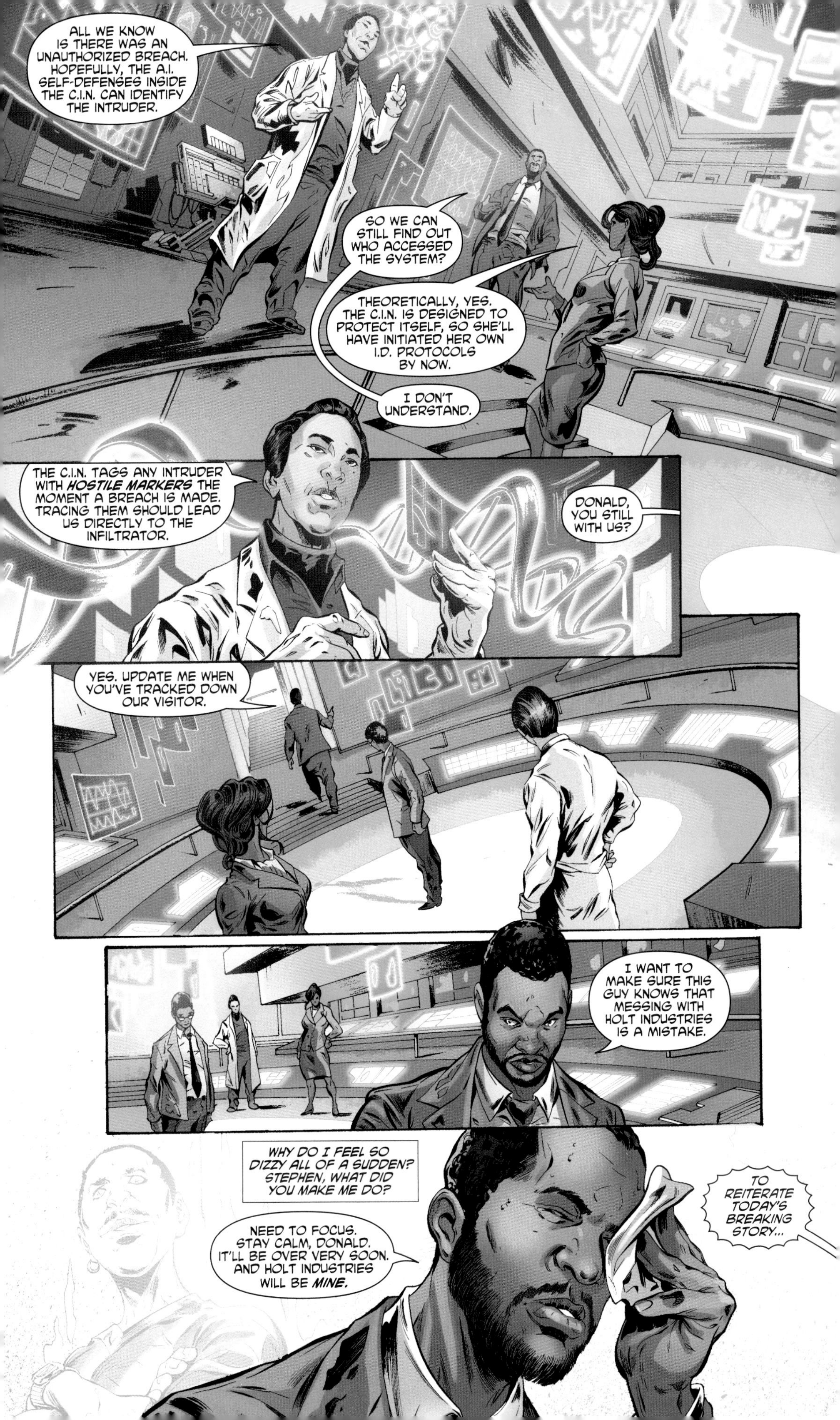
ALL WE KNOW IS THERE WAS AN UNAUTHORIZED BREACH. HOPEFULLY, THE A.I. SELF-DEFENSES INSIDE THE C.I.N. CAN IDENTIFY THE INTRUDER.
SO WE CAN STILL FIND OUT WHO ACCESSED THE SYSTEM?
THEORETICALLY, YES. THE C.I.N. IS DESIGNED TO PROTECT ITSELF, SO SHE'LL HAVE INITIATED HER OWN I.D. PROTOCOLS BY NOW.
I DON'T UNDERSTAND.
THE C.I.N. TAGS ANY INTRUDER WITH HOSTILE MARKERS THE MOMENT A BREACH IS MADE. TRACING THEM SHOULD LEAD US DIRECTLY TO THE INFILTRATOR.
DONALD, YOU STILL WITH US?
YES. UPDATE ME WHEN YOU'VE TRACKED DOWN OUR VISITOR.
I WANT TO MAKE SURE THIS GUY KNOWS THAT MESSING WITH HOLT INDUSTRIES IS A MISTAKE.
WHY DO I FEEL SO DIZZY ALL OF A SUDDEN? STEPHEN, WHAT DID YOU MAKE ME DO?
NEED TO FOCUS. STAY CALM, DONALD. IT'LL BE OVER VERY SOON. AND HOLT INDUSTRIES WILL BE MINE.
TO REITERATE TODAY'S BREAKING STORY...

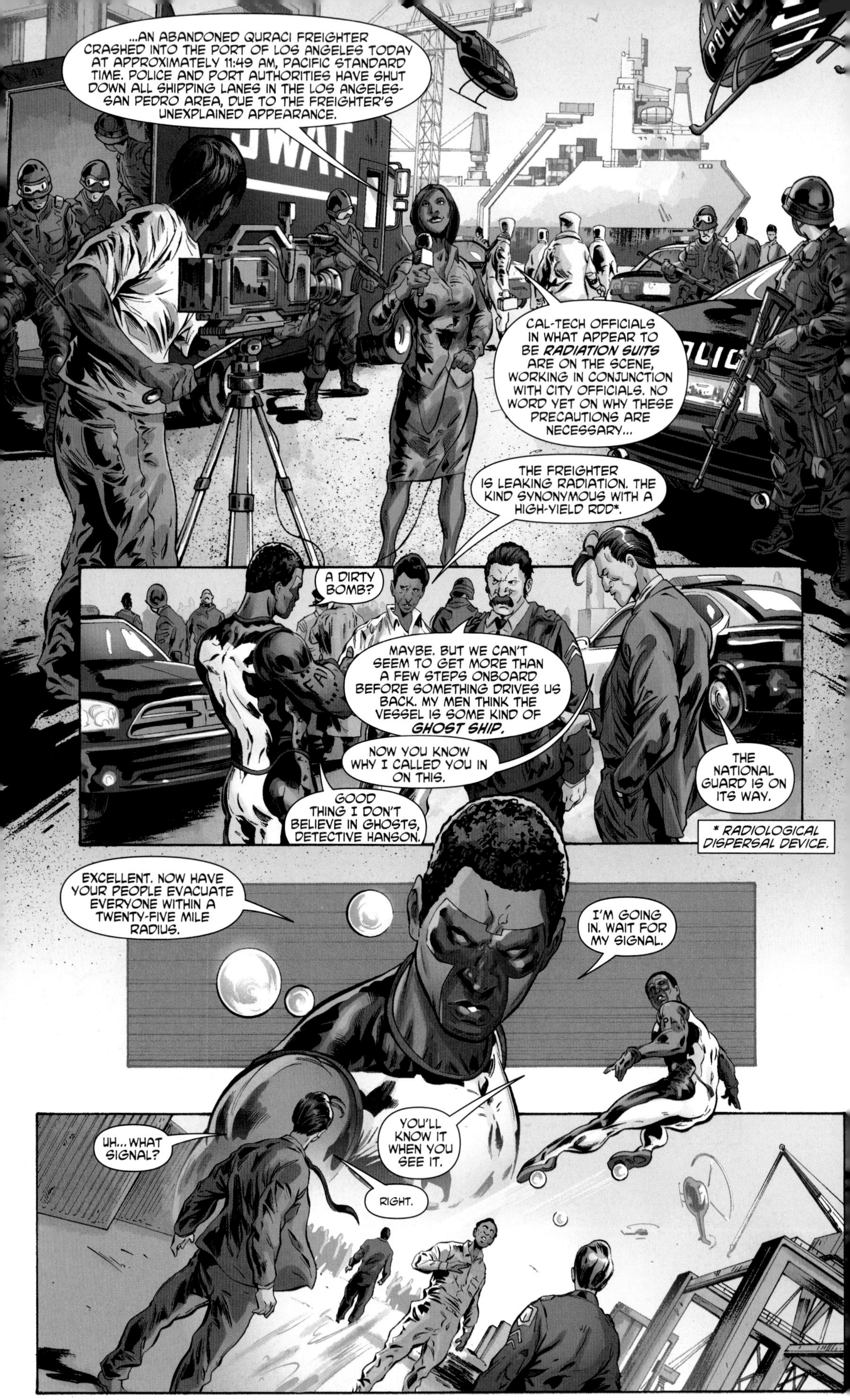
...AN ABANDONED QURACI FREIGHTER CRASHED INTO THE PORT OF LOS ANGELES TODAY AT APPROXIMATELY 11:49 AM, PACIFIC STANDARD TIME. POLICE AND PORT AUTHORITIES HAVE SHUT DOWN ALL SHIPPING LANES IN THE LOS ANGELES-SAN PEDRO AREA, DUE TO THE FREIGHTER'S UNEXPLAINED APPEARANCE.
SWAT
POLICE
CAL-TECH OFFICIALS IN WHAT APPEAR TO BE *RADIATION SUITS* ARE ON THE SCENE, WORKING IN CONJUNCTION WITH CITY OFFICIALS. NO WORD YET ON WHY THESE PRECAUTIONS ARE NECESSARY...
THE FREIGHTER IS LEAKING RADIATION. THE KIND SYNONYMOUS WITH A HIGH-YIELD RDD*.
A DIRTY BOMB?
MAYBE. BUT WE CAN'T SEEM TO GET MORE THAN A FEW STEPS ONBOARD BEFORE SOMETHING DRIVES US BACK. MY MEN THINK THE VESSEL IS SOME KIND OF ***GHOST SHIP.***
NOW YOU KNOW WHY I CALLED YOU IN ON THIS.
GOOD THING I DON'T BELIEVE IN GHOSTS, DETECTIVE HANSON.
THE NATIONAL GUARD IS ON ITS WAY.
* *RADIOLOGICAL DISPERSAL DEVICE.*
EXCELLENT. NOW HAVE YOUR PEOPLE EVACUATE EVERYONE WITHIN A TWENTY-FIVE MILE RADIUS.
I'M GOING IN. WAIT FOR MY SIGNAL.
UH... WHAT SIGNAL?
YOU'LL KNOW IT WHEN YOU SEE IT.
RIGHT.

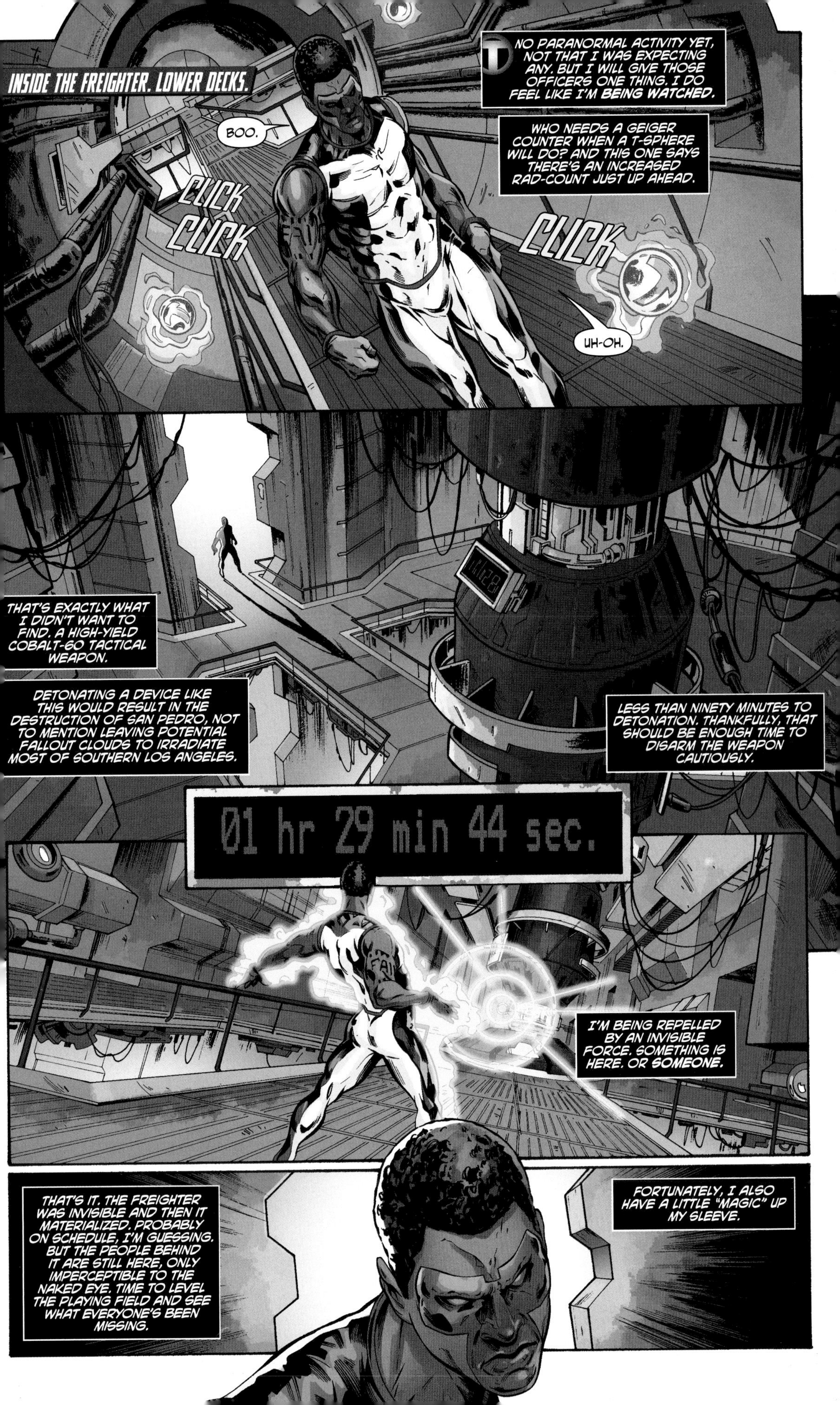

INSIDE THE FREIGHTER. LOWER DECKS.
NO PARANORMAL ACTIVITY YET, NOT THAT I WAS EXPECTING ANY. BUT I WILL GIVE THOSE OFFICERS ONE THING. I DO FEEL LIKE I'M BEING WATCHED.
BOO.
WHO NEEDS A GEIGER COUNTER WHEN A T-SPHERE WILL DO? AND THIS ONE SAYS THERE'S AN INCREASED RAD-COUNT JUST UP AHEAD.
CLICK
CLICK
CLICK
UH-OH.
THAT'S EXACTLY WHAT I DIDN'T WANT TO FIND. A HIGH-YIELD COBALT-60 TACTICAL WEAPON.
DETONATING A DEVICE LIKE THIS WOULD RESULT IN THE DESTRUCTION OF SAN PEDRO, NOT TO MENTION LEAVING POTENTIAL FALLOUT CLOUDS TO IRRADIATE MOST OF SOUTHERN LOS ANGELES.
LESS THAN NINETY MINUTES TO DETONATION. THANKFULLY, THAT SHOULD BE ENOUGH TIME TO DISARM THE WEAPON CAUTIOUSLY.
01 hr 29 min 44 sec.
I'M BEING REPELLED BY AN INVISIBLE FORCE. SOMETHING IS HERE. OR SOMEONE.
THAT'S IT. THE FREIGHTER WAS INVISIBLE AND THEN IT MATERIALIZED. PROBABLY ON SCHEDULE, I'M GUESSING. BUT THE PEOPLE BEHIND IT ARE STILL HERE, ONLY IMPERCEPTIBLE TO THE NAKED EYE. TIME TO LEVEL THE PLAYING FIELD AND SEE WHAT EVERYONE'S BEEN MISSING.
FORTUNATELY, I ALSO HAVE A LITTLE "MAGIC" UP MY SLEEVE.

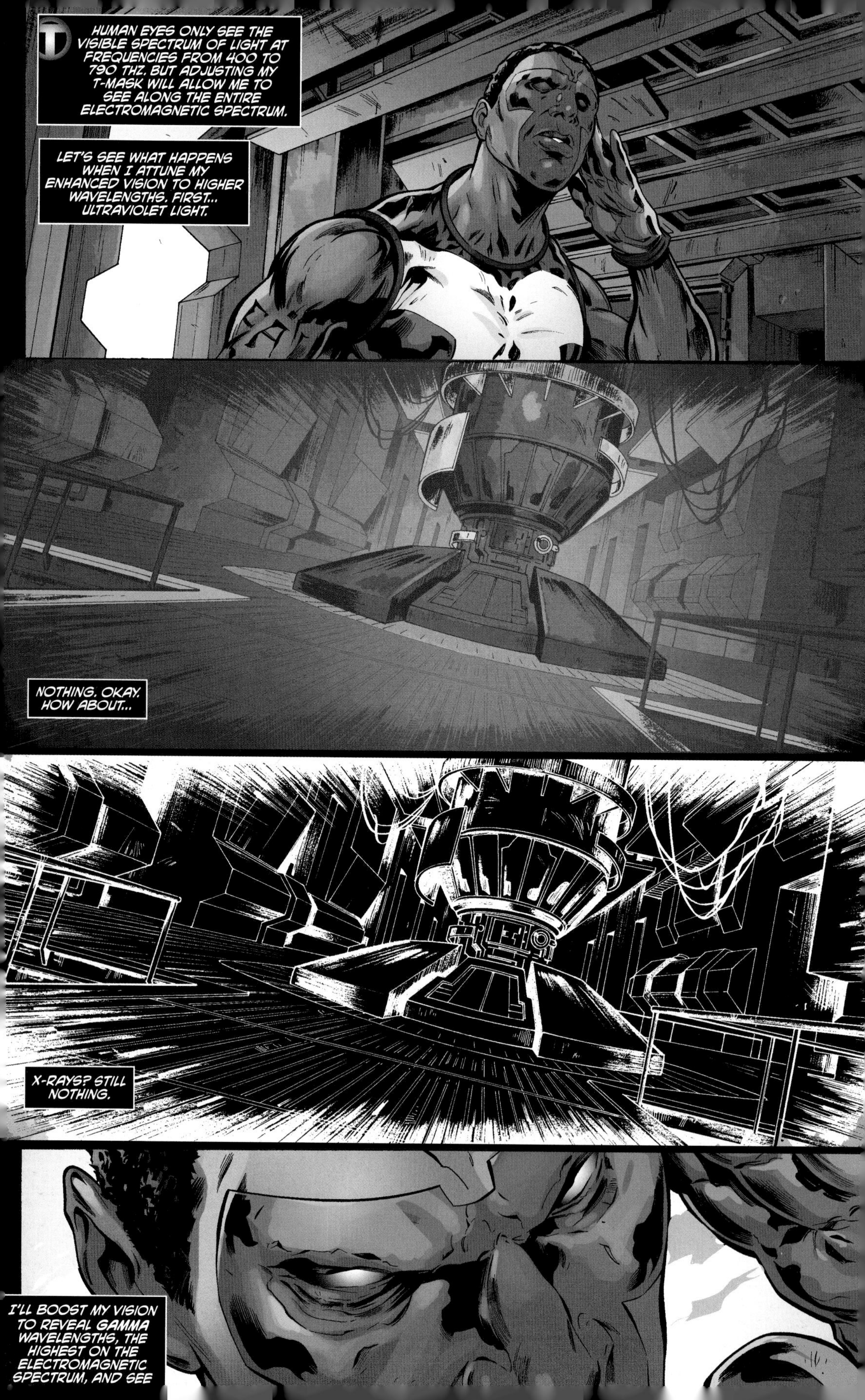
HUMAN EYES ONLY SEE THE VISIBLE SPECTRUM OF LIGHT AT FREQUENCIES FROM 400 TO 790 THZ. BUT ADJUSTING MY T-MASK WILL ALLOW ME TO SEE ALONG THE ENTIRE ELECTROMAGNETIC SPECTRUM.
LET'S SEE WHAT HAPPENS WHEN I ATTUNE MY ENHANCED VISION TO HIGHER WAVELENGTHS. FIRST... ULTRAVIOLET LIGHT.
NOTHING. OKAY. HOW ABOUT...
X-RAYS? STILL NOTHING.
I'LL BOOST MY VISION TO REVEAL GAMMA WAVELENGTHS, THE HIGHEST ON THE ELECTROMAGNETIC SPECTRUM, AND SEE

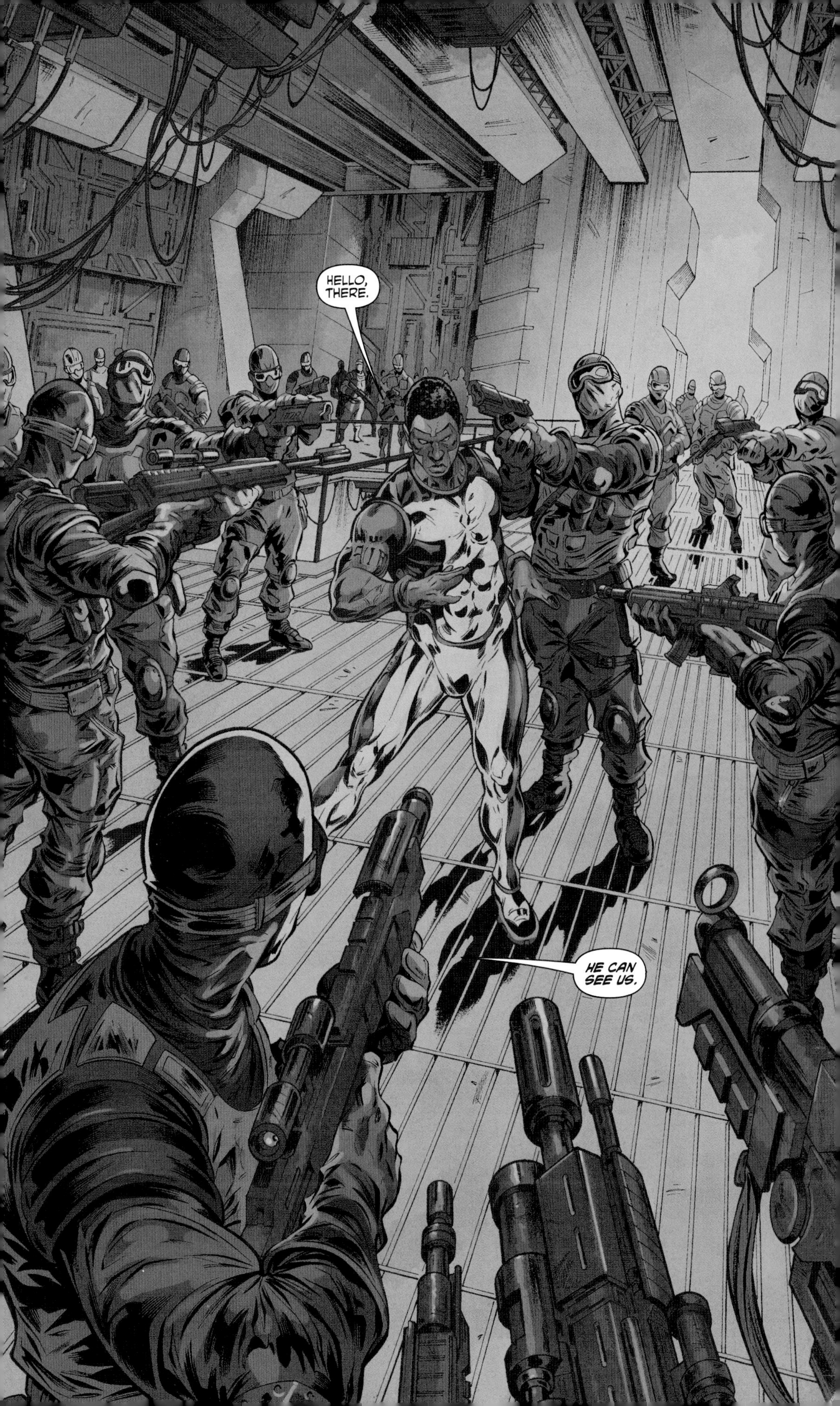
HELLO, THERE.
HE CAN SEE US.

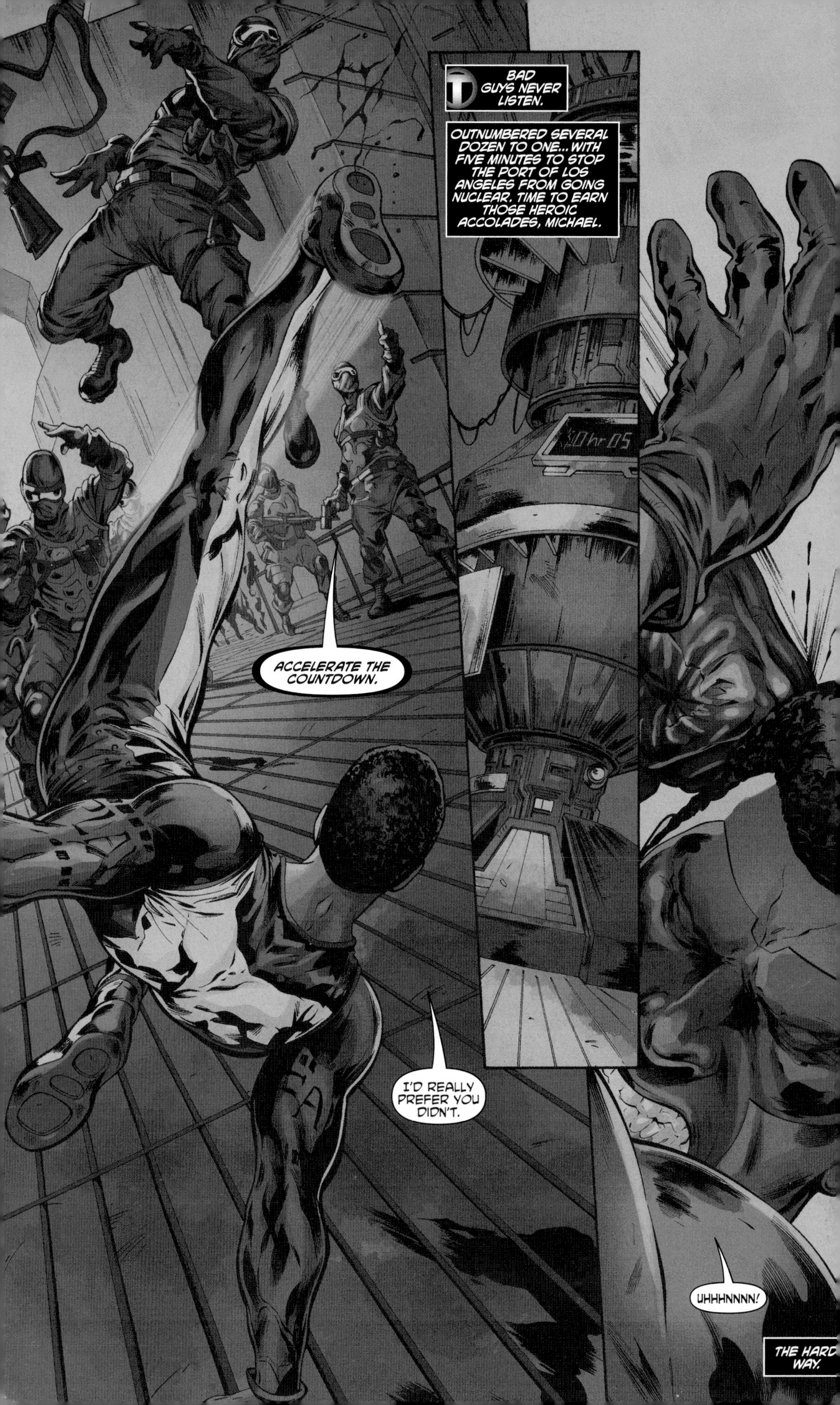
BAD GUYS NEVER LISTEN.
OUTNUMBERED SEVERAL DOZEN TO ONE... WITH FIVE MINUTES TO STOP THE PORT OF LOS ANGELES FROM GOING NUCLEAR. TIME TO EARN THOSE HEROIC ACCOLADES, MICHAEL.
ACCELERATE THE COUNTDOWN.
I'D REALLY PREFER YOU DIDN'T.
UHHHNNNN!
THE HARD WAY.

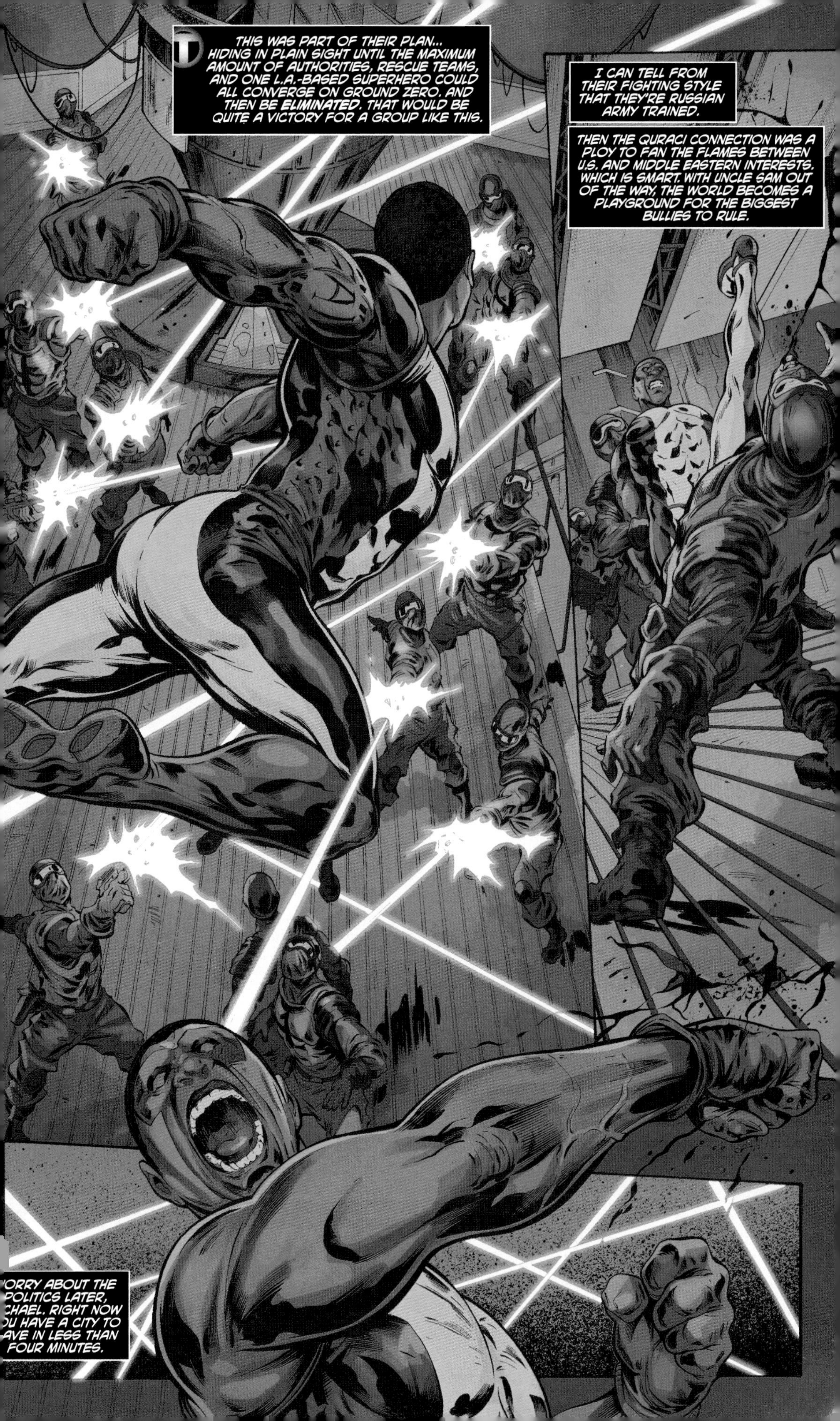
THIS WAS PART OF THEIR PLAN... HIDING IN PLAIN SIGHT UNTIL THE MAXIMUM AMOUNT OF AUTHORITIES, RESCUE TEAMS, AND ONE L.A.-BASED SUPERHERO COULD ALL CONVERGE ON GROUND ZERO. AND THEN BE ELIMINATED. THAT WOULD BE QUITE A VICTORY FOR A GROUP LIKE THIS.
I CAN TELL FROM THEIR FIGHTING STYLE THAT THEY'RE RUSSIAN ARMY TRAINED.
THEN THE QURACI CONNECTION WAS A PLOY TO FAN THE FLAMES BETWEEN U.S. AND MIDDLE EASTERN INTERESTS. WHICH IS SMART. WITH UNCLE SAM OUT OF THE WAY, THE WORLD BECOMES A PLAYGROUND FOR THE BIGGEST BULLIES TO RULE.
ORRY ABOUT THE POLITICS LATER, CHAEL. RIGHT NOW OU HAVE A CITY TO AVE IN LESS THAN FOUR MINUTES.

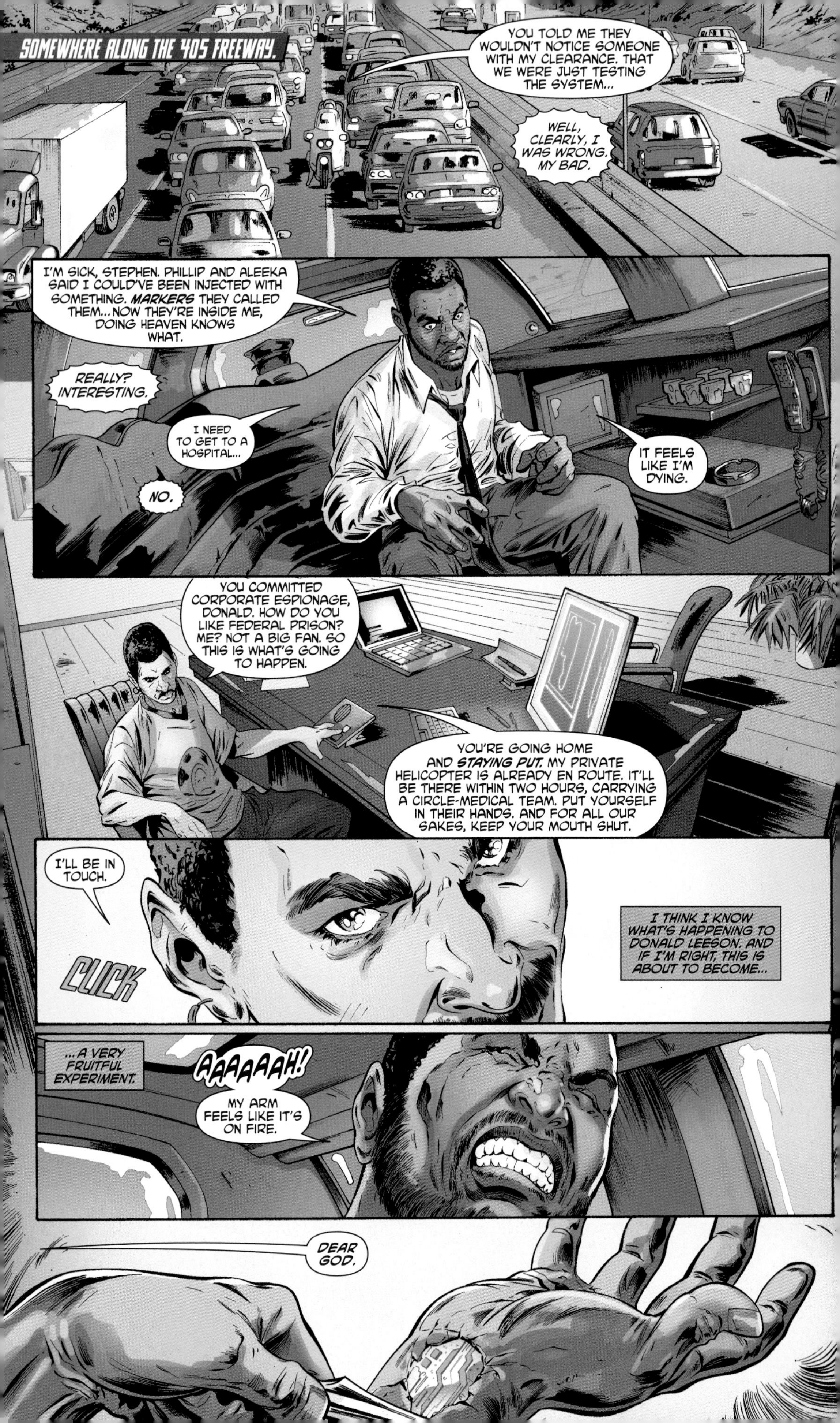
SOMEWHERE ALONG THE 405 FREEWAY.
YOU TOLD ME THEY WOULDN'T NOTICE SOMEONE WITH MY CLEARANCE. THAT WE WERE JUST TESTING THE SYSTEM...
WELL, CLEARLY, I WAS WRONG. MY BAD.
I'M SICK, STEPHEN. PHILLIP AND ALEEKA SAID I COULD'VE BEEN INJECTED WITH SOMETHING. MARKERS THEY CALLED THEM...NOW THEY'RE INSIDE ME, DOING HEAVEN KNOWS WHAT.
REALLY? INTERESTING.
I NEED TO GET TO A HOSPITAL...
NO.
IT FEELS LIKE I'M DYING.
YOU COMMITTED CORPORATE ESPIONAGE, DONALD. HOW DO YOU LIKE FEDERAL PRISON? ME? NOT A BIG FAN. SO THIS IS WHAT'S GOING TO HAPPEN.
YOU'RE GOING HOME AND STAYING PUT. MY PRIVATE HELICOPTER IS ALREADY EN ROUTE. IT'LL BE THERE WITHIN TWO HOURS, CARRYING A CIRCLE-MEDICAL TEAM. PUT YOURSELF IN THEIR HANDS. AND FOR ALL OUR SAKES, KEEP YOUR MOUTH SHUT.
I'LL BE IN TOUCH.
CLICK
I THINK I KNOW WHAT'S HAPPENING TO DONALD LEESON. AND IF I'M RIGHT, THIS IS ABOUT TO BECOME...
...A VERY FRUITFUL EXPERIMENT.
AAAAAAH!
MY ARM FEELS LIKE IT'S ON FIRE.
DEAR GOD.

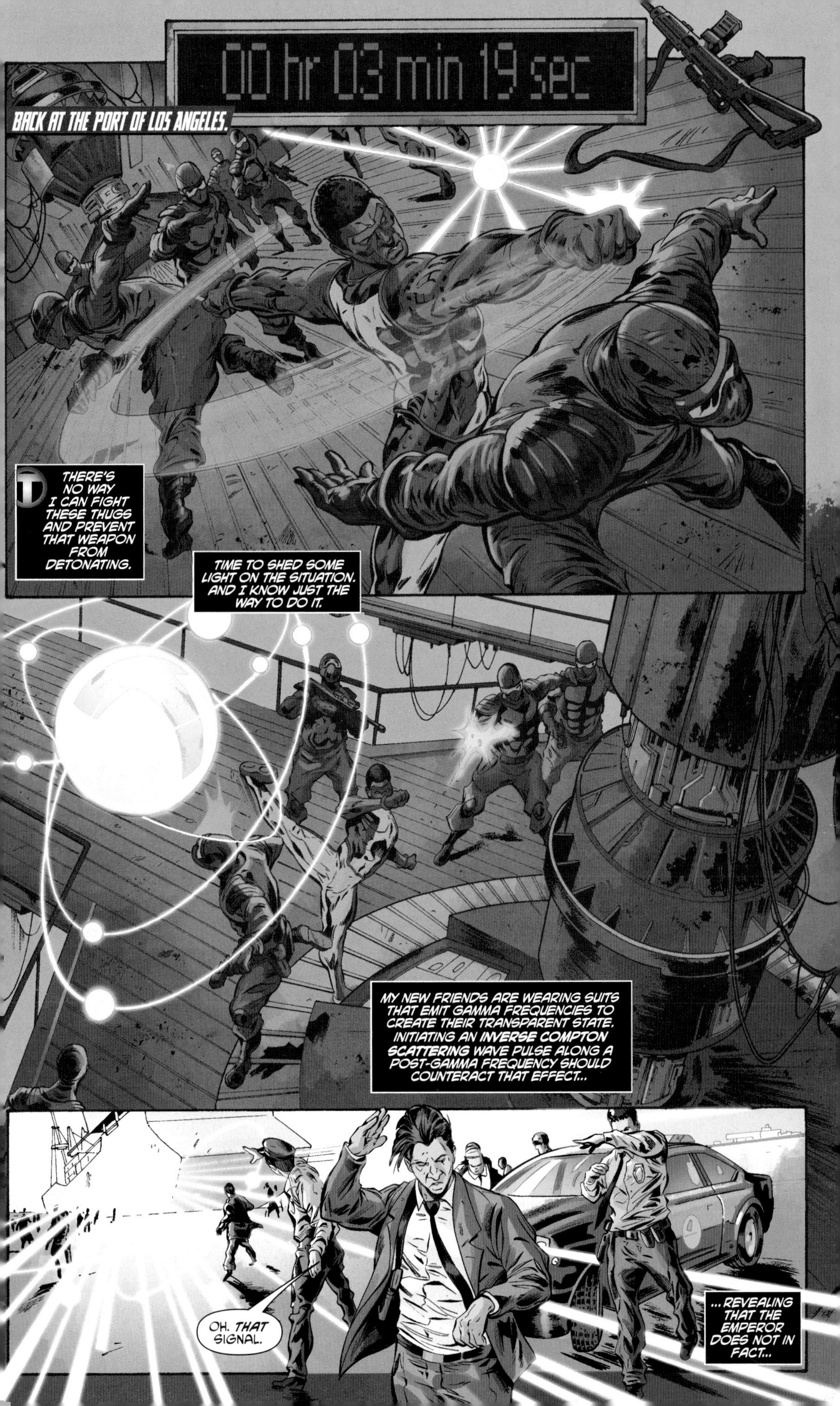
00 hr 03 min 19 sec
BACK AT THE PORT OF LOS ANGELES.
THERE'S NO WAY I CAN FIGHT THESE THUGS AND PREVENT THAT WEAPON FROM DETONATING.
TIME TO SHED SOME LIGHT ON THE SITUATION. AND I KNOW JUST THE WAY TO DO IT.
MY NEW FRIENDS ARE WEARING SUITS THAT EMIT GAMMA FREQUENCIES TO CREATE THEIR TRANSPARENT STATE. INITIATING AN INVERSE COMPTON SCATTERING WAVE PULSE ALONG A POST-GAMMA FREQUENCY SHOULD COUNTERACT THAT EFFECT...
OH. THAT SIGNAL.
...REVEALING THAT THE EMPEROR DOES NOT IN FACT...

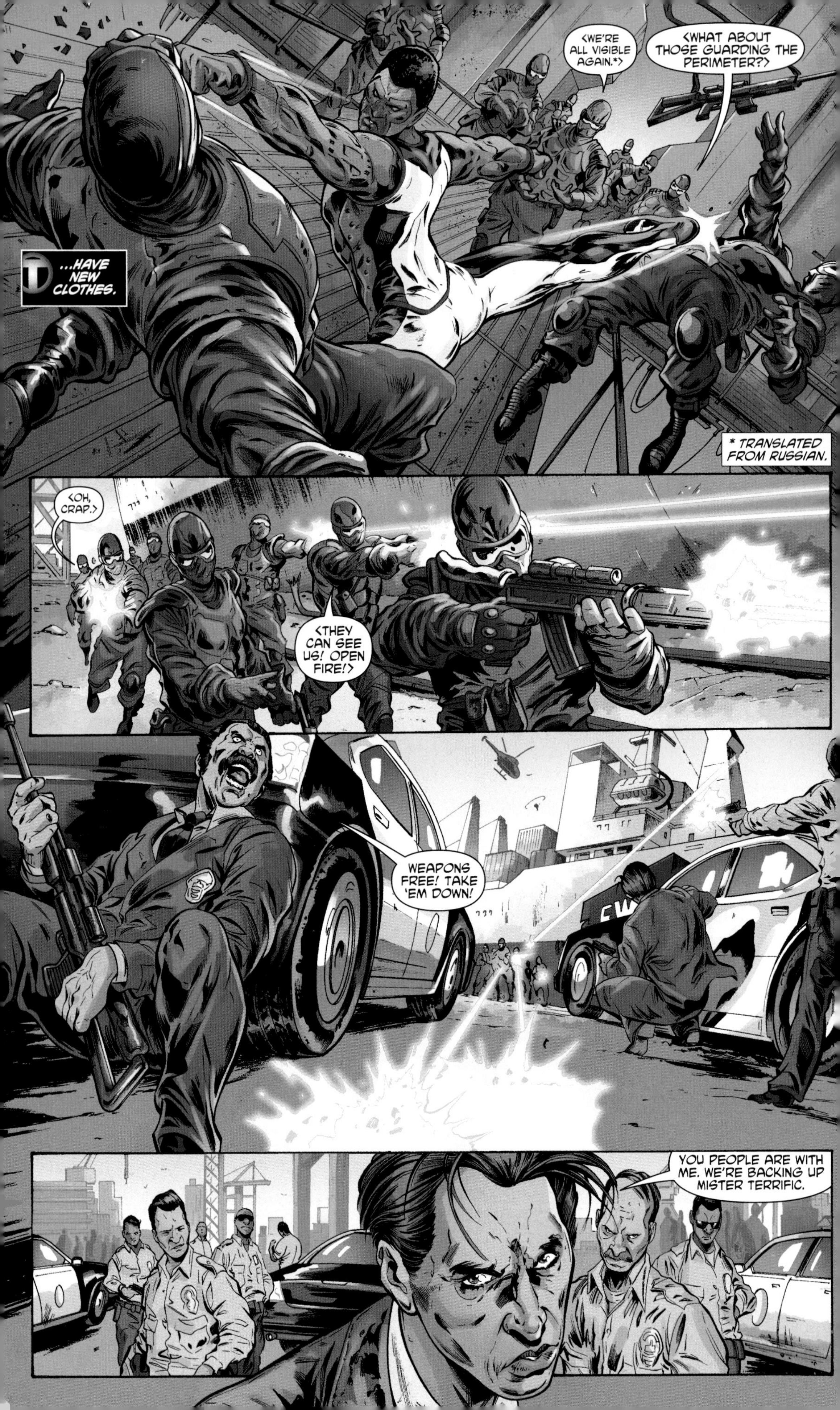
...HAVE NEW CLOTHES.
<WE'RE ALL VISIBLE AGAIN.*>
<WHAT ABOUT THOSE GUARDING THE PERIMETER?>
* TRANSLATED FROM RUSSIAN.
<OH, CRAP.>
<THEY CAN SEE US! OPEN FIRE!>
WEAPONS FREE! TAKE 'EM DOWN!
YOU PEOPLE ARE WITH ME. WE'RE BACKING UP MISTER TERRIFIC.

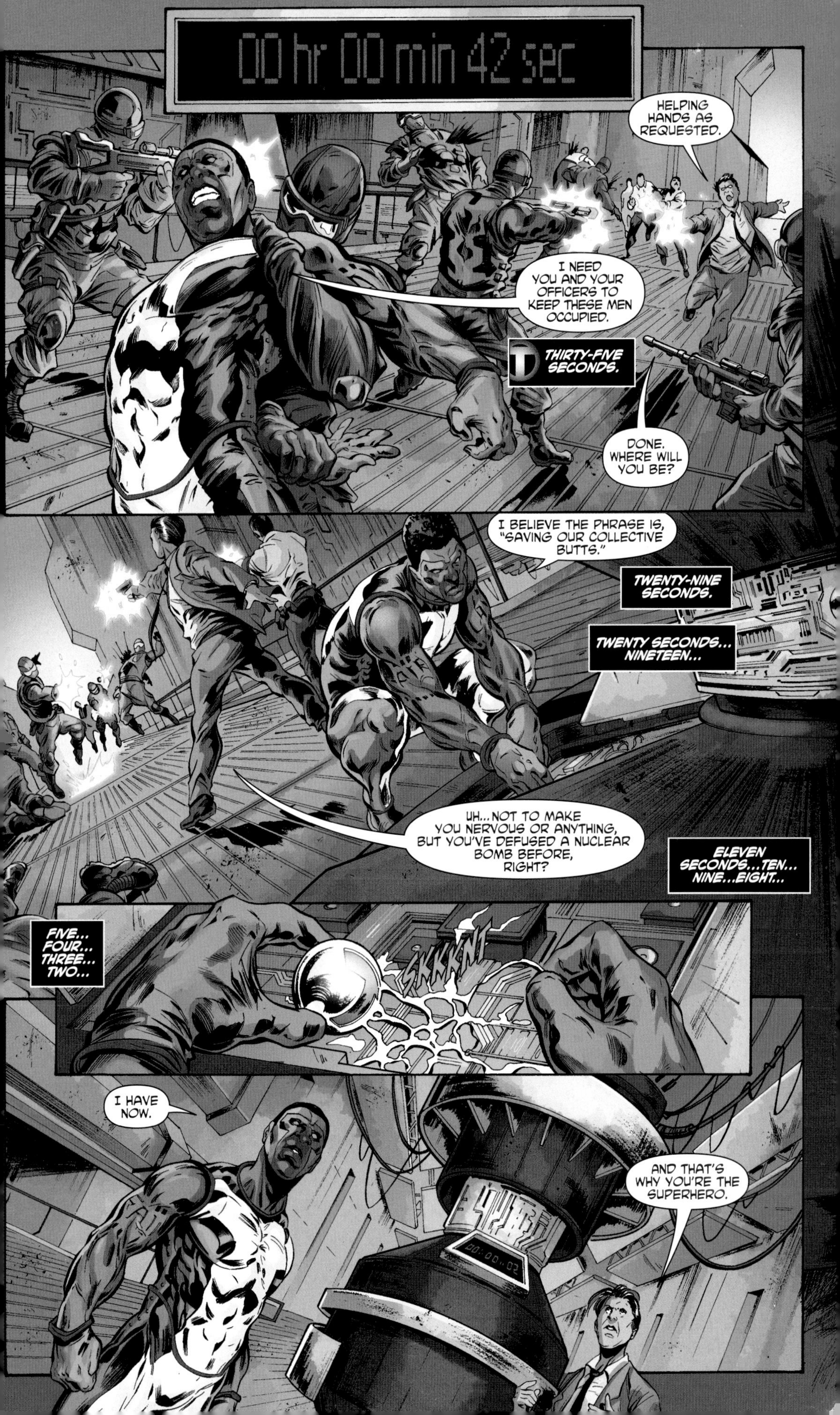
00 hr 00 min 42 sec
HELPING HANDS AS REQUESTED.
I NEED YOU AND YOUR OFFICERS TO KEEP THESE MEN OCCUPIED.
THIRTY-FIVE SECONDS.
DONE. WHERE WILL YOU BE?
I BELIEVE THE PHRASE IS, "SAVING OUR COLLECTIVE BUTTS."
TWENTY-NINE SECONDS.
TWENTY SECONDS... NINETEEN...
UH... NOT TO MAKE YOU NERVOUS OR ANYTHING, BUT YOU'VE DEFUSED A NUCLEAR BOMB BEFORE, RIGHT?
ELEVEN SECONDS...TEN... NINE...EIGHT...
FIVE... FOUR... THREE... TWO...
SKKKZT
I HAVE NOW.
AND THAT'S WHY YOU'RE THE SUPERHERO.

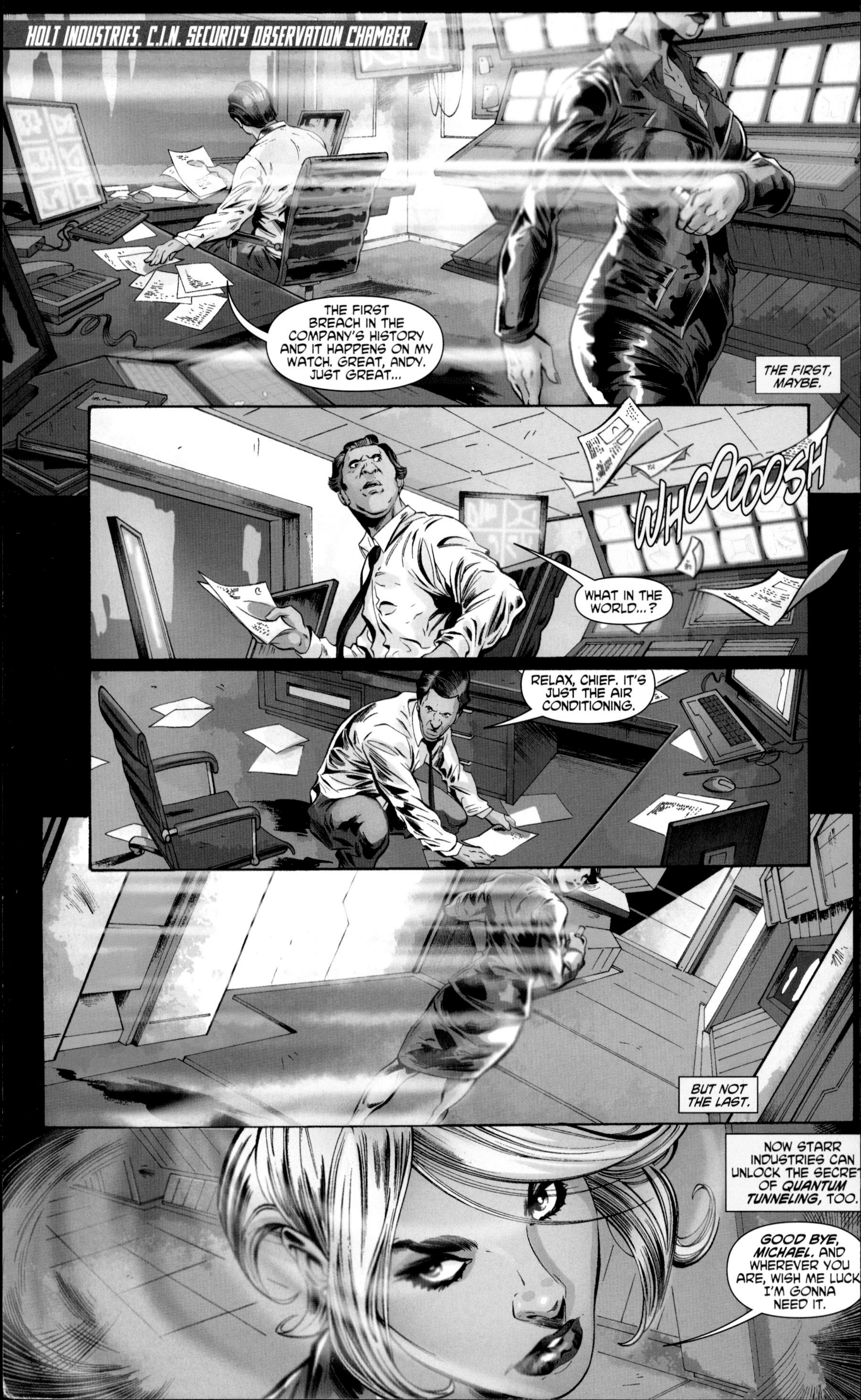
HOLT INDUSTRIES. C.I.N. SECURITY OBSERVATION CHAMBER.
THE FIRST BREACH IN THE COMPANY'S HISTORY AND IT HAPPENS ON MY WATCH. GREAT, ANDY. JUST GREAT...
THE FIRST, MAYBE.
WHOOOOOOSH
WHAT IN THE WORLD...?
RELAX, CHIEF. IT'S JUST THE AIR CONDITIONING.
BUT NOT THE LAST.
NOW STARR INDUSTRIES CAN UNLOCK THE SECRET OF QUANTUM TUNNELING, TOO.
GOOD BYE, MICHAEL. AND WHEREVER YOU ARE, WISH ME LUCK. I'M GONNA NEED IT.

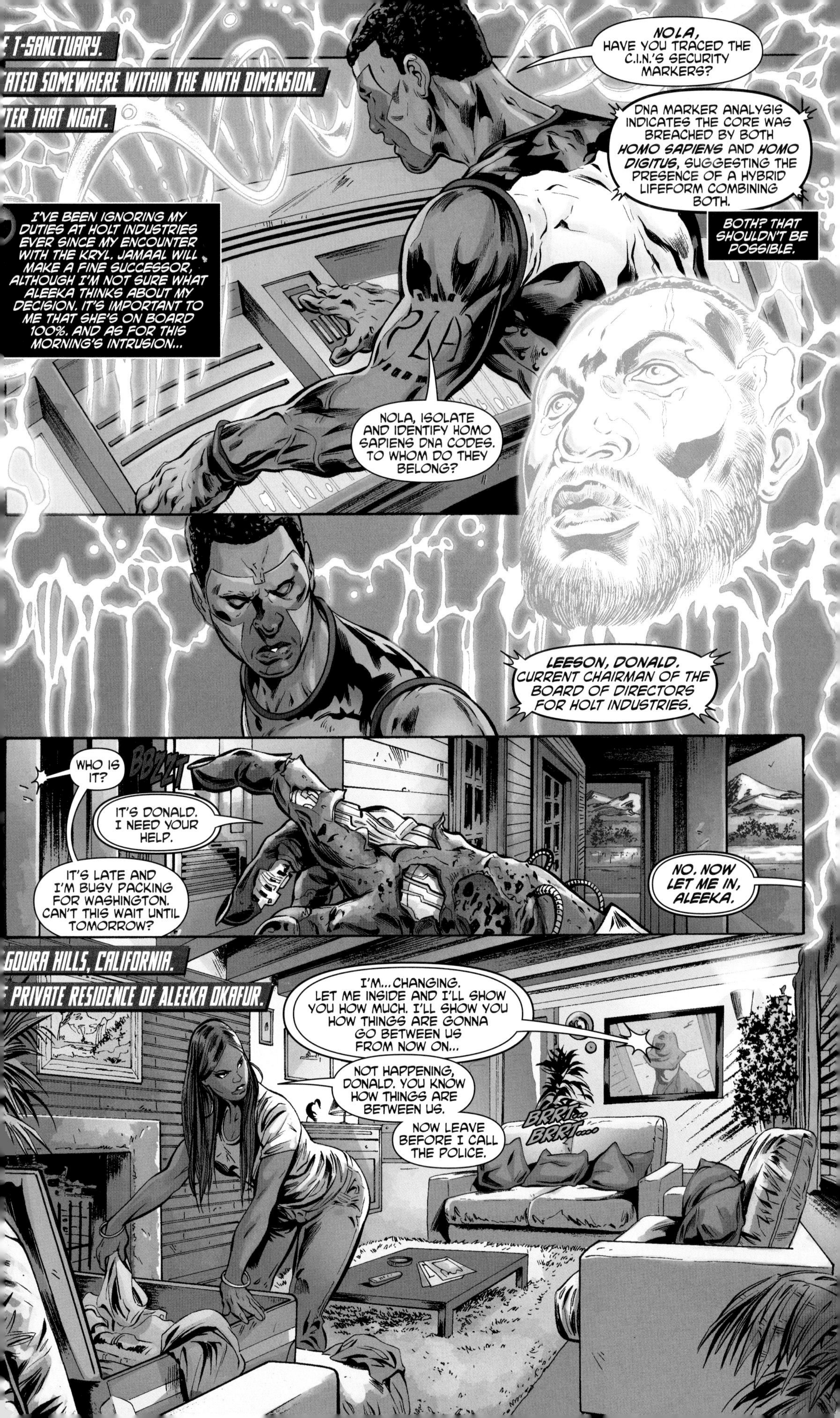

...E T-SANCTUARY.
...ATED SOMEWHERE WITHIN THE NINTH DIMENSION.
...TER THAT NIGHT.
NOLA, HAVE YOU TRACED THE C.I.N.'S SECURITY MARKERS?
DNA MARKER ANALYSIS INDICATES THE CORE WAS BREACHED BY BOTH HOMO SAPIENS AND HOMO DIGITUS, SUGGESTING THE PRESENCE OF A HYBRID LIFEFORM COMBINING BOTH.
BOTH? THAT SHOULDN'T BE POSSIBLE.
I'VE BEEN IGNORING MY DUTIES AT HOLT INDUSTRIES EVER SINCE MY ENCOUNTER WITH THE KRYL. JAMAAL WILL MAKE A FINE SUCCESSOR, ALTHOUGH I'M NOT SURE WHAT ALEEKA THINKS ABOUT MY DECISION. IT'S IMPORTANT TO ME THAT SHE'S ON BOARD 100%. AND AS FOR THIS MORNING'S INTRUSION...
NOLA, ISOLATE AND IDENTIFY HOMO SAPIENS DNA CODES. TO WHOM DO THEY BELONG?
LEESON, DONALD. CURRENT CHAIRMAN OF THE BOARD OF DIRECTORS FOR HOLT INDUSTRIES.
BBZZT
WHO IS IT?
IT'S DONALD. I NEED YOUR HELP.
IT'S LATE AND I'M BUSY PACKING FOR WASHINGTON. CAN'T THIS WAIT UNTIL TOMORROW?
NO. NOW LET ME IN, ALEEKA.
...GOURA HILLS, CALIFORNIA.
...PRIVATE RESIDENCE OF ALEEKA OKAFUR.
I'M...CHANGING. LET ME INSIDE AND I'LL SHOW YOU HOW MUCH. I'LL SHOW YOU HOW THINGS ARE GONNA GO BETWEEN US FROM NOW ON...
NOT HAPPENING, DONALD. YOU KNOW HOW THINGS ARE BETWEEN US.
NOW LEAVE BEFORE I CALL THE POLICE.
BRRT... BRRT....

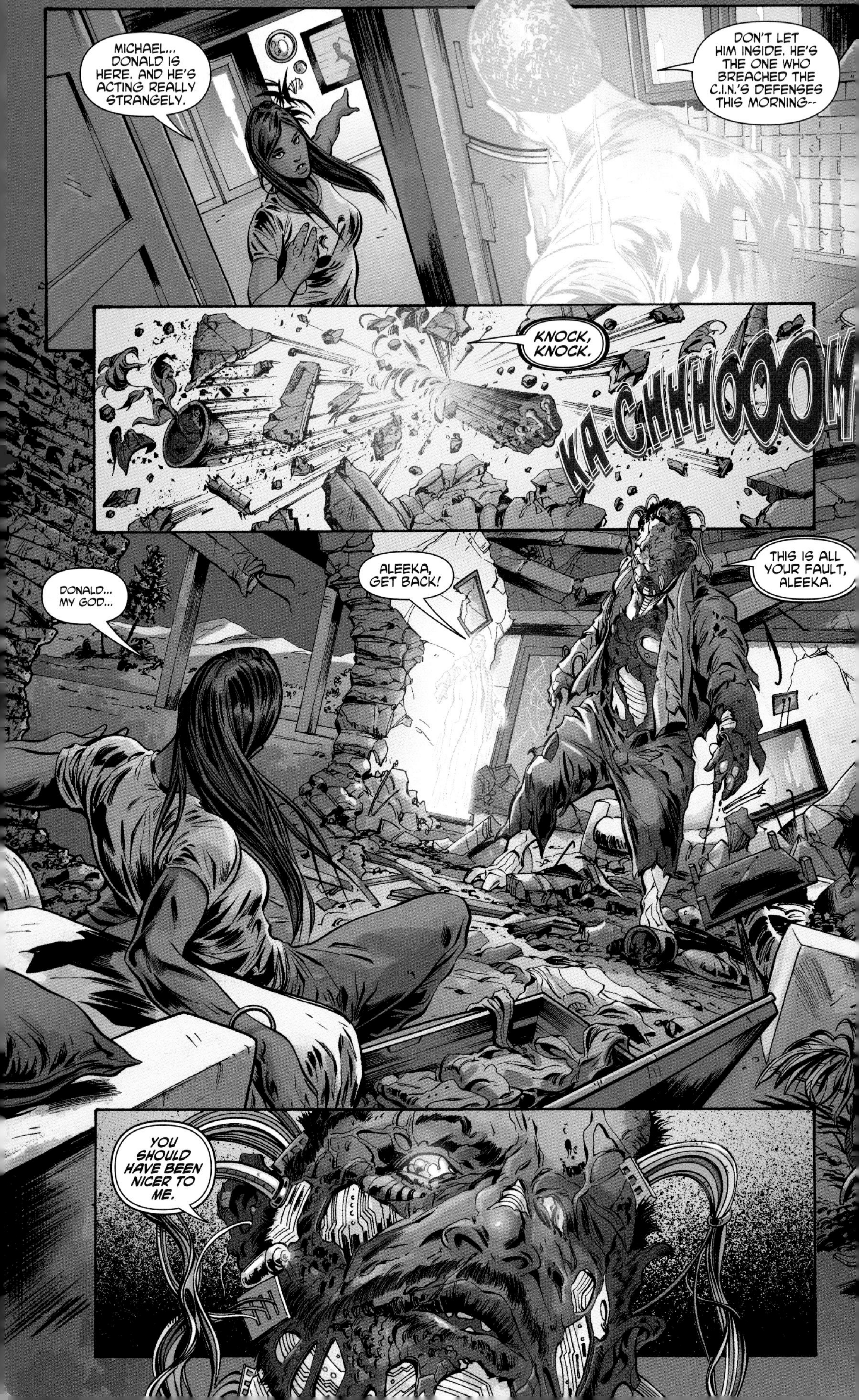
MICHAEL... DONALD IS HERE. AND HE'S ACTING REALLY STRANGELY.
DON'T LET HIM INSIDE. HE'S THE ONE WHO BREACHED THE C.I.N.'S DEFENSES THIS MORNING--
KNOCK, KNOCK.
KA-CHHHOOOM
DONALD... MY GOD...
ALEEKA, GET BACK!
THIS IS ALL YOUR FAULT, ALEEKA.
YOU SHOULD HAVE BEEN NICER TO ME.

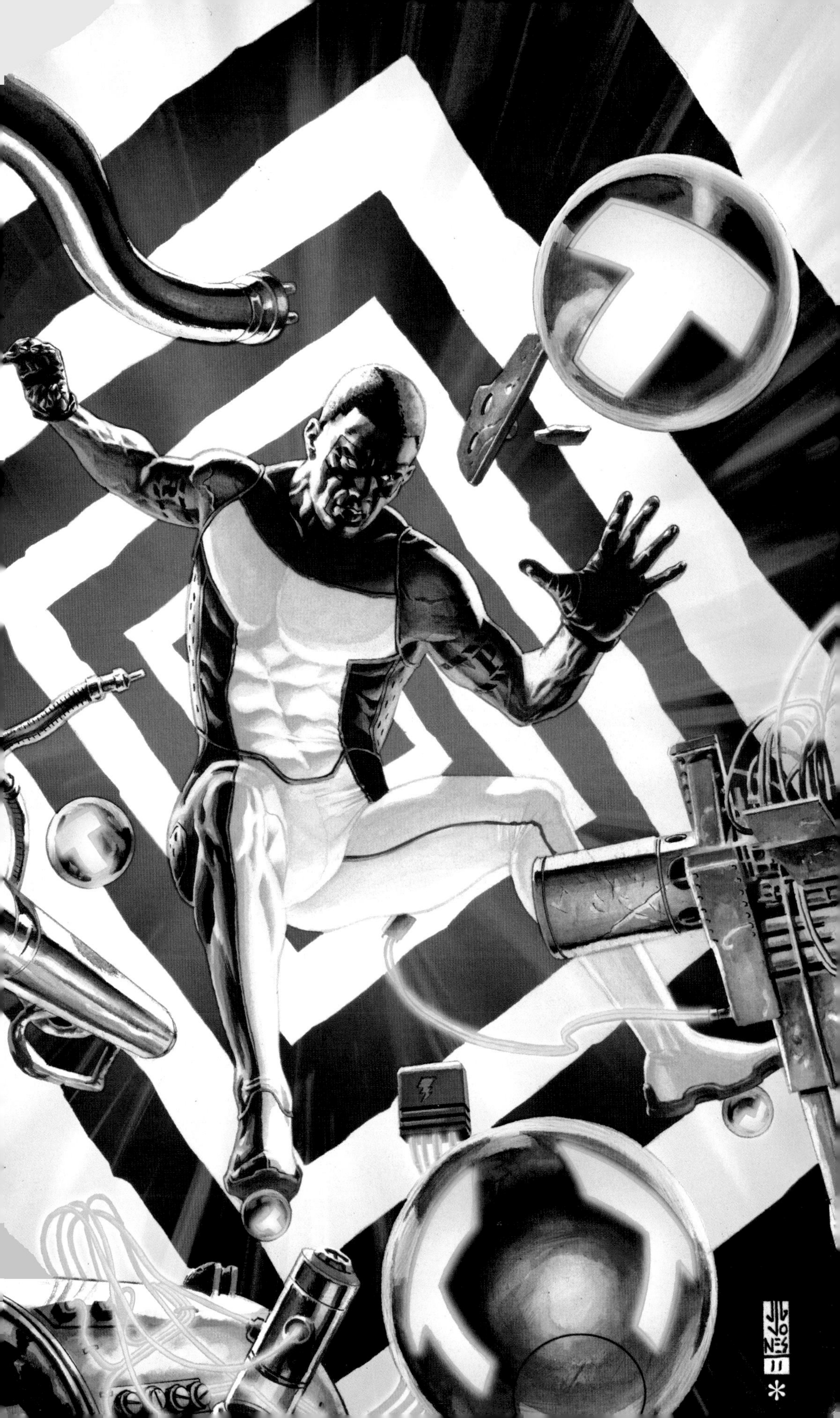

THE TRUTH IS OUT THERE

ERIC WALLACE writer **GIANLUCA GUGLIOTTA** penciller **WAYNE FAUCHER** inker
cover art by **J.G. JONES** with colorist **HI-FI**

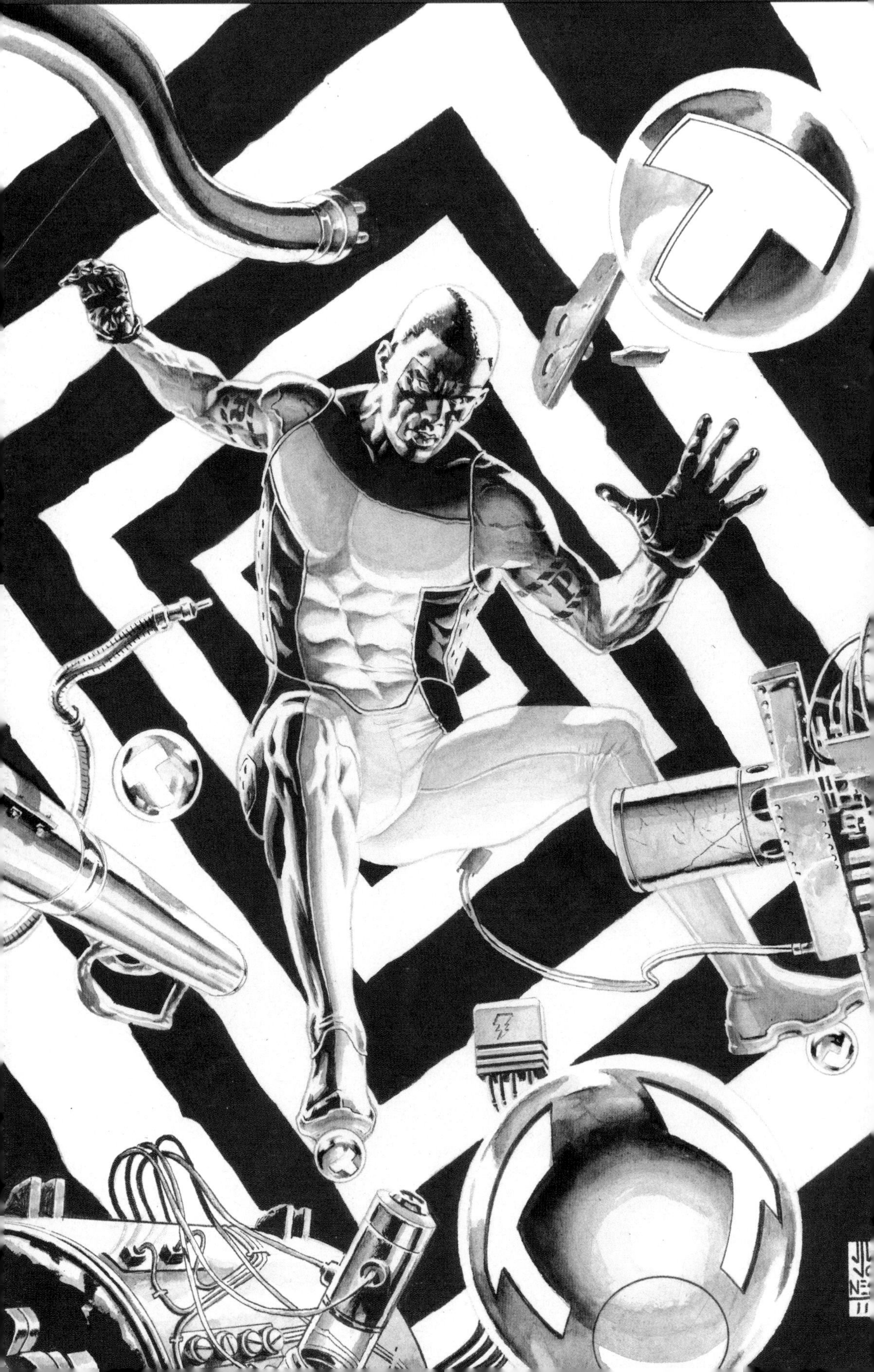

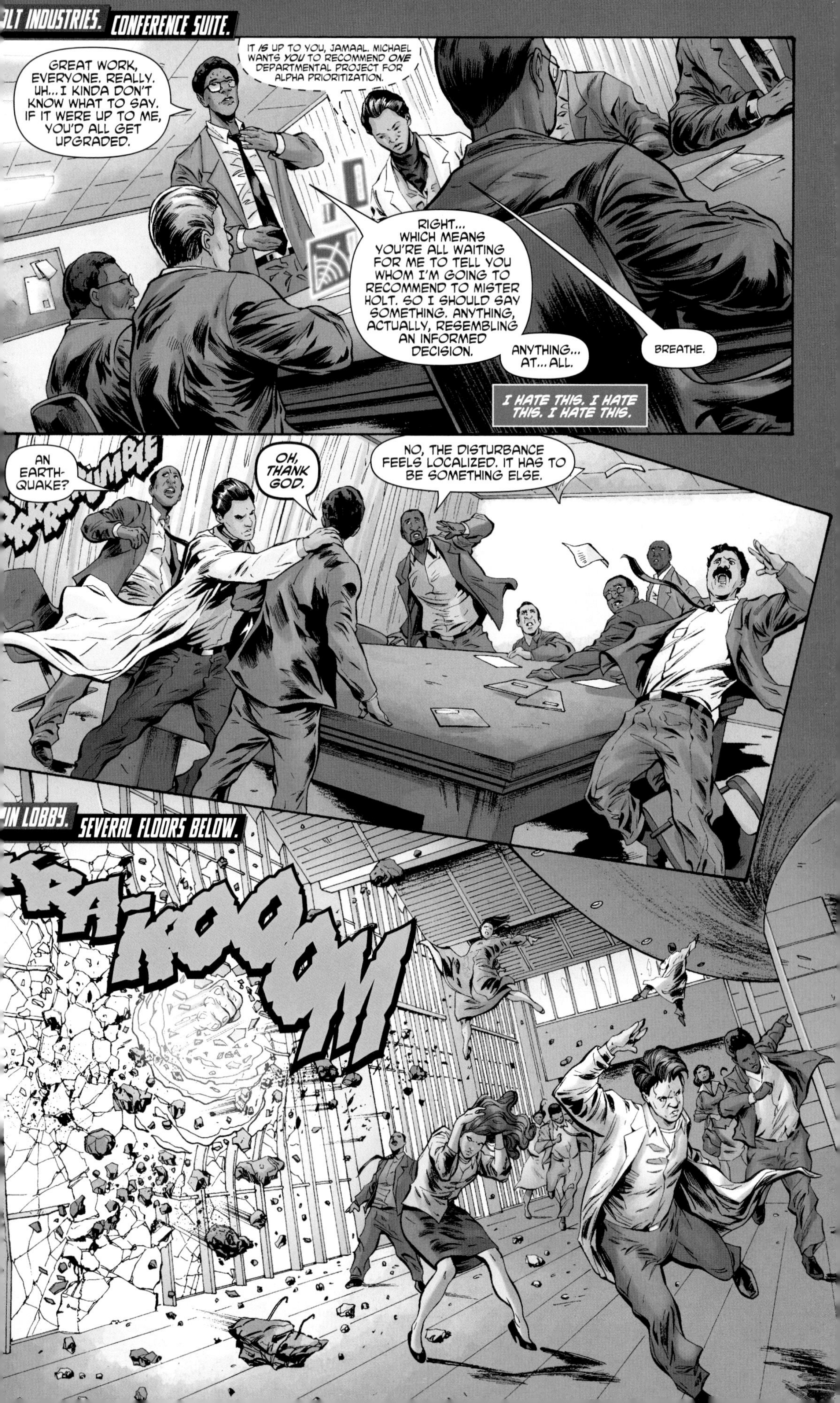

OLT INDUSTRIES. CONFERENCE SUITE.
GREAT WORK, EVERYONE. REALLY. UH...I KINDA DON'T KNOW WHAT TO SAY. IF IT WERE UP TO ME, YOU'D ALL GET UPGRADED.
IT IS UP TO YOU, JAMAAL. MICHAEL WANTS YOU TO RECOMMEND ONE DEPARTMENTAL PROJECT FOR ALPHA PRIORITIZATION.
RIGHT... WHICH MEANS YOU'RE ALL WAITING FOR ME TO TELL YOU WHOM I'M GOING TO RECOMMEND TO MISTER HOLT. SO I SHOULD SAY SOMETHING. ANYTHING, ACTUALLY, RESEMBLING AN INFORMED DECISION.
ANYTHING... AT... ALL.
BREATHE.
I HATE THIS. I HATE THIS. I HATE THIS.
AN EARTH-QUAKE?
OH, THANK GOD.
NO, THE DISTURBANCE FEELS LOCALIZED. IT HAS TO BE SOMETHING ELSE.
IN LOBBY. SEVERAL FLOORS BELOW.

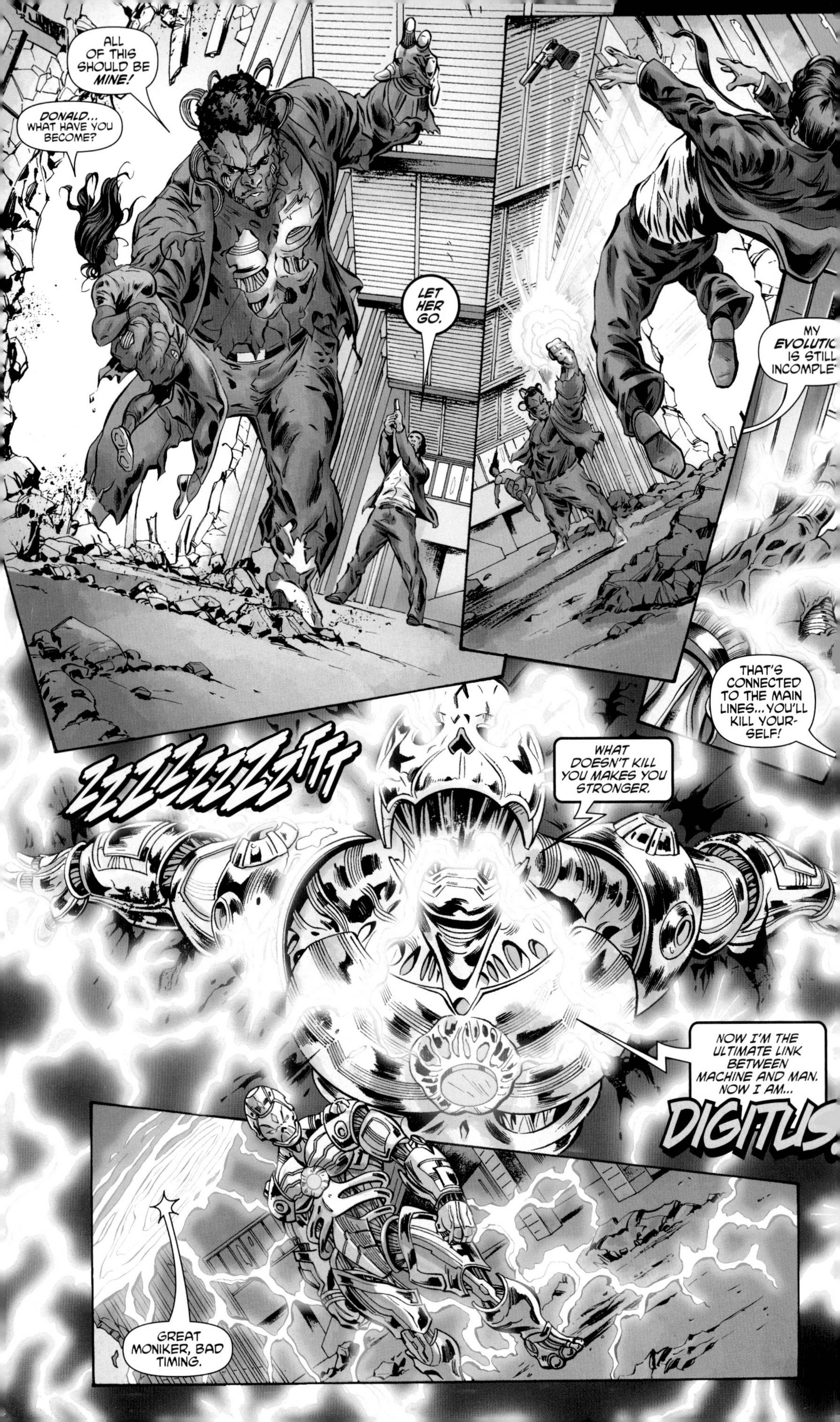
ALL OF THIS SHOULD BE MINE!
DONALD... WHAT HAVE YOU BECOME?
LET HER GO.
MY EVOLUTIC IS STILL INCOMPLE
THAT'S CONNECTED TO THE MAIN LINES... YOU'LL KILL YOURSELF!
ZZZZZZZZZTTT
WHAT DOESN'T KILL YOU MAKES YOU STRONGER.
NOW I'M THE ULTIMATE LINK BETWEEN MACHINE AND MAN. NOW I AM...
DIGITUS
GREAT MONIKER, BAD TIMING.

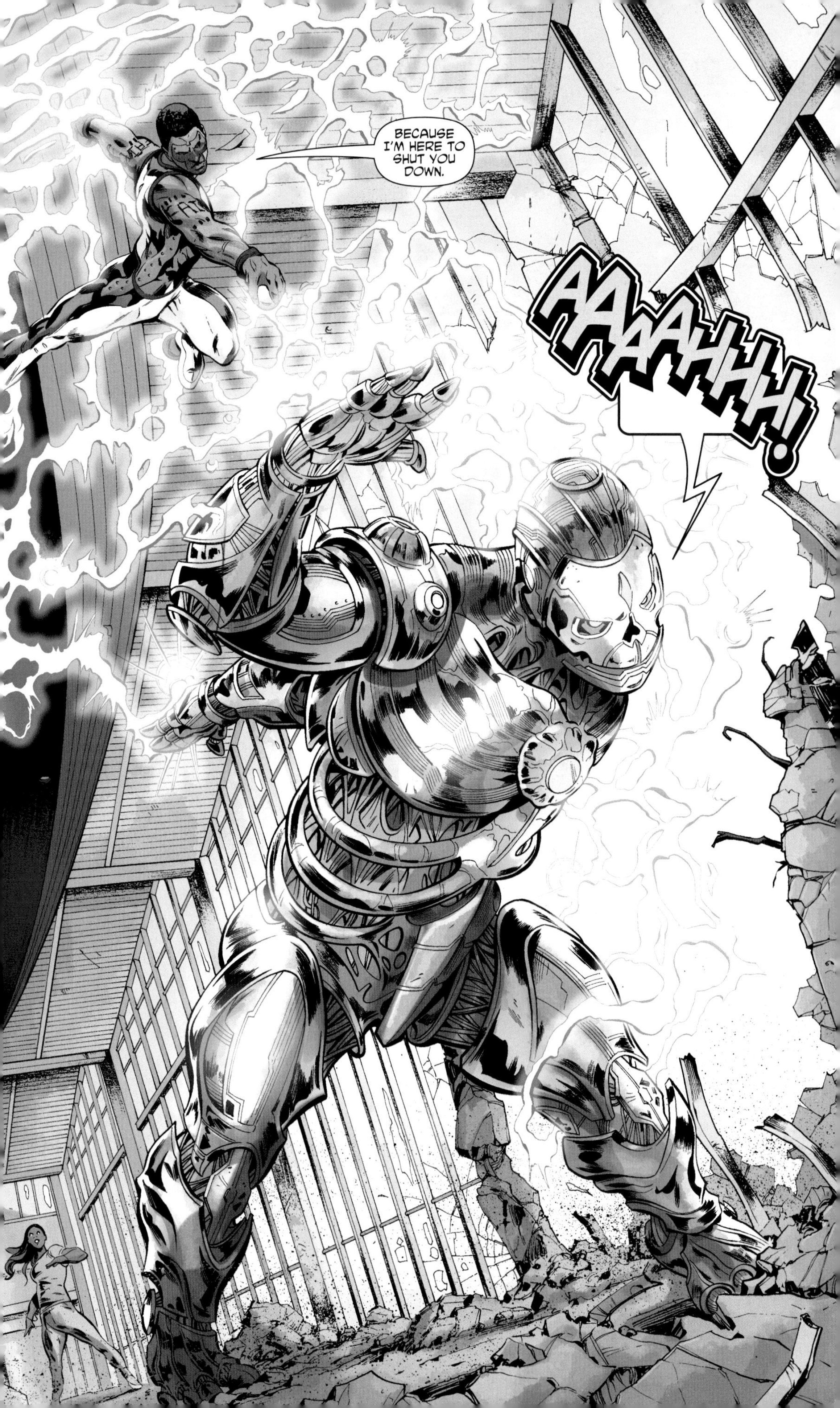

BECAUSE I'M HERE TO SHUT YOU DOWN.
AAAAHHH!

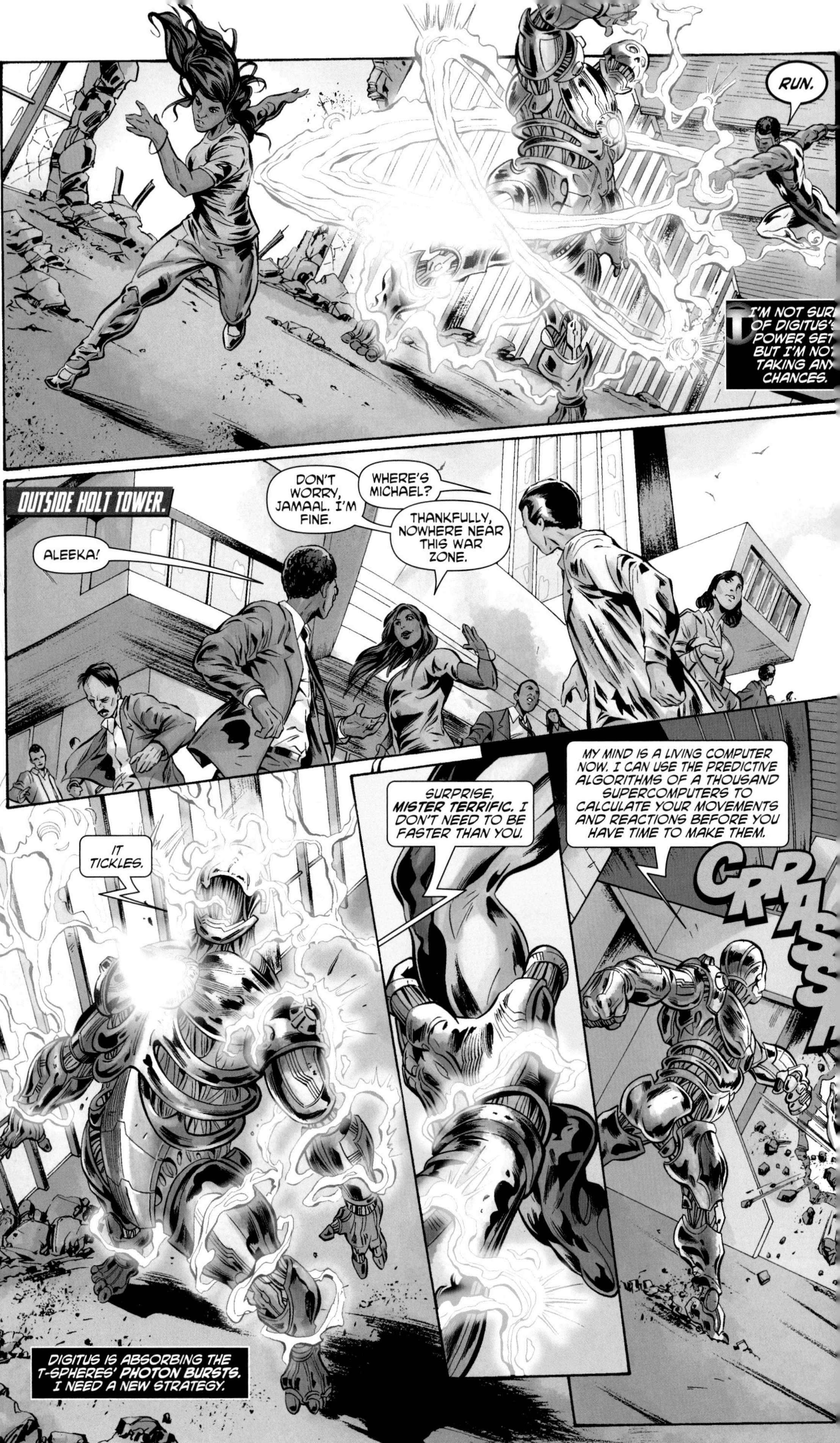

RUN.
I'M NOT SUR
OF DIGITUS'S
POWER SET
BUT I'M NOT
TAKING ANY
CHANCES.
OUTSIDE HOLT TOWER.
ALEEKA!
DON'T WORRY, JAMAAL. I'M FINE.
WHERE'S MICHAEL?
THANKFULLY, NOWHERE NEAR THIS WAR ZONE.
IT TICKLES.
SURPRISE, MISTER TERRIFIC. I DON'T NEED TO BE FASTER THAN YOU.
MY MIND IS A LIVING COMPUTER NOW. I CAN USE THE PREDICTIVE ALGORITHMS OF A THOUSAND SUPERCOMPUTERS TO CALCULATE YOUR MOVEMENTS AND REACTIONS BEFORE YOU HAVE TIME TO MAKE THEM.
CRASS
DIGITUS IS ABSORBING THE T-SPHERES' PHOTON BURSTS. I NEED A NEW STRATEGY.

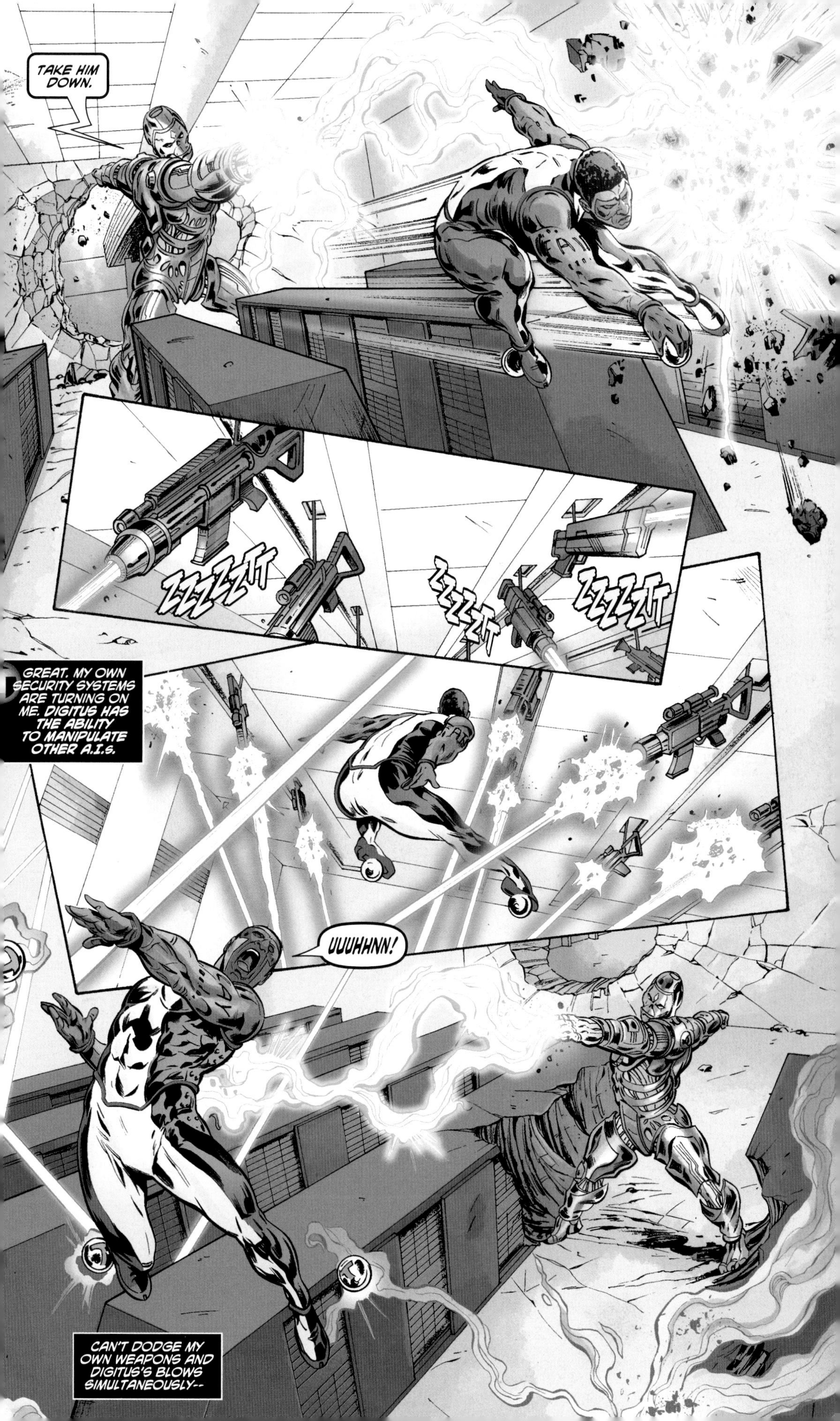
TAKE HIM DOWN.
ZZZZZZTT
ZZZZZTT
ZZZZZTT
GREAT. MY OWN SECURITY SYSTEMS ARE TURNING ON ME. DIGITUS HAS THE ABILITY TO MANIPULATE OTHER A.I.s.
UUUHHNN!
CAN'T DODGE MY OWN WEAPONS AND DIGITUS'S BLOWS SIMULTANEOUSLY--

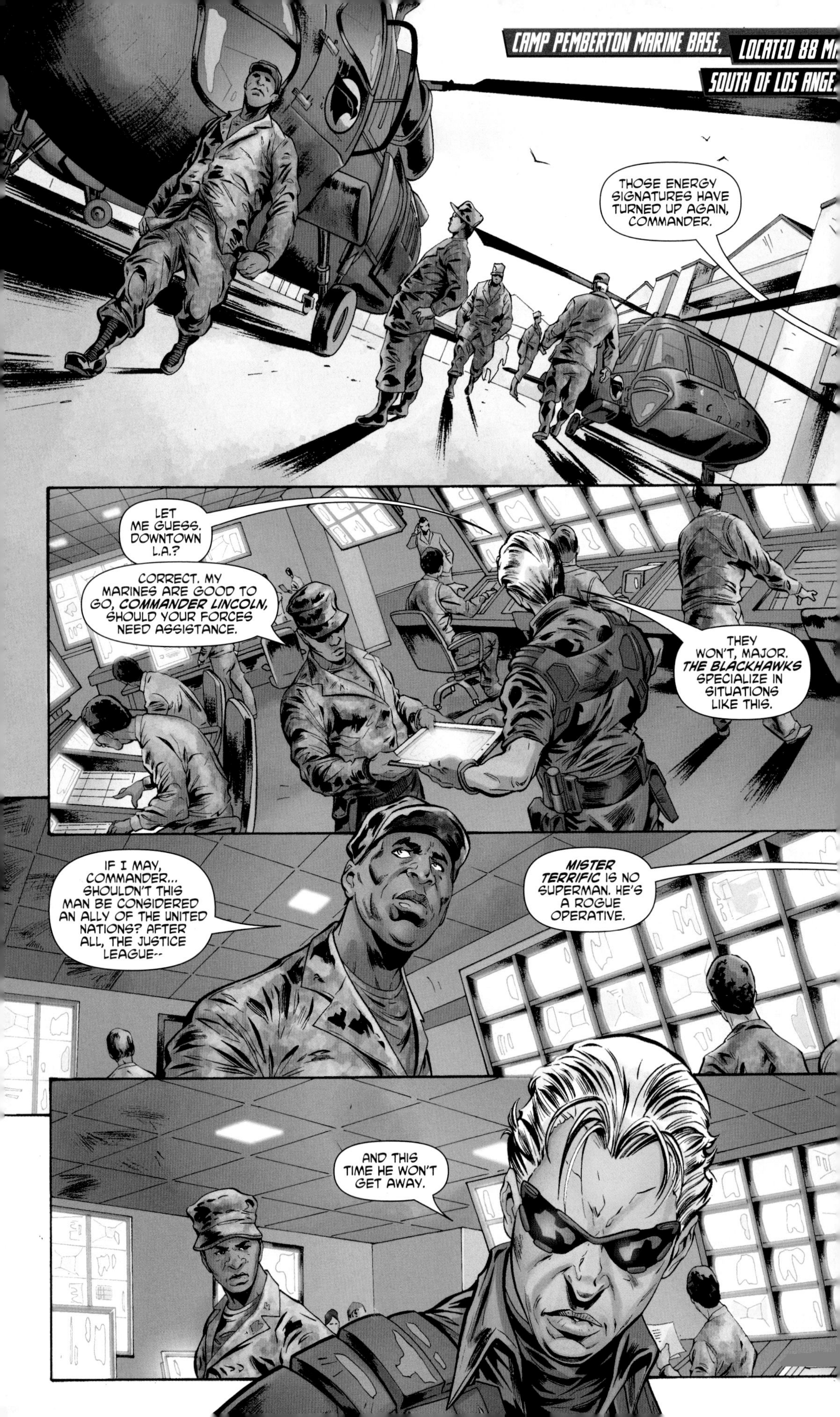
CAMP PEMBERTON MARINE BASE, LOCATED 88 MI
SOUTH OF LOS ANGE
THOSE ENERGY SIGNATURES HAVE TURNED UP AGAIN, COMMANDER.
LET ME GUESS. DOWNTOWN L.A.?
CORRECT. MY MARINES ARE GOOD TO GO, COMMANDER LINCOLN, SHOULD YOUR FORCES NEED ASSISTANCE.
THEY WON'T, MAJOR. THE BLACKHAWKS SPECIALIZE IN SITUATIONS LIKE THIS.
IF I MAY, COMMANDER... SHOULDN'T THIS MAN BE CONSIDERED AN ALLY OF THE UNITED NATIONS? AFTER ALL, THE JUSTICE LEAGUE--
MISTER TERRIFIC IS NO SUPERMAN. HE'S A ROGUE OPERATIVE.
AND THIS TIME HE WON'T GET AWAY.

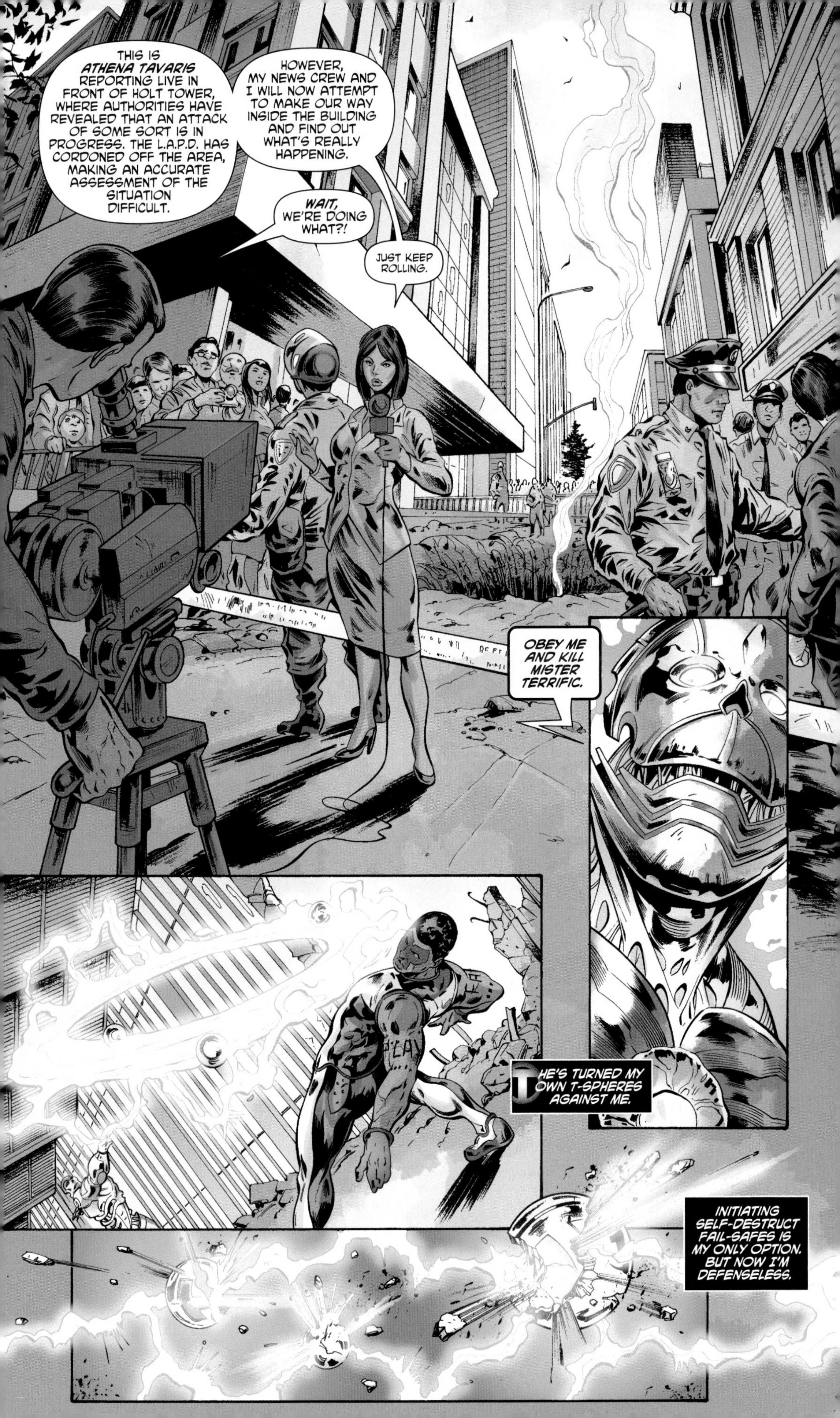

THIS IS ATHENA TAVARIS REPORTING LIVE IN FRONT OF HOLT TOWER, WHERE AUTHORITIES HAVE REVEALED THAT AN ATTACK OF SOME SORT IS IN PROGRESS. THE L.A.P.D. HAS CORDONED OFF THE AREA, MAKING AN ACCURATE ASSESSMENT OF THE SITUATION DIFFICULT.
HOWEVER, MY NEWS CREW AND I WILL NOW ATTEMPT TO MAKE OUR WAY INSIDE THE BUILDING AND FIND OUT WHAT'S REALLY HAPPENING.
WAIT, WE'RE DOING WHAT?!
JUST KEEP ROLLING.
OBEY ME AND KILL MISTER TERRIFIC.
HE'S TURNED MY OWN T-SPHERES AGAINST ME.
INITIATING SELF-DESTRUCT FAIL-SAFES IS MY ONLY OPTION. BUT NOW I'M DEFENSELESS.

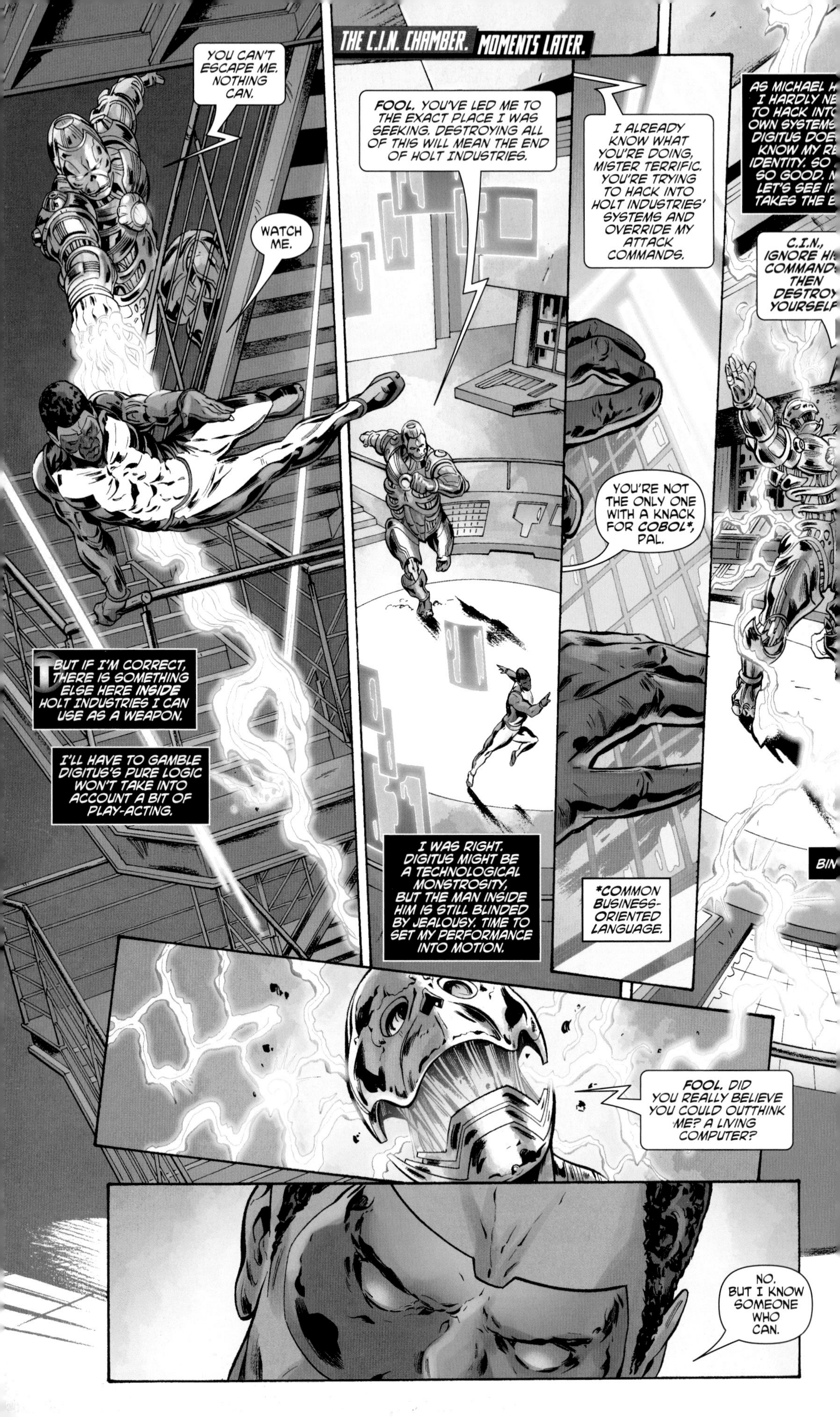
YOU CAN'T ESCAPE ME. NOTHING CAN.
WATCH ME.
BUT IF I'M CORRECT, THERE IS SOMETHING ELSE HERE INSIDE HOLT INDUSTRIES I CAN USE AS A WEAPON.
I'LL HAVE TO GAMBLE DIGITUS'S PURE LOGIC WON'T TAKE INTO ACCOUNT A BIT OF PLAY-ACTING.
THE C.I.N. CHAMBER. MOMENTS LATER.
FOOL. YOU'VE LED ME TO THE EXACT PLACE I WAS SEEKING. DESTROYING ALL OF THIS WILL MEAN THE END OF HOLT INDUSTRIES.
I WAS RIGHT. DIGITUS MIGHT BE A TECHNOLOGICAL MONSTROSITY, BUT THE MAN INSIDE HIM IS STILL BLINDED BY JEALOUSY. TIME TO SET MY PERFORMANCE INTO MOTION.
I ALREADY KNOW WHAT YOU'RE DOING, MISTER TERRIFIC. YOU'RE TRYING TO HACK INTO HOLT INDUSTRIES' SYSTEMS AND OVERRIDE MY ATTACK COMMANDS.
YOU'RE NOT THE ONLY ONE WITH A KNACK FOR COBOL*, PAL.
*COMMON BUSINESS-ORIENTED LANGUAGE.
FOOL. DID YOU REALLY BELIEVE YOU COULD OUTTHINK ME? A LIVING COMPUTER?
NO. BUT I KNOW SOMEONE WHO CAN.

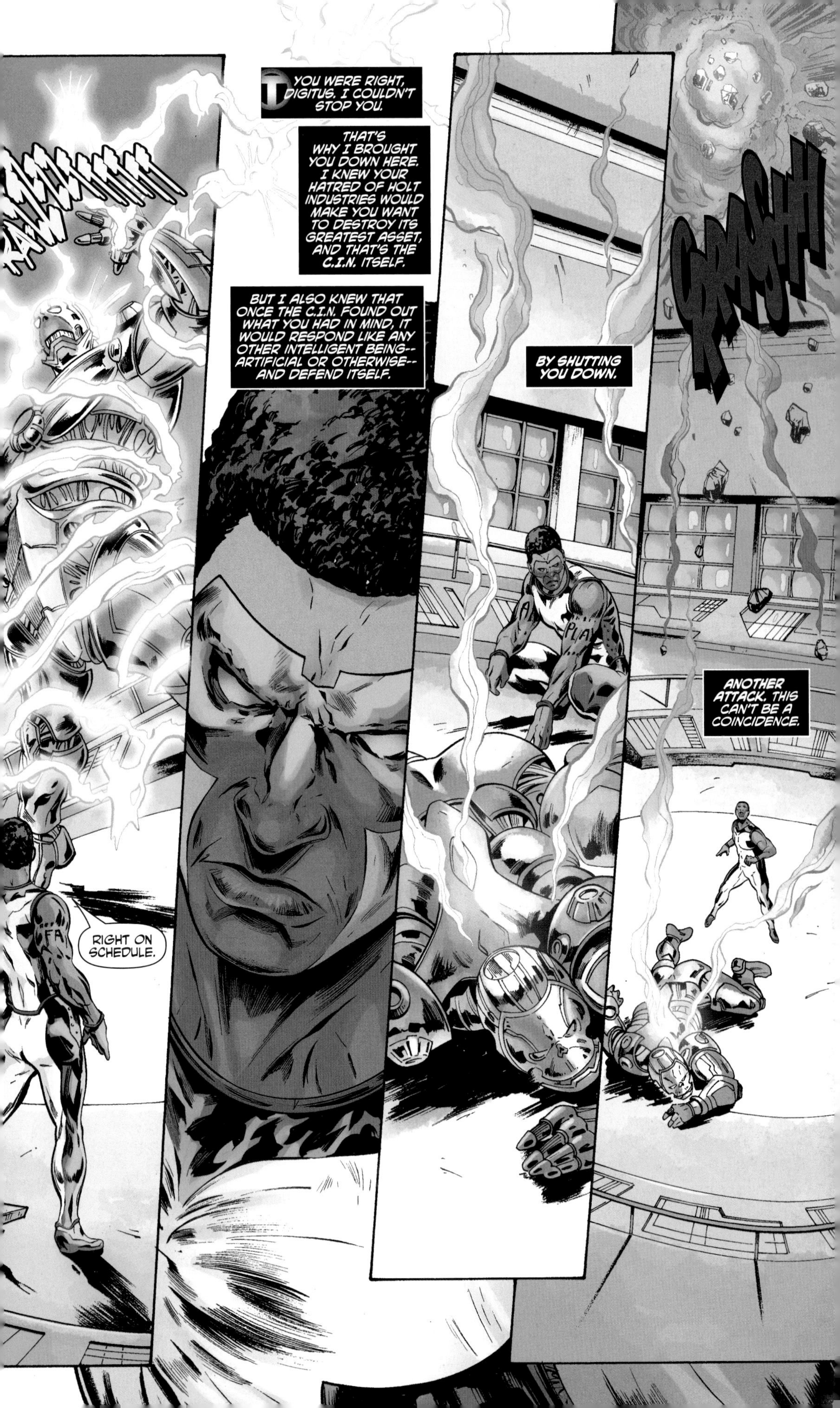

RAZZCHHH
RIGHT ON SCHEDULE.
YOU WERE RIGHT, DIGITUS. I COULDN'T STOP YOU.
THAT'S WHY I BROUGHT YOU DOWN HERE. I KNEW YOUR HATRED OF HOLT INDUSTRIES WOULD MAKE YOU WANT TO DESTROY ITS GREATEST ASSET, AND THAT'S THE C.I.N. ITSELF.
BUT I ALSO KNEW THAT ONCE THE C.I.N. FOUND OUT WHAT YOU HAD IN MIND, IT WOULD RESPOND LIKE ANY OTHER INTELLIGENT BEING--ARTIFICIAL OR OTHERWISE--AND DEFEND ITSELF.
BY SHUTTING YOU DOWN.
CRASSHH
ANOTHER ATTACK. THIS CAN'T BE A COINCIDENCE.

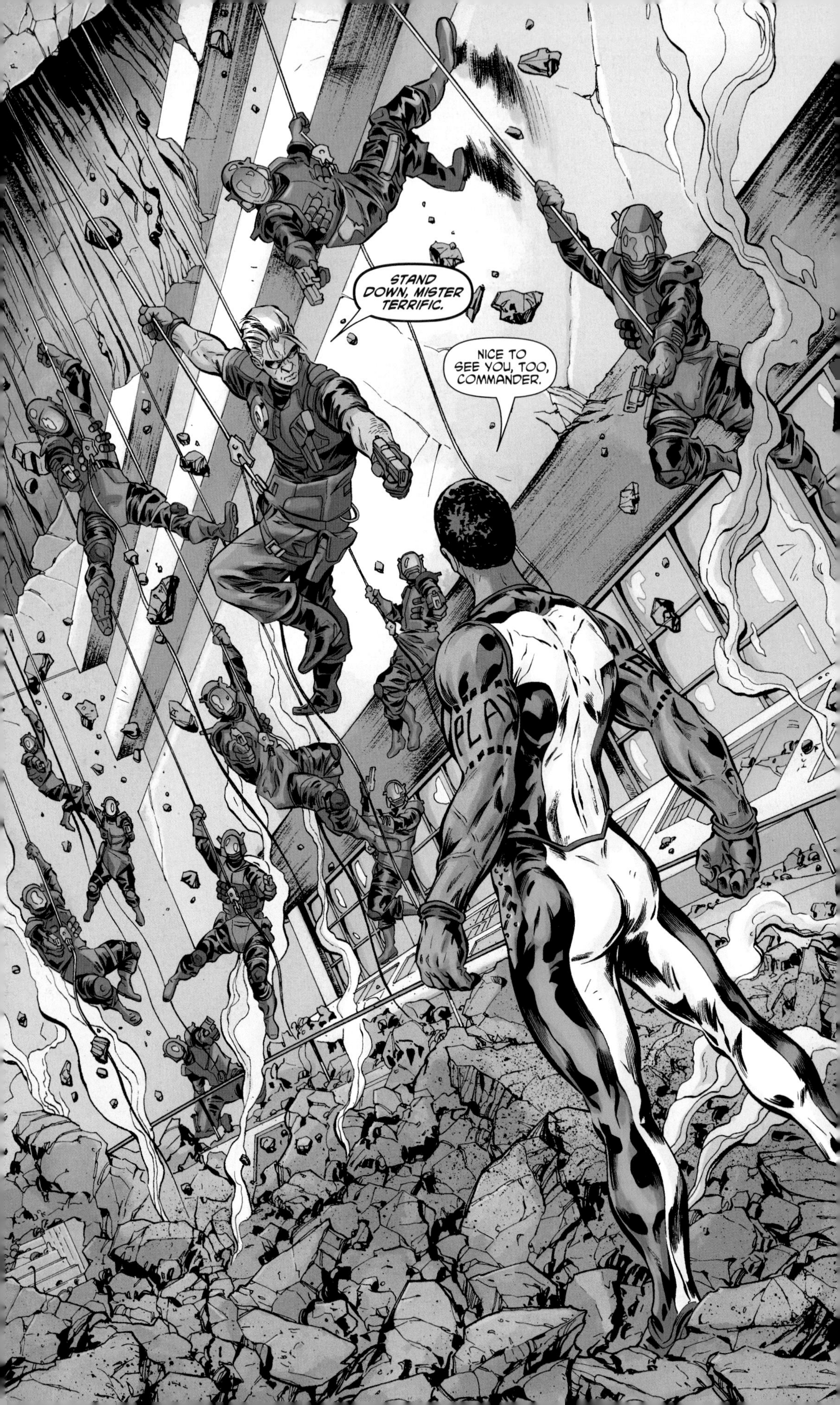
STAND DOWN, MISTER TERRIFIC.
NICE TO SEE YOU, TOO, COMMANDER.

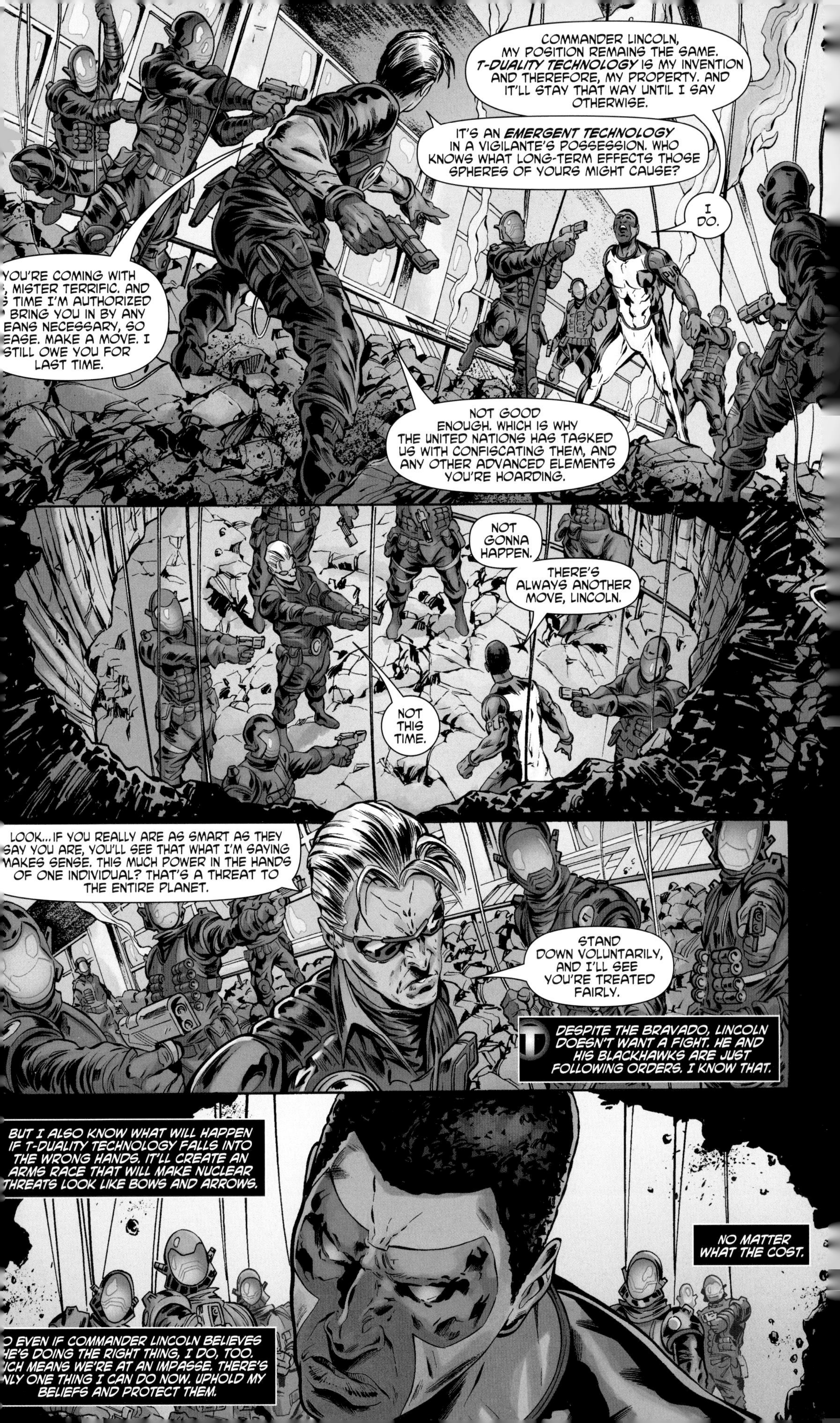

COMMANDER LINCOLN, MY POSITION REMAINS THE SAME. T-DUALITY TECHNOLOGY IS MY INVENTION AND THEREFORE, MY PROPERTY. AND IT'LL STAY THAT WAY UNTIL I SAY OTHERWISE.
IT'S AN EMERGENT TECHNOLOGY IN A VIGILANTE'S POSSESSION. WHO KNOWS WHAT LONG-TERM EFFECTS THOSE SPHERES OF YOURS MIGHT CAUSE?
I DO.
NOT GOOD ENOUGH. WHICH IS WHY THE UNITED NATIONS HAS TASKED US WITH CONFISCATING THEM, AND ANY OTHER ADVANCED ELEMENTS YOU'RE HOARDING.
YOU'RE COMING WITH , MISTER TERRIFIC. AND TIME I'M AUTHORIZED BRING YOU IN BY ANY EANS NECESSARY, SO EASE. MAKE A MOVE. I STILL OWE YOU FOR LAST TIME.
NOT GONNA HAPPEN.
THERE'S ALWAYS ANOTHER MOVE, LINCOLN.
NOT THIS TIME.
LOOK... IF YOU REALLY ARE AS SMART AS THEY SAY YOU ARE, YOU'LL SEE THAT WHAT I'M SAYING MAKES SENSE. THIS MUCH POWER IN THE HANDS OF ONE INDIVIDUAL? THAT'S A THREAT TO THE ENTIRE PLANET.
STAND DOWN VOLUNTARILY, AND I'LL SEE YOU'RE TREATED FAIRLY.
DESPITE THE BRAVADO, LINCOLN DOESN'T WANT A FIGHT. HE AND HIS BLACKHAWKS ARE JUST FOLLOWING ORDERS. I KNOW THAT.
BUT I ALSO KNOW WHAT WILL HAPPEN IF T-DUALITY TECHNOLOGY FALLS INTO THE WRONG HANDS. IT'LL CREATE AN ARMS RACE THAT WILL MAKE NUCLEAR THREATS LOOK LIKE BOWS AND ARROWS.
NO MATTER WHAT THE COST.
EVEN IF COMMANDER LINCOLN BELIEVES HE'S DOING THE RIGHT THING, I DO, TOO. ICH MEANS WE'RE AT AN IMPASSE. THERE'S NLY ONE THING I CAN DO NOW. UPHOLD MY BELIEFS AND PROTECT THEM.

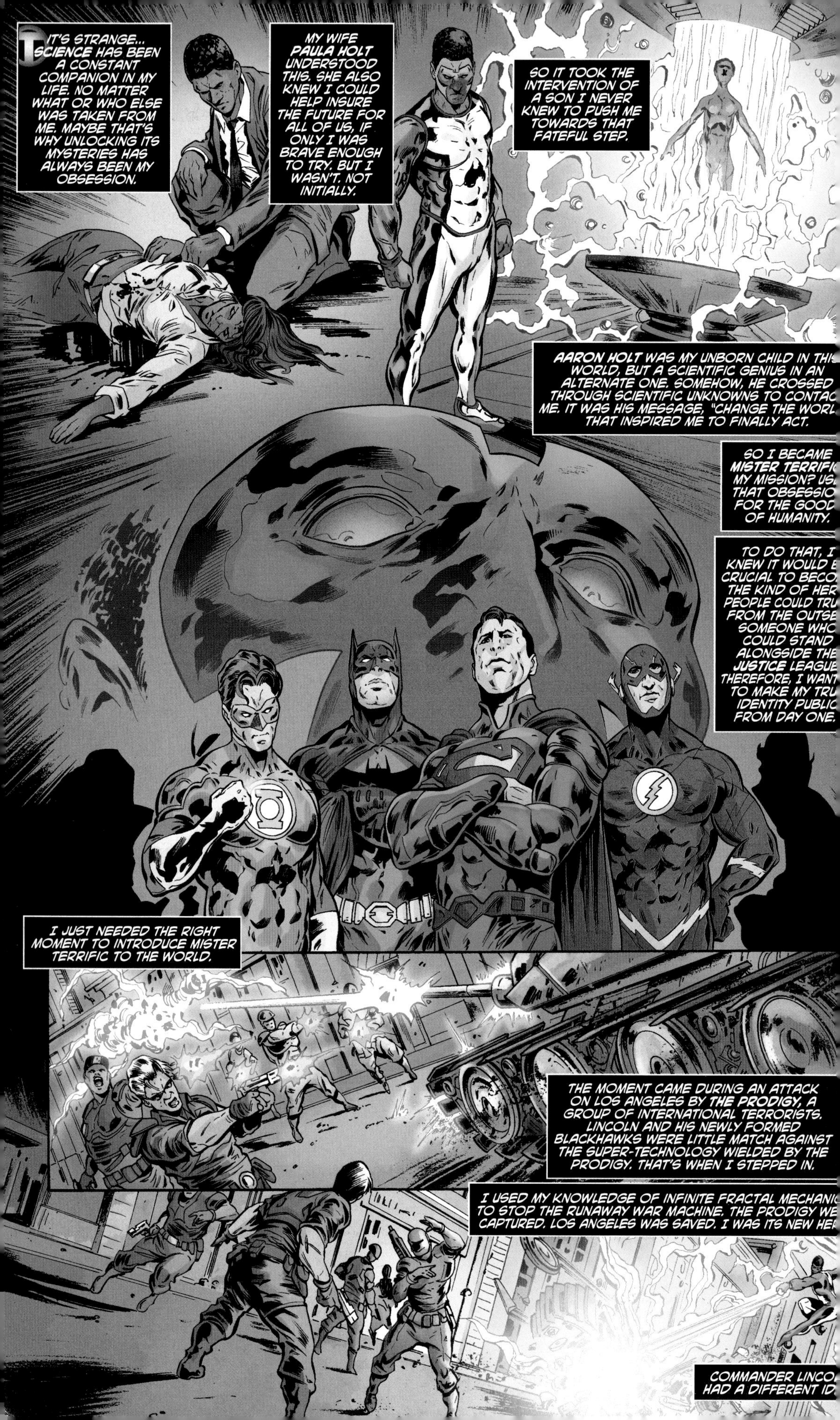
IT'S STRANGE... SCIENCE HAS BEEN A CONSTANT COMPANION IN MY LIFE. NO MATTER WHAT OR WHO ELSE WAS TAKEN FROM ME. MAYBE THAT'S WHY UNLOCKING ITS MYSTERIES HAS ALWAYS BEEN MY OBSESSION.
MY WIFE PAULA HOLT UNDERSTOOD THIS. SHE ALSO KNEW I COULD HELP INSURE THE FUTURE FOR ALL OF US, IF ONLY I WAS BRAVE ENOUGH TO TRY. BUT I WASN'T. NOT INITIALLY.
SO IT TOOK THE INTERVENTION OF A SON I NEVER KNEW TO PUSH ME TOWARDS THAT FATEFUL STEP.
AARON HOLT WAS MY UNBORN CHILD IN THIS WORLD, BUT A SCIENTIFIC GENIUS IN AN ALTERNATE ONE. SOMEHOW, HE CROSSED THROUGH SCIENTIFIC UNKNOWNS TO CONTAC ME. IT WAS HIS MESSAGE, "CHANGE THE WORL THAT INSPIRED ME TO FINALLY ACT.
SO I BECAME MISTER TERRIFI MY MISSION? US THAT OBSESSIO FOR THE GOOD OF HUMANITY.
TO DO THAT, I KNEW IT WOULD B CRUCIAL TO BECO THE KIND OF HER PEOPLE COULD TRU FROM THE OUTSE SOMEONE WHO COULD STAND ALONGSIDE THE JUSTICE LEAGUE THEREFORE, I WANT TO MAKE MY TRU IDENTITY PUBLIC FROM DAY ONE.
I JUST NEEDED THE RIGHT MOMENT TO INTRODUCE MISTER TERRIFIC TO THE WORLD.
THE MOMENT CAME DURING AN ATTACK ON LOS ANGELES BY THE PRODIGY, A GROUP OF INTERNATIONAL TERRORISTS. LINCOLN AND HIS NEWLY FORMED BLACKHAWKS WERE LITTLE MATCH AGAINST THE SUPER-TECHNOLOGY WIELDED BY THE PRODIGY. THAT'S WHEN I STEPPED IN.
I USED MY KNOWLEDGE OF INFINITE FRACTAL MECHANI TO STOP THE RUNAWAY WAR MACHINE. THE PRODIGY WE CAPTURED. LOS ANGELES WAS SAVED. I WAS ITS NEW HE
COMMANDER LINCO HAD A DIFFERENT ID

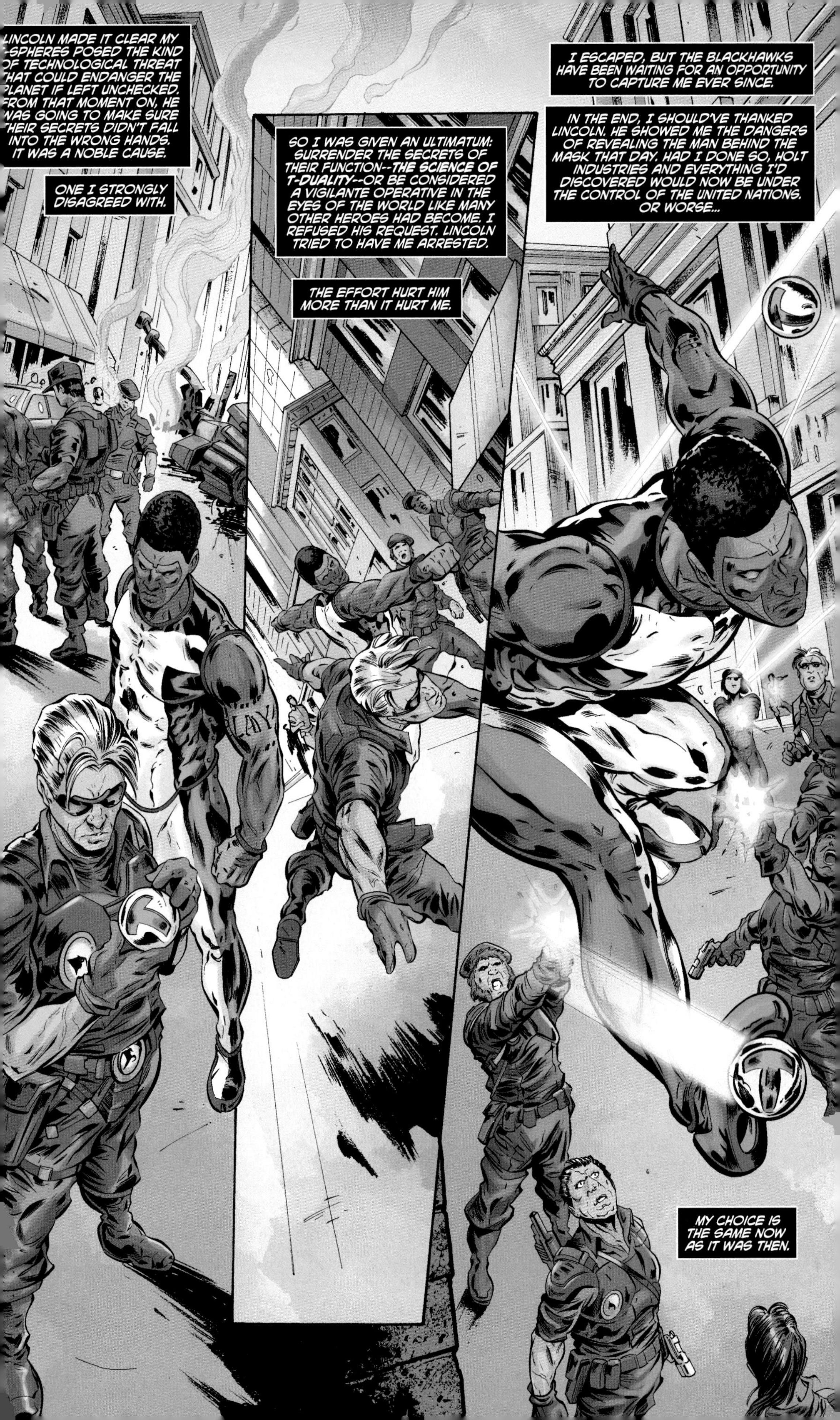
LINCOLN MADE IT CLEAR MY T-SPHERES POSED THE KIND OF TECHNOLOGICAL THREAT THAT COULD ENDANGER THE PLANET IF LEFT UNCHECKED. FROM THAT MOMENT ON, HE WAS GOING TO MAKE SURE THEIR SECRETS DIDN'T FALL INTO THE WRONG HANDS. IT WAS A NOBLE CAUSE.
ONE I STRONGLY DISAGREED WITH.
SO I WAS GIVEN AN ULTIMATUM: SURRENDER THE SECRETS OF THEIR FUNCTION--**THE SCIENCE OF T-DUALITY**--OR BE CONSIDERED A VIGILANTE OPERATIVE IN THE EYES OF THE WORLD LIKE MANY OTHER HEROES HAD BECOME. I REFUSED HIS REQUEST. LINCOLN TRIED TO HAVE ME ARRESTED.
THE EFFORT HURT HIM MORE THAN IT HURT ME.
I ESCAPED, BUT THE BLACKHAWKS HAVE BEEN WAITING FOR AN OPPORTUNITY TO CAPTURE ME EVER SINCE.
IN THE END, I SHOULD'VE THANKED LINCOLN. HE SHOWED ME THE DANGERS OF REVEALING THE MAN BEHIND THE MASK THAT DAY. HAD I DONE SO, HOLT INDUSTRIES AND EVERYTHING I'D DISCOVERED WOULD NOW BE UNDER THE CONTROL OF THE UNITED NATIONS. OR WORSE...
MY CHOICE IS THE SAME NOW AS IT WAS THEN.

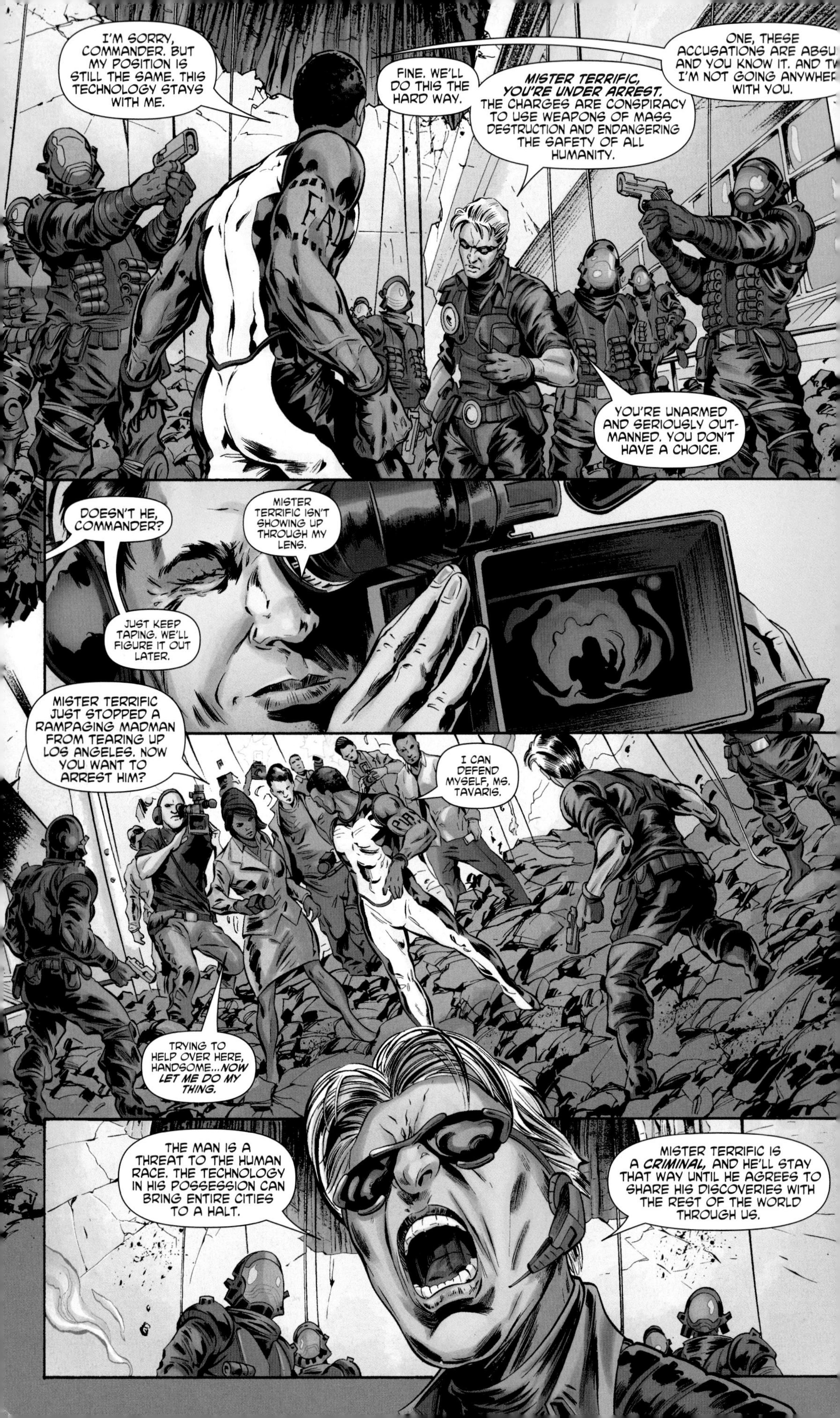
I'M SORRY, COMMANDER. BUT MY POSITION IS STILL THE SAME. THIS TECHNOLOGY STAYS WITH ME.
FINE. WE'LL DO THIS THE HARD WAY.
MISTER TERRIFIC, YOU'RE UNDER ARREST. THE CHARGES ARE CONSPIRACY TO USE WEAPONS OF MASS DESTRUCTION AND ENDANGERING THE SAFETY OF ALL HUMANITY.
YOU'RE UNARMED AND SERIOUSLY OUT-MANNED. YOU DON'T HAVE A CHOICE.
DOESN'T HE, COMMANDER?
MISTER TERRIFIC ISN'T SHOWING UP THROUGH MY LENS.
JUST KEEP TAPING. WE'LL FIGURE IT OUT LATER.
MISTER TERRIFIC JUST STOPPED A RAMPAGING MADMAN FROM TEARING UP LOS ANGELES. NOW YOU WANT TO ARREST HIM?
I CAN DEFEND MYSELF, MS. TAVARIS.
TRYING TO HELP OVER HERE, HANDSOME...NOW LET ME DO MY THING.
THE MAN IS A THREAT TO THE HUMAN RACE. THE TECHNOLOGY IN HIS POSSESSION CAN BRING ENTIRE CITIES TO A HALT.
MISTER TERRIFIC IS A CRIMINAL, AND HE'LL STAY THAT WAY UNTIL HE AGREES TO SHARE HIS DISCOVERIES WITH THE REST OF THE WORLD THROUGH US.

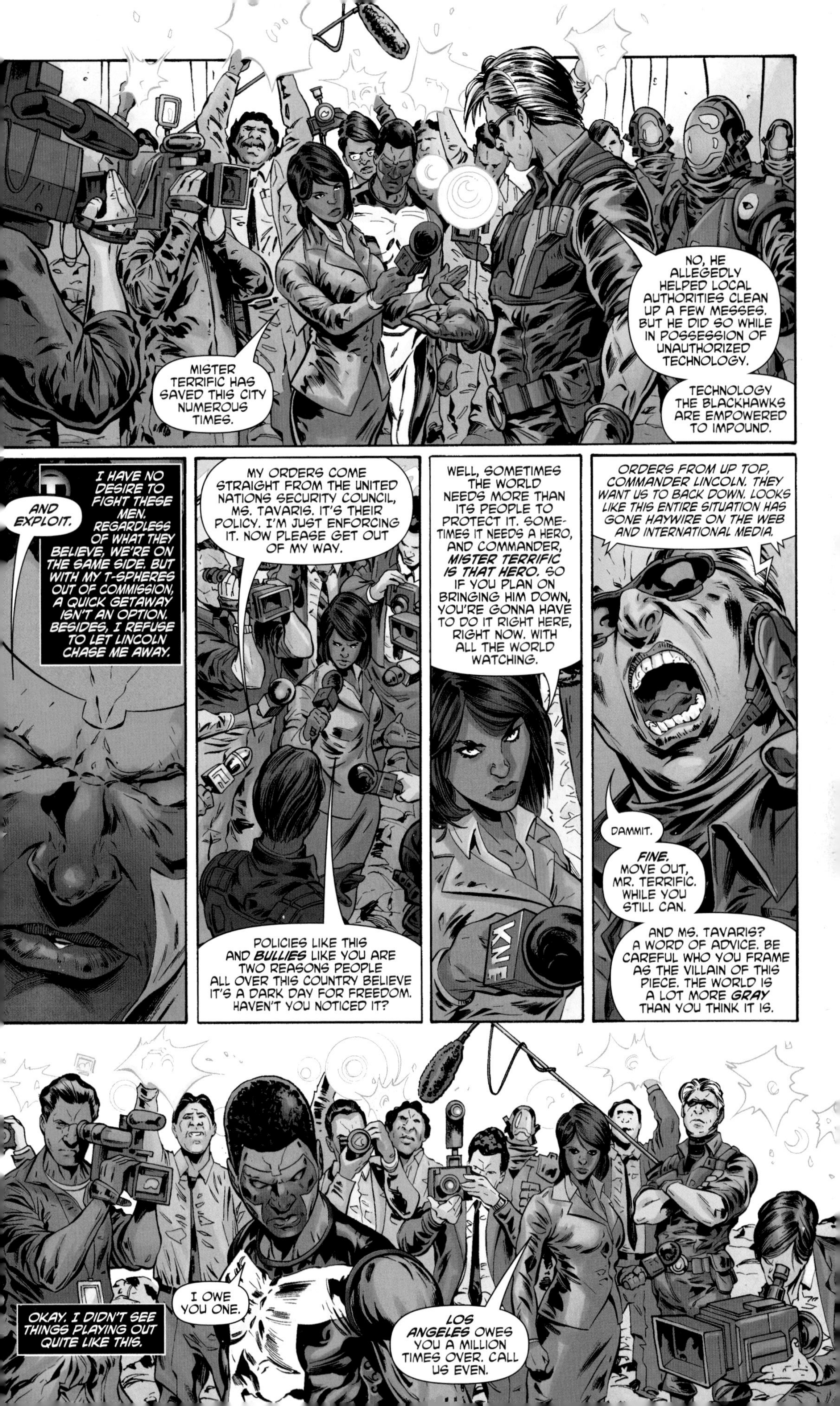
MISTER TERRIFIC HAS SAVED THIS CITY NUMEROUS TIMES.
NO, HE ALLEGEDLY HELPED LOCAL AUTHORITIES CLEAN UP A FEW MESSES. BUT HE DID SO WHILE IN POSSESSION OF UNAUTHORIZED TECHNOLOGY.
TECHNOLOGY THE BLACKHAWKS ARE EMPOWERED TO IMPOUND.
I HAVE NO DESIRE TO FIGHT THESE MEN.
AND EXPLOIT.
REGARDLESS OF WHAT THEY BELIEVE, WE'RE ON THE SAME SIDE. BUT WITH MY T-SPHERES OUT OF COMMISSION, A QUICK GETAWAY ISN'T AN OPTION. BESIDES, I REFUSE TO LET LINCOLN CHASE ME AWAY.
MY ORDERS COME STRAIGHT FROM THE UNITED NATIONS SECURITY COUNCIL, MS. TAVARIS. IT'S THEIR POLICY. I'M JUST ENFORCING IT. NOW PLEASE GET OUT OF MY WAY.
POLICIES LIKE THIS AND BULLIES LIKE YOU ARE TWO REASONS PEOPLE ALL OVER THIS COUNTRY BELIEVE IT'S A DARK DAY FOR FREEDOM. HAVEN'T YOU NOTICED IT?
WELL, SOMETIMES THE WORLD NEEDS MORE THAN ITS PEOPLE TO PROTECT IT. SOMETIMES IT NEEDS A HERO, AND COMMANDER, MISTER TERRIFIC IS THAT HERO. SO IF YOU PLAN ON BRINGING HIM DOWN, YOU'RE GONNA HAVE TO DO IT RIGHT HERE, RIGHT NOW. WITH ALL THE WORLD WATCHING.
KNE
ORDERS FROM UP TOP, COMMANDER LINCOLN. THEY WANT US TO BACK DOWN. LOOKS LIKE THIS ENTIRE SITUATION HAS GONE HAYWIRE ON THE WEB AND INTERNATIONAL MEDIA.
DAMMIT.
FINE. MOVE OUT, MR. TERRIFIC. WHILE YOU STILL CAN.
AND MS. TAVARIS? A WORD OF ADVICE. BE CAREFUL WHO YOU FRAME AS THE VILLAIN OF THIS PIECE. THE WORLD IS A LOT MORE GRAY THAN YOU THINK IT IS.
OKAY. I DIDN'T SEE THINGS PLAYING OUT QUITE LIKE THIS.
I OWE YOU ONE.
LOS ANGELES OWES YOU A MILLION TIMES OVER. CALL US EVEN.

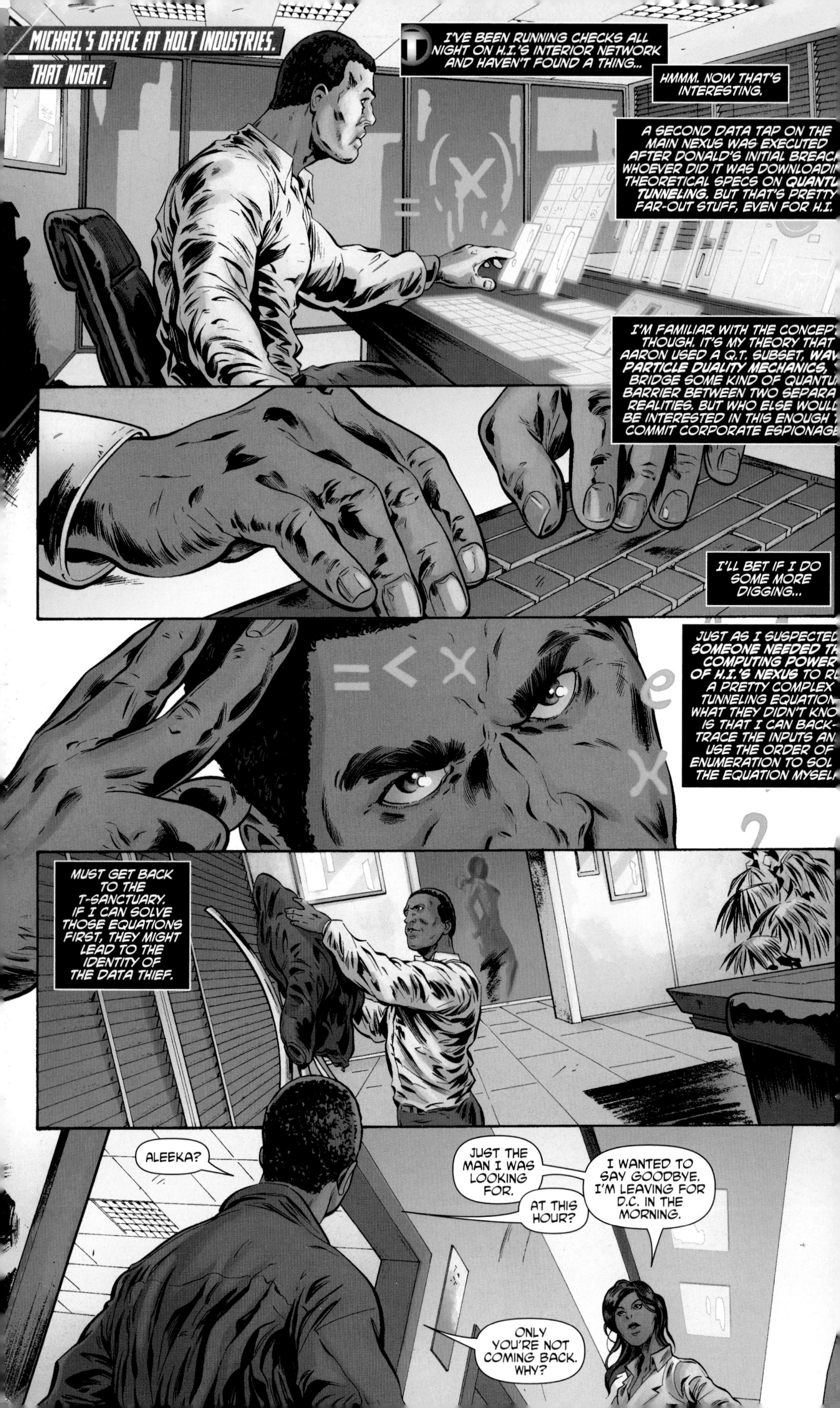

MICHAEL'S OFFICE AT HOLT INDUSTRIES.
THAT NIGHT.
I'VE BEEN RUNNING CHECKS ALL NIGHT ON H.I.'S INTERIOR NETWORK AND HAVEN'T FOUND A THING...
HMMM. NOW THAT'S INTERESTING.
A SECOND DATA TAP ON THE MAIN NEXUS WAS EXECUTED AFTER DONALD'S INITIAL BREAC WHOEVER DID IT WAS DOWNLOADI THEORETICAL SPECS ON QUANTU TUNNELING. BUT THAT'S PRETTY FAR-OUT STUFF, EVEN FOR H.I.
I'M FAMILIAR WITH THE CONCEP THOUGH. IT'S MY THEORY THAT AARON USED A Q.T. SUBSET, WAV PARTICLE DUALITY MECHANICS, BRIDGE SOME KIND OF QUANTU BARRIER BETWEEN TWO SEPARA REALITIES. BUT WHO ELSE WOUL BE INTERESTED IN THIS ENOUGH COMMIT CORPORATE ESPIONAG
I'LL BET IF I DO SOME MORE DIGGING...
JUST AS I SUSPECTE SOMEONE NEEDED T COMPUTING POWER OF H.I.'S NEXUS TO R A PRETTY COMPLEX TUNNELING EQUATION WHAT THEY DIDN'T KNO IS THAT I CAN BACK-TRACE THE INPUTS AN USE THE ORDER OF ENUMERATION TO SOL THE EQUATION MYSEL
MUST GET BACK TO THE T-SANCTUARY. IF I CAN SOLVE THOSE EQUATIONS FIRST, THEY MIGHT LEAD TO THE IDENTITY OF THE DATA THIEF.
ALEEKA?
JUST THE MAN I WAS LOOKING FOR.
AT THIS HOUR?
I WANTED TO SAY GOODBYE. I'M LEAVING FOR D.C. IN THE MORNING.
ONLY YOU'RE NOT COMING BACK. WHY?

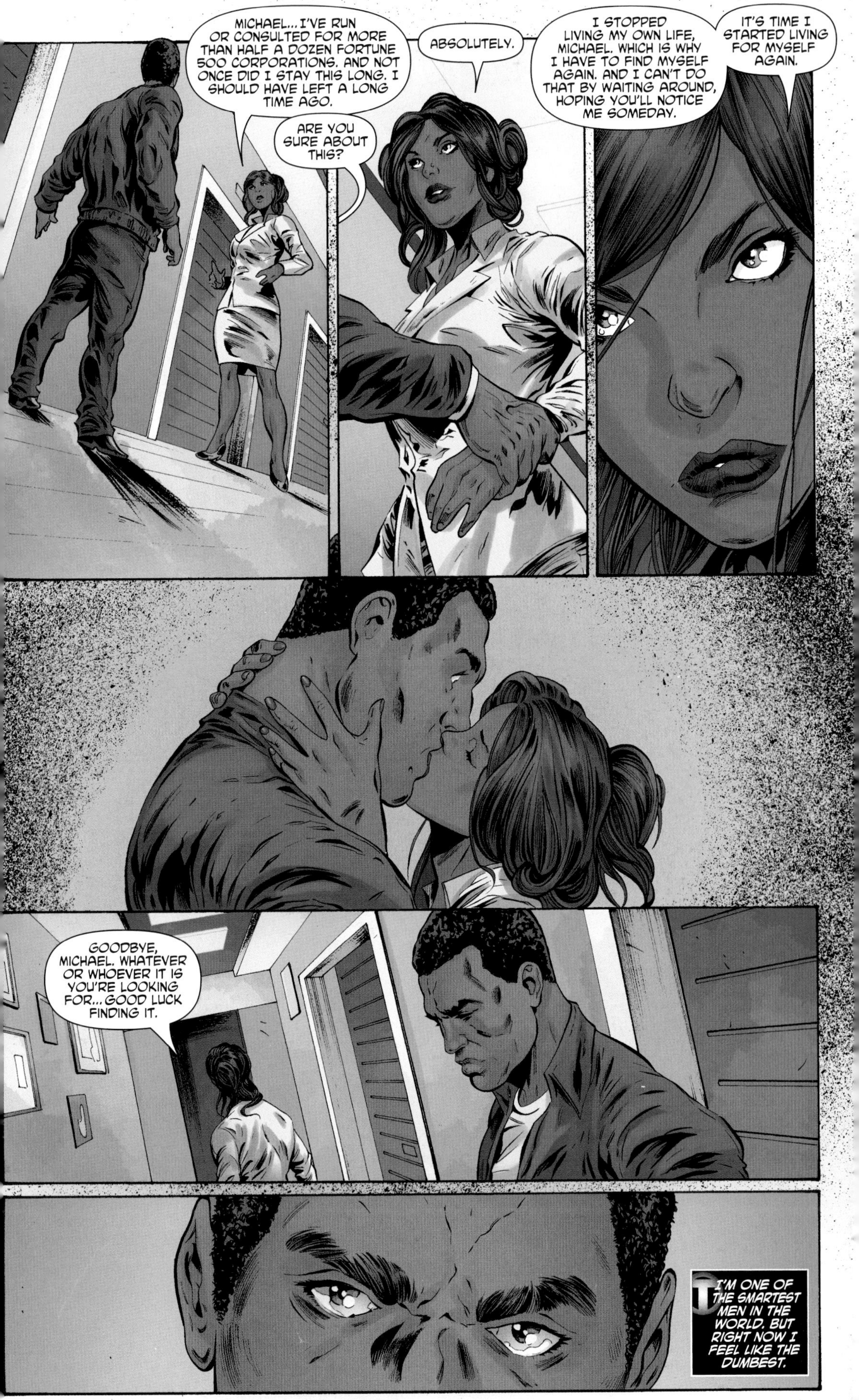
MICHAEL... I'VE RUN OR CONSULTED FOR MORE THAN HALF A DOZEN FORTUNE 500 CORPORATIONS. AND NOT ONCE DID I STAY THIS LONG. I SHOULD HAVE LEFT A LONG TIME AGO.
ARE YOU SURE ABOUT THIS?
ABSOLUTELY.
I STOPPED LIVING MY OWN LIFE, MICHAEL. WHICH IS WHY I HAVE TO FIND MYSELF AGAIN. AND I CAN'T DO THAT BY WAITING AROUND, HOPING YOU'LL NOTICE ME SOMEDAY.
IT'S TIME I STARTED LIVING FOR MYSELF AGAIN.
GOODBYE, MICHAEL. WHATEVER OR WHOEVER IT IS YOU'RE LOOKING FOR... GOOD LUCK FINDING IT.
I'M ONE OF THE SMARTEST MEN IN THE WORLD. BUT RIGHT NOW I FEEL LIKE THE DUMBEST.

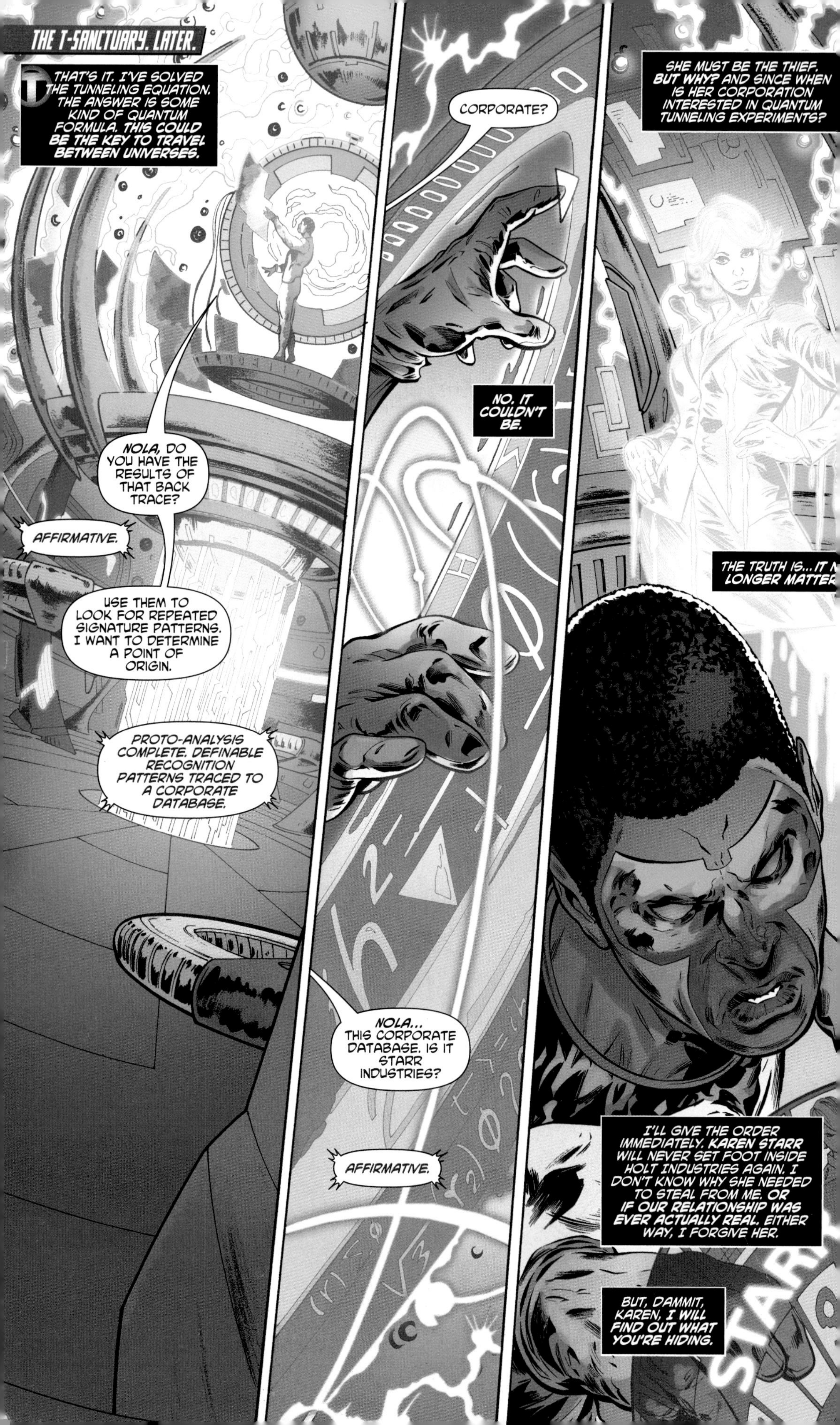
THE T-SANCTUARY. LATER.
THAT'S IT. I'VE SOLVED THE TUNNELING EQUATION. THE ANSWER IS SOME KIND OF QUANTUM FORMULA. THIS COULD BE THE KEY TO TRAVEL BETWEEN UNIVERSES.
NOLA, DO YOU HAVE THE RESULTS OF THAT BACK TRACE?
AFFIRMATIVE.
USE THEM TO LOOK FOR REPEATED SIGNATURE PATTERNS. I WANT TO DETERMINE A POINT OF ORIGIN.
PROTO-ANALYSIS COMPLETE. DEFINABLE RECOGNITION PATTERNS TRACED TO A CORPORATE DATABASE.
CORPORATE?
NO. IT COULDN'T BE.
NOLA... THIS CORPORATE DATABASE. IS IT STARR INDUSTRIES?
AFFIRMATIVE.
SHE MUST BE THE THIEF. BUT WHY? AND SINCE WHEN IS HER CORPORATION INTERESTED IN QUANTUM TUNNELING EXPERIMENTS?
I'LL GIVE THE ORDER IMMEDIATELY. KAREN STARR WILL NEVER SET FOOT INSIDE HOLT INDUSTRIES AGAIN. I DON'T KNOW WHY SHE NEEDED TO STEAL FROM ME. OR IF OUR RELATIONSHIP WAS EVER ACTUALLY REAL. EITHER WAY, I FORGIVE HER.
BUT, DAMMIT, KAREN, I WILL FIND OUT WHAT YOU'RE HIDING.

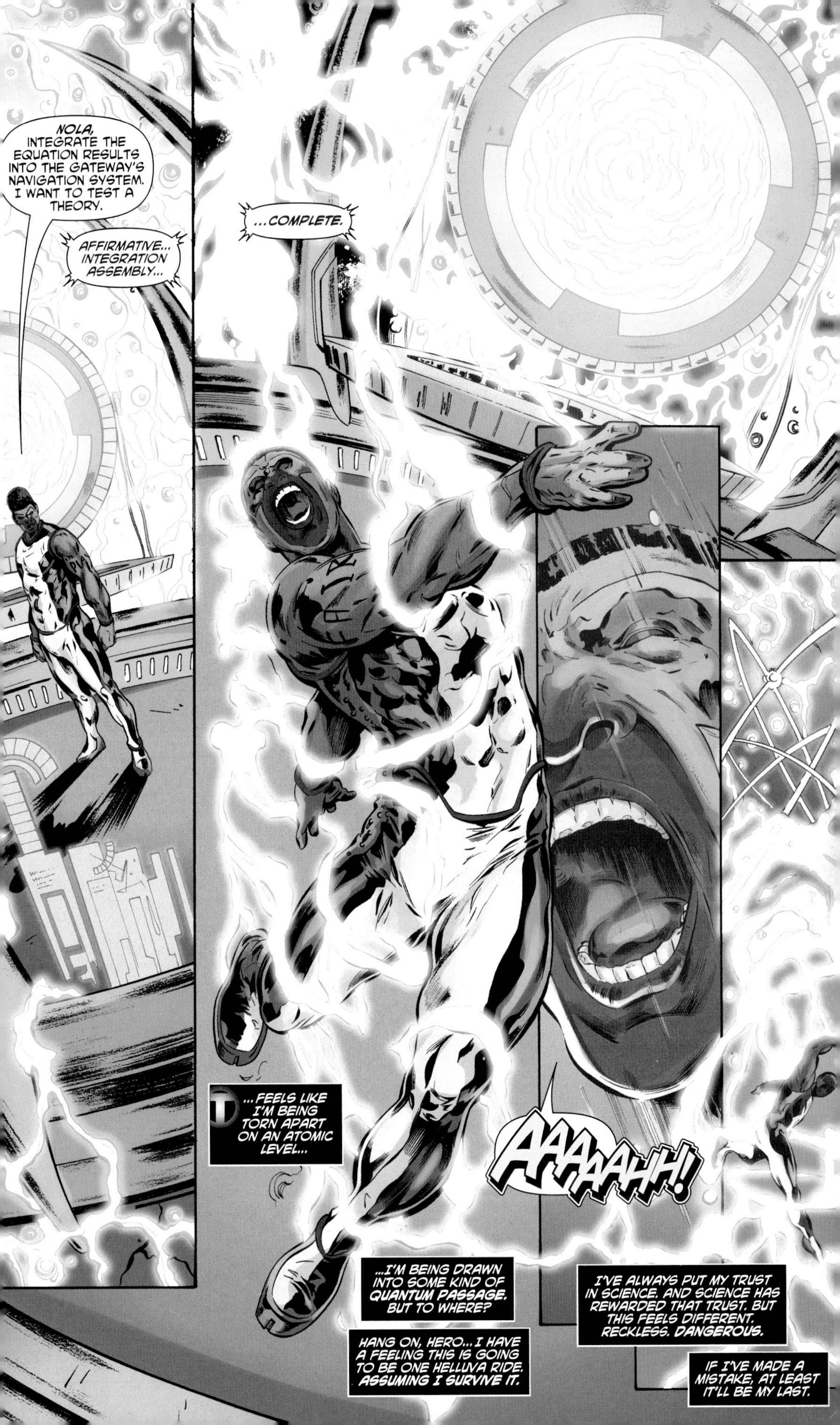
NOLA, INTEGRATE THE EQUATION RESULTS INTO THE GATEWAY'S NAVIGATION SYSTEM. I WANT TO TEST A THEORY.
AFFIRMATIVE... INTEGRATION ASSEMBLY...
...COMPLETE.
...FEELS LIKE I'M BEING TORN APART ON AN ATOMIC LEVEL...
AAAAAHH!
...I'M BEING DRAWN INTO SOME KIND OF QUANTUM PASSAGE. BUT TO WHERE?
HANG ON, HERO... I HAVE A FEELING THIS IS GOING TO BE ONE HELLUVA RIDE. ASSUMING I SURVIVE IT.
I'VE ALWAYS PUT MY TRUST IN SCIENCE. AND SCIENCE HAS REWARDED THAT TRUST. BUT THIS FEELS DIFFERENT. RECKLESS. DANGEROUS.
IF I'VE MADE A MISTAKE, AT LEAST IT'LL BE MY LAST.

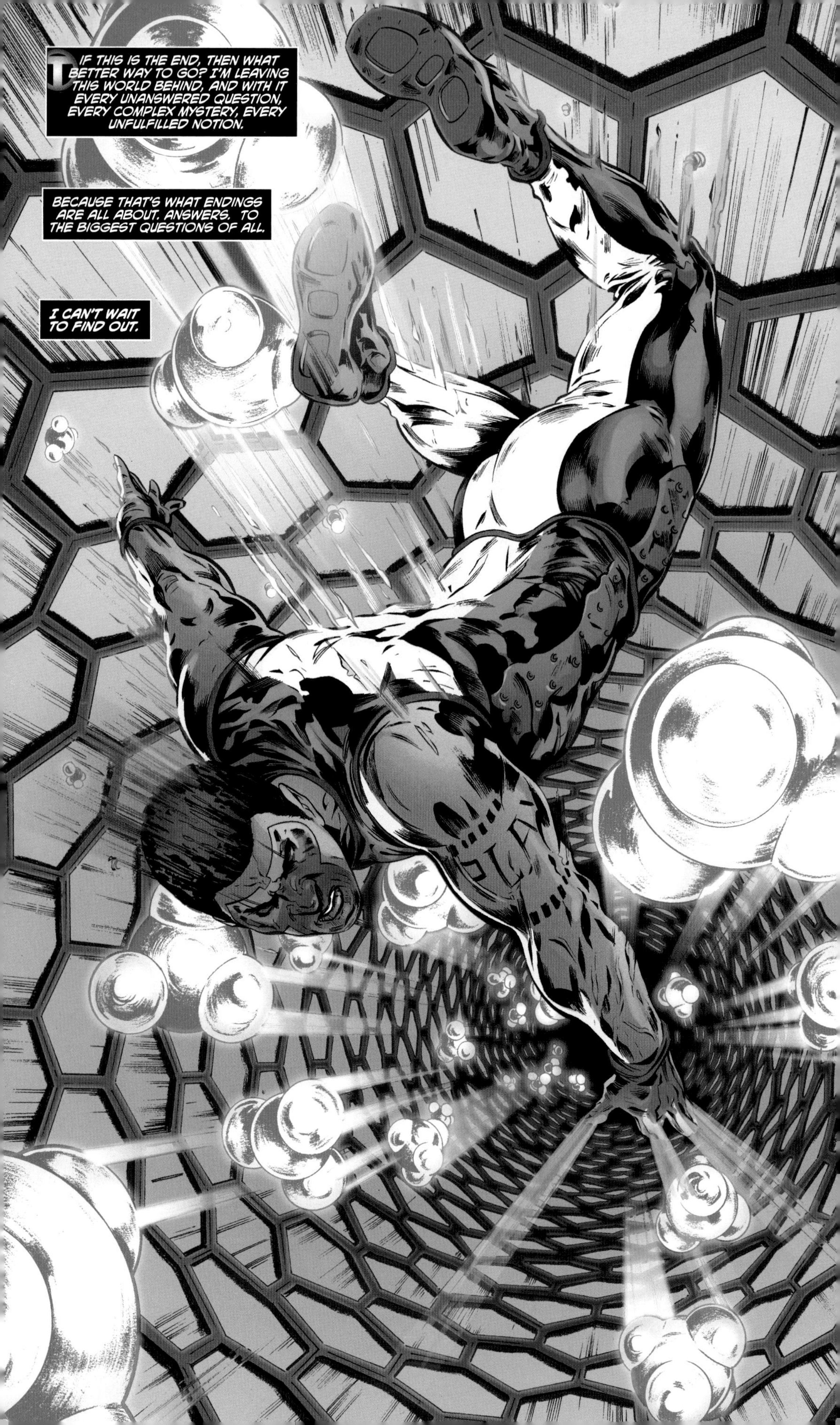
IF THIS IS THE END, THEN WHAT BETTER WAY TO GO? I'M LEAVING THIS WORLD BEHIND, AND WITH IT EVERY UNANSWERED QUESTION, EVERY COMPLEX MYSTERY, EVERY UNFULFILLED NOTION.
BECAUSE THAT'S WHAT ENDINGS ARE ALL ABOUT. ANSWERS. TO THE BIGGEST QUESTIONS OF ALL.
I CAN'T WAIT TO FIND OUT.

MISTER TERRIFIC CHARACTER DESIGNS
"ALIENS IN THE NINTH DIMENSION" KRYL AND HARMONY DESIGNS BY GIANLUCA GUGLIOTTA

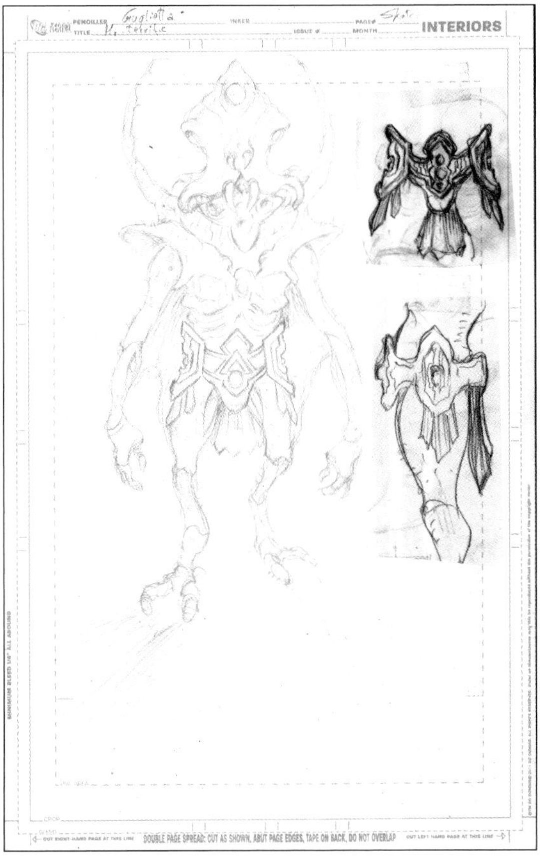
PENCILLER
INKER
PAGE#
ISSUE #
MONTH
INTERIORS
DOUBLE PAGE SPREAD: CUT AS SHOWN, ABUT PAGE EDGES, TAPE ON BACK, DO NOT OVERLAP

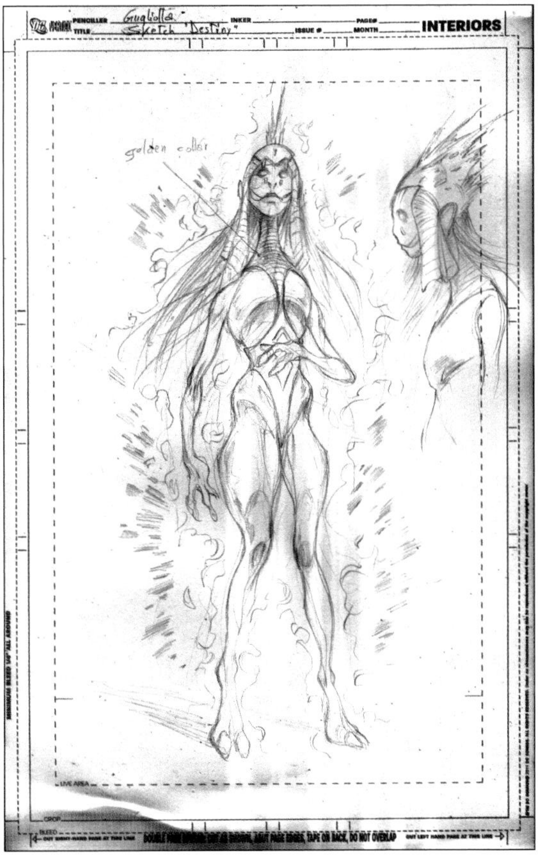
PENCILLER Gugliotta
TITLE Sketch "Destiny"
INKER
PAGE#
ISSUE #
MONTH
INTERIORS
golden collar
DOUBLE PAGE SPREAD: CUT AS SHOWN, ABUT PAGE EDGES, TAPE ON BACK, DO NOT OVERLAP

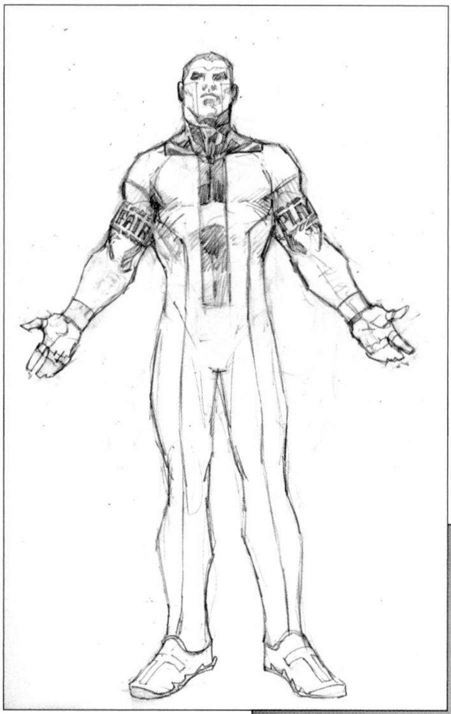

Jim Lee

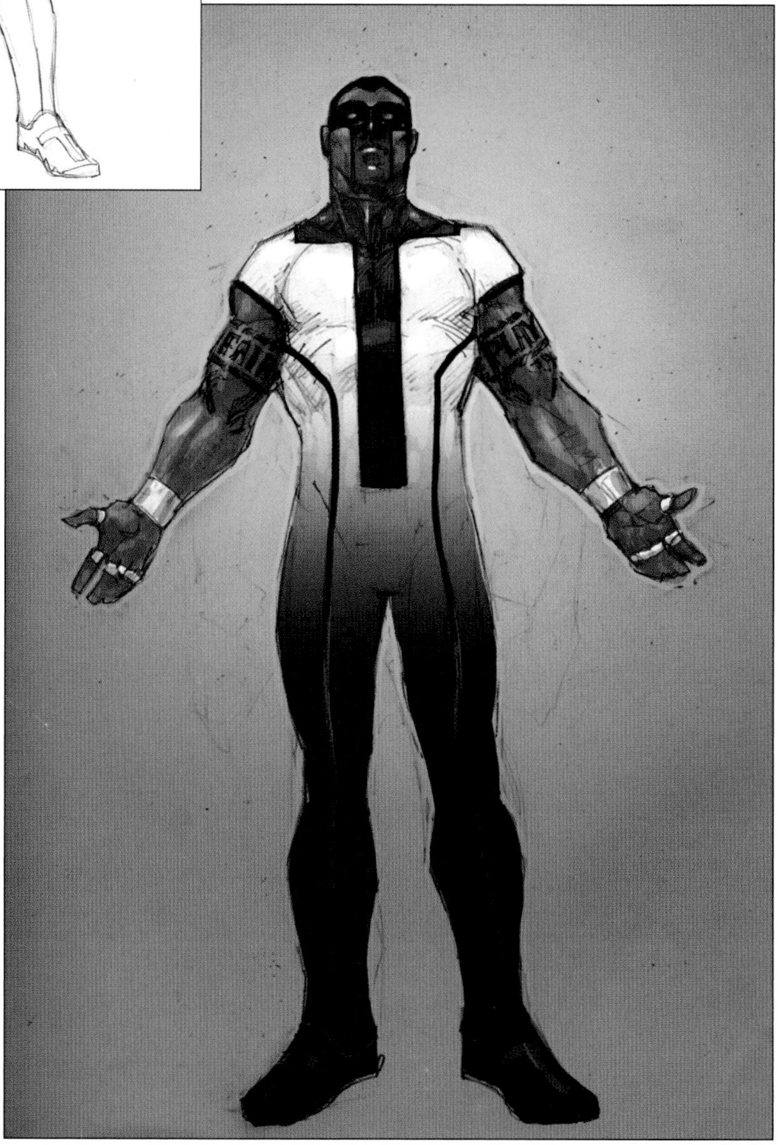

Jim Lee

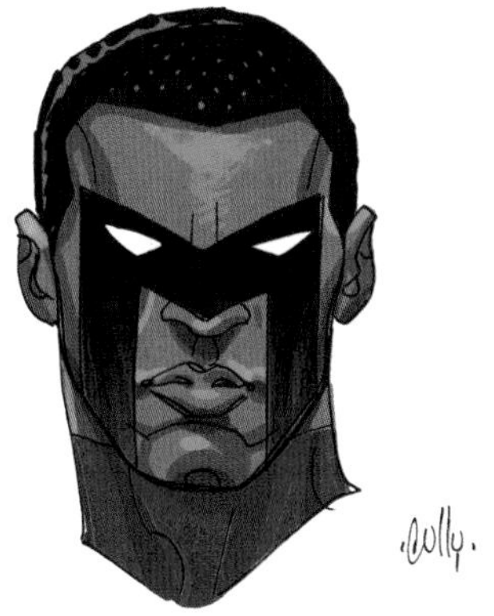
Cully.

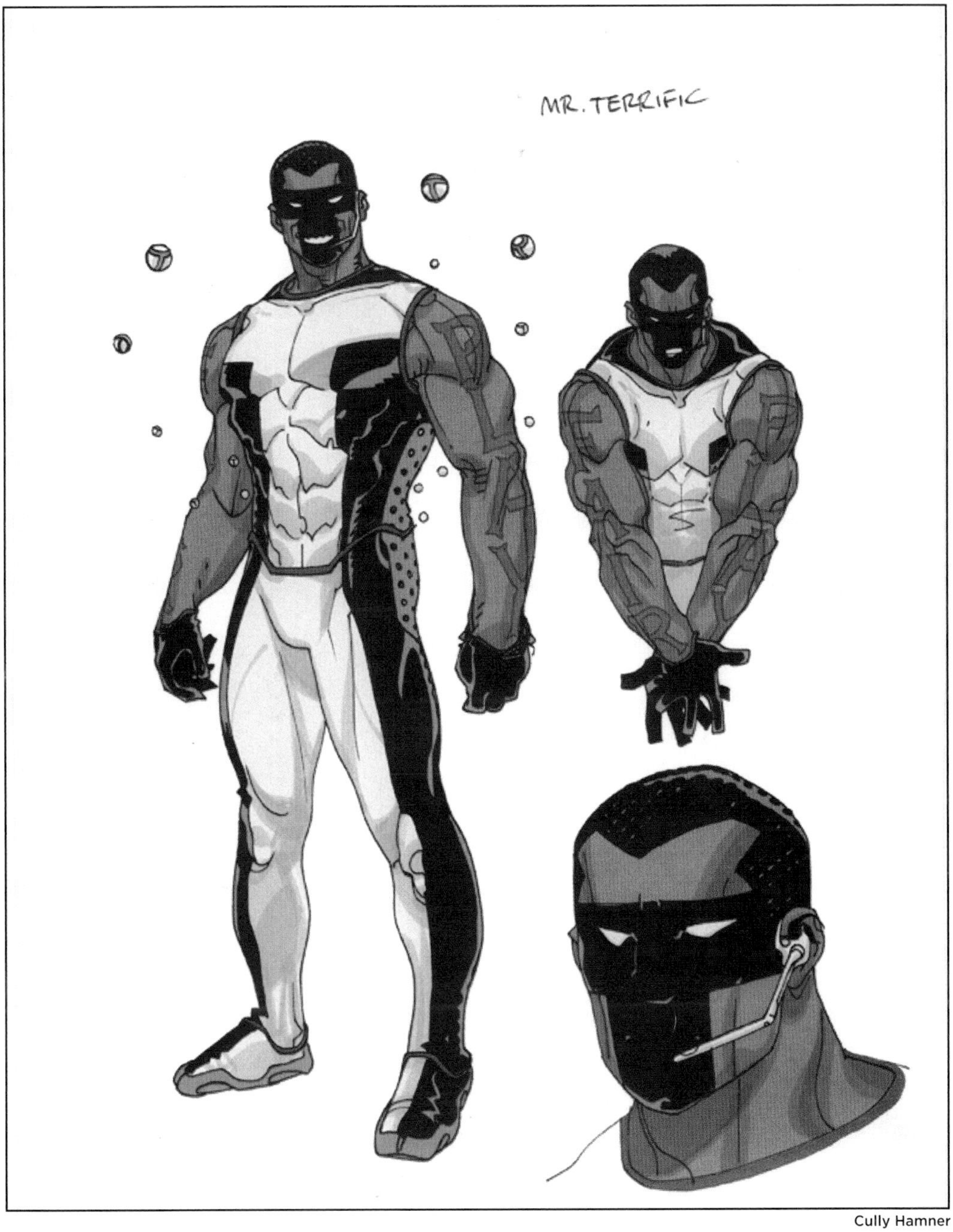
MR. TERRIFIC

Cully Hamner

MISTER TERRIFIC

COVER SKETCHES BY J.G. JONES

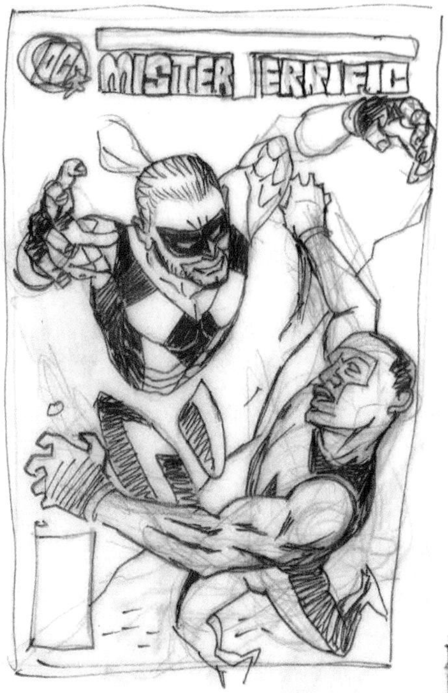
MISTER TERRIFIC

MR. Terrif
holds onto
ice surface-

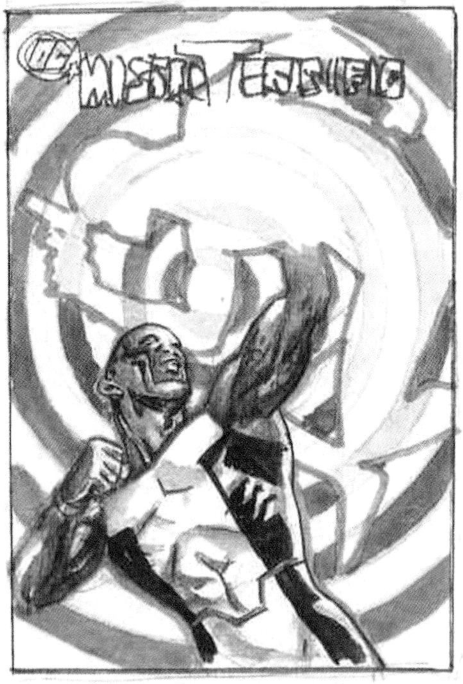

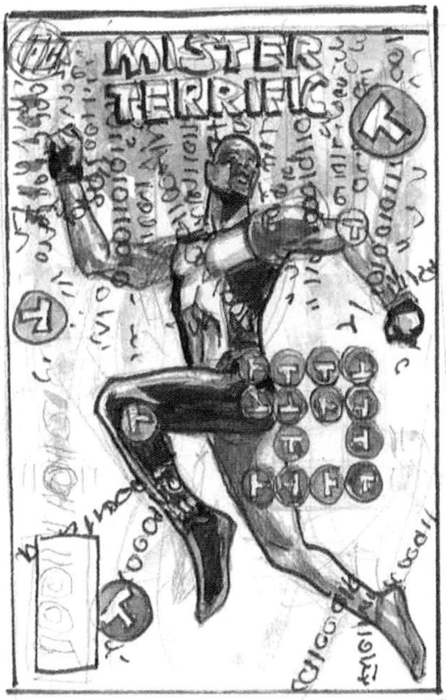
MISTER
TERRIFIC

MR. Terrific
Bound by
Binary
Bonds

1001101110001

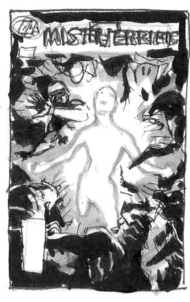

MR. T →

← surrounded by weird Aliens

MISTER TERRIFIC

↑ CIRCUIT BOARD BACKGROUND

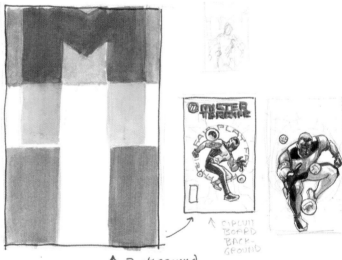

↑ Background Colored like This. Color overlaid on bkgrnd. art.

#4

MISTER TERRIFIC

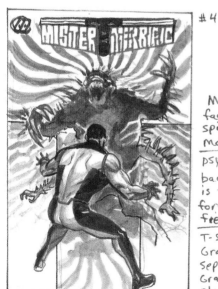

Mr. Terrific faces spiny monster

psychedelic background is the force field

T-shaped Graphic separates Graphic elements

MISTER TERRIFIC

PENCILS FROM MISTER TERRIFIC #5 AND #7 BY GIANLUCA GUGLIOTTA

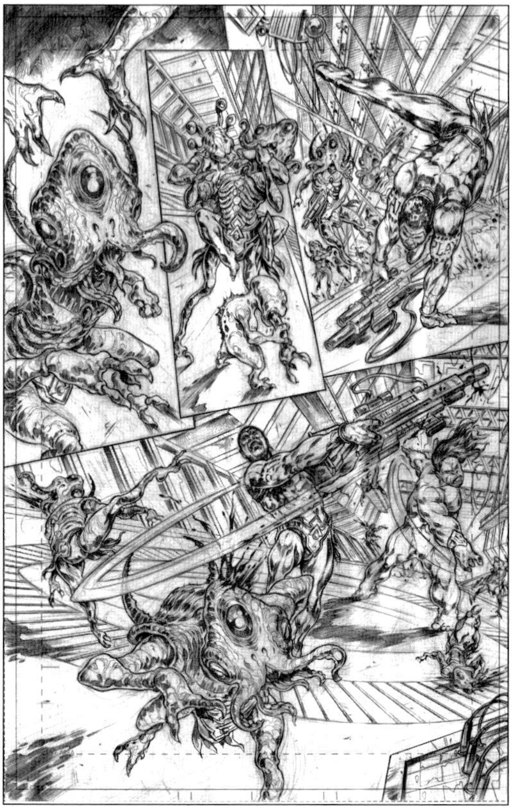

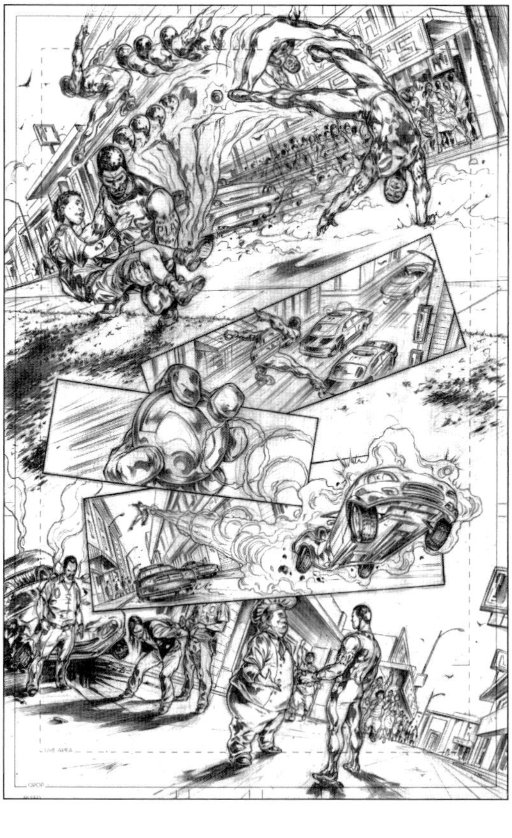

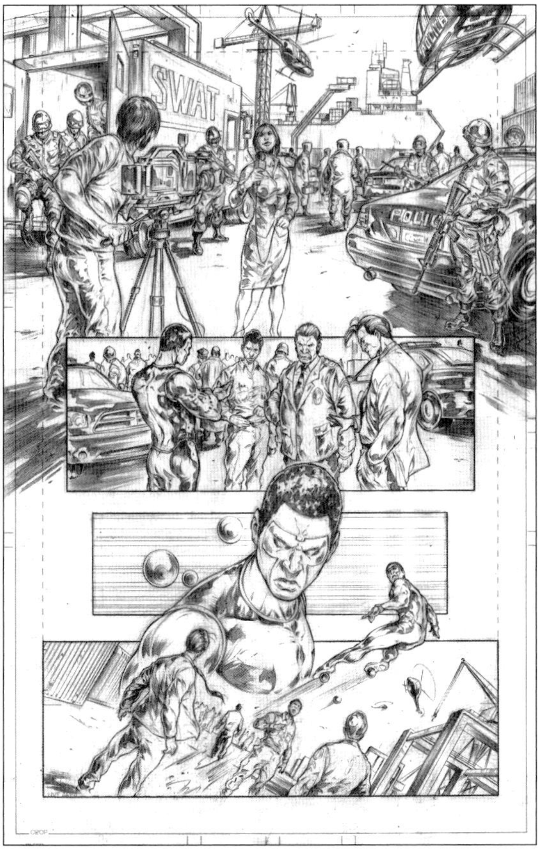
SWAT

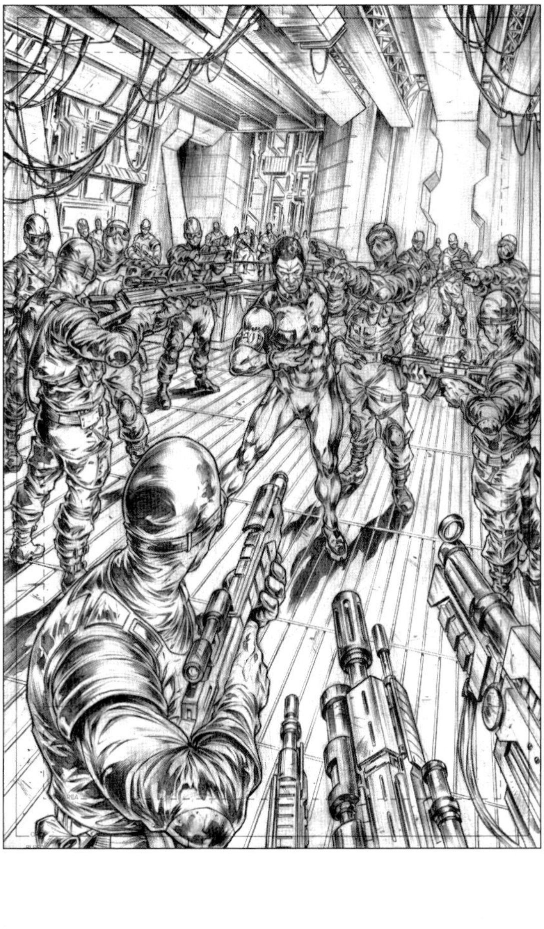

MISTER TERRIFIC

SPREAD PENCILS FROM MISTER TERRIFIC #4

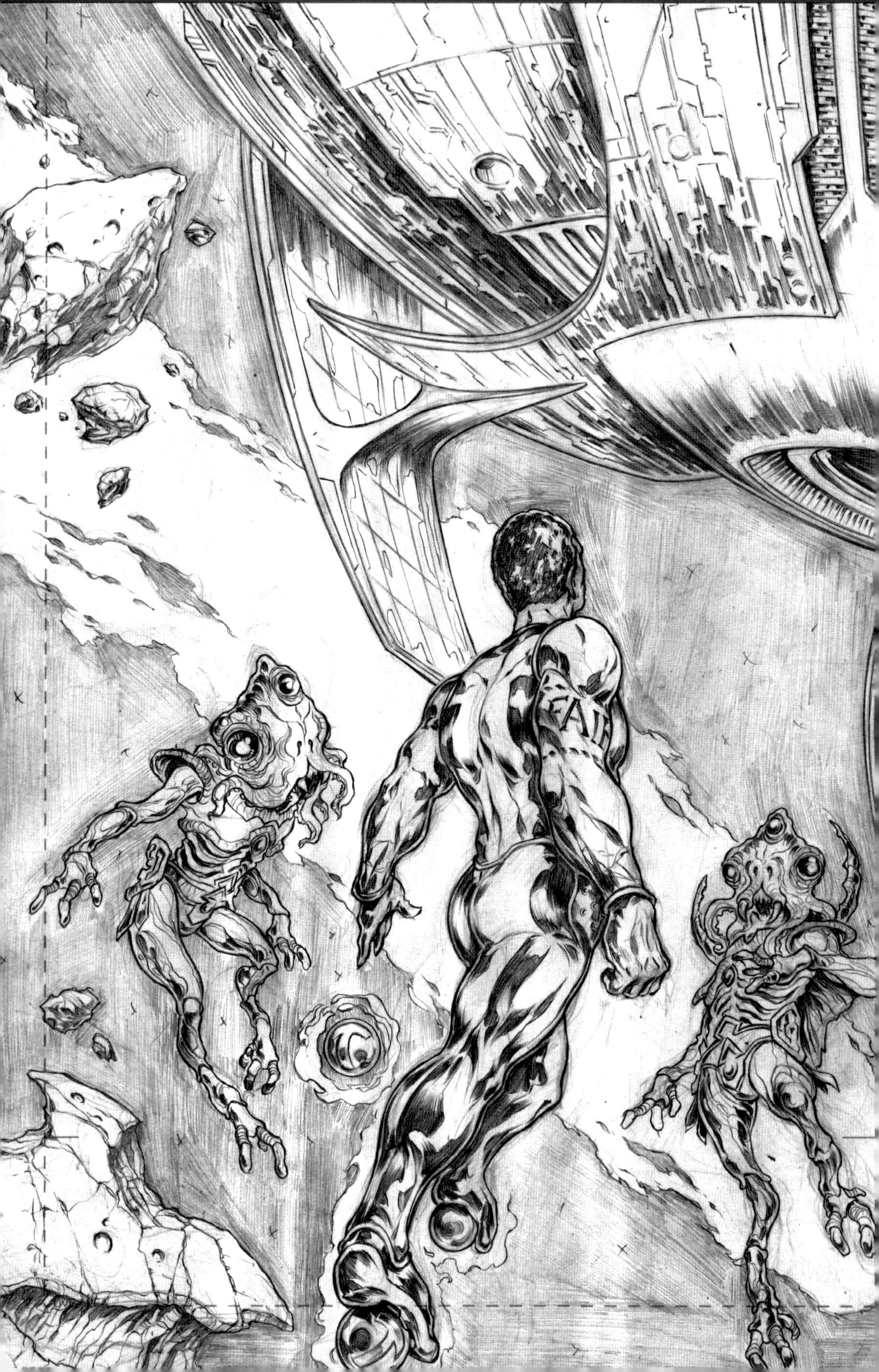

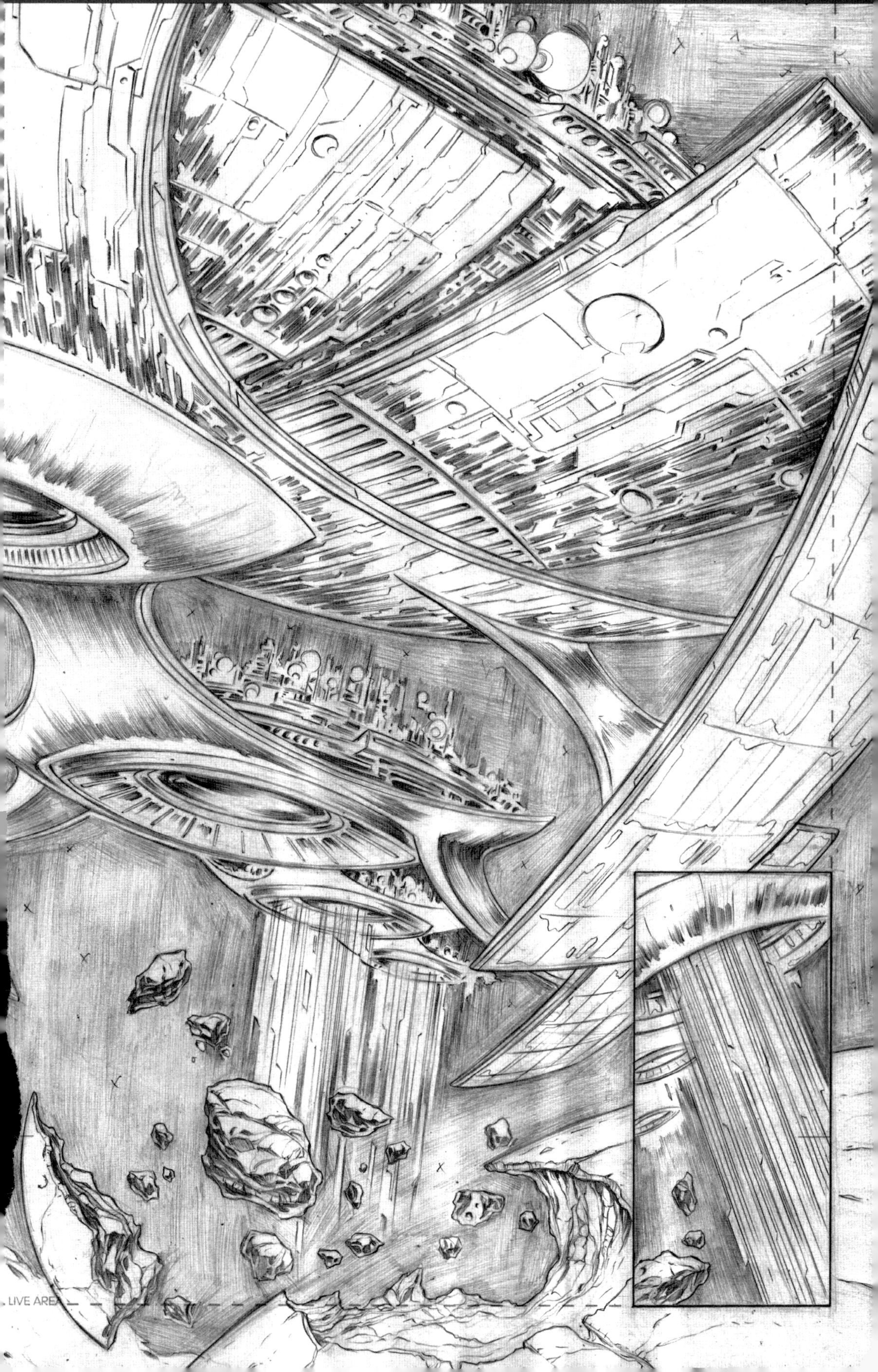
LIVE AREA

MISTER TERRIFIC

PENCILS FROM MISTER TERRIFIC #4, #7, #8 BY GIANLUCA GUGLIOTTA

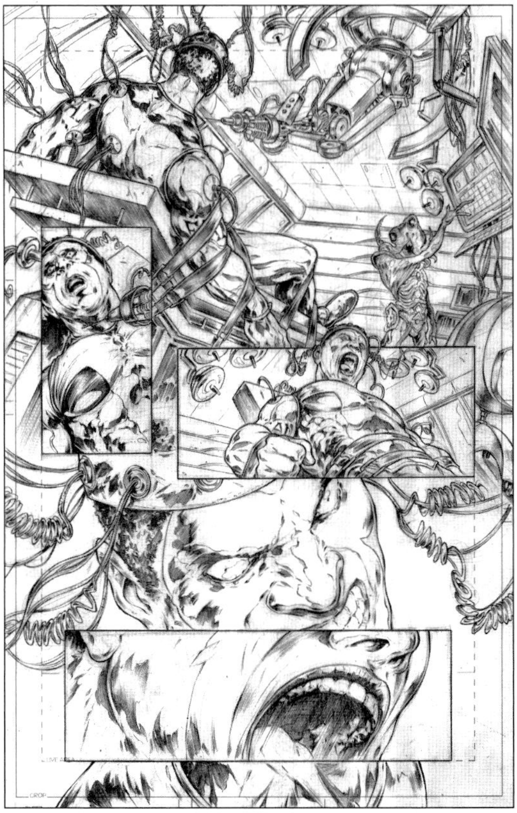

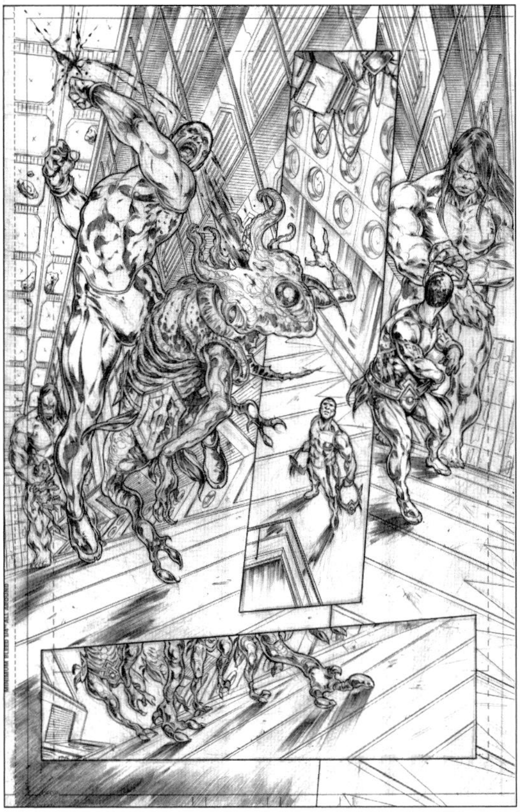

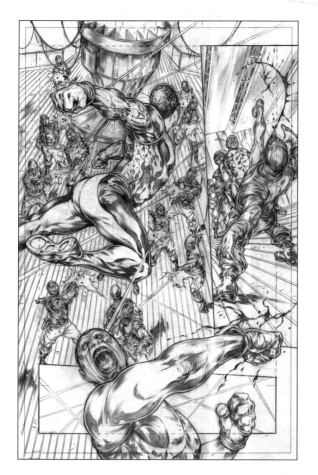

MISTER TERRIFIC

PENCILS FROM MISTER TERRIFIC #8 BY GIANLUCA GUGLIOTTA

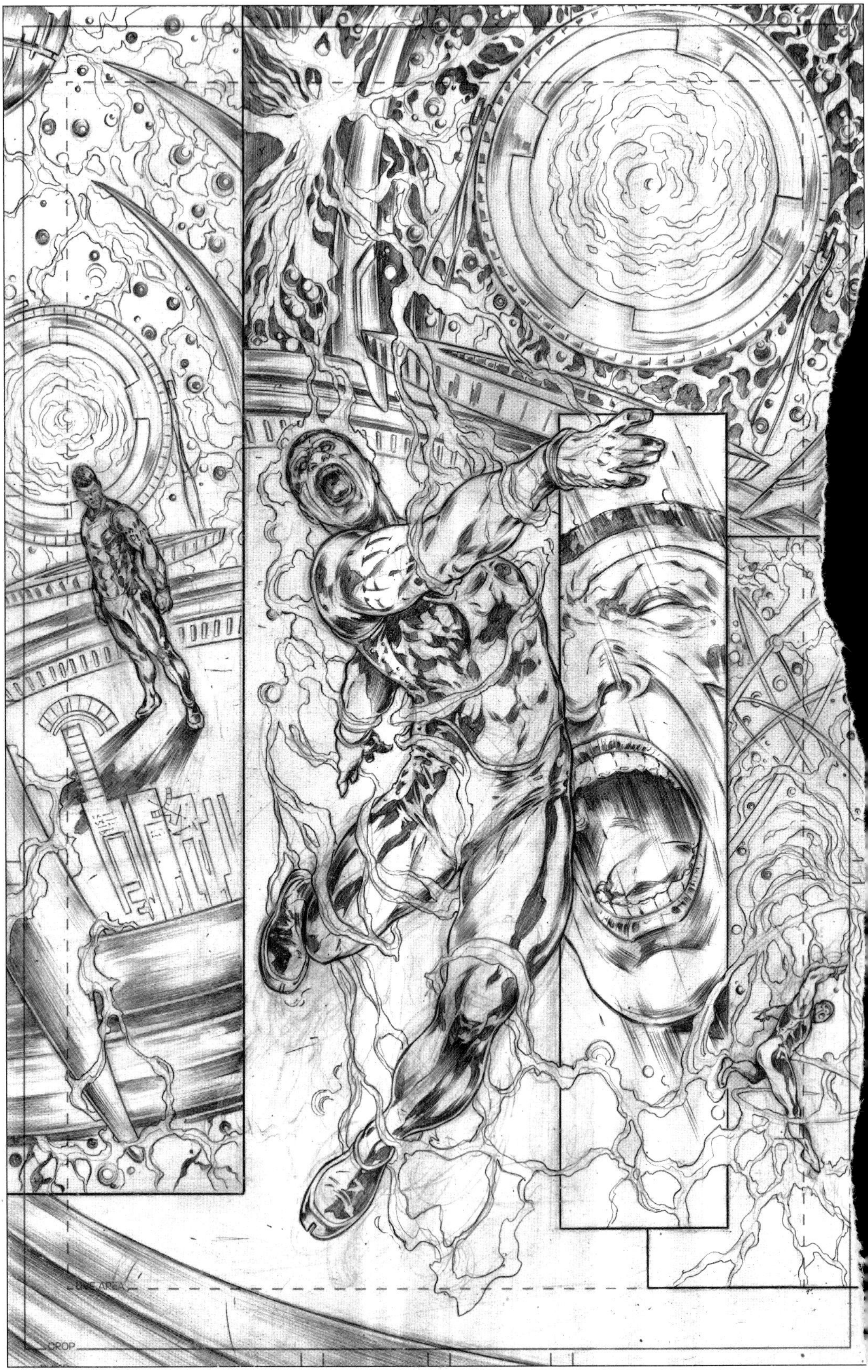